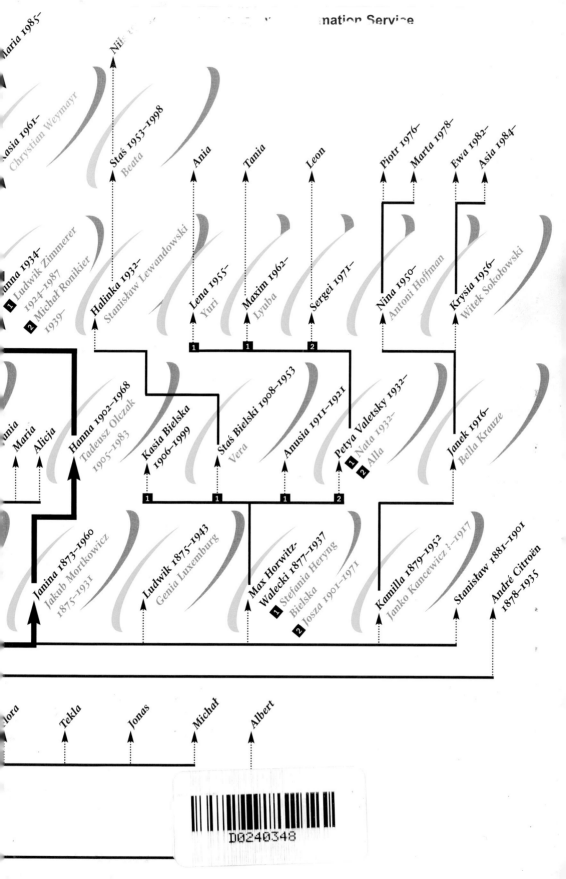

Maria 1985–

Kasia 1961–
Christian Weymayr

Niba

Staś 1953–1998
Beata

Ania

Tania

Leon

Piotr 1976–

Marta 1978–

Ewa 1982–

Asia 1984–

Hanna 1934–
1 *Ludwik Zimmerer 1924–1987*
2 *Michał Ronikier 1939–*

Halinka 1932–
Stanisław Lewandowski

Lena 1955–
Yuri

Maxim 1962–
Lyuba

Sergei 1971–

Nina 1950–
Antoni Hoffman

Krysia 1956–
Witek Sokołowski

1

1

2

Hanna 1902–1968
Tadeusz Olczak 1905–1983

Kasia Bielska 1906–1999

Staś Bielski 1908–1953
Vera

Anusia 1911–1921

Petya Valetsky 1932–
1 *Nata 1932–*
2 *Alla*

Janek 1916–
Bella Krauze

Mania

Maria

Alicja

1

1

1

2

Janina 1873–1960
Jakub Mortkowicz 1875–1931

Ludwik 1875–1943
Genia Luxemburg

Max Horwitz-Walecki 1877–1937
1 *Stefania Heryng Bielska*
2 *Josza 1901–1971*

Kamilla 1879–1952
Janko Kancewicz ?–1917

Stanisław 1881–1901

André Citroën 1878–1935

Flora

Tekla

Jonas

Michał

Albert

IN THE GARDEN OF MEMORY

IN THE GARDEN OF
MEMORY

A Family Memoir

———————— ✳ ————————

JOANNA OLCZAK-RONIKIER

Translated by Antonia Lloyd-Jones

Weidenfeld and Nicolson
LONDON

First published in Great Britain in 2004
by Weidenfeld & Nicolson

First published in Poland in 2001
by Spoleczny Instytut Wydawniczy ZNAK

A CIP catalogue record for this book
is available from the British Library.

ISBN 0 297 64549 8

Typeset and printed in Great Britain by
Butler and Tanner Ltd, Frome and London

Weidenfeld & Nicolson
The Orion Publishing Group Ltd
Orion House
5 Upper Saint Martin's Lane
London WC2H 9EA

943.
805

www.orionbooks.co.uk

CONTENTS

————— ✳ —————

All illustrations are the private property of Joanna Olczak-Ronikier

Endpapers: Family Tree

ACKNOWLEDGEMENTS

———————— ✳ ————————

The author wishes to thank the heroes of this book:

Monika Bychowska-Holmes, for the passion, energy and effort she has put into bringing our family closer.

Jan Kancewicz, for his stories, valuable information and comments.

And also all our Polish, American and Russian relatives, for their help, for providing documents and photographs, and for their kind cooperation.

TRANSLATOR'S NOTE

―――――――――✳―――――――――

Some of the historical background to this story may be unfamiliar to the non-Polish reader, so here are some brief facts about the context.

The author's grandmother, Janina Horwitz, was born in 1873, when Poland was partitioned between the empires of Russia, Austria–Hungary and Prussia. The Russian partition was known as the Congress Kingdom of Poland, and centred on Warsaw; the Austro-Hungarian partition encompassed Galicia and included Kraków, and the Prussian partition centred on Posen – in Polish, Poznań.

In 1830 and 1863–4 uprisings against the occupying Russian empire had been brutally crushed, followed by the execution or exile to Siberia of thousands of Poles and stern Russification and Germanisation policies in the Russian and Prussian partitions. The uprisings and their outcome also fuelled the Romantic and Positivist movements in Polish art and literature.

These were followed between the 1890s and 1910s by the 'Young Poland' cultural trend. In the same era the struggle for independence was led by new political forces such as the Polish Socialist Party (led by Józef Piłsudski) and its right-wing rival the Endecja, or National Democracy (led by Roman Dmowski).

Following the First World War, in 1918 Poland regained independence with Piłsudski as head of state. Initially the new republic fought several wars to establish its borders, including the 1919–20 war with the Soviet Bolsheviks, when a miraculous Polish victory at the Battle of Warsaw was the prelude to Poland regaining a large part of its traditional territory to the east. However, after Piłsudski's retirement the country suffered from political infighting and economic difficulties. In 1926 Piłsudski staged a military coup and introduced the Sanacja regime, which dealt fiercely with its political opponents.

At the outbreak of the Second World War Poland was invaded by Germany from the west and the Soviet Union from the east. Parts of western Poland were annexed to the Reich, with the central area becoming the so-called General Government, run by German administration as a source of labour. Millions of Poles and Jews were murdered in the concentration camps. The eastern part of Poland was occupied by Soviet troops, and many thousands of Poles were deported to Siberia. In June 1941 when Germany attacked the Soviet Union, these Poles were freed and allowed to form an army, which, led by General Anders, was evacuated via the Middle East to fight in Europe.

Throughout the war Poland's Home Army, under orders from the Polish government-in-exile in London, led resistance action within Poland. The Ghetto Uprising in Warsaw was the tragic last-ditch attempt of the remaining Jews to resist being exterminated. Shortly before Poland was finally liberated in 1944, the resistance staged the desperate Warsaw Uprising against the occupying Nazis, after which the Germans razed the city to the ground before retreating. Meanwhile Soviet troops waited outside the city for Polish resistance to be destroyed, as the Germans' final action could only make it easier for Soviet influence to take over the devastated country.

At the Tehran conference in November 1943 the Allied powers agreed with Stalin that after the war the Soviet Union would retain the Polish territory it had initially annexed. As a result, after the war Poland's map was redrawn, and all its borders were shifted westwards, with the loss of cities including Wilno (Vilnius) to Soviet Lithuania, and Lwów (Lviv) to Soviet Ukraine.

In the 'Polish People's Republic', as communist Poland was officially known, those who returned from the free Polish forces and people who had been active in the resistance were imprisoned or sent to the Gulag. The communist regime lasted until 1989, when Poland regained independence.

Antonia Lloyd-Jones

For Kasia and Maria

VIENNESE BLOOD

———————— ✱ ————————

On Tuesday, 28 October 1998, at the Jewish Cultural Centre in Kraków, I had a metaphysical experience, when my great-great-grandfather, or rather the shadow of his ghost, made a brief, unexpected appearance. Earlier, in the programme for the *Encounters with Jewish Culture Month*, I had read that on that very day at 6 p.m. there would be a meeting with Paul Chaim Eisenberg, the Chief Rabbi of Austria, entitled 'Life will return with songs'. So off I ran, thinking, Who knows? What if?

There was nothing metaphysical about the meeting as such, no great revelations of the theological or philosophical kind. For two hours Paul Chaim played his own guitar accompaniment as he sang familiar Jewish songs in Yiddish, such as 'Az der rebe lakht...', or 'Tumbalalayka', mixing the singing with equally familiar anecdotes about devout Jews who had sought the rabbi's advice. In spite, or maybe because, of this, the evening was a great success. The assembled audience clapped and sang along to the songs, and at the end a very young Jewish girl from Kazakhstan who had been sitting among them came up on stage and sang a few more popular songs. After that the people slowly began to disperse. As the rabbi too was starting to make his way to the exit I went up to him, making an unpardonable blunder in the very first moment by offering my hand while introducing myself, something that in such an instance a woman should never, ever do.

'A hundred and seventy years ago my great-great-grandfather was the Chief Rabbi of the Jewish community in Vienna,' I said. 'His name was Lazar Horwitz. Would there be any chance of finding traces of him?' I asked.

'Horowitz,' he corrected me. 'What do you mean? His traces don't take much finding. I have his portrait hanging in my office above my desk. He's a very well-known figure, a man of intellect,

I

one of our greatest rabbis. He became famous for changing the ritual regulations that were in force for circumcision; despite the objections of Orthodox Jews he ordered the blood flow to be staunched with a sponge, instead of having it sucked out of the wound by the mohels who performed the operations, which often gave babies lethal infections. As soon as I get back to Vienna I'll have a photograph of the portrait taken, and I'll send it to you. Please give me your address.'

And although he never sent the photograph, he resurrected a person who barely existed in my memory; but the more I found out about him, the more distinct he became.

The *Encyclopaedia Judaica* devotes at least a dozen pages to the Horowitzes. They were descendants of the tribe of Levites, 'the Servants of the Temple'; at one time they carried the nickname Ha-Levi, and for centuries they produced long dynasties of priests and scholars. In modern times they spread throughout Europe, with one branch of the clan settling in the Czech town of Horowice. That was the source of the name conferred on them towards the end of the eighteenth century by the Austrian authorities. It changed its form to Horwitz, Hurwitz and even Gurwicz, depending on the country where individual branches of the family later settled. My great-great-grandfather still had two 'o's in his name, whereas my great-grandfather only had one.

Lazar (Eleazar) Horowitz was born in 1804 in the town of Floss in Bavaria, the son and grandson of a rabbi, and in 1828 when he was just twenty-four years old he became a rabbi for the Jewish community in Vienna. He was an advocate of Reformed Judaism, which tried to modernise medieval Jewish customs by accepting European dress, secular education and participation in the life of Christian society without abandoning one's own religion. He wrote a great deal and left to posterity many volumes of Talmudic commentaries published under the title *Yad Eleazar*, in which he defended his progressive views on matters of ritual, which exposed him to fierce attack from Orthodox members of the community. He was characterised by determination and courage; he was actively involved in the problems of Austrian Jews, and made an effort to improve their legal and social situation.

He was forty years old – not a young man in those days – when in 1844 my future great-grandfather, Gustav, came into the world. The boy graduated from Vienna University with the degree of Doctor of Philosophy and Theology, and wrote his doctorate on

Spinoza. So why did he end up in Warsaw as a clerk in the office of Izaak Kleinmann, a merchant with a monopoly on the import of salt from the mine at Wieliczka, near Kraków, to the Congress Kingdom (as the Russian partition of Poland was called)?

Probably because the learned Viennese Talmudist had eight children and had to see to their future; his son, the young philosopher, was not a very resourceful fellow. So a wife with a dowry was sought for him, because of the fear that he would not find a lucrative enough job in Vienna to be able to maintain a family. Kleinmann meanwhile, the father of eleven children, had money and was casting around Europe for suitable husbands for his eight daughters. An emancipated Jew, modern and cosmopolitan, he was more fluent in German than Polish and felt more at home in Berlin or Vienna than in Warsaw. He disliked the Polish Jews for the fanaticism of the Orthodox circles, while those who advocated assimilation were, to his mind, too obsequious towards the Poles, whom in turn he despised for their disdainful attitude to the Jews. The Misses Kleinmann received a thorough private education, knew foreign languages, were pretty and had dowries, so he had no trouble in finding husbands for them among the Dutch, German and French Jews – educated people without any complexes. The prettiest Kleinmann girl, Amalia, made the best match, marrying Louis Citroën, a banker who came from Holland but lived in Paris. Their son André founded the famous Citroën car firm.

How did the union between my future great-grandmother Julia and my future great-grandfather come about? Because of his commercial contacts, Izaak Kleinmann travelled a great deal and often visited Vienna. For all his progressive views he was a religious man, and must certainly have associated with his Viennese coreligionists. Perhaps he met Rabbi Lazar Horowitz there? Or maybe one of their mutual friends acted as a go-between? Or else it was a professional matchmaker, a *shadkhan*. A union with a famous rabbinical family must have appealed to Kleinmann's vanity. Money plus intellect: the very best combination.

No one will ever know when and where Julia first set eyes on Gustav. Their fathers must have arranged a few meetings for the young people to become better acquainted. Did they like each other? She certainly liked him. He was handsome, well educated, and full of melancholy charm, which women always find fascinating. He had pale eyes and romantic sideburns shading his solemn young face. He was said to look like the Polish romantic poet Cyprian Norwid, or maybe an insurgent from Artur Grottger's paintings of the 1863 Uprising. And what did the young rabbi's son think of the young lady? That she was not bad-looking, not unintelligent, that she inspired confidence and was sure to be a good wife and to bear him healthy, capable children. That was perfectly adequate. He was reluctant to leave for the gloomy Russian city that went by the name of Warsaw, but he did not protest. He was a God-fearing man and he knew that his fundamental task in life was to start a family. What about happiness? Happiness was the result of well-performed duties.

By a miraculous turn of fate their engagement announcement has survived, printed on vellum decorated with embossed lacy edging and garlands of flowers. In Warsaw my grandmother sacredly preserved two large bundles of her parents' engagement correspondence, but discretion never allowed her to acquaint herself with their contents. It was all burned in 1944 during the Warsaw Uprising, along with the entire family archive. Only a couple of letters have survived, written in exquisite calligraphy, sent from Vienna to Warsaw and from Warsaw to Vienna. They wrote to each other in German: *Geliebte Julienchen! Verehrte und geliebter Gustav!* ('My beloved little Julia!' 'My adored and beloved Gustav!')

In 1867 their wedding ceremony was held at the synagogue in Vienna and was registered with the Viennese municipal authorities. She was twenty-two, and he was twenty-three years old. They settled in Warsaw, at 49 Królewska Street, a stone's throw from the Saxon Gardens, in a tenement building that belonged to her parents. What did they live on? On the interest on Julia's dowry, which was invested in the family business, and on Gustav's modest income as an employee in his father-in-law's office. Nowadays, instead of philosophical essays, he wrote out invoices for hundredweight after hundredweight of salt.

The bookshelves in their flat were filled with countless volumes in green bindings, the works of Lazar Horowitz, and in the drawing room hung a large oil portrait of the eminent sage, amid a sea of family photographs in round black frames. The interior was decorated with wedding gifts from the Viennese family: silver candlesticks, trays, little baskets, sugar bowls and porcelain vases in the

Biedermeier style. All Lazar's mementoes were destroyed by fire during the war. The only thing to have survived from generation to generation is a story about his dashing wife, Karolina, who while visiting her son in Warsaw encountered a patriotic demonstration. When the Cossacks charged the crowd, she ran into the street, shouting at the top of her voice, '*Schämen Sie sich, Herren Kosaken!*' ('Shame on you, Cossacks!')

Lazar died in 1868 in Vosslau, on the outskirts of Vienna, a year after his son's wedding. That same year Gustav's first daughter, Flora, was born. Over the next fourteen years another nine children were born (one died in infancy).

'*Fünf Töchter ist kein Gelächter*' ('Five daughters is no joke'), they said, when the fifth girl, my future grandmother, was born in 1873. Two years later a sixth child was born, a boy at last. Overjoyed that he finally had a son, Gustav went to the café to boast to his friends, and was told amid gales of laughter: 'Go home and look carefully, Mr Horwitz – you must be mistaken, it's sure to be another daughter!' Two years later another boy was born, then a daughter, and then another son.

In tune with the spirit of the era, the older girls were given flower names: Flora and Róża (Rosa); while the younger ones had distinctly foreign names: Gizella, Henrietta, and Żaneta (Jeanette). The first-born son was named after his grandfather, Lazar, but his entire life he used the name Ludwik. The next was called Maksymilian, a typically Austrian name; then came Kamilla, another botanical name, and finally the youngest son's name, Stanisław, can be seen as a conscious decision to polonise the family.*

From childhood onwards my grandmother could not stand her foreign-sounding name, Żaneta, and insisted on being called by the Polish version, Janina. What her father called her is not known. She did not retain many memories of him. He had more conversations with his older daughters, and all she remembered of him was the general impression of a quiet, gentle, timid man who, lost and alien within the huge family, did not interfere in domestic matters or in his children's upbringing.

---

* Translator's note: Polish first names have various diminutive forms, some of which are not instantly identifiable. While the diminutives of Kamilla and Gizella are Kamilka and Gizelka, Ludwik's diminutive is Lutek and Stanisław's is Staś (or Stach). Later in the book we find the diminutives of: Gustaw – Gucio; Joanna – Joasia; Jan – Janek or Jaś; Maria – Mania; Hanna – Hania or Hanka; Flora – Florcia; Ryszard – Ryś; Paweł – Pawelek; Krystyna – Krysia; Monika – Monisia; Katarzyna – Kasia, etc.

However, as the descendant of rabbis he demanded scrupulous observance of all manner of religious regulations. My grandmother could still remember the candles that were lit on Friday evenings before the Sabbath dinner, and Saturdays, on which any sort of work was forbidden; Passover, when the only bread they could eat for a whole week was matzos; Yom Kippur, when the adults observed a total fast, and other traditional rites and festivals.

❧

Gustav Horwitz never acclimatised to Warsaw. To the very end he remained a foreigner, lost in an alien city. Nor can he have been too happy dealing with commercial correspondence about salt. For consolation he used to read Goethe and Heine. Was he happy at least in his marriage to Julia, who had inherited her father's energy and resourcefulness, qualities of which Gustav himself was utterly bereft? The distance between parents and their offspring and the discretion that was the norm in those days did not allow the children to ask any questions, so no information on this subject was handed down to the next generation. Nothing is known about the couple's fifteen years of married life, but nor was there any memory of quarrelling or conflict, or even of raised voices. One small detail that oddly stuck in my grandmother's memory typifies her father's impracticality and her mother's imperious demeanour in a striking way. It concerned reprimanding a maid who had committed some offence or other.

'*Sage ihr…*' ('Tell her…'), said Gustav quietly.

'*Sage du ihr. Warum immer ich?*' ('You tell her. Why do I always have to?') protested her mother loudly.

While he was alive, the family spoke German at home. This was how all the children gained their superb knowledge of literary German, tinged with a slight Viennese accent. He read a lot, and the next generations inherited his love of German literature, culture and art. Years later, a fascination with the poetry of Heine would unite my grandmother and my grandfather, Jakub Mortkowicz, and one of the first authors to be published by the company he founded was Friedrich Nietzsche.

In August 1940 my grandmother was summoned to Gestapo headquarters on Warsaw's Szuch Avenue for interrogation. The problem was that a street vendor had some books on his stall by German authors that had been published in the past by Mortkowicz, but had since been banned by the Nazis. The books had been confiscated, and although my grandmother was no longer the official owner of either the publishing firm or the bookshop she used to run, and had nothing to do with it, they demanded an explanation from her. She behaved in such a stately manner, and spoke impeccable German with such fluency, that she inspired deep respect in the officer interrogating her. Despite being aware of her racial origin, somehow he smoothed the matter over and let her go home. Only a few months later that would have been impossible.

In October 1940 the Nazis issued the order to establish the Warsaw Ghetto. Throughout the war, while in hiding in the provinces, my mother and grandmother pretended not to understand a single word of German. Suspiciously good knowledge of that language could only have been harmful.

In Kraków, where we lived after the war, I refused to listen to the story of Jaś Orłowski, a twenty-year-old insurgent who had died in the cellar of the house at 59 Mokotowska Street, where, after countless vicissitudes during the occupation, my mother and grandmother had ended up during the Warsaw Uprising. A large bomb had hit the tenement building's five-storey annexe, which had collapsed, burying the people in the flats in rubble. Only the rooms on the ground floor were saved, where there was an insurgents' hospital, and those who managed to escape into the cellars survived. All around, hell had broken loose. Corpses pulled from the ruins were carried into the courtyard, where families sought their relatives among them, and the wounded were carried down to the cellars, including the badly burned Jaś. There were no dressings or anaesthetics, nor any medicines.

'I want to go home, to my mother,' he cried in his fever. A few days earlier, when the houses on Moniuszko Street had been on fire, while saving people from the upper floors he had fallen with some burning roof beams and would have been burned to death if not for a heroic friend who had carried him out of the fire.

'Your voice is like my mother's. Please come here and hold my hand, please say something to me,' he begged my grandmother. So she began to recite poetry. She knew all the great works of Polish, French, Russian and German poetry by heart. She was an expert at declamation, the now outdated art of interpreting a text by modulating the voice, using mime and gesticulation. As a child I could listen to her endlessly, so I can well imagine her comforting that boy with the words of Lermontov, melodiously crooning in the Russian manner: *'No otiets tvoy stary voin, zakalen v boyu, spiy malyutka, bud spokoyen, bayushki bayu...'* ('Your father is an old warrior, inured to battle, / Sleep, little one, rest peacefully, hushaby now.') Or maybe she raised her voice to a shout as she intoned the words of Hagar in Kornel Ujejski's patriotic poem: 'The sunbeams of fires have charred my head over, I cry out to thee, Jehovah, Jehovah...'

This declamation of hers had a miraculous effect. The people who were crowded into the cellar, maddened with pain, fear, helplessness and despair, calmed down and began to listen. Now, as I write this, I realise that the word 'declaim' comes from the Latin *clamare*, to cry out. *'De profundis clamavi ad te, Domine'* – 'Out of the depths have I cried unto thee, O Lord!' Once my grandmother was exhausted and had to stop, my mother took over, because the boy kept imploring her, 'Please go on, please don't stop...' Of the entire vast repertoire of poems recited on that occasion the most appropriate was by Goethe:

Höchstes Glück der Menschenkinder
Ist doch die Persönlichkeit.
Jedes Leben sei zu führen
wenn man sich nicht selbst vergisst.
Alles könne man verlieren,
wenn man bleibe, was man ist.

[The greatest fortune known to man
Is the human personality.
No man's life is led in vain
If he keeps his identity.
A man can lose all that he owns
If her remains the man he is.]

Jaś, an architecture student, knew German. And probably, as he squeezed my grandmother's hand, he repeated, 'A man can lose all that he owns, if he remains the man he is.'

I couldn't bear this story. I hadn't been there with them in that cellar, and I couldn't imagine a nightmare that I myself had not lived through. I refused to think about it. All I wanted was to forget the experiences of the occupation as quickly as possible.

And besides, I was irritated by the hidden moral of the story. German poetry versus German cruelty? Human dignity versus violence? I have the utmost difficulty and confusion in describing this episode. Even now it still seems to me a touch too maudlin and bombastic.

But my grandmother was like an ancient Roman and loved moral messages. It would have been out of character for her to fail to come up with this particular memory of the occupation the first time I brought my future husband, Ludwig Zimmerer, to visit her in 1957. I spent years reminding him that he had only proposed to me because he was so shocked by the symbolic meaning of that conversation and the lack of any anti-German resentment on my family's part. At the time, various friends of theirs were outraged by this friendship. 'After what you've been through, how can you invite a German into your home, and agree to let him marry Joasia, who was only whisked from the jaws of death by a miracle?' they would drip-feed into my mother's ear. By a paradoxical coincidence she had written her doctorate about Wanda, the legendary queen of Kraków who refused to marry a German prince. I must admit that when I first got to know Ludwig, I felt some trepidation when I asked if I could invite him home, but my grandmother just beamed and said, 'At last I'll have someone to talk German to again.'

Gustav Horwitz died in 1882, when he was barely thirty-eight. A minor surgical procedure performed at home, as was the norm in those days, in the dining room, on a table covered in a white sheet, ended in a blood infection. On his deathbed he insisted on bidding farewell to all his children, so they went up to his bed in turn: first the oldest, fourteen-year-old Flora, then Róża, who was a year younger, then Gizella and Henrietta, nine-year-old Żaneta, seven-year-old Lutek, five-year-old Maks, and three-year-old Kamilka. He placed his hand on each of their heads and said: '*Bleib fromm!*' ('Stay devout.') His wife, with the youngest, one-year-old Staś, in her arms, cried: 'You shall bless them at their weddings. You're not leaving us!'

Apparently there was a large crowd of poor Jews at the funeral, whom in his lifetime he had helped without letting his father-in-law know.

In their hearts he left a sense of sorrow and sympathy, in their memories the image of his rounded shoulders hunched over his desk, a hand shading his permanently reddened eyes from the light, and in their ears the monotonous tapping of his shoes along the wooden pavement under the window, as he set off for the office early in the morning and came home weary late in the afternoon. That was all he meant to anyone, it seemed. Even his dying request – '*Bleib fromm*' – was not fulfilled by any of his children. But he had brought a longing for something more than just a comfortable existence into the worldly, prosaic life of the Warsaw merchant's family. Future generations would be indebted to him for a spiritual unease that could sometimes be hard to bear, but also for the conviction that thanks to art and literature life can be much more bearable, and that is quite a gift.

Izaak Kleinmann, that energetic man of the world and businessman, died not long after his quiet son-in-law. They were buried side by side in the Jewish cemetery in Warsaw. Meanwhile, at the age of thirty-seven, my great-grandmother Julia Horwitz was left on her own with nine children.

THE CHILDREN FROM KRÓLEWSKA STREET

————————————*————————————

Julia's desperate weeping could be heard for many nights to come. My grandmother never forgot how her mother cried out at her dying husband's bedside, 'You're not leaving us! You can't leave me alone!' She must have loved him very much, and she must have suffered greatly, but she never spoke to anyone about her pain. It is telling that after Gustav's death she stopped observing religious rules and did not expect her children to, as if she had taken offence at God for refusing to save him. She also stopped talking to the children in German, and Polish became the main language at home.

At this point she made a choice that determined the future for the next few generations. She decided to polonise the family. However, although she dropped the Jewish traditions and customs, she did not change her faith and remained, at least formally, an adherent of Judaism, although being christened would have made it easier for her children to gain access to Polish society. She had no wish to renounce her identity or erase all trace of her origin. She was very proud, and did not need a crutch to lean on, either in the form of Judaism or any other religion. Whether or not she had ever had faith in God's protection, from now on she believed only in her own strengths. Whenever some sadness or drama occurred in her closest family circle, she never encouraged humility or patient submission to fate. She always gave the person in despair the same advice: '*Kopf hoch!*', meaning, 'Head up!' This favourite expression of hers, repeated year after year ad nauseam, ended up as the motto of the entire family. Successive generations down the line would think of it at their toughest moments, and perhaps it was just what kept them going and helped them to survive.

Where did this German catchphrase come from? Did Gustav bring it with him from Vienna? Did his father, the wise rabbi, bid him farewell with these words, guessing that his son's life would be quite painful, at the mercy of his rich father-in-law, in a strange, barbarian country? Or is it more likely to have been his impetuous mother, Karolina, who feared no one, not even the Cossacks, who so firmly told him not to lose heart?

The invocation 'Head up!' can be understood in two ways: as an encouragement to show strength and courage, meaning, 'You'll manage, you'll cope with the situation,' and also as a reminder never to forget your own dignity, but to go through life with your chin up, looking others straight in the eye. Wherever the saying came from and whatever it meant, it undoubtedly played a very important role in shaping the mentality of all the heroes of this story. It stuck in their minds, marking the bottom line, and whenever disaster occurred, stopped them from floundering helplessly, wringing their hands or capitulating. It may even have been that very phrase that allowed my great-grandmother to find the strength and wisdom to bring up her nine children.

She was not left entirely alone. In Warsaw she still had her mother, father and three brothers. While he was alive, her father felt responsible for Julia, managed her dowry, regularly paid her the interest it earned and often added generous hand-outs from his own funds; but when he died his wife, Miriam Kleinmann, inherited his money, and she was a mean and selfish woman to whom it never occurred to support her daughter financially. Julia's brothers, Bernard and Michał, who were private bankers, took on the care of their widowed sister, but evidently they discharged their duties badly, because the household was under constant financial pressure; so Julia decided to get involved in business herself.

With her brothers' help she began to turn her dowry to profit by lending money at a rate of interest. This trade, common in those days, and as a rule conducted by Jews, even now is still regarded with contempt by some people, who associate it with usury and exploitation, although it does not have to mean preying on human weakness and indigence at all. No one ever heard of Julia being ruthless or grasping, yet her own family regarded her occupation as shameful, and avoided mentioning it by name. It must have been a painful problem for the children. They hated Bernard and Michał's frequent visits to the house, when they would shut themselves up in the kitchen with their sister and hold raucous conversations in an incomprehensible language. They often seemed to be shouting at her, arguing or demanding something in raised voices. After such conversations Julia was always upset and had reddened eyes.

She was aware of the odium that was incumbent on this sort of business, but she had no other opportunity to earn a living. While earning the money to buy food and an education for her offspring in this way, she knocked it into their heads, sometimes literally, that the most important things in life are knowledge, diligence and ambition; she also sternly suppressed anything that might be termed cunning or scheming. When she was informed that thirteen-year-old Maks was working as a ticket tout outside the theatre in the Saxon Gardens to obtain the money for a show he wanted to see, she stood by the kitchen door, which was the children's way into the house, waited for the boy to come home, and struck him a few powerful blows with a piece of firewood, shouting, 'My son! That's the last time you'll ever get involved in any sharp practice.' Then she explained: 'I'm having to bring you up without a father and that makes me all the more responsible for your conduct.'

She brought them up in her own way, according to her own principles. She herself was unusually resourceful, enterprising and shrewd, but in the hierarchy of values that she inculcated in her children, material goods came last. She did not want them to get involved in 'shady dealings'. She believed first and foremost in the importance of education, the only thing that could guarantee them a decent place in Polish society. She spoke to her parents and brothers in German or Yiddish, and she spoke Polish with a distinct Jewish accent, but she sent her own children to Polish schools, where they learned faultless Polish and acquired knowledge of Polish literature and history. Only the oldest son, Ludwik, began his education at a Jewish school, which must have been in accordance with his father's wishes. Later he transferred to a private Polish high school run by Wojciech Górski, where the two youngest, Maks and Staś, were also pupils. On the other hand, all the girls went to schools that were renowned for their patriotism.

This showed incredible determination. It would have been far more convenient to bring all nine up to be cosmopolitans, to push them out of Poland, an enslaved and oppressed country, and into the free, wide world – to their father's rabbinical family in Vienna, or to Berlin, Paris or Amsterdam, where their wealthy aunts could help their nieces and nephews make a start in life; but evidently Julia believed that people are meant to belong to the place where they were born, and to endure the consequences.

13

What was life like for those nine children, crowded into a flat of limited size and living in fairly modest conditions? What means did their mother use to ensure that life proceeded normally, without any upsets, quarrels or shocks, and that the issues of health, nourishment, education and upbringing did not cause any particular problems? My grandmother, who spent her post-war years in Kraków, began to write her memoirs shortly before her death, and so her stories of her childhood in nineteenth-century Warsaw have been preserved in all their bright colours. They tell of the children's games and arguments, of their domestic habits, and the walks they took in long-since non-existent streets, places and landscapes.

Despite being badly off they had domestic servants; at breakfast Fryderyka the cook used to come into the dining room carrying a huge copper pan of boiling milk and a basket of rolls, all of which vanished in a matter of seconds. There was no shortage of food in the house, as two separate anecdotes prove. Their neighbour on Królewska Street was a Mrs Gancwol, the wife of a well-known industrialist, who spent all day long playing the piano, wearing a beautiful white lacy dressing gown. Whenever her sons, Lutek and Olek, reminded her about meals, she would say, 'Go and see Mrs Horwitz, she'll feed you.' So they would come and sit at the table with the entire family. At suppertime, when there were rolls with smoked sausage, a ravening horde of other neighbours, the little Luksemburgs, would regularly invade the dining room, as if on an errand, headed by Róża – Rosa, the future communist revolutionary.

There was more of a problem with clothing; only the oldest daughter, Flora, was given new dresses, and then they were passed on from one girl to the next. Flora was fourteen when her father died, and was a great help to her mother in caring for her younger siblings. Every morning before leaving for classes she buttered ten rolls for their mid-morning break, two for each of the five children who were at school. She also darned the stockings and socks, which that great herd wore out mercilessly. Róża, who was one year younger, also helped her mother; she was the prettiest of all the siblings, as well as being modest and extremely kind.

As a rule the older children taught the younger ones to read and write. They had to do their school homework diligently and thoroughly. Henrietta, who was top of her class, impressed everyone by getting up at dawn before her exams and revising all her notes. To avoid oversleeping, she tied a piece of string to her foot and fastened the other end to the cook's bed, because she was the earliest riser. The tugging on the string must have woken her from a very deep sleep.

My grandmother's memoirs reveal that in her concern for her children's health and correct development, both mental and physical, her mother observed the most up-to-date principles of hygiene. The children's bedclothes had to be aired every day. The positioning of the beds was dictated by the children's state of health: those who tended to catch colds slept in sunny rooms. She took thorough care of their eyesight and teeth. Each child was regularly taken to the best dentist in Warsaw, Franciszek Kobyliński, on Count Berg Street (later renamed Traugutt Street), for check-ups and any necessary fillings. Afterwards, their consolation prize was to drop in at Lourse's café on Krakowskie Przedmieście (an elegant street in central Warsaw) for chocolate, and thus a visit to the dentist ceased to be a nightmare.

In each of the nine siblings the genes of the less resourceful, sensitive intellectuals, the Horwitzes, and the strong, upwardly mobile arrivistes, the Kleinmanns, combined in a different way. The oldest daughter, Flora, energetic, determined and bossy, was the most like her mother. The second one, Róża, had inherited Julia's practicality and Gustav's mild nature. The third, Gizella, dreamy, quiet, secretive and inclined towards melancholy, seemed a faithful copy of her father. The fourth, red-headed Henrietta, had a complex nature; she would start quarrels, and then complain that no one loved her. Janina, impetuous like her mother, inherited intellectual fervour from the Horwitzes, and her greatest passion from childhood onwards was books. The youngest girl, Kamilka, outwardly the quietest and least troublesome, later turned out to have the strongest character of all the children.

The boys were even more different from one another. Lutek and Staś were like their father in their quietness and dislike of conflict. Maks, quick-tempered, brave and confident, was afraid of nothing and no one. From earliest childhood he was highly temperamental. He always seemed to be involved in fights and arguments. His exploits were legendary. Unusually strong physically, at only just three years old he could move the heaviest objects in the flat. Intelligent, capable and sharp, he could memorise very long poems after a single hearing. When at their father's funeral the oldest son, seven-year-old Lutek, was supposed to say the Kaddish over the grave but was too unnerved by the crowd of people to utter a word, five-year-old Maks pushed him aside and unhesitatingly recited the Hebrew prayer from memory. He caused his mother the most worries, and perhaps that was why she loved him the most.

Julia aimed to nurture vitality in her children and a firm grasp of reality – the features of her own personality, so much at odds with Gustav's general disposition, which had tended towards daydreaming. She regarded her husband's characteristic lack of initiative as a misfortune, maybe even as the cause of his premature death. She must have more or less consciously felt a grudge against him for making her a widow so young and for leaving her with a flock of children to bring up, so she strictly discouraged anything that seemed to show evidence of inner disorder, such as indolence, a tendency to split hairs, or any sort of 'I don't want to...', 'I won't...' or 'I can't...'.

She wanted to protect them from the ruinous effects of life in the spiritual sphere alone. She cared about balance. My future grandmother, who obsessively read anything that fell into her hands, was constantly being reminded not to ruin her eyes in poor light; quite often the book was torn from her hands and she was sent to help with the cleaning or the mangle. Her sister Róża, who preferred household to intellectual occupations, would be thrown out of the kitchen and told to go and read a book. There certainly was the occasional row or some conflict, but they never disturbed the domestic peace for long. Amazingly, Julia was in favour of fights among the boys, as she reckoned they helped build up their muscles, and was in general a great advocate of physical exercise. She extremely rarely meted out stern punishments, which made them all the more terrifying when she did. Beating was not one of her teaching methods, though that one time the wretched Maks was hit with a piece of firewood, and another time Flora was slapped in the face for disobedience. Julia was very bossy and did a lot of shouting; from morning to evening she delivered orders, commands and prohibitions in a raised voice. Maks, who was most often at the thick end of it, used to encourage her: 'Shout, Mama, shout, some of it will always stick, something will always remain!'

I think if it hadn't been for the iron firmness that she used to implement her educational programme, where there was no room for doubts and indecision, she would never have managed to 'make people out of the children', as she used to say at the time. However, that iron firmness must have been accompanied by great and intelligent love. Despite financial problems and worries, which she never lacked, an atmosphere of warmth and sincerity prevailed in the house, guaranteeing a sense of security.

Yet one memory that always remained a thorn in my grandmother's flesh bears witness to the fact that, for all her love, Julia sometimes hurt the children's feelings. One day the school needlework teacher told her pupils to bring in some tulle for embroidery. So little Żaneta, already an aesthete, carefully lined a shiny tobacco tin with a piece of pink tissue paper. She dreamed of laying the transparent white material in it. Then she would have her own, hand-embroidered serviette. Simply the word 'tulle', as she told the story, made her feel ecstatic. But when she asked for some money for the object of her desire, her mother responded by saying, 'That sort of frippery is a luxury. In a house with nine children where I have to take care of everything on my own, each of you should help me. Look how many of your stockings and socks need darning. Take those to your sewing lesson and learn how to darn properly. It'll be useful to you in life.'

One can imagine the shame of that nine-year-old little girl, bringing a pile of torn children's socks to school instead of a piece of white tulle in pink tissue paper. She hated needlework for ever after, but she did learn to darn properly; and though she never sewed on a button in her life, I have a perfect memory of her in the post-war years, putting on her glasses and opening a Russian tea tin, taking out a darning mushroom, a thimble, some red worsted and a thick needle, which I had to thread for her, and carefully, slowly and neatly darning my winter socks.

Only in this one single tale of the family home was there a faint note of bitterness. All the other stories were full of affection, gratitude and admiration — for the considerate way in which her mother took care of one of her daughter's frost-chapped hands, another girl's watering eyes, or a third one's over-anxiety; for the fact that when any of them was more seriously ill than usual, she sat up all night by the sick child's bed, and never let anyone take her place; and for her extraordinary medical intuition, thanks to which she always made perfect diagnoses concerning her children's health. To the end of her days she could never forgive herself for the fact that, although she had been against her husband's operation, she had finally given in to the persuasion of Warsaw's two most eminent doctors of the era, the specialist Ignacy Baranowski and the surgeon Julian Kosiński, which ended in tragedy.

Maybe that was why she did not lack the courage to stand up to the authorities when Maks had an accident that led to unpleasant complications. At the age of seven he bet his peers in the courtyard that he could jump down from a tall wooden outhouse. He jumped, and hit his knee so hard that it swelled up, seriously injured. The infection lasted a long time, with the boy's condition growing steadily worse, until finally a consultation group of top surgeons decided that the child's life could only be saved by amputating his leg. Julia refused to give her consent and decided to act alone. She left her home and children and took the sick boy to Berlin, to consult the German surgeons. Their treatment saved the leg from amputation, although it remained stiff and Maks walked with a limp for the rest of his life.

A source of constant delight and joy was the garden at the back of the tenement building on Królewska Street, which my grandmother remembered to the end of her days as a childhood paradise. It seemed to be ownerless, with no gardener or caretaker, so the children could do what they liked there. There were apple and pear trees growing there, as well as cherries, plums, gooseberry bushes, blackcurrants and roses. Once carefully cultivated and tended, it had since gone wild, which made it an even greater attraction. No fruits in the world ever tasted so sweet, my grandmother used to say, as the ones in the garden on Królewska Street, no roses ever had such a delightful scent. They didn't have to go away to a holiday resort in summer: ... *the comings and goings, games and fun of our childhood years, the whispers and confidences of teenage girls against the background of our 'own' secret garden had the untold charm of unrestrained, untroubled freedom*, she wrote in her memoirs. *In winter Mama had a skating rink made on the largest lawn. A copious flood of water froze splendidly, and the young folk, who first learned to skate pushing along small chairs for balance, in time developed into nimble skaters who later showed off their skills at the fashionable skating pond in the Saxon Gardens.*

In a ground-floor flat in the annexe an old man with a white beard often used to stand at a window overlooking that paradise, watching the children play. He was Chaim Zelig Słonimski, grandfather of the famous Polish poet, Antoni Słonimski.

The tenement building on Królewska Street was near the Saxon

Gardens, and the children often went there for after-dinner walks. In the 'Fruit' avenue there was a kiosk selling sweets and lemonade. In the 'Literature' avenue there was a well, from which the wards of the Charitable Society drew the most delicious water in the world and sold it for a few pennies to thirsty passers-by. In the 'Main' avenue a clump of massive chestnut trees rustled their leaves and fluff showered down from trees in bloom. Sunlight was refracted in the streams of water gushing from the fountain, creating magical rainbows. Elegantly dressed little girls with balls or skipping ropes ran down the avenues, in the care of their French nursemaids. My future grandmother used to gaze at them enviously, and dreamed of making friends with one of them. Once she gathered her courage, went up to the lovely Stefcia Krysińska, daughter of a famous lawyer, and asked: 'Would you like to play with me, Miss?' The reply was a curt 'No', and for the rest of her life she never forgot the insult.

In their school years they used to cross the Saxon Gardens twice a day, on the way to school and on the way back. By the pond, where pure white swans were swimming, and where people skated merrily in winter, they came out onto Niecała Street and continued across Teatralny Square, where the older sisters held the younger ones tightly by the hand and looked round carefully as they crossed the road, to make sure they didn't fall under a cart or a droshky. Then they went on, via Senatorska Street, to the corner of Miodowa Street, where Sołtyk Palace stood.

THE MYSTERY OF THE TORN PHOTOGRAPH

———————— ✳ ————————

Sołtyk Palace, an enormous old mansion, was the former residence of the Bishops of Kraków. The new owner rented out the rooms to innumerable tenants. On the ground floor on the Senatorska Street side were the most elegant shops in town: Izdebski's glass and porcelain store, Thonnes's ladies' clothing, and Lilpop's watchmaker's studio. One could spend hours gazing into the shop display windows, but the Misses Horwitz never stopped in front of them, for fear of being late for class. Little Żaneta, however, often forced her sisters to make a short stop in front of Hoesick's bookshop. Then she would visually devour the colourful covers of the children's books displayed there: *Maniusia's Dolls*, *Mrs Grypska's Box*, *Kazio's Toys*, *The Flash of Light*, *Campanella*, *Laura's Diary* and *The Little Princess*, titles she remembered for the rest of her life. That childish, unsatisfied hunger for books was the reason why, later on in life, as the owner of her own publishing firm, she devoted so much attention to children's books. The next generation of children would gaze at the window display at Mortkowicz's bookshop on Mazowiecka Street, engrossed in the titles of the books she had translated.

Once they had torn themselves away from the bookshop window, the young ladies turned into Miodowa Street and entered the huge mansion gates. On weekdays they ran towards the courtyard, from where they rushed up the kitchen stairs, two steps at a time, to the first floor of the building. On days celebrating the beginning and end of the year, their headmistresses' name-days or other important school events they walked slowly in pairs up the front staircase, which led to a door with a brass plaque inscribed 'Leokadia and Bronisława Kosmowska's private school for girls'.

Girls' private schools were an important part of the intellectual landscape of the era. In 1882, when my grandmother started her schooling, the tsarist Russification policy within the Russian empire was at its height. Its relentless executors were Warsaw's infamous Governor-General Yosif V. Hurko and the curator of the Warsaw School District, Alexander Apukhtin, who on taking up his post in 1879 announced that in ten years' time no mother in the country would be speaking to her child in Polish – and he was doing everything he could to keep his promise. Pupils at government secondary schools were the most badly terrorised. 'A school that's run according to Apukhtin's system will produce either cretins or heroes,' they used to say in Warsaw. The torment suffered by the children is described in Stefan Żeromski's *Sisyphean Labours*, Janusz Korczak's *Ill-Starred Week*, and Wiktor Gomulicki's *Memoirs of a Sky-Blue Uniform*. When Henryk Sienkiewicz delivered a story entitled *From the Diary of a Warsaw Crammer* to the editorial office of the literary journal *Niwa* ('The Soil'), the censors would not pass it for publication. 'I'll have to take [it] to Poznań,' he said, as Poznań was in the less restrictive Prussian partition. 'Maybe they won't get the idea and will let it through.' And indeed, the story came out in instalments under the title *From the Diary of a Poznań Teacher*.

The Russian textbooks taught contempt for Polish history and tradition. Plain-clothes inspectors used to raid the pupils' lodgings to check if the young people were reading any books that had been banned by the censors. The pupils were forbidden to speak in Polish, not just during school breaks but in any public place. The slightest infringements were punished with detention, a flogging or expulsion from the school. The intellectual and moral standards of the Russian teachers cried out for vengeance. The obtuse, relentless demands that they made on the children, their constant repression and mortification, quite often led to suicides among school pupils. As a result, people were reluctant to send their children to government secondary schools. Girls from the landed gentry usually had governesses and domestic teachers. Those from the middle classes were sent to private schools, although they were more expensive than state schools and graduating from them did not entitle one to enter university. But if a girl wanted to get higher education, her wish was regarded as a passing whim; in any case, university studies were not open to women in the Congress Kingdom. Thus the task of a private school was to turn out enlightened wives and mothers, in a pleasant atmosphere, free of fear and humiliation; and that was just the sort of atmosphere that

Julia Horwitz was looking for when she enrolled her daughters at Leokadia Kosmowska's school. The school's strong idealism, the spirit of resistance to the invader that prevailed there, its devotion to the idea of independence and to romantic poetry all had an effect on the young ladies' imaginations and inspired a love of Poland, among the Jewish pupils too. But love, as everyone knows, is not always requited.

⬥

In the same mansion lived Ferdynand Wilhelm Hoesick and his family, the owner of the bookshop into whose window Żaneta used to gaze with such delight. His son – and only child – Ferduś, or Ferdynand Hoesick, a future writer and critic, wrote a memoir entitled *My Parents' House*, in which he described the games he played with his contemporaries who lived in the same building. In the huge courtyard they used to play tipcat, rounders, tag, and heads and tails, and were also keen on bullying their small neighbours, the Weinkranzes, for example by 'christening' them under the water pump. *Simply because they were Jews, they were regarded by all the other boys as something inferior, and as by nature they did not err on the side of bravery, time and again they had to put up with all sorts of mischievous pranks of ours*, he writes with disarming sincerity. Sometimes the boys sought entertainment in town. *We, or rather some of my friends, particularly enjoyed fighting the little Jewish boys on Infant Jesus Square. I remember that on the way back from school we always went that way, with our rulers hidden up our sleeves, to take the opportunity to hit the Jewish boys with them; there was always a crowd of them there at a certain time of day, because they had just come out of a Jewish school*, the subtle humanist movingly continues.

What was it like to live with a constant sense of threat? To find out as a child, that in the country where you live you are regarded as 'something inferior' and might be insulted for that reason alone? I never asked this question, so I do not know the answer. I can only imagine that it was necessary to choose one's paths in life and one's friends wisely, to have as little inevitable unpleasantness as possible.

Half my school friends were of Semitic origin, which in view of their total assimilation was of no importance and was never mentioned or pointed out by the teachers, my grandmother stressed approvingly. She clearly regarded this fact as unusual.

She ended up at the Kosmowskas' school because of her own obstinacy, in rather dramatic circumstances. Four of her sisters, Flora, Gizella, Róża and Henrietta, had already been pupils there for a few years, but Żaneta was enrolled at a school run by Izabella Smolikowska, later Hewelke, because it was nearer home, and the little girl had to start school while her mother was away in Berlin with the sick Maks, seeking the help of the local doctors.

Their father had died only a few months earlier, and his nine-year-old daughter had not forgotten the religious strictures that he observed. School activities began on a Monday. The new pupil, clever and obedient, coped superbly with the teachers' instructions – until Saturday. On Saturday the children were told to write an essay. She alone did not open her exercise book, but sat idly doing nothing. She explained to the astounded teacher that on the Sabbath she was not allowed to take pen in hand. He complained to the headmistress, who declared that she would not tolerate such behaviour in her school. In reply the haughty child, who would one day be my grandmother, put her books in her satchel and without a word went home. Next day, Żaneta informed her sisters that she would not cross the threshold of Miss Smolikowska's school again. A few days later, when the girls realised that the little one was adamant, they took her with them to the Kosmowskas' school. Evidently, her principles were taken more seriously there, or treated more indulgently, and she herself soon gave them up. Regretfully? Or not? I do not know.

Both headmistresses, the Kosmowska sisters, dignified, well on in years – or so it seemed to me – great patriots, were especially keen on moral educational issues. We respected them deeply, and they had great authority. I cannot remember any of the pupils showing any defiance or having a critical attitude to their head-mistresses. We particularly esteemed the stern, but always fair, Miss Leokadia, wrote my grandmother in her memoirs. Here too, like in the government schools, the official language of instruction was Russian, but the teachers, ignoring the bans, conducted the lessons in Polish; during lessons supposedly devoted to needle-work and drawing, as a rule they secretly taught the so-called 'motherland subjects', Polish literature, history and geography. A surprise inspection and discovery of the slightest breach of the reg-ulations could mean a severe penalty, including closure of the school, so the young ladies were also well versed in the principles of conspiracy. At an agreed signal forbidden books were concealed in special hiding places, and all sorts of ruses were used to fool the inspectors. Whenever one appeared, the girls began to chatter in Russian during breaks, and in class the teacher would always call on the same star pupil to answer – the one who was able to recite perfectly all the titles of the Tsar and his enormous family.

The Polish teachers were enlightened people with broad horizons. For example, one who taught the history of Poland – secretly, of course – was Jadwiga Szczawińska, later Dawidowa, a famous educational and social activist, future creator of the Flying University, the illegal higher-educational establishment for women. Not just facts and dates were crammed into the young heads. Above all they were instilled with the fundamental precepts of positivism, which declared that one should live for others, not for oneself. While teaching social commitment, responsibility, unselfishness and self-sacrifice, at the same time the educators of the day knew how to inspire curiosity and enthusiasm for learning in their pupils. From those school years my grandmother gained an impressively wide range of knowledge and interests. For example, she had a passion for botany and was able to identify plants and dry them in a herbarium, and knew the Polish, Russian and Latin names of every herb and flower she came across on walks in the meadows. She would bring huge bouquets of flowers back with her, and then lovingly and expertly describe the nature and characteristics of each individual species.

She always liked to read, but her fascination with poetry was born at school, as well as her habit of writing out poems that made a special impression on her into thick copybooks in beautiful calligraphy. These copybooks kept her company throughout her life. At first they were very modest school notebooks bound in oilcloth, but later on they were elegant albums in morocco and brocade covers. During the war she used to glue together odd sheets of paper – whatever she came across – and after the war she would take over my half-filled flimsy school exercise books with dingy covers.

The content of these copybooks changed with the times too. The first writers to appear there were the Polish and German classic poets: Juliusz Słowacki, Cyprian Norwid, Goethe and Heine. Later came Teofil Lenartowicz, Władysław Syrokomla, Kornel Ujejski and Maria Konopnicka, all major Polish nineteenth-century poets. Later still came Kazimierz Przerwa Tetmajer, who aroused 'strange thrills'. Next came contemporary authors issued by her own publishing house: Leopold Staff, Julian Tuwim, Bolesław Leśmian and Maria Pawlikowska-Jasnorzewska. During the war Krzysztof Kamil Baczyński appeared (who died aged 23 in the 1944 Warsaw Uprising), and after it came Tadeusz Różewicz, a poet who would seem to be completely alien to her tastes but was sincerely beloved and was her neighbour for a while on Krupnicza Street in Kraków after the war. Goodness knows why she wrote all these poems out, because she knew them by heart. I spent my entire childhood listening to lines such as: 'Three times has the golden moon gone round...' (Juliusz Słowacki), 'And when Stach went to war...' (Maria Konopnicka), 'In his court at Suza King Darius is feasting...' (Kornel Ujejski), and 'Old rascal that I am, I'm roasting in the sun...' (Julian Tuwim).

Later on, the Mortkowicz publishing firm would issue its own mini-anthologies of poetry entitled *Lira i Lirenka* ('The Lyre and the Little Lyre'), including all the most beautiful poems written in Polish. Sometimes I have a dream about finding a tiny volume in a yellowing leather binding in a second-hand bookshop, and I am filled with a wonderful feeling of bliss; but I always wake up empty-handed.

My grandmother always remembered her school years with great pleasure. She loved to describe her school adventures and her own displays of patriotic resistance. Despite the relative freedom, knowledge of the Russian language and Russian literature was strictly enforced. These subjects were taught by native Russian speakers. In her memoirs she describes the result of being overly familiar with Professor Yurashkievich: *He was even quite good-natured and liked to chat with us, which once got me into big trouble. We were jokingly teaching him Polish pronunciation and at one point I said, 'How come you've lived in Poland for such a long time but you haven't been able to learn Polish?' To which, his joking tone immediately changing to a sharp one, he replied fiercely in Russian, 'It's not me that lives in Poland, but you that live in Russia.' This incident was reported to the headmistress, who gave me a severe reprimand, ascribing all the blame to me, because 'one does not hold such conversations with a "Moskal"'* [as the Russians were commonly known].

Our farewell to our headmistress after finishing school was a very festive, moving occasion. 'Now pass on what you have been given

here to others,' she said in parting with us, writes my grandmother; and she goes on to tell how immediately afterwards the young school-leavers ran off to have their photograph taken as a souvenir, round the corner at Mieczkowski's photographic studio, which was in the mansion's annexe and was the shape of a large, glazed summer house. It was 1888. She was fifteen years old.

Ah, that souvenir photograph! What a pity it did not survive, but was lost with all our other belongings in the rubble of the Warsaw Uprising. I have such a vivid memory of it. I can see every detail so perfectly – every one of the small group of friends who finished school with me, she wrote regretfully almost seventy years later, then added a list of names.

In 1960 this very extract from her memoirs appeared in the *Ekspres Wieczorny* ('Evening Express'), a Warsaw evening newspaper. Soon after, a miracle occurred. An old lady called the editorial office to complain that she had not been mentioned in the text, although she went to the same school as the author and was in the same class. To prove it, she could provide the very same photograph, in which she herself featured. My grandmother's niece, Karolina Beylin, who worked for the newspaper, took the matter in hand. She sent the office caretaker to fetch the photograph, and then delivered it to Kraków.

It was actually half a photograph, with the left side torn off, but luckily it reached my grandmother a couple of weeks before her death and she was still able to rejoice in the resurrection of such a dear souvenir. However, she was already feeling too unwell to thank the contributor. Later on, the letter with the lady's name and address on it got lost. Only the yellowed photograph remained in the family archives. Written on it in a stranger's hand is the date 1889, which conflicts with my grandmother's account, in which she claimed that she finished school the year before. It does not make any vital difference. However, another error of memory is revealed on the back. It turns out that the young ladies did not have their souvenir picture taken at Mieczkowski's studio, but at Rembrandt Art Photography, 151 Marszałkowska Street. Indeed, one can see that the photographer was an artist. He has very carefully stage-directed every gesture and pose, the arrangement of the hands, the facial expressions and gazes. It was a serious matter, so none of the girls is smiling – and thus they remain, frozen for ever in a picturesque group, dressed for the occasion, buttoned up to the neckline, squeezed into corsets and staring straight ahead of them.

The girl sitting in the middle is clearly an 'emancipated woman'. She is not wearing a corset, her curly hair is cut short, and she is wearing a fancifully tied spotted bow round her neck. She is Ada Kosmowska, the headmistresses' niece, who later became an actress in the Kraków theatres. To her left sits my future grandmother, with a book on her knees. Beside her, holding a book, stands Helena Hirszfeld, *a quiet, fragile, highly refined girl*, sister of the famous Bolesław Hirszfeld, a fervent Polish patriot of Jewish origin, a rich industrialist and also a generous philanthropist, political and social activist, whom Stefan Żeromski called 'the Son of Immortality' in his story *The Legend of the Itinerant Labourer*. At Ada Kosmowska's feet sits my grandmother's dearest friend, Mania Ziembińska, *a beautiful black-eyed, black-haired girl*, daughter of the cashier at a firm called Krzysztof Brun and Sons. Beside her stands Tola Chwat, daughter of a famous Warsaw doctor. At the end sits Madzia Goldfluss, *diligent, intelligent, later a first-class librarian in Lwów*.

Thanks to information left by my grandmother and my mother I can identify most of the schoolgirls shown in the picture; but who is the young lady standing on the far left, the one who has been torn in half diagonally? Is she Stasia Adamska? Or Wacia Mazurowska, or maybe Mania Buszkowska, *daughter of a prominent lawyer, exemplary in every regard*? Or perhaps she is the forgotten friend? I shall never know. Judging from the composition of the photograph and from the names given in the memoirs, the portraits of at least three or four girls were lost for ever with the torn-off left half.

This photograph is full of mysteries. On the back a note has been scribbled in handwriting that I do not recognise, saying: *Extracted in 1945 from under a thick layer of soiled books and papers*. I do not know who found it, or where. Was it in the rubble of a ruined house, or in a buried cellar perhaps? Was it already damaged when it was found? Or did that lady tear it in half, keep the half with herself on it, and give my grandmother the other half, hoping that in exchange her existence would be recorded in writing?

More than a hundred years have passed since the young schoolgirls had their photograph taken at Rembrandt's, but the stubborn spirit of that nameless girl refuses to depart and dissolve into nonexistence. She keeps haunting me, begging to be remembered – and apparently not in vain. After I had finished this chapter, I found a lost trace – evidence of her existence – among the family papers, in the form of a letter from Karolina Beylin to my grandmother:

Warsaw, 27 September 1960

Dearest Auntie,
I'm sending you this charming photograph, which is a fine illustration for your memoirs [...]. Your friend, Mrs Wrzesińska (she didn't say what her maiden name was), lives on Akademicka Street.

FOUR WEDDINGS WITHOUT A FIFTH

—————————— * ——————————

There is a moving scene in one of Carlos Saura's films where the adult heroine peeps through a half-open door into the dining room of her childhood. The whole family is gathered at table, including her long-dead parents and herself as a very little girl. The wind, or maybe the flow of time, sets the cut-glass pendants of the chandelier hanging above the table in motion. The crystal sound makes the child look up towards the door. For a split second the past and the future are looking at each other, as they meet in the present, and the viewer feels an unearthly shudder. Right now I am trying to pull off an even harder trick than stepping back into the world of my own childhood, because my aim is to open the door into my great-grandmother Julia Horwitz's flat over a century ago.

The year is 1888. The place is Warsaw, 49 Królewska Street, on the first floor at the front of the building. On the door there is a white plaque with a name written in black Gothic letters: 'Gustav Horwitz, dr philosophie'. Gustav has been dead for six years now, but his widow has not removed the plaque from the door. This creates the illusion that there is a husband and father in this home. His study has remained exactly as it was: the bookcase is full of works of philosophy and volumes of German poetry. In the corner stands a fine old clock in an ash-wood case, and above the sofa hangs a gilded Biedermeier-style mirror – wedding presents from Gustav's family in Vienna.

The children take refuge in their father's study when they need silence and solitude. Life at home is focused on a room called the parlour, which is a combination of a dining room and a drawing room. The parlour is also a passage, leading to the rest of the flat, and so it is constantly full of motion. Each of the nine siblings has a lot of personal matters to attend to, and a crowd of friends as well, who drop in without warning and sit down to supper together, each shouting louder than the others, arguing and making up again. Nowadays it is hard to imagine life revolving from morning to evening around such a large flock, but in those days no one complained of a lack of privacy. If the girls wanted to discuss secrets of the heart, they would go out to the kitchen stairs, into the garden or the courtyard. But their mother used to herd them back into the house; she preferred to have control of them.

In the parlour, where an oil portrait of their grandfather, the Viennese rabbi, hung on the wall, and the bookshelves were full of green-bound volumes of Talmudic commentaries that he wrote, there was a cabinet that housed the collected works of the greatest Polish poets Adam Mickiewicz, Juliusz Słowacki and Zygmunt Krasiński, published by Brockhaus in Leipzig in the Library of Polish Classics series. That publisher's services to Polish culture and national consciousness were invaluable. Thanks to him, readers could get hold of the works of Polish poets that were banned in the Congress Kingdom or were published only after being mutilated by the tsarist censors. Copies smuggled across the border in small numbers were hard to get, a much sought-after treasure. It is significant for the history of the family's assimilation that thirteen-year-old Ludwik Horwitz received this priceless gift as a bar-mitzvah present from his uncle, who himself had not yet learned to speak Polish very well. Now, besides the beloved poems of the contemporary poets, such as Maria Konopnicka, Adam Asnyk, Władysław Syrokomla and Teofil Lenartowicz, my future grandmother could declaim patriotic classics such as Mickiewicz's 'Ordon's Redoubt', 'My Testament' and 'Agamemnon's Grave' (both by Słowacki) at social events.

There was also a piano in the parlour, a prerequisite in any middle-class home. The young ladies played on it four-handedly, with each other or with their suitors. Sometimes their neighbour, Lutek Gancwol, played dance music for their parties. As he played, he gave the dancers instructions: 'Gentlemen to the right! Ladies to the left! *Chaîne! Changer des dames! En avant!*' How innocent the customs of those days were. One day, when he tried to kiss my fifteen-year-old future grandmother on the hand, she tore herself free and cried indignantly: 'Go to the devil!'

☙

It is the evening. At a round table covered in red plush the household are gathered in the light of an oil lamp. The younger children are doing their homework. Seven-year-old Staś has only just started school. Nine-year-old Kamilka goes to Miss Jadwiga Sikorska's school. Eleven-year-old Maks is at Wojciech Górski's renowned private school on Hortensja Street. The teachers cannot cope with him. He is highly temperamental. His illness and the resulting infirmity have not held him back at all. He always seems to be in some sort of a fight or fuss. When he began school, he was still walking on crutches, but after getting hit over the head once or twice, his schoolmates soon stopped calling him 'cripple'. Anti-Semitic taunts will send him into a fury. When a teacher, who meant nothing bad by it, quietened the class down by saying, 'You're not at the cheder now,' Maks took him to task for his religious intolerance. Intelligent and well read, he always seems to be having intellectual arguments with the teachers and often wins the upper hand. Maybe resentment about his racial origin and his physical handicap make him constantly feel the need to prove that he is not inferior to others, but superior, stronger and more intelligent. As a small boy he already liked to be in charge.

Tranquil, absent-minded, always rather distracted, thirteen-year-old Ludwik is a pupil at the philological secondary school No. III. From time to time a school inspector calls at the house to inspect Lutek's shelves and drawers in search of banned reading matter. Everyone finds this offensive, but that is the cost of studying at a state secondary school. However, the state-secondary-school matriculation qualifies one for higher education.

Fifteen-year-old Żaneta, my future grandmother, who is now called Janina, is blushing as she reads the latest instalment of *The Third Woman*, Henryk Sienkiewicz's new novel, published in the *Kurier Codzienny* ('Daily Courier'). Her mother tears the newspaper from her hands – the novel is quite unsuitable for young ladies. And besides, there is a pile of her younger siblings' socks waiting to be darned. Despite having a reputation for being bold and independent, Janina is afraid of her irascible mother, so she furiously gets down to work. Her older sisters are already grown up. Flora is twenty, Róża is nineteen, Gizella is eighteen and Henrietta seventeen. They spend the whole time whispering secrets to one another, blushing or bursting into laughter. The younger girls alter their old dresses to look new, according to the patterns in the latest issue of *Bluszcz* ('Ivy'). They are going to wear them at Flora's wedding, because Flora, thank God, is engaged, and the first big stone has fallen from their mother's heart.

After supper someone suggests a game of lotto or forfeits. They have a fun time. But at a fixed, fairly early hour they must carry out a daily duty. On the second floor Granny Kleinmann is waiting. Since her husband's death she refuses to sleep alone in her huge, eight-room flat, so one of her granddaughters must go and stay the night with her. Janina is sent up to her most often. She is reluctant to go, despite the fact that her grandmother, though not greatly liked by her grandchildren, is very loving to her. She is always offering her cakes and sweets, and once even bought her some summer clothes at Wlodkowski's famous shop on Czysta Street, a dress made of white calico with grey stripes and a navy-blue overcoat with a matching hat. It was the first new outfit my future grandmother had ever owned. Until then she had always worn her older sisters' dresses. That must have been why the colour and style of the clothes stayed in her memory for the rest of her life.

Miriam Kleinmann, though rich, was generally very mean, and her grandchildren were not very fond of her. As her own daughter explained to her: 'If you want them to love you, do something for them, give them something – you know how many things they need. The children should know that there is someone in the world apart from me who cares about them.' Very little came of these hints, although Miriam was fully aware that their poor financial situation made it difficult to get her granddaughters married off. According to Jewish tradition, finding suitable husbands for one's daughters was a basic parental duty. Marriage was too serious a matter to be contracted for love. After all, it concerned two people's future, and that of their offspring. The older generation took charge of bringing the couples together, involving family, friends and a professional matchmaker. Before any decision was made, the advantages and disadvantages of both sides were discussed in detail, and all the pros and cons were weighed up in a businesslike way. The young people did not have much say in the matter. The main prerequisite for the marriage contract was the dowry. The smaller it was, the worse the chances of finding a suitable partner. The Misses Horwitz had many advantages: pretty and educated, they came from a good, rabbinical family, which was highly valued among Jews. Unfortunately, however, they could not count on having decent dowries.

Their mother was very upset about this. If any of her daughters were to end up an old maid it would be a catastrophe. But her opportunities for action were fairly limited. Foreign resorts and fashionable holiday locations, where it was easiest to make matrimonial acquaintances, did not come into play for financial reasons. Her modest social position excluded elegant public balls. So the entire family was involved in the search, including the more distant relatives based in Paris, Germany and Holland, as well as the nearest ones in Warsaw, and also friends from the same social circles. Mothers who were friends with each other and had similar problems used to take turns to organise private receptions combined with dances and popular party games, to which they invited young people of both sexes. At such gatherings friendships were made, sometimes leading to marriage. If a girl got to know a bachelor and he made a good impression, he could pay a visit to the young lady at her home. Whenever a suitor for one of the older sisters came to Królewska Street, the rest of the siblings were driven out of the parlour. Often the conversation between the young people did not take off, and then Janina would be called in to declaim some poetry, usually her star turn, Lenartowicz's 'The Country Maid'.

When private contacts failed to produce a result, a professional matchmaker came to call. For some unknown reason he always had an umbrella with him, which he left in the hall, then settled down in the kitchen and sang his favourite's praises to Mrs Horwitz. The girls would listen at the door and then, in fits of laughter, imitate his proposals. But it was laughter through tears; they hated all this fuss about their future, which made them feel like goods for sale. They dreamed of true love, like in Maria Rodziewicz's romantic novels, and yet they did appreciate their mother's efforts. They knew that only a reliable man with a future could guarantee them a secure existence. How much hope and how much fear there was in their hearts we shall never know.

None of these girlish whispers, confidences, hesitations, sorrows and joys made their way into the pages of my grandmother's memoirs. Where emotional matters were concerned she always maintained utter discretion, so I do not know how Flora's future husband, Samuel Beylin, came into her life. She chose him from among several candidates presented to her. But who introduced them? The matchmaker? The family? Or friends? He was undoubtedly a good match. He used to buy hops in the Congress

Kingdom and export them to Russia and Germany. He had his own hop-drying plant in Leszno so he was wealthy, and on top of that he was likable. Did Flora love him? All I could find out from family accounts was that after finishing school she very much wanted to go on studying. She was extremely able, and while he was alive her father had supported her plans; but after his death she had to help care for her younger siblings, and there was no longer any question of further studies.

In November 1888 she married Samuel and became a wealthy person overnight. Even before the wedding, her loving fiancé rented a beautiful flat on Elektoralna Street, furnished it carefully and hired some servants. As a wedding present he took his wife on honeymoon to Vienna, knowing it was her dream to visit her father's home city. They set off just after the wedding, from their new flat. In the carriage that was taking them to the station serving the Warsaw–Vienna line, Flora realised that she had forgotten her galoshes, so they went home for them. Using their own key to open the door without ringing the bell, they noticed that the flat was brightly lit and heard the animated sound of a large number of party-goers coming from the dining room. The servants had invited their own guests and, without even waiting for the master and mistress to be properly on their way, were having a ball. The inexperienced mistress of the house took fright and gave her husband a beseeching look. He realised how terrified she was, and that making a fuss would cause them to be late for the train, or even make it impossible for them to depart. So he grabbed the galoshes from their place in the corridor and they sneaked out again, silently closing the door behind them.

The trip was a great success. The newly-weds visited the Viennese relatives, toured the museums and sights of Vienna, and attended a performance at the Vienna Opera, where they saw the Archduke Rudolf and his wife in the royal box. Three months later he tragically shot himself and his lover at Mayerling, and Flora kept endlessly having to repeat what the unfortunate heir to the throne had looked like, how he was dressed and how he behaved. 'It's no good being narrow-minded,' she used to insist. What a lot of impressions and experiences she might have missed if she had taken the servants to task that time.

My grandmother left no description of her oldest sister's wedding service and celebration. She used to excuse herself by saying that she could not remember much about it, as she was too thrilled with her first ball dress to notice anything else. The dress was made of muslin, with a sky-blue sash around the waist, and although it had been converted from one of her older sisters' hand-me-downs, it inspired universal admiration. But how and where was the wedding ceremony held? It must have been conducted according to the full ritual. Samuel was a believer and a very devout Jew. Throughout his life he remained faithful to his religion, observed the traditional customs and spent a lot of time praying. How interesting an account of that picturesque celebration from over a century ago would be. Unfortunately, despite being sensitive to the charms of life and inclined to celebrate even the most humble excuse for rejoicing, my grandmother never told me about the romantic Jewish festivals and religious ceremonies that she remembered from childhood.

As she writes in her memoirs: *After our father's death, our family home was no different from other Polish homes.* She abridges and simplifies the difficult process of assimilation. After all, those who kept their Jewish religion also kept up the basic traditional customs: the brothers celebrated their bar mitzvah, wedding ceremonies were conducted by a rabbi and relatives were buried at the Jewish cemetery. Naturally, the children spoke in Polish and did not know Yiddish, went to Polish schools and read Polish literature, but they went on living among people of Jewish origin. The names that appear in the memoirs are almost exclusively Jewish: Klingsland, Sterling, Askenazy, Hirszfeld, Handelsman, Lauer and Landau.

People from this environment, assimilated members of the intelligentsia, shared similar interests, but also similar problems. They were hurt by the mistrust, ill will and disdainful attitude of Polish society to 'intruders'. I am not surprised that my grandmother was reluctant to turn her thoughts back to those days. At the age of eighty-three she did write the following: *Broaching the subject of my racial origin does not cause my any difficulties. I have no personal grudges or complexes in this regard. I am quite simply not ashamed of it.* Yet she left everything to do with her Jewish past out of her memoirs. I do not believe that she had no complexes or grudges. When one's dignity and self-respect are wounded from childhood onwards, a sense of shame is inevitable. I think she probably felt ashamed to admit that shame to herself.

In 1889 the Beylins' son was born and, according to Jewish tradition, inherited the name Gustaw from his late grandfather. The same year the second of my grandmother's sisters, the lovely Róża, got married – not out of common sense, but for love. She had gone to Holland to visit her aunt who was married to a Dutchman, and there she met a Dutch Jew called Jakub Hilsum, and fell hopelessly in love with him. Julia did not like her future son-in-law at all, but could not persuade Róża to change her mind. A few months after she came home, Róża's wedding was held in Warsaw, at puzzling speed. Could that sensible, modest young girl, once removed from her mother's control, have 'forgotten herself', and given in to the cajolery of a seducer whom she hardly knew? It was the only marriage in the family to result from a fit of passion, and it was the only one to fall apart. I shall never know how many tears and tempests preceded this hasty union, but having finally given her consent Julia put a brave face on it. The wedding celebration was very festive, and a large number of guests were invited. A memorable anecdote tells how the bride went to change into her wedding dress, but did not emerge from the bathroom for such a long time that the worried bridegroom began to bang on the door, only to find her in her white dress, brought all the way from Paris, and her white wedding veil, doing her daily duty of washing her little brothers' ears and necks for the last time ever.

The dress was supplied by the aunt who lived in Paris, Amalia Citroën, Julia's dearest sister. She was also generous to her other nieces, giving Gizelka a sky-blue silk Parisian dress trimmed with brown ostrich feathers, and Janina her first evening outfit, made of white silk. To go with it, she was given her first pair of long white gloves. This outfit and the compliments it inspired made a greater impression on her than the company of Samuel Adalberg, famous in the future as the author of *The Book of Polish Proverbs*, who was her neighbour at the wedding dinner.

In the summer of 1892 the entire Horwitz family set off for a holiday at Otwock, where they rented a flat in a boarding house. The younger children had a happy time playing in the woods and by the water, while the young ladies carefully prepared their summer outfits in the hope of a social life, new friends and maybe even flirtations. Unfortunately, Granny Kleinmann insisted that she would rather go to Ciechocinek, and demanded that nineteen-year-old Janina keep her company. Her granddaughter categorically refused – she preferred to spend the summer in the company of the other young people. So the offended Miriam went with her son Jonas, a not very bright, rather eccentric fellow. In wretched Ciechocinek she suffered a twisted bowel after eating a colossal plateful of raspberries and departed this life. For years on end my grandmother had pangs of conscience about her refusal to go, and could not bear to eat raspberries.

The funeral was held at the Jewish cemetery in Warsaw. All Miriam's daughters came from abroad: Eleonora and Flora from Holland, Anna, Balbina and Amalia from Paris, and Tekla from Germany. Their Warsaw relatives had them to stay. It was the last big gathering of the Kleinmann family, a splendid ceremony in *fin de siècle* style, dominated by the rich foreign ladies in their huge black feathered hats and rustling silk and taffeta dresses from the top fashion houses. They brought huge trunks with them full of outfits, dressing gowns, fur coats and stoles, as well as expensive gifts. The older girls secretly tried on the Parisian dresses, while the younger children romped about among the glad rags, ribbons and fripperies that were strewn about the flat.

During the funeral ceremony there was a lot of sobbing and wailing, as custom dictated, but it was fairly conventional grief. No one was particularly upset about the death of the dried-up, selfish Miriam Kleinmann. However, it caused a major change in the Horwitz family's life. The rich siblings behaved extremely decently, renouncing all rights to inherit from their mother in favour of Julia. And so, from one day to the next – as happens only in novels – she became very rich.

She inherited the tenement building on Królewska Street and a lot of capital. She no longer had to worry about dowries for the girls, or about money for her sons' education. She could allow herself and the children luxuries they had previously been denied. This made it possible for Janina to take her first trip abroad. For ages she had wanted to visit her beloved sister Róża, who was now living in Amsterdam, but there had been no money for it. Besides, she could not have set off on such a long journey alone, but one of the Dutch aunts who was going home after the funeral took her with her.

Her stay in Holland lasted a whole six months. Perhaps it had a secret purpose, either social or matrimonial? If so, in a certain sense it fulfilled its aim, because that was when my future grandmother discovered her second favourite passion in life after literature: art. She loved the Dutch and Flemish paintings that she saw for the first time in her life, and it was from her love of Bruegel, Hals and Rembrandt that the most important love of her life would later arise. But that is another story.

In 1894 the third sister, Gizella, was married to Dr Zygmunt

Bychowski, a neurologist. He was a very learned man, a good doctor, an able scientist and a generous social activist. Yet for a long time Gizelka, so quiet and mild, refused to agree to the match. Was she in love with someone else? Was she afraid of Zygmunt's quick temper and bossy side? Or were they divided by their very different attitudes to their common origins? The young Horwitzes were proud of their Polishness in a fairly exalted way. Of course they did not hide their recent past, but they regarded it as a sort of lower rung of development, from which, with a huge effort, they had gone up a level. Zygmunt, on the other hand, always emphasised his Jewish identity.

He was the son of Samuel Bychowski, a learned Talmudist from Volhynia. Brought up in an Orthodox atmosphere, he had gone to religious schools, the cheder and the yeshiva, and later continued his Talmudic studies in Saint Petersburg and Warsaw. At the age of seventeen he had rebelled and decided, against his father's wishes, to gain a secular education. After passing his matriculation, he had run away to study medicine in Vienna, for which his devout father had renounced his unnatural son. Later on they had been reconciled, Zygmunt had completed his studies in Warsaw and begun work in a Jewish hospital. He was active in Jewish academic and social organisations and associations, was a member of the board of the Jewish community in Warsaw, and was involved in all sorts of initiatives concerning Jewish society.

Nowadays this sort of attitude seems proof of independence and dignity, but in those days an assimilated young lady might have regarded this marriage as a possible misalliance. In fact, Zygmunt was an excellent match. I do not know why my future grandmother encouraged her sister to refuse him. Perhaps she knew of some essential reasons why she should resist? When it came to light that she was 'intriguing' against the candidate hotly supported by their mother, she got a slap in the face from her – for the first and last time ever. At that point she stopped interfering, and Gizelka said yes to Zygmunt.

Two years later, the fourth sister, red-haired Henrietta, got married to Julian Margulies, a doctor of chemistry, with whom she moved to Insdorff in Austria. My future grandmother was twenty-three by now – in other words she had gone past the 'fatal second decade', regarded in those days as the borderline of youth – and her mother began to worry about her future.

SEARCHING FOR THE MEANING OF LIFE

———————— ✗ ————————

The advent of the terrible twentieth century was very slow, as time went by unhurriedly. The usual, everyday impressions were still to the fore, and there were only as many of them as one's mind could embrace at the ordinary pace of nature. That must have been why the colours, form and flavour of events stayed in the memory with such intensity. How expressively my grandmother describes that long youth of hers, with all its occupations, amusements, jolly trips to summer resorts, occasional journeys abroad and beautiful clothes. In my mind's eye I can see the cut of the dresses, feel the touch of the striped linen and woollen materials, hear the buzz of girlish voices and the clack of wooden mallet against ball during games of croquet at the summer resort. The girls are surrounded by young men, who smile alluringly. Their intentions are not clear, and they cannot be trusted; but their glances, compliments and courtship are very sweet.

Although she did not hurry into marriage, Janina was not indifferent to the charms of the gentlemen. The heightened sentimental and sexual atmosphere that prevailed in a house so full of marriageable young ladies must have helped, and men make frequent appearances in her memoirs. When she was still a schoolgirl she used to gaze in delight at *the fine blue eyes, walnut-coloured moustache and full red lips* of her mathematics teacher, Edward Glass. She proudly describes how she was courted in Ciechocinek by a student at Zurich Polytechnic, Arnold Teichfeld, and how he was the object of her first girlish sighs. Later on, Adolf Wertheimer, a German from Nuremberg, who was a colleague of her brother-in-law Samuel Beylin, made a great impression on her. He was young, handsome and friendly, a born flirt who was more than willing to visit a house with so many pretty girls in it and was made very welcome by their mother, who must have seen a potential son-in-law in him. Sitting next to Janina at dinner, he stroked her hand under the table, and – as she admits in her memoirs with disarming sincerity – she did not tear it away because it felt very nice. It later turned out that Adolf – a philanderer – had seduced several young ladies at once; caught in a tender embrace with the red-haired Henrietta, he was expelled from the house once and for all.

I always revelled in the story of the amorous activities of the unfaithful Michał Muttermilch, the fiancé of Mela Klingsland, the future painter Mela Muter. In those days Mela was a very young, lovely slender girl, with long raven-black plaits and a pink-and-white complexion; Michał loved her immensely, and his love was reciprocated. However, during a party at Mela's parents' house he secretly thrust a billet-doux into my future grandmother's hands. Ah, what sweet, innocent times! She felt insulted – after all, she was his fiancée's closest friend. Who did he take her for, abusing the principles of decent behaviour so crudely? Giving the good-for-nothing a look of thunder she ostentatiously ripped the little note to shreds; but she did not throw it away. She secretly hid the scraps in her bag and when she got home she carefully stuck them together again. The love poem he had written must have made quite an impression on her, because she remembered the words for ever. Sometimes she let herself be persuaded, and with a mixture of shame and pride, she would recite that poetical declaration of love from years ago:

My lady, you have a lovely gaze,
Your eyes are limpid as a doe's
Whenever your pretty head you raise,
So saintly your expression grows.
I send your looks a tribute in praise,
My lady, you have a lovely gaze.
Whenever a glance from your glowing eyes
Is joined by a graceful smile,
In my heart the hopes arise,
My dreams awake in rapid file.
I dream that, fast as starlight's rays,
Merged in one spirit to heaven we're flying,
My lady, you have a lovely gaze!

Not long after, the faithless Michał married Mela. They settled in Paris, but divorced a few years later. She became famous as a very good painter. He changed his name to Merlé and became a communist.

❧

It is such a pity that the piles of black notebooks in which, from her earliest youth, day after day, my grandmother used to note down all her experiences and thoughts, were burned in the Warsaw Uprising. They would have been an invaluable source of information on the people, events and atmosphere of the era, as well as an interesting record of the experiences of this granddaughter of a Viennese rabbi, born in the Russian partition, who became a publisher of Polish literature. I knew her as a strong person, full of optimism, aware of her own merits and achievements. She never allowed herself or anyone else to indulge in weakness, hesitation or indecision. Like Evagrius of Pontus, the monk who lived in the desert, she severely condemned depression and self-pity. In the memoirs written in her old age she was very happy to turn her thoughts back to the things that brought her pleasure, which is why dresses, journeys, flirtations and men's compliments occupy so much space in them; but at the same time she admitted that her youth was not a cheerful time for her at all. She suffered painfully from a sense of inferiority.

Worries that you are inferior to other people, that you do not deserve to be socially accepted and that you are not equal to the demands of life are the usual anxieties of adolescence – troublesome, but luckily they pass. How very painful and humiliating it must have been to feel that nothing would change with the years, that despite your achievements and successes you would never attain full approval or respect, you would always be someone inadequate, alien and undesirable. Your greatest efforts to be just like the rest of society would be of no help at all – your 'unfavourable ancestry' would always be pointed out, and you would not be able to avoid annoyances, provocation, stupid jokes, and at best patronising contempt.

Youth is a time of discord and rebellion, with raging ambitions, oversensitivity, and mood swings from euphoria to despair. Add to this an awareness of your ethnic stigma and it must have been very difficult to find the ground beneath your feet. Youth also involves a search for your own identity, and here being assimilated placed you at a crossroads. Julia's decision to break with the Jewish

41

religion and customs was certainly a deep shock for the children. Before they had had time to cope with the physical loss of their father, they had to part with his spiritual presence. As the cult objects and ritual customs disappeared from their home, as they stopped celebrating religious holidays and conducting the ceremonial rites to which he attached such weight, as the religious bans and injunctions that he so scrupulously observed no longer counted, he gradually died a second death.

Parting with their father also meant parting with God. The age-old system of beliefs and principles that put the world in order, created a sense of security and gave a meaning to life was rejected. No other religion replaced Judaism, so they were left with a void in their souls, which had to be filled somehow, by finding their own, secular hierarchy of values, their own signposts and anchors. 'Honesty, industry, discipline and perseverance! That's what you must learn if you want to grow up into decent people!' Julia's ringing voice would cry from dawn to dusk. Meanwhile, the ghost of their father, Gustav, would slink about the house and whisper to his offspring, 'Man does not live by bread alone.'

In the souls of these newcomers from another world, eager to embrace Polishness, there must have been a good deal of confusion. They would have to mobilise all their vital energy – inherited from their mother – to find a place for themselves in life, without losing their father's inner culture, his sensitivity and good breeding in the process. The aim was to go forward without elbowing past others, and without trampling on anyone along the way; to be proud of your achievements, without mistaking pride for conceit; to fight against your sense of inferiority without slipping into arrogance; not to let bitterness turn into rancour; and to be sure of being liked by people without being obsequious or hypocritical. In the most general terms, it meant being internally reconciled to your fate, while maintaining your spirits and your dignity. It all sounds extremely grandiloquent, but in those days life was taken very seriously.

The years of their birth plainly had an influence on the mentalities of the young Horwitzes. The four older sisters, Flora, Róża, Gizella and Henrietta, grew up in the 1880s, when the ideal of the woman as high priestess of the family hearth was still in force. They accepted the reality in which they were destined to live, although it was not always benevolent. They sought support and refuge from the world at home, in the traditional family, in marriage and in bringing up children. They fulfilled their duties scrupulously and that kept them in good spirits. They were typi-fied by great psychological resilience, which made it easier to accept the trials that life brought in its wake.

The youngest siblings, Lutek, Maks and Kamilka, grew up in the last decade of the century, when attitudes to young people under-went a violent revolution. This generation refused to put up with political and social pressure passively, but got involved in various different forms of rebellion and struggle. As a schoolboy Maks was already active in illegal underground independence groups, issuing handwritten patriotic newspapers, and like all young rebels reading banned literature by Marx, Liebknecht and Bebel, and organising secret meetings of a 'literary circle' at the house on Królewska Street, whose participants read their own compositions or recited Polish patriotic verse. His older brother, Lutek, was also a member of the circle, but their sisters were not admitted to the meetings. As a schoolgirl, Janina used to gaze longingly after the teenage youths as they went through the parlour, and sometimes she succeeded in overhearing how emotionally her usually sneering, spiteful brother could declaim Mickiewicz and Słowacki.

In age she was in the middle of the siblings, and in terms of her outlook on life too. Much more emancipated than her older sisters, she aimed to have a broader sphere of activity than just a family. Unlike the younger ones, she was not inclined towards rebellion and ideological commitment. However, she did not want to live for herself alone. Her school played a huge role in shaping her per-sonality. It aroused not only a thirst for knowledge, but inculcated in her a system of moral principles typical of that era, to which she remained faithful for the rest of her life. The main one of these principles stated that a fully successful life must be a creative life. This stipulation included the duty to be active and sensitive to the needs of others, as well as rigorous, with internal discipline, and above all never to stop developing, both intellectually and spiritually.

After finishing school, she longed to continue her studies, but women were not allowed to attend Warsaw's Imperial University. A few extremely determined women went to study abroad, but she did not have well-enough-defined interests or enough courage to decide on such a step. If her father had been alive, she might have found him willing to discuss her future. Her mother was too absorbed in getting her older sisters married off to worry about her problems, so she had to take decisions on her own. Undeniably, she took on innumerable duties with huge determination.

She had always had a special fondness for teaching, so she and her friend Andzia Askenazy, sister of Szymon, a well-known historian, decided to attend to their younger siblings. They took the children, Kamilka and Staś Horwitz, Róża and Henio Askenazy, to the mineral-water garden at the Saxon Gardens. People taking cures used to come and drink the water in the early morning, and after that it was quiet and peaceful there. The children listened to stories told by their carers, then played, while the young ladies used the time to educate themselves, reading German and French classics aloud, as they both knew those languages.

Later on, Janina took the famous 'Fröbel courses' given by Mrs Kazimiera Jahołkowska, a pupil of German educator Friedrich Fröbel (who founded the kindergarten system), and ran a study group, something like a private mini-kindergarten for her family's and friends' children. At the same time, introduced into social work by the renowned activist Ester Gold, later Stróżecka, she taught a poor Jewish girl how to read and write.

Most importantly, however, in 1890, two years after leaving school, thanks to the intervention of her former teacher, Jadwiga Szczawińska-Dawidowa, she enrolled at the Flying University. This famous clandestine institution, co-organised and run by Szczawińska, played a huge role in educating young people, especially girls. Secret lectures given by the best university professors were held at private homes and paid for from audience subscriptions. The talks given by Adam Mahrburg, a historian of philosophy, enjoyed the greatest acclaim. He was not just a superb expert in his subject, but also an excellent lecturer. Apparently he captivated his audience with his eloquence. More for this reason than for love of the subject, Miss Janina Horwitz decided to study philosophy under him.

She had an unfortunate start. She turned up at the classes in the middle of the academic year, not until the fourteenth lecture. She was completely unprepared, so she just made careful notes and tried, without much success, to understand what the professor was saying. After a month of these classes came 'repetition', when she would have to recount the main points of Descartes and Hume's philosophical systems. The chaotic notes were not much use, and it came to light that Janina had no idea about the subject. Deeply humiliated in front of the other students, she approached

Mahrburg in a free moment and asked if, in view of the fact that she had not attended the lectures from the start, it made any sense for her to continue her studies. He replied that studying was limitless, with no end or beginning; one could start the journey wherever one happened to be and, by overcoming the difficulties, keep going ahead. He advised her not to be discouraged and to keep working. So she continued to attend lectures on psychology, history, philosophy, logic and the theory of knowledge, achieving such progress within a few years that Mahrburg commissioned her to translate an essay by the German philosopher Siebeck, 'Metaphysical Systems in their Relation to Experience', which was published in the next volume of the *Library of Philosophy*.

Astonishingly, I have a copy of it at home, though it is a very dog-eared, tatty little pamphlet. On the title page there is a dedication, reading: *To Mrs Janina Horwitz-Mortkowicz, a Nestor of philosophy at the house of 130 bards in Kraków, in memory of an evening in early spring 1945, with deep respect and gratitude.* The signature is illegible. It is dated 6 March 1946. I do not know what happened on that gratefully remembered evening in early spring 1945. The war was still on and, lost after the Warsaw Uprising, I was waiting in the town of Siedlce for someone to find me at last and take me away from my paternal uncle; but by March 1946 I was in Kraków, and I do remember a frail old man appearing at the door of our flat at 22 Krupnicza Street, the Writers' House, holding a bouquet of violets and that pamphlet. He was an old admirer of my grandmother's and had found the book in a second-hand shop; thrilled with his find, he had hurried over to call on her. But that very afternoon the drunken poet Konstanty Gałczyński had gone mad at our house, and was screaming that he was going to kill the lot of us. 'I'll shoot Mrs Mortkowicz, I'll shoot Hania and I'll shoot Joasia. There'll be nothing left in this country but crappy cooperatives,' he cried. When he saw the old man, transparent as a ghost, he took fright and calmed down. Then they sat at the table together for ages, while Gałczyński complained about something, and my grandmother's admirer whispered something to him. And that is how they have remained in my memory. The only obscure proof that I didn't dream it all is that mouldering pamphlet.

❧

As he handed Julia Maks's matriculation certificate, the boy's venerable headmaster, Wojciech Górski, said in farewell: 'You are removing a crown of thorns from my head.' Not long after, the seventeen-year-old left for Ghent, to study mathematics and physics. He was eighteen when in 1895 he joined the Union of Polish Socialists Abroad, an émigré organisation that brought together socialists living abroad. It was there that he suffered repression for his political convictions for the first time. When the owners of the flat where he had rented a room saw that he had hung a portrait of Karl Marx on the wall, they gave him notice to quit, and he had to look for a more liberal landlord.

Four children were left at Królewska Street: fifteen-year-old Staś, who was still at school, seventeen-year-old Kamilka, who had just taken her matriculation exam, Lutek, who was twenty-one and was studying geology at Warsaw University, and twenty-three-year-old Janina. Her intellectual caprices had moved into the background, when Kamilka began to cause trouble in her turn. This quiet girl proved the most stubborn of all six daughters. As a child she had already made up her mind to become a doctor, but no one in the family took her seriously. When after finishing school she announced that she had to take the exam to gain her matriculation certificate, without which she would not be accepted for higher education, her request was treated as a harmless whim. In a single year she worked her way through the four-year secondary-school course in Russian and took her matriculation exam before an unfriendly committee without making a single mistake, for which she won a gold medal. Everyone congratulated her wholeheartedly for this success, but when she informed them that in the autumn she wanted to start her studies abroad, in Zurich, because that was the only place where girls were accepted for medicine, the house was filled with dismay.

Julia announced that she would never give her consent. Medicine was no profession for a woman. Kamilka would be a laughing stock, the butt of coarse jokes on the part of the professors and students. She would go off the rails and ruin her life. As she said, or rather angrily shouted all this, she met with silent, dogged resistance, something she had never encountered before from her children and which she was unable to break down.

In the summer of 1896 she took Janina and Kamilka on a trip abroad. Was it just for pleasure? Or did that journey too have some more or less hidden purposes? Why were young ladies taken abroad in those days? In the hope that some life-changing opportunity might be waiting for them there, in the form of an attractive, wealthy suitor. Like every Jewish mother, Julia knew of nothing more important than caring for her offspring and dreaming of their happiness. Perhaps at a fashionable resort fate would smile on the older girl? Perhaps the charms of society would distract the younger one from daydreaming about studies that were so unsuitable for ladies?

They stayed at Baden-Baden, then one of the most fashionable health resorts. Ah, those sweet, long-lost trips to 'take the waters'. A morning wander to one of the many medicinal springs, filling crystal glasses with the invigorating liquid, and then slowly sipping it through a little tube during a walk that lasted until one could feel the desired effects and it was necessary to run home as fast as possible. At noon there was lunch at a communal table, where acquaintances and friendships were made. Later came a walk along the promenade and a concert in the band-shell, where the spa's resident orchestra played a pot-pourri from the Viennese operettas. In the evening there were *'réunions'* at the 'Kurhaus' – in other words, dance parties at the spa's main building. Kamilka spent the whole time sitting in the boarding house with her nose in her medical books and refused to take part in social life. So her mother only took Janina out 'into society' in the evenings.

A very strict ritual was in force during parties at the 'Kurhaus'. The *maître de cérémonie* would approach the older lady and ask if she would allow him to present a certain gentleman, who would very much like to be acquainted with both ladies. With *Madame's* permission, the young man would be introduced to her, and would ask if she in turn would present him to *Mademoiselle*. Only after completing these formalities could he canvass for the right to dance with the young lady. All this took place within firing range of the watchful gazes of the other mothers gathered in the ball-room and their jealous daughters, and must have been of doubtful appeal. Nor can conversation with a completely strange young man have been among the greatest of pleasures, so none of the health-resort dancers was able to win the heart of my fastidious future grandmother.

Poor Julia. Kamilka was adamant that she would never renounce her studies, and it was obvious that she would not give way. Janina complained that she was bored. Her third daughter, Róża Hilsum, kept writing her mother desperate letters begging for her help. Her husband had suffered a great financial disaster in Amsterdam, so they had moved to Paris under the protective wing of aunt Amalia

Citroën. Róża was unhappy, because Hilsum had been unfaithful to her, made a scene and left home. She could not get over the loss of her first-born, beloved son Gucio, although she had already given birth to two more boys, René and Lucien. She was at her wits' end, and wanted to return to Warsaw. From Baden-Baden Janina was sent to Paris for the sisters to discuss the situation. Meanwhile, Julia took Kamilka back to Warsaw, in the hope that at home she would convince the unruly child to see sense.

I do not know the details of Hilsum's escapades, but they must have been so scandalous that Aunt Amalia, the mediator in family matters, had decided that Janina should not witness them, and took her niece to stay at her house. Amalia was very kind to her Warsaw relatives, although she herself had brought up five children alone because her husband had committed suicide while suffering a nervous breakdown.

My grandmother remembered her stay at the Citroëns' house with the greatest delight, and would go into raptures about the elegance and affluence that reigned there. She was escorted about Paris by Amalia's youngest son, seventeen-year-old André. One day they went to Versailles together. At the entrance they were told that the palace was closed to the public that day. Without a second thought, her cousin tipped his bowler hat and said firmly: 'La presse'. They were let in immediately. At the time she thought: 'You'll get by in life, my boy!' And she was right.

Aunt Amalia was very fond of her niece and looked after her kindly, taking her to her friends' houses, to famous fashion stores, where she bought her many beautiful outfits, and to visit museums and exhibitions. She urged her to stay in Paris and promised to guide her future. Róża's problems suddenly went into the background, because Janina sensed that she had finally discovered her vocation. Fascinated by the Louvre, the art galleries and the atmosphere of the Latin Quarter, where she made friends with some Poles who were studying in Paris, she decided not to return to Warsaw, but to stay at her aunt's and enrol at the Sorbonne to study art history.

She had found her vocation. She had finally discovered what she wanted to do, and was determined to defend her plans. She sat down at the desk to write and inform her mother of her intentions, and had just sealed the envelope when a messenger came with a letter from Warsaw. In it, Julia despairingly reported that Kamilka had stuck to her guns and gone abroad. Under the family pressure she had given up medicine, but had enrolled in the natural sciences faculty in Berlin, where Tekla Neufeld, Julia's sister who lived there, had promised to take care of her.

It was a bolt from the blue for my future grandmother. All her dreams were shattered, all her promising plans lay in ruins. She tore up her long letter arguing in their favour, because she could not inflict another shock on her mother. She knew there was no question of both girls going out into the world and leaving her on her own, so she left Paris in despair, not even rejoicing at the thought of the impression her Parisian dresses would make in the streets of Warsaw. As well as feeling resentful about her fate, she was jealous that her little sister, six years her junior, had the nerve to be so determined, while she was wasting her life away and would never achieve anything. She arrived in Warsaw feeling sad and embittered.

A RED CLOAK AND A BANNER
MADE FROM A RED TABLECLOTH

———————✻———————

After the death of Julia's mother, Miriam, the Horwitzes moved from the first floor to the second, into the Kleinmanns' eight-room flat. It was much bigger and more comfortable, but, brought up with a different aesthetic, the Horwitz family found its nouveau-riche ostentation rather garish. Instead of a cosy parlour there was a proper drawing room full of furniture made of ebony edged in gilt and upholstered in amaranthine damask. It was decorated with mirrors and columns, on which stood candleholders made of gilded bronze. Heavy amaranthine curtains with golden tassels hung in the windows, and artistically wrought jardinières and palms in enormous flowerpots stood on the costly carpets.

The plaque inscribed 'Gustav Horwitz, dr philosophie' in Gothic lettering was no longer on the front door. Fortunately, the mementoes of Gustav did make their way upstairs from the old flat, including the portrait of the Viennese rabbi in its black frame, the library full of beloved books and the ash-wood Biedermeier furniture from Vienna. On one of the drawing-room walls hung a new acquisition: a huge portrait of a young lady painted in the extremely expressive Secession style. It showed a life-sized female figure dressed in scarlet and black, against a golden background. The main feature of her costume was a floor-length red cloak, folded open to reveal a black silk lining. The lady was wearing a black hat with a fancifully turned-up brim and a black satin band. From under the hat a cloud of frizzy fair hair and a young face loomed out. The portrait had a green frame, which heightened the intensity of its gold, red and black hues. The model for it was my future grandmother.

That elegant, rather extravagant outfit came from the best fashion house in Brussels. Ever since their financial situation had so greatly improved, mindful of Janina's future, her mother had had no qualms about spending money on her clothes. By now she had given up trying to persuade her youngest daughter, Kamilka, to appear 'in society', but she had not yet lost hope of making a favourable match for her older daughter – and time was passing.

In the summer of 1898 they travelled together to Ostend, the Belgian maritime resort, which was very fashionable in those days. On the way they stopped for a few days in Brussels to equip the young lady with suitable outfits, and bought summer suits made of white piqué and blue linen, straw hats and also a bathing suit of thick navy-blue wool, consisting of bloomers that came down to the ankles and a blouse with a sailor's collar and elbow-length sleeves. Appearing before a man in such a costume was inadmissible, so in order to bathe, ladies rented a horse-drawn cab with a hood to shield them from peeping Toms. Inside they changed into their costumes, then the driver whipped the horse and drove the cab into the sea. Only then could they dive into the water. Once they had splashed about in the waves, the ladies got back into the cab and put on their corsets, drawers, petticoats, blouses, skirts, jackets, gloves and veiled hats. Only fully kitted out, holding the inseparable lacy parasol to keep off the sun, could they appear on the beach.

Once a Frenchman tried to take a photograph of my future grandmother while she was bathing. He was fiercely upbraided for his insult to morality by a chance witness to his shameless behaviour.

The many exquisite costumes bought in Brussels included that red cloak. It does not appear to have helped my future grandmother to conquer Ostend, but it certainly produced a sensation in Warsaw when she got home. People turned to look at her in the streets and asked for the address of the shop where she got her clothes, and after one of the Wednesday concerts at the Musical Society the famous portrait painter Leon Kaufman asked through a common acquaintance – such arrangements were never made directly – if she would like to pose for a portrait in that highly original get-up.

The decision depended on Julia, who luckily gave her consent. Obviously, a young lady could not spend time alone in an artist's studio, so her friend Niusia Nelkenbaum went with her as a chaperon. The painter was a very popular figure in Warsaw. *He is so charming, talented and handsome, and his life is full of freedom,* the very young Zofia Nałkowska wrote in her diaries. Women worshipped him. He used to walk along Nowy Świat Street in central Warsaw with a red rose in his crimson lips. I imagine the young ladies' hearts beating fast as they ran to the first sitting. Unfortunately the alluring painter was so engrossed in his work that they never once felt the slightest threat to their innocence. After about a dozen sittings the portrait was finished. Pleased with the result, Kaufman exhibited his work at the newly opened Zachęta Gallery (headquarters of the Warsaw Fine Arts Society). A very complimentary article about the painting appeared in Aleksander Świętochowski's literary periodical *Prawda* ('Truth'), written by the art critic Michał Muttermilch – the same fellow who in a previous chapter tried to seduce my future grandmother. Once the exhibition was over, Julia bought the portrait of her daughter, which was then hung in the drawing room on Królewska Street.

In autumn 1898 it was in this drawing room, at an oval table covered in a red tablecloth, on ebony gilded chairs, that almost the entire family sat down again, as in the past. Four of the children were living with their mother – Janina, Lutek, who was still a student, Staś, who was still at school, and Maks, who had come home after completing his doctorate at the physics and mathematics faculty of Ghent University.

Despite his outstanding mathematical talents, the newly appointed doctor did not go in for academic work, but took a post as head of a crafts school for Jewish youths. However, but his main occupation was his political work. Once back in Warsaw, he became one of the most active members of the Warsaw branch of the Polish Socialist Party. *A talented mathematician, thoroughly educated, intelligent, lively and amusing, though a great chatterbox [...]. A first-class organisational and educational talent* – as his Party comrade Józef Grabiec described him in his book *Red Warsaw*. This was when 'Comrade Piotr' – Maks Horwitz's Party pseudonym – got to know 'Comrade Wiktor', ten years his senior, i.e. the future president of independent Poland, Józef Piłsudski. Grabiec writes: *Horwitz, who would one day be Wiktor's sworn enemy, at the start of his political activity was his supporter, his uncritical, fanatical admirer.*

This is confirmed by my grandmother. She notes: *As I have*

*already mentioned, my politically active siblings did not initiate
me into their conspiratorial activities. I was only occasionally
trusted... Once Maks suggested that I take part in a spring outing.
I went by chaise and listened to the animated conversation of
several participants, of whom one in particular caught my attention, because of his outward appearance as well as his wit. Only
once we were back at home did my brother inform me secretively:
'Do you know who that was? Józef Piłsudski, the man who
escaped from exile recently.' At the time he was still enchanted
by him, which completely changed later on.*

Piłsudski, *young, fair and slender with a small beard, keen,
bright blue eyes and an unusually calm, abstemious way of life,*
was famously endowed with unusual charisma, hypnotised people
with his patriotic ardour and met with universal adoration. Maks,
a twenty-two-year-old *romantic captivated by the idea of independence,* was able to love him, despite his own contrariness and
arrogance. The fact that Piłsudski had no anti-Semitic prejudices
and did not divide people into Jews and non-Jews also attracted
Maks to him.

෨

That day Julia's married daughters, Flora Beylin and Gizella
Bychowska, had come to pay a visit to Królewska Street. They were
always happy to drop in at their mother's flat, but this time the
reason for the meeting was serious: Róża Hilsum had come from
Paris and Kamilka from Berlin because both were causing concerns
that the family council wished to discuss. Róża had decided to
leave her unfaithful husband and move to Warsaw, and had
brought her children with her, René and Lucien, who were playing
under the table with their little cousins. One of them was Gucio
(Gustaw) Beylin, a future lawyer who would defend the writer and
scholar Tadeusz 'Boy' Żeleński in a famous case over author's
rights (described below in the chapter entitled 'The Independence
Years'); the other was Gucio (Gustaw) Bychowski, a future psychoanalyst, who would study under Sigmund Freud and Eugen Bleuler.

The conversation was difficult. There had never been a divorce
in the family before, so they began to deliberate. How did Róża
plan to organise her life? Where would she and the children live?
What would she live on? Naturally her mother would help her; she
had already been sending large sums of money to Paris since the
problems began. But should her husband be entirely freed of

financial responsibility for his family? And could Róża say for sure if she loved Hilsum or not?

These considerations could be spun out ad infinitum, so the other problem was debated. The topic for discussion was nineteen-year-old-Kamilka. After two years studying natural history in Berlin she had come home to announce that she was moving to Zurich. Only there could she enrol for her dream study of medicine. Her mother was adamantly opposed to this plan. All this time she had been deluding herself that in Berlin her youngest daughter would meet someone interesting, get married and give up her daydreams of emancipation. She had not realised what a strong character Kamilka had, and was still trying to persuade her. She should understand her mother's fears. It was no longer even the wretched medicine that was the issue, but that she could not go alone to a foreign city where she had no relatives and no one to care for her. Nonsense, replied Kamilka – young ladies were more and more often going abroad alone and managing perfectly well. Then came the final argument: it would be interesting to know what she was going to live on, as she was not getting a single penny from home for her flights of fancy.

Flora, Gizella and Róża supported their mother. Maks, as usual, was on his youngest sister's side. Lutek and Staś kept quiet, to avoid getting told off by either side. My future grandmother was irritated. It was she who had always had the reputation of being an individualist. Meanwhile Kamilka was proving for the second time that she knew what she wanted. Janina felt additionally humiliated by the fact that none of the family was taking any notice of the new painting hanging on the wall; and as she refused to play second fiddle in any situation, she quietly slipped out of the drawing room. Shortly after, she came back in, wearing the outfit in which she had posed for her portrait. She liked theatrical effects, so she imagined that once she was standing right by the painting, in the same pose and in the same costume, she would arouse exclamations of delight; but, absorbed in their debate, the family ignored her. Only Maks gave her a second glance. 'How do I look?' she asked coquettishly, pirouetting in her red cloak. 'Like a peacock,' replied her dearest little brother curtly.

Oh, that Maks! Too clever by half, perverse, malicious and arrogant. High-minded, obsessed with other people's adversity, dedicated to the·Cause, self-sacrificing. The Party delegated him to agitation work among the poor Jews from the Warsaw districts of

Nalewki and Praga. Small craftsmen, shopkeepers and pedlars maintaining large families on the few pennies they earned, isolated from Polish society by language, religion and custom, they had no chance of ever changing their social status, gaining an education or earning enough for a reasonable existence; and from the Poles they met with contempt, disgust and mistrust.

Apparently the shock of discovering areas of such hopeless human indigence caused the young man to renounce his career and thoughts of his own happiness and decide to devote his life to fighting against the system that allowed people to be so abased. His Party comrades laughed at his rather too graphic way of expressing his obsession with the fate of the ghetto inhabitants. *He was often reminded of a speech he made in which he was particularly gushing about the indigence of the Jewish proletarian, what a poor, wretched child it was from birth, scrofulous and suffering from rickets in a filthy, torn rag of a shirt*, wrote Grabiec. Maks must sometimes have been comically bombastic. After all, he was only twenty-one.

As paradox would have it, the Socialist Party, which was in favour of Jewish assimilation, sent mainly comrades of Jewish origin to work among the Jewish proletariat; these people had generally been born into assimilated families and were unable to communicate with their charges. A year earlier Maks, then still a student and a member of the Union of Polish Socialists Abroad in Belgium, wrote about this problem in a letter sent to Poland: *The Jewish movement entirely lacks any Jewish intellectuals who known the jargon.* The situation was so difficult that in order to catch the mistakes in propaganda brochures aimed at the Jews, Leon Wasilewski, a socialist from an aristocratic family, learned Yiddish. So Maks too had to learn the language he had run away from, in order to bring his kinsmen into the Polish society that rejected them – rather a perverse twist of fate.

What did the family, so proud of its assimilation progress, think of this? Julia believed in her son. He was fighting for national and social justice. It is hard to imagine finer ideals. His older sisters reckoned he was ruining his own life, but Lutek and Kamilka understood him perfectly. They had followed his example and joined the Party. In those days the Polish Socialist Party gave a sense of brotherhood to people of the most varied social backgrounds. It was fighting for a free, democratic Poland, where all race and class differences would disappear. Belonging to the movement, quite apart from hopes for a better future, gave the Jews an immediate guarantee of integration with the progressive faction of Polish society. A common struggle, shared aims and quite often a shared prison cell – all this engendered their longed-for acceptance and ennoblement.

The idea captivated some people with its sense of justice and attracted others from the artistic side, while others associated it with their dreams of performing some sort of heroic deed. That is a quote from sociologist and political activist Ludwik Krzywicki's *Memoirs.* He is actually talking about the beginnings of the movement, but his definition, comparing socialist doctrine with the manifestation of a new cult, whose advocates bravely sought the martyr's crown, allows one to understand better the now unimaginable blind faith in supposedly infallible prophets and sacred tomes that prevailed. He continues: *... coming into contact with socialism produced the same result everywhere: just as dry tinder bursts into flames when sparks fall upon it, so in the course of a few days any young person who was a champion of labour became a socialist. To be more precise, he became the adherent of a new religion – the religion of labour, the religion of solidarity. I use the term 'religion' quite knowingly, because their emotional state was as exalted as a state of deep religious faith. There were some who, on getting hold of* Das Kapital *for the first time, were so moved that they kissed the book in greeting.*

Fortunately, my future grandmother was resistant to all ideological temptations. She was not interested in politics, and combined social activity and society life without a clash. Her brother loved to mock her for her 'bourgeois hypocrisy' and 'double-edged morality'; but it was to him that she owed her contact with the left-wing circles of Warsaw's 'non-submissives'.

She was very active at the famous free lending libraries run by the Warsaw Charitable Society, where young people from the intelligentsia did social work as librarians. She was attracted to this work by the woman who ran the lending library on Dzielna Street, the wife of a Dr Oppenheim. Dzielna Street adjoined Smocza, Gęsia and Muranowska Streets, which was exactly where Maks performed his agitation activities. It was a district inhabited almost exclusively by poor Jews, who were the main patrons of the lending library. There was no need to encourage them to read. The young librarian's role was to suggest suitable books and to explain why they were worth getting to know. The customers were extremely receptive, sensitive and grateful for the slightest show of interest; and so Janina loved this work and devoted every Sunday morning to it.

At the same time she was happy to take advantage of the entertainments offered her by her mother. They used to go to the theatre together, to musical evenings and charity balls. In spring they would go for drives by droshky down the broad and elegant Ujazdowskie Avenue, and were always attending summer concerts at Szwajcarska Dolina ('Swiss Valley', a garden with a café and a band-shell, a popular place for society to take walks in summer or skate in winter). 'Attendance' required suitable outfits, so they both ran about the fashion houses, where it turned out that Julia, the harassed mother of nine, who at the age of fifty was already looking old, had extremely good taste, and the costumes she chose for her daughter aroused universal admiration. Among her friends Janina was known as one of the most elegant young ladies, and even the popular writer Kazimierz Przerwa Tetmajer himself – the idol of schoolgirls who read his erotica with flushed cheeks – on seeing her at Swiss Valley cried out in earnest, 'That girl! That girl! Just look at her. That girl and no other! I must make her acquaintance!'

In her red cloak she made a terrific impression on the men. At a Wednesday concert at the Musical Society a German, newly arrived from Breslau (now Wrocław in Poland), fell in love with her at first sight. He found some friends in common and through them asked if he might be permitted to visit the house. Before answering, her perspicacious mother wrote to her late husband's family in Breslau to ask who this unknown fellow was. The reply was extremely encouraging: *'Ein feiner musikalischer Herr, vieler Millionär'* ('A refined, musical gentleman, a multi-millionaire'). So, with her daughter's consent, Julia invited him to Sunday morning tea. However, without giving warning of her intentions, Janina went out to the lending library on Dzielna Street, as she did every Sunday. She later justified herself by saying that this weekly obligation seemed to her more important than conversing with a stranger, with whom, as she put it, she could have nothing in common.

∞

The Musical Society appears in this story again. One autumn day in 1898 a messenger brought a sealed envelope to Królewska

Street. In it were two tickets for the next Wednesday concert, and a letter from Kamilka. She was writing to tell her mother that, although she had not gained her consent, she was leaving for Zurich. She could not give up her plans, which to her were the most important thing in life. She had obtained the money for her journey by selling the gold medal she had won for passing her matriculation exam so faultlessly. Once there, she would try to get by somehow on her own resources. She did not want any support from home, apologised for her wilfulness, gave assurance of her love, and asked for understanding. She enclosed the tickets her mother had requested the day before, which she had bought on her way to the station.

To give Julia her due credit, she was a magnanimous and forbearing person. She soon came to terms with her daughter's decision and hurried to provide her with financial help. She was later very proud of her, and in the final years of her life, when Kamilka was already working as a doctor in Munich and Berlin, she spent a lot of time with her abroad.

As soon as she reached Zurich, Kamilka immediately became involved in political activity, joining the youth section of the Union of Polish Socialists Abroad. Not long after, when he finished his studies in Warsaw, Lutek went to Switzerland to be a junior academic. Taking advantage of the Easter holidays, he and Kamilka rushed to Warsaw and took part in the First of May demonstration. As usual, the tsarist police attacked and held up the marchers, but did not arrest them on the spot, just checked their identity documents. The details of both young Horwitzes were taken down. That evening, fearing the consequences, they both bolted from Warsaw to Zurich. Next day the gendarmes turned up at Królewska Street with an order to arrest the *buntovshchiki* – the Russian word for 'rebels'. On failing to find them there, they took Julia away with them. Her family were shocked. They were afraid that a person of her age might pay for her imprisonment with a serious illness. It was a few days before they managed to have her freed from the prison at the town hall. There was no end to their complaints and expressions of sympathy. Julia, however, did not think she had been treated unjustly at all. On the contrary, she too felt like 'a rebel'.

She admitted that when the march had come down Królewska Street and past her building on its way to Teatralny Square, when she had heard them shout, 'Long live freedom! Long live brotherhood! Down with the power of capital! Down with exploitation!', when among the red flags she had seen her own children with red stars in their lapels, she had forgotten that she herself was a capitalist and exploiter. She had been so moved that she had torn the red cloth from the drawing-room table and begun to wave it out of the window like a banner.

After migrating from Królewska Street, the portrait of Janina in her red cloak adorned her future drawing rooms. It also hung on the wall at our home in Okólnik Street when I was a little girl. In 1940 it was hanging in her flat in the building on the Old Town Marketplace in Warsaw, which before the war had been the site of the Mortkowicz publishing firm's printing press and warehouse. After the bombing raids of September 1939, which left the house on Okólnik Street without a roof, we had moved to the Old Town, with all our portable property. My grandmother took a lot of trouble over organising our new home, hanging up pictures, putting the books in order and arranging keepsakes and knick-knacks on the ash-wood tables. She was convinced we would live out the war there peacefully and she reckoned that, as long as we were alive, we should live in fine surroundings. A few months later we had to escape from there and hide from the Germans in all sorts of places, in conditions that were not altogether in harmony with my grandmother's aesthetic requirements; and during the Warsaw Uprising the portrait went up in flames in the Old Town, along with all our other family property. Not a trace of it was left, no reproduction or photograph. So let there appear here at least, on these pages, the ghost of its existence.

A PALE GHOST, AN ETHEREAL SHADOW

———————✳———————

How sad it is that old people love to talk about their past, but young people, if they condescend to listen at all, do not listen carefully, do not remember much or ask about the details, and immediately forget what they have heard. I cannot understand why, absorbed in my youth by my own problems, I did not encourage my grandmother to speak, I did not draw her out and write down all those stories that were her life, but which also represented a part of history, culture and literature. Today all that is left of those memories is some vague sketches. I would love to give them clearer contours and fill in the background with all the colourful details, but it is too late.

I regret, for example, that I know so little about one particular sentimental adventure that happened in the summer of 1899. *That year Zakopane* [then, as now, a popular resort in the Tatra Mountains] *was transformed into a privileged literary salon* en plein air, *where almost everything that deserves to be dubbed 'the brains of society' appeared all at once... Every tenth person whom one met on Krupówki Street was a celebrity*, reported the Kraków publication, *Czas* ('Time'). The old Julian Klaczko, a contributor to *Revue des deux mondes* and author of *Causeries florentines* (about Italian art and culture), went for drives about Zakopane in a three-wheeled bath chair pushed by a servant. Henryk Sienkiewicz and his children had fun here while he was engrossed in writing *The Crusaders*, as did the writers Leon Wyczółkowski, Teodor Axentowicz, Lucjan Rydel and Stefan Żeromski. That year was the apogee of the 'Young Poland' movement – the very fruitful literary and cultural trend of that era – and so Zakopane was swarming with 'decadents'. On the veranda of a fashionable café on Płonka Street one might encounter the young poet Jerzy Żuławski, the young playwright Maciej Szukiewicz and future writer Tadeusz

Żeleński, then a medical student. At the centre of attention, as usual, were the famous romantic writer and 'Bohemian' Stanisław Przybyszewski and his beautiful Norwegian wife Dagny. Everyone was talking about them and nothing else, which was most upsetting for Sienkiewicz.

Apart from their fame, it is hard to envy the Przybyszewskis anything; nor is fame exactly a reason to rejoice. Dagny was ill, frightened and helpless, with no money or hope of any sort of stability in life, and since June had been living with their two children, four-year-old Zenon and two-year-old Iwi, at Dr Chramec's acclaimed hydrotherapeutic clinic. In June that year, in Lwów, Stanisław, known as Stach for short, in an alcoholic trance, had become entangled in an unfortunate affair with the wife of his best friend, the poet Jan Kasprowicz, and had at the same time seduced the painter Aniela Pająk.

Dagny wrote to him from Zakopane as follows: *My darling! My darling! I beg you, please don't be sad, come to me as soon as you can. I am waiting for you with arms open wide, I miss you and I love you.* And then, *My love! I am so sad and full of gloom since you left that it's beyond all measure... Today I had a new misfortune. The landlady rented out my rooms, so I have nowhere to live again, and worse still, as you know, I have no money... Can you send me 50 florins?... I know how hard it is, but what am I to do... I love you endlessly.*

There was nowhere to go home to, because Stach, harassed by the demands of his creditors, had just liquidated their beautiful, four-room flat in Kraków, and despite his wife's pleas had sold for a pittance or given away their valuable furniture and fittings – their entire property. He was drinking. As he wrote to Jadwiga Kasprowicz: *Destroy my letters, otherwise I'm lost. And send me 10 guilders.* To Aniela Pająk he wrote: *Send me even about 10 guilders. Just hurry, my dearest, I've no money left for cigarettes now. Despair.*

But what does any of this domestic hell have to do with my future grandmother? That same year, so disastrous for the Przybyszewskis, she spent the summer in Zakopane with her mother, her closest friend Niusia, and Lutek, Kamilka and Staś, who were already studying abroad but had come home for the summer. Zakopane was still an extremely exotic place for Varsovians, so very careful preparations were made for the trip. They needed passports to cross the border between the Congress

Kingdom of Poland and Galicia (which was in the Austro-Hungarian partition). They had to get special shoes made of canvas or strong leather with thick soles (heels were out of the question), rubber raincoats, thick woollen capes with hoods, warm underwear because the evenings could be cold, hats with veils and parasols for the ladies because the mountain sun was fierce, metal-tipped walking sticks for the gentlemen for mountain hikes, binoculars to admire the beauty of the mountains, and supplies of tea, sugar, arrack and candles, just in case.

First of all, Kraków provided the new arrivals from over the border with some unforgettable impressions, both patriotic and aesthetic. After that the railway took them to Chabówka. There they had to hire a two-horse wagon with a thick white canvas hood stretched above it to protect against rain, heat and dust. It was a long journey, and along the way they ate sandwiches, hard-boiled eggs and roast chicken.

They stayed at the villa 'Podlasie' on the corner of Krupówki Street, where today there is a post office. At the time, my future grandmother was twenty-six. Zakopane enchanted her then for the rest of her life. She was always sensitive to the beauty of nature, so she ran about as if intoxicated on group outings and solitary walks, climbing up to the mountain pastures and the Regle dales. Her cultural and social adventures were just as exciting. Kazimierz Przerwa Tetmajer, the idol of the young ladies, was reading extracts from his latest novel, *The Abyss*, at the Tourist Hotel. When he finished he was showered in flowers. Jerzy Żuławski spoke about Słowacki's rhapsody *King-Spirit* at the Tatra Station hall. Every evening there were concerts, poetry readings and humorous performances. On Tuesdays there were dances at Dr Chwistek's therapeutic clinic, on Thursday's at Dr Chramec's, and on Saturdays at Dr Bauer's in Klemensówka. They used to dine at Mrs Libkin's on Chałubiński Street, the boarding house where all the literary and artistic eminences of the day were staying; and that was when Fate assigned Janina a place at table beside no less a person than Dagny Przybyszewska.

She wrote about it in her memoirs as follows: *She was on her own with two small children, waiting for her husband to arrive. Quite apart from the fame that surrounded her, she enchanted me with the first conversation and her indescribable personal charm. To this day I cannot explain why she liked talking to me so much. We conversed at all the communal dinners, and we never lacked a topic for our chat. I think being able to communicate with me easily in the German language was one of the reasons why we became close. Moreover, at the time she was feeling very lonely, as everyone knows ... I remember one of the purely female conversations we had about a famous Warsaw beauty, Siena Reichman, the daughter of a well-known Warsaw doctor, who was sitting opposite us. Dagny did not share the generally ecstatic opinion of her beauty. 'Sie ist banal,' she said, 'banale blaue Augen, banales rosiges Antlitz. Selbst die Bluse die sie trägt is banal blau.' ('She is banal, with banal blue eyes, a banal rosy face, and even her blue blouse is banal.') Here she pointed to my blouse, which was also blue, and said that its colour had character. She used to pay me compliments of this kind, flattering me beyond measure.*

Towards the end of July Stanisław Przybyszewski arrived in Zakopane and moved in with Dagny and the children. It might have looked as if he had come to his senses, finished his affair with Jadwiga Kasprowicz and returned to his wife. But the next bit of my grandmother's memoirs bears witness to his habitual philandering:

On the first day after his arrival I was standing on the veranda, looking through the window at him as he spoke to the other people in the room. Out of snobbery and a sort of coquetry I thought in a childish way, 'I want him to look at me and come out here to me.' And that is what happened. He looked up and at once broke off his conversation and came out to me on the veranda. I cannot remember what he said to me, but that evening we met at a dance. He sat down next to me and, pointing to Dagny, who was dancing, said to me in his husky whisper: 'I like her, but I like you too.' I did not encourage him to make further outpourings. Next day, I found a new issue of Życie ('Life') pushed under the door, including a piece he had written entitled 'At the time of a miracle'. That was all. From this unusual friendship I was left with a photograph, inscribed, 'In memory of some pleasant times spent together'.

I feel a shudder of horror when I think what those 'pleasant times' might have led to. Luckily, tormented by his woes, Przybyszewski was probably just up to his usual tricks out of habit. And my grandmother was a very self-controlled person. Her memoirs continue: *My friendship with Dagny had a sequel. Two years later, just before her tragic departure for the Caucasus, she came to Warsaw, where she sought me out. She was posing for a*

*portrait by Konrad Krzyżanowski and asked me to escort her to
the sittings, during which we amused ourselves with conversation. The painting was very interesting and was bought by a
collector, Bernard Lauer, and hung in his flat for a long time.*

That portrait, painted in spring 1901, and later destroyed during
the war, was considered one of Krzyżanowski's best works.
Nowadays it is only known from reproductions, but even so it
makes a stunning impression, as if the painter had a presentiment
of death haunting Dagny. Or perhaps she herself could feel that it
was the end. She had already been through so many tragic and
humiliating experiences: separation from her husband and children, chaotic roaming about Europe in search of somewhere to
settle, vague and unsuccessful emotional adventures with other
men who were hopelessly in love with her, and a lack of any sort of
prospects in life – all this is drawn on her face, where there is no
trace of her former beauty. She has a black mourning dress, buttoned up to the neck, sharpened features, compressed lips, and
unseeing eyes. What did those two young women chat about
during the sittings? The decadent, scandalous femme fatale, the
unhappy muse of the Young Poland movement who had lost in
life, and the principled young lady who took reality so seriously.
Did they talk about blouses again? It's hard to believe they did. A
few weeks later, on 4 June 1901, Władysław Emeryk took his own
and Dagny's life in Tiflis. My grandmother did not like to talk
about it. The whole affair was so contrary to her own philosophy of
life, yet she always felt a fondness for Dagny and was quite proud
of that fleeting acquaintance.

What was my grandmother's outlook on life at the end of the
century? It must have been a mixture of influences typical of that
era. She still had the slogans of the positivist educators ringing in
her ears, who insisted on patient, hard work for the future. The
socialists, in the person of her brother, demanded renunciation of
one's own happiness and prosperity in the name of the fight for
freedom and justice. Day in, day out her mother reminded her that
a woman's role was to found a family and was ever more insistently urging her to get married. Meanwhile, the voice of ambition was
crying out about the need to achieve something in life, and the
sense of inferiority resulting from her ethnic origin was whispering
that whatever her achievements she would always be an outsider

in the country of her birth. Pride bade her fight against that feeling, and find herself a worthy place in society.

I imagine that for someone who was excessively anguished by their own and other people's demands on them, contact with the Young Poland environment must have been fascinating. Down with the philistines! 'Down with the dull side of life! *Evviva l'arte!* Let us be intoxicated by the moment, let us live for art! Art as a religion, with the artist as its priest'; the entire magical world of Przybyszewski made a huge impression, and the young disciples centred around him – 'the children of Satan' – in their black cloaks and black hats made an even greater one. So it is not surprising that one of these satellites of the Master, a Kraków poet whom she occasionally encountered in Zakopane, in the street, at cafés, at readings and at dances, should have enchanted her. There was a meaningful exchange of glances, then a conversation, then a meeting, and finally a walk together – and then a parting. Towards the end of the summer she left Zakopane and went via Kraków to Vienna. Near Vienna, at Isendorff, she spent a few weeks staying with her sister Henrietta. From there she wrote to the poet, who was still in Zakopane. For those days it was rather a brave step to take. She must have known Przybyszewski's work by heart, because the beginning of the first romantic letter is unfortunately a faithful imitation of his style: *And now a time of dreams and reveries has come, 'the time of a miracle'. Here I am dreaming, or rather being lulled into dreams by new, unfamiliar impressions. We were sitting, and for a long time your gaze wandered in dream-like musing, until your dreamy eyes, intoxicated with beauty, shone into my soul...*

She received an answer, to a poste restante address in Vienna. He wrote: *Why did your voice fly here to me and let forth gentle music all around? I parted with you, my lips whispering mutely, as so many times before I have parted with a pale ghost, an ethereal shadow that walks behind me and before me, and shall never again place a hand on my brow or fall asleep on my heart... So may you remain mute. In your silence I would hear the sweetest, most beautiful song. And you would be one of those who, walking about my meadow, do not tread on the flowers, but give them colour and scent... After your 'goodnight for ever' I wanted to say 'good day' to you on the morrow at Hala Gąsienicowa [a high mountain pasture]. But you were not there, so now I repeat it to the pensive forests and I listen...*

What did she write back? Did she make a declaration of love? In the next letter he confided: *Might I have found love? I am quaking all over at yesterday's memories, but I am afraid to open my eyes to it... Today I went for a long walk in the Regle dales and about Walowa Glade, where gentians the colour of your eyes are still in bloom. You were there with me and you spoke to me. There I read your letter for the second time, for I treat each one of them like a sybarite. I imbibe it and close my eyes. It comes in a wave and shakes my soul, and then you are mistress of it... Why are you as you are? Why are your thoughts so pure? Why do you know how to speak so that when I hear you I cannot adopt the usual smile of irony and can hardly hold back a spasm of weeping that seeps not from my lips but from my mind?*

This is how the needs of my romantic imagination were gener-ously satisfied, wrote my grandmother in her memoirs. *Now I could freely confess my wasted youth, my hunger for love and my longings. I wrote: 'I can see the force and beauty of the things you show me, but I do not have the wings to rise up to them.'*

And he replied: *'You do have the wings. A seagull's white wings. Even the sharp talon of irony that lies hidden in their down does not wound but soothe...'*

What a wonder, a new world of impressions and emotions had opened up to me. I was so bewildered by them that while watching a production of Romeo and Juliet *at the Burgteater I whispered to my companion, my Viennese cousin, that I had seen more beautiful love letters than Romeo's declarations. She looked at me anxiously, in case I were raving... Oh! those yellowed envelopes addressed to Janina, Vienna, Poste restante (he didn't know my surname). How many impressions I owe you!...*

I went home to Warsaw engrossed in my experiences. But reality put an end to it all pretty quickly. While I was still, as he put it, 'waiting for the song of my loving troubadour' he began to write more and more painful letters, complaining that he was no longer worthy of my dreams. And I for my part was making inquiries and discovering more and more opinions of my mysteri-ous 'troubadour', whom I only knew from glances and poetic words. And in the end it came to a break, which I justified with the cruel words, 'I cannot have anything in common with a contributor to Czas and Kraj.*'*

Czas ('Time'), published in Kraków, and *Kraj* ('Country'), published in Saint Petersburg, both encouraged the policy of conciliation and loyalty to the partitioning powers and condemned all forms of resistance, even the most innocent ones involving educational activity. My future grandmother moved in the circles of the liberal intelligentsia, which were opposed to the authorities. After her romantic summer in Zakopane came a gloomy Warsaw winter.

In those days, just as now, differences in world outlook divided people radically and uncompromisingly, and just as today, social relations with ideological enemies were out of the question; but this adventure in correspondence did have sentimental meaning for Janina, and I think the decision to end it must have been very painful.

From Druskienniki, where she spent the summer of 1900, she wrote to the poet for the last time, asking him to return her letters. He wrote back in a rather frivolous tone: *I received your letter at Zakopane. How beautiful it is there! There even mankind's worthless clay seems an immaculately beautiful element. At Plonka's I saw you in the same chair as a year ago. I saw the same contours of your body that made me shudder a year ago. Are you blushing? But that's how it was.* However, this imaginary adventure had ceased to amuse her by now. She dryly demanded: *Please send me my letters by return, to Druskienniki, poste restante.* She got them, without any message.

Yet she did not return the letters the poet wrote to her. She sacredly preserved the entire correspondence for the rest of her life. When in 1939 she gathered up the most valuable things from her flat in Warsaw that had been wrecked in a bombing raid, among the items she took with her to her new home in the Old Town Marketplace was a small case full of those yellowed envelopes and pages filled with poetic effusions; and just before moving out of Warsaw on her occupation-era wanderings she sat down at the old-fashioned tiled stove and burned all the letters, one by one. She did not want them to fall into the wrong hands. She did not want a stranger to read those platonic confessions. She was afraid someone might misunderstand and draw false conclusions that would cast a shadow on her love for her husband.

What unusual subtlety of feelings – but what importance she must have attached to those letters, how many times she must have read them if, at the age of eighty-three, she could still quote each one of them in her memoirs. Clearly she wanted some trace of this story to survive, so I do not think I am doing her any posthumous damage by including extracts of this Young-Poland-style correspondence, or by betraying the fact that her admirer was Maciej Szukiewicz, a critic, poet, playwright, and later custodian of the museum dedicated to the painter Jan Matejko in Kraków. He died in 1943, surviving his letters by three years.

AT LAST!

———————— ✳ ————————

It feels strange to go back through the mists of time and trace the means used by Destiny to bring together two people to whom, indirectly, one owes one's existence. One day in the autumn of 1899 Maks Horwitz brought home a friend and introduced him to his sister, Janina. 'You're both interested in art, so you'll have something to talk about,' he said rather scornfully; as befitted a professional revolutionary, he regarded their interest in art as an extravagant whim.

The young man was twenty-four years old, with intelligent eyes and a soulful, rather Christ-like face behind the shadow of a curly beard. A year earlier he had come back from Antwerp, where he had graduated from the Commercial Academy. Before that he had spent two years studying political and social sciences in Munich. Now he was working at the Wawelberg Bank in Warsaw as a foreign correspondent, but he was finding the job deadly boring. It was very soon apparent that he and Miss Horwitz shared the same passions. They had similar aesthetic tastes, and both loved the Dutch and Flemish painters, such as Vermeer, Rubens, Rembrandt and Frans Hals. She had got to know them in Amsterdam on her visit to her sister, while he had come across them during his studies in Belgium, when he had deepened his knowledge of art by subscribing to the refined periodical *The Studio*, published in London, and to the famous *Yellow Books* illustrated by the best graphic artists of the day. She did not know these publications, so on his next visits he brought them along, and together they marvelled at the ethereal, rather mannered works of Henri Fantin-Latour, Edward Burne-Jones and Pierre Cécile Puvis de Chavannes, and drawings by Arthur Rackham, Eduard Dulac and Aubrey Beardsley.

His visits became more and more frequent. She persuaded him

to sign up for courses at the Flying University, and he attended Adam Mahrburg's lectures on the theory of knowledge, which that year were being held in the parlour of the house on Królewska Street. By that time she was already one of the best female students, and he gazed at her in rapture as she shone with erudition, elegance and beauty.

They were also brought together by the whole wide-reaching sphere of social activity. She was active in the secret educational movement and worked at the Warsaw Charitable Society's free lending libraries, where she was a member of the catalogue committee, which oversaw the intellectual standard of the libraries' collections. She also belonged to the secret Circle of Women of the Kingdom of Poland and Lithuania. All this made a great impression on the young bank employee.

Jakub Mortkowicz (or Jakób, as his first name was spelled in those days) also had some major achievements in this sphere. While still in Radom, where he went to secondary school, he had belonged to underground self-educational circles. Later in Belgium he had been active in the student socialist movement, which was how he had come into contact with Maks Horwitz. He had never joined the Party, but he was heavily involved in underground activities. His flat in Warsaw (where there were three photographs on the wall, of the Winged Victory of Samothrace, Eleonora Duse and Karl Marx) was used to store socialist and independent underground literature, smuggled over the border or printed in Warsaw on secret small presses, for distribution among the workers and young people.

He took his political activities seriously, but his underground pseudonym, 'Decadent', reveals a spark of self-irony smouldering beneath his solemnity. He could sense, fortunately, that politics was not his vocation.

Where would one find such idealism nowadays? It makes one want to sigh with nostalgia. Where on earth would one expect to find a person of not much more than twenty who has studied abroad, is fluent in four languages, has a good profession, intellectual and artistic interests and a calling for social involvement, is honest and disinterested, and to cap it all is handsome to boot? Where did this paragon of virtue spring from, who fortunately, like every mortal, did also have a few shortcomings?

He was born in 1875 in Opoczno, into a Jewish family, about which, unfortunately, I know very little. He had a lot of siblings.

What were their names? Edzia was the youngest; then there was Hela, whose granddaughter, Krysia Wasserman, is now the custodian of a museum in Washington; Michał; Oleś; Samuel, who left for America; Henryk, who as a young man set off into the world and disappeared somewhere; perhaps someone else too?

Jakub's father, Eliasz, had a new and second-hand bookshop in Radom, which must have been the source of his son's intellectual aspirations and love of books; but based on the fact that so little was ever said in our home about my grandfather's family, and so much was said about my grandmother's, I am inclined to suppose they were a little bit ashamed of the Mortkowiczes. Perhaps they were regarded as being of lower social standing. When Jakub opened his own publishing house, he brought his father to Warsaw and gave him a job in his bookshop, but behind the scenes, in the office, not 'at the front', so he would not have any contact with the customers. My mother had a childhood memory of him as a white-haired, gentle old man with bleary, bloodshot eyes, sitting over the invoices, on the sidelines of life as it hummed around him; but she did not devote a single word to him in her exhaustive book on the publishing house's activities, entitled *At the Sign of the Ear of Corn*. Why not? If not for Marianna Mlekicka, who wrote her doctoral thesis on Jakub Mortkowicz, I would not even know that my grandfather came from Opoczno and that his father was a bookseller too.

There is no need to hide the fact that, among Jews who had decided to assimilate, a huge role was played by ambitions relating to the level of Polonisation they had achieved. When the parents, through their looks, language and religious customs, were a reminder of the environment that the children had made such an effort to get out of, family love and loyalty were severely put to the test.

Nowadays it is hard to imagine how painful this process of tearing oneself away from one's roots must have been, how many humiliations one must have had to endure on the way to becoming Polish, how many betrayals, disloyalties, greater and lesser insults one had to commit with regard to one's forsaken kin on this climb to the peak of an icy mountain. How many complexes, prejudices and regrets must have been seething away in there. How many imaginary rungs on the social ladder divided Eliasz Mortkowicz, who still spoke with a Yiddish accent and was kept out of sight in the office, from the poet Julian Tuwim, already so domesticated in his 'Polish motherland' as he took confident steps, under the gaze of his admiring public, towards Jakub Mortkowicz's 'sapphire study' to discuss the graphic design for his new collection, *Socrates Dancing*.

My grandfather's sister, the sweet, radiant Edzia, whom I remember very well, clearly stood higher on that ladder than her own father. By profession she was a dentist, but she preferred to work for her brother's firm. Rosy, plump and smiling, she served the customers at the counter. In 1939 she went to America to stay with her brother Samuel. If she had stayed in Poland she would certainly have been killed, like their siblings Hela, Michał and Oleś, who lived in Łódź.

But what would inevitably happen is still a long way off. For now, Miss Janina is holding subtle conversations with the young banker about art and life's ideals. There is no hint of any declaration of love yet. He is too timid for that, and she still prefers to live in her imagination and to send sentimental epistles to the Kraków poet. She is awoken from her emotional slumber by a shock, similar to the one we experienced in Poland eighty-two years later in December 1981, when martial law was imposed.

On 23 December 1899, just before Christmas, the tsarist police arrested several dozen people in Warsaw from the circles of the progressive intelligentsia who were involved in underground educational activity. Among those who ended up in prison were Ludwik Krzywicki and Adam Mahrburg, both lecturers at the Flying University, writers and social activists Janusz Korczak and Stefania Sempołowska, and also Maks Horwitz and, ever dearer to Janina's heart, the young banker Jakub Mortkowicz.

The arrests were connected with a great public scandal that had been revolving around the activities of the Warsaw Charitable Society's free lending libraries for a year now. As so often happens in Poland, the conflict, involving a clash between two contradictory ideological trends, had degenerated into an ugly business, in which instead of sober, polemical arguments, people were using invective, slander and denunciation.

The traditional Charitable Society volunteers – people from conservative and clerical circles – believed that the lending libraries for Warsaw's poor, which had existed for forty years, should have in their collections nothing but religious, morally improving reading matter to teach patience, gratitude and humility to the needy.

When in 1892 young people from intelligentsia circles took on work in the lending libraries, they were shocked by the content of these crude collections. A specially assembled catalogue committee devised a list of valuable, intellectually improving books, which they gradually began to introduce into the lending-library stock. The official annual fund for this purpose totalled forty-five roubles. Money was now collected for new purchases, thanks to the volunteers' own contributions or donations from wealthy patrons.

Students, young ladies from intelligentsia and middle-class homes or teachers, named or anonymous, but always enthusiastic, the volunteers now worked Sunday shifts in the city's poorest districts, encouraging the Polish and Jewish proletariat to read the works of Henryk Sienkiewicz, Stefan Żeromski, Bolesław Prus, Balzac, Victor Hugo and Dumas. Instead of devotional pamphlets, popular science books explaining Darwin's theories or the laws governing the economy, and sometimes even socialist reading matter were endorsed.

The chairman of the Society, Prince Michał Radziwiłł, was alarmed by reports reaching him from clerical circles about corrupting the populace and arranged a church inspection of the lending-library collections. Many books were discovered there that were 'unsuitable' or that were on the church's index of prohibited books. The right-wing press blew the matter up to the extreme. The periodicals *Przegląd Katolicki* ('Catholic Review') and *Rola* ('The Scroll') did not mince their words. They warned not just the public, but also the tsarist authorities that a 'Jewish-Masonic clique of non-believers [was] promulgating revolutionary activity at the lending libraries by disseminating books that [were] prohibited by the censors and condemned by the Church'. They also published the names of the catalogue committee members, 'the spiritual sons of the great revolution and the commune'.

Prince Radziwiłł backed this report by warning the Governor-General, Prince Imeretinsky, that the activities of the lending libraries should not be left in the hands of people propagating atheism and nihilism among the readers. As a result of these denunciations the tsarist authorities conducted searches at all the lending libraries. Nothing prohibited was found. Then *Rola* announced that, thanks to a warning about the searches, basketfuls of banned books had been removed from the premises during the night. This unprecedented betrayal of national solidarity in favour of the partitioning powers aroused universal outrage. Even in the right-wing press this mean, infamous deed was stigmatised. However, it was no help at all, and arrests were made among the Warsaw 'non-submissives'.

I have a perfect memory of that day, except that I do not remember the date, when after finding out that the prisoners would be transported from Pawiak prison to the Tenth Pavilion in the Citadel [Warsaw's infamous fortress where many rebels were imprisoned or executed], *from early morning I stood outside the prison on Pawia Street with my eyes glued to a hole in the gate. Now I wonder why none of the policemen or constables, who were so zealous in those days, did not forbid me to stay there. I waited for the prisoners to come out and be put in the carriages that stood ready for them in the large prison forecourt. I can clearly see the calm, self-controlled figure of Maks and Mortkowicz's profile in a light Belgian cloak with a camera hanging over his shoulder,* wrote my grandmother.

As the year 1900 began, Maks was awaiting sentence in the Tenth Pavilion in the Citadel, and Jakub Mortkowicz had been exiled to the Caucasus. For the first but not the last time, reality had brutally intruded into Janina's life. The dancing parties, visits to fashion houses and drives down Ujazdowskie Avenue were over, and so were her activities at the lending library, because they had all been closed down. The tsarist authorities arranged for them to be combined into one single central establishment, to be run by the clerical administration of the Charitable Society. The Flying University lectures were over too, because the lecturers were under arrest, and the exalted correspondence with the Kraków poet had lost its charm.

Every Friday Janina took parcels, books and letters to the gendarmerie on Krucza Street for her brother. Her mother wrote:

Dear Son,
I am sending you two pairs of boots, two brushes and two tins of polish. One brush and tin are for cleaning the boots and the other is for polishing the floor. That is so you will exercise your arm and leg muscles, because not using them for so long is bad for you.

Or:

Dear Son,
I am sending you a book that has just come out, Żeromski's
Homeless People. *Read it and write to say what you think of it.*
I liked it very much.

Both ladies also went to visit Maks at the Citadel. My grandmother remembered with horror for the rest of her life the thick,
damp walls and the conversations through bars in the presence of
guards. Maks was gloomy and had changed. Somewhere along the
way he had lost his sometimes tiresome but also charming tendency to tease and joke. Something was gnawing at him.
Something had touched him deeply. Did imprisonment have such
a strong effect on him?

Józef Grabiec writes that it was at this point that Maks
Horwitz's ideological metamorphosis began. The apologist for
Polishness, the romantic who dreamed of independence, came out
of prison a different person. He began to emphasise his Jewish
identity, idealised the merits of the Jews, reacted violently to any
attempt to criticise them, denied the sense of assimilation and
revolutionised his own convictions.

This change was probably the result of a nasty incident that he
experienced while under arrest. When he began to assert himself,
he was maltreated by the police and called a *parshivy yevrey*,
which translates from Russian as 'filthy Jew'. In Grabiec's ironical
tone I cannot sense any particular warmth or sympathy for his
Party comrade, but I understand perfectly that no one wants to be
called a 'filthy Jew' in Russian or in Polish, or in any language at
all, and that anyone who had this experience would start to look
elsewhere for the solution to problems that did not matter to the
struggle his comrades were fighting, but were personally relevant
to himself.

He did not discuss any of this with his family. He was learning
English, translating Poincaré's *Science and Hypothesis*, and writing
articles for Warsaw periodicals under a pseudonym. My future
grandmother was determined to shorten the long, drawn-out
months for herself by doing translation work. She was translating
Siebeck's 'Metaphysical Systems', as mentioned earlier.

Finally Jakub reappeared in Warsaw. He went back to his job at
the bank and to his conversations with the beautiful young lady.

Now they were united not only by their aesthetic interests, but also by the fear and longing they had experienced; but there was still no question of making any declarations of love. Towards the end of July it had been possible to secure Maks's release from arrest against bail. Surely fearing that in Warsaw he would get involved in yet another political scandal, his mother sent him under Janina's care to the resort of Druskienniki for a rest. He could not get his fill of enjoyment at being free. He flirted with the girls, went for long walks, made new friends and debated into the small hours with anyone he found to talk to.

Janina spent the mornings at a little table under a great oak tree finishing off her translation, and the afternoons alone by the River Niemen, staring at the sky, lost in thought. Meanwhile, elegant copies of the periodical *The Studio* kept arriving regularly from Warsaw.

In August 1900, worried that her daughter's acquaintance with a man in a poor situation and with no property was growing more intimate, her mother fetched her from Druskienniki and took her to Paris. The World Exhibition was being held there to celebrate the start of the new century. Both ladies enthused over the remarkable attractions on show, were horrified by 'the monstrosity', that great feat of engineering known as the Eiffel Tower, and visited the Parisian museums, art exhibitions and fashion houses. Janina, who loved to travel, would have been happy if she hadn't been aware of the hidden purpose of the trip. Her Parisian aunts, with her mother's tacit approval, were conducting a rather persistent search for a candidate for their niece's hand in marriage, arranging apparently accidental meetings with a great variety of bachelors. Finally they found someone who seemed the ideal partner, a Swiss engineer of Jewish descent, based in Geneva and determined to marry a well-bred young lady. So the kind Amalia Citroën gave a big family dinner party, to which she invited the engineer and sat him next to Janina.

The elegant *dîner* was socially an utter fiasco. Conversation between the young people did not take off. The older generation, with artificial animation, kept putting forward new topics for them to talk about, in the hope that one of them would catch on, but instead the atmosphere became more and more awkward. Cousin André did nothing to hide his amusement at the embarrassing situation. For the umpteenth time in her life, my future grandmother felt terribly humiliated. She had nothing at all in common with this strange man. Why was she expected to win his respect? Why should she spend her life with him? And that was when she finally realised that there was someone in Warsaw with whom she had a great deal in common, someone who was just waiting for a sign from her. So she wriggled out of visiting an exhibition with the Swiss engineer, and never saw him again.

The next day she bought a reproduction of Burne-Jones's painting *King Cophetua and the Beggar-Maid*, and once back in Warsaw she presented this souvenir to the banker, who adored the Pre-Raphaelites. This gift – a silent declaration – was the turning point in their relationship. She had made up her mind – at last! And so, as the new century dawned, into the life of my future grandmother came my future grandfather.

DECISIONS

———————— ✳ ————————

The year was 1901. The British were at war with the Boers. A plague was raging in Naples. In Warsaw Caruso was singing and Ciniselli's Circus was giving its inaugural performance in a renovated building on Ordynacka Street. And on Krakowskie Przedmieście construction work finished on a modern, five-storey hotel, named the Bristol. In a new black notebook, in an even, slanting hand my future grandmother noted down her resolutions for the new year, and for the new century. By now she was engaged to Jakub Mortkowicz and was taking their future together very seriously.

The magical date marking the advent of the new century prompted people to reflect, take stock of the past and make decisions for the future. Few people in partitioned Poland were satisfied with the current state of affairs. It felt as if their captivity would last for generations, while Russification and Germanisation eradicated the national character. Political repression, social conflict, the sense of impotence and hopelessness – all together it was hard to bear. The optimists reckoned that even in the toughest circumstances one could always achieve some good. Those who were weak and not psychologically resilient – *souls like frail rushes, full of despair and disappointment* – ran away from painful reality into decadence, spleen and alcohol, often to their deaths. The radicals claimed that one should blow up the old order and build a new and just one on its rubble.

In the autumn of 1901 an unusual scene was enacted at the flat on Królewska Street. A photographer appeared in the family drawing room with some complicated apparatus. In an ebony chair upholstered in amaranthine plush sat my great-grandmother, Julia Horwitz, with her daughters gathered around her. The youngest, Kamilka, was then twenty-two, Janina was twenty-eight, Gizella thirty-one, and Flora thirty-three. Twenty-six-year-old Lutek was

standing in the second row. Róża was missing – she had decided to
be reunited with her husband and had returned to Paris – and so
were Henrietta, who still lived in Austria, and the youngest, Staś,
who was studying natural history in Leipzig and had not come
home for the holidays.

Dressed in black and wrapped in a black headscarf, Julia has
white, smoothed-back hair and, though barely fifty-six, looks like
an old woman. Lutek, the 'eternal student', is buttoned up to the
neck in an academic uniform, modelled on Russian military uniforms. Janina, my future grandmother, smart as ever, is wearing a
dress in the latest fashion, embellished with lots of tucks, folds,
pleats and little buttons. Her long, curly hair is pinned up.
Kamilka, for three years now a medical student in Zurich, has
short hair and is wearing a modest blouse of masculine cut as
befits an emancipated woman. Flora Beylin and Gizella
Bychowska, the married women, have come with their children.
There are three little Beylins: twelve-year-old Gucio, eleven-year-
old Genia and nine-year-old Mania. Gucio Bychowski is six. The
youngest generation are lined up at the front, girls in the middle
and boys on either side.

The main hero of events is twenty-four-year-old Maks, who has
taken his place beside his mother in the middle of the group, in the
foreground. His long hair, Christ-like beard and sideburns shading
his slender face make him look like an Italian Carbonaro. Or like
Nadson, the then fashionable Russian revolutionary poet, full of
disenchantment and *Weltschmerz*, on whom he modelled himself.
And behind him, at the back, stand two tsarist gendarmes – in
uniform, with huge revolvers tucked into their belts.

The photographer is hiding beneath a piece of black material
covering a wooden box. He asks them not to move, not to bat an
eyelid, but to smile. No one smiles. There is a flash of magnesium,
and the family portrait is recorded, with representatives of the
regime in the background. In each of the related homes there was a
copy of that photograph, but they were all lost amid the upheavals
of the Second World War. Ours was burned during the Warsaw
Uprising. Fortunately, in her memoirs my grandmother left a
detailed description of the photograph, and of the circumstances in
which it was taken.

The family came together on that occasion for a very sad reason.
That day the gendarmes were taking Maks from the prison in the
Citadel to the Saint Petersburg railway station. From there, under

their escort, he was to leave for Siberia. On the way they allowed him to stop off at home to say goodbye to his mother. Undoubtedly their benevolence was the result of a generous bribe. The bail that a year earlier had led to his release from prison had been paid in vain. Once at liberty he had returned to Party activity and had been detained again. This time he was sentenced to three years in exile.

He was to have been dispatched to the place of exile in stages, which meant travelling for months on end, from one stopping place to the next, in the company of common felons and criminals, freezing cold and hungry. With his stiff, shorter leg he would never have been able to survive such a journey, so his mother took matters into her own hands and went to Saint Petersburg. She did not know Russian and had no friends there, but she spent such a long time banging at one ministry door after another, not sparing a penny to bribe the officials, that finally she managed to wheedle permission for her son to make the journey under guard by passenger train at his own cost.

Maks's home visit must have been planned in advance, because she had ordered a photographer to come and immortalise the farewell gathering. She was afraid she would not live to see her son's return, and she wanted to have a souvenir of their final meeting. Were the gendarmes in the shot because they refused to let the prisoner out of their sight? Or was their presence supposed to emphasise the drama of the situation? The thought of a three-year separation was tearing the relatives' hearts in two. They stifled their tears while the representatives of authority were present, but when the prisoner was led away the women began to sob desperately. The children cried too, and asked the adults: 'Why has Uncle Maks been sentenced to Siberia?'

'Because he was fighting for a free Poland!' replied Janina, my future grandmother.

'No!' Kamilka corrected her. 'Because he was fighting for socialism.'

Maks's niece, Mania Beylin, never forgot this scene and mentioned it in her memoirs. The event she witnessed had an influence on the rest of her life. That day she heard the word 'socialism' for the first time. She writes that although at the time she did not understand what it meant, she associated it with a great and sacred cause, worth fighting and suffering for. From that September day her uncle-the-revolutionary became for her the highest authority,

an example to follow. Ten years later she herself became a socialist, and later, in his footsteps, a communist. Despite all the dramas
that she witnessed, despite her own tragic experiences, she con-
fesses that to her mind that word always retained the radiance that
had so enchanted her in childhood.

But what exactly did it mean? Judging from the clash between
the sisters, it meant something different to each of them. To
Kamilka it was the fight for social justice, while to Janina it was
the fight for independence. Their difference of opinions was a
reflection of the debate then current among Polish socialists, and
which in a few years' time would lead to a dramatic split in the
Polish Socialist Party. Here, in the family forum, the difference in
views was determined not so much by ideological influences as by
date of birth and the two girls' different psychological make-up.

Kamilka was by nature serious, down-to-earth and sensitive, but
not sentimental, as well as six years younger than Janina. Her generation was more and more loudly demanding political, social and
moral changes. The slogan 'women's liberation' was not a plati-
tude for her; since childhood she had known that she wanted to be
a doctor, and she reckoned she was fully entitled to choose her
own path in life. Having joined the Polish Socialist Party as a
student, she shared the views of those activists who claimed that
gaining independence would not solve all the problems, and that
only an international revolution could do away with exploitation,
poverty and class and racial discrimination.

Janina did not have the temperament or the mentality of a revolutionary. She was shaped by the influences of her positivist teachers, who enjoined toiling patiently for the future. Her instructors
had taught her ardent patriotism and social commitment. However, she was not inclined towards asceticism, she loved the
world's attractions, elegant clothes, beautiful objects and travel,
and she had no intention of renouncing her own pleasures for the
general good. She expressed her patriotic dreams in a rather exalted
way, specific to the era. At the classes she held for children in the
family she promised her little nieces and nephews: 'When Poland
rises from the dead we shall all put on white dresses, let down our
hair, place garlands of flowers on our heads and dance for joy. And
after that we shall try very hard for our motherland to be the most
beautiful, happiest country in the world.' Maks and Kamilka reckoned, not without reason, that her vision of the future was rather
sketchy.

The passenger train to Saint Petersburg left at 12.33 Warsaw time. In Saint Petersburg there was a change of train, to the Nizhny Novgorod line. That was where the train journey ended. The next stage was by ship to Kazan, and from there up the River Kama to Perm, the provincial capital of Eastern Siberia. Did someone accompany Maks to the station? Whenever prisoners left for Siberia crowds of their friends, comrades and relatives turned up on the platform to give them encouragement, mementoes and good advice, and to receive their final instructions. His mother had already provided him with warm clothing, snacks for the journey, money and food supplies; but the young man's luggage consisted mostly of books, mainly on the exact sciences. He took over one hundred volumes with him, and before his departure he gave the family a huge list of professional periodicals on astronomy and physics, with a request to subscribe to them for him and send them on to his place of exile. From there every few days he sent popular science articles to the Warsaw publication *Wszechświat* ('The Universe'). It is hard to believe the tsarist regime treated its opponents so mildly.

Julia had not yet recovered from parting with Maks when tragic news came from Leipzig. Her youngest son, her beloved Staś, had taken his own life. He was only just twenty. 'Why? Why?' everyone kept repeating endlessly. 'Why?' cried his mother in despair, before losing consciousness and falling to the floor. She never fully recovered from this misfortune, nor were the reasons for the suicide ever explained. The boy was buried in a Leipzig cemetery. His grave, marked by a monument recording his dates of birth and death, was carefully maintained and visited by the family until the outbreak of the Second World War. Nowadays there can be no trace of it left.

Did family legend idealise Staś a bit, or was he really an enchanting creature? He remained in their memories as an unusually good, sensitive boy, full of charm. He was a great help to his mother in countless matters to do with running the home on Królewska Street. He was always thinking of others, never of himself. None of his siblings ever fell out with him – he was always willing to make concessions. If anyone met with misfortune he was the first to run up and comfort them. He was extremely considerate to poor and disadvantaged people. He secretly put a

Joanna Olczak, 1946

Lazar (Eleazar) Horowitz,
Gustav's father

Karolina Horowitz,
Gustav's mother

Gustav Horwitz

A group of sixth-form pupils from Miss Kosmowska's school. Sitting first on the left is Janina Horwitz.
To her right are: Helena Hirszfeld, Adela Kosmowska, Antonina Chwat, Maria Ziembińska and Matylda Goldfluss.

Świder, near Warsaw, 1894. From the left: in the arms of her wet-nurse, Mania Beylin; in the hat, Gustaw Beylin; sitting, Kamilla Horwitz. Above them: Róża Hilsum; her son Gucio; little Genia Beylin; Flora Beylin holding the fan. Above them: Gizella Horwitz; Janina Horwitz; and on the stair rail, Wacław Kirszrot.

From the left:
Flora Beylin,
Gizella Bychowska,
Róża Hilsum
and Henrietta
Margulies, *circa*
1898.

Janina Horwitz, *circa* 1898

Jakub Mortkowicz as a school pupil
in Radom

Maksymilian Horwitz, Ghent, 1898

Stanisław Horwitz, *circa* 1901

Janina and Jakub Mortkowicz, 1901

Jakub Mortkowicz and Hanna

Stefania and Karolina Beylin,
circa 1903

Samuel Beylin and his
children Karolina,
Gustaw, Genia and
Mania, *circa* 1903

Dr Zygmunt Bychowski, mobilised as
a doctor in the tsarist army during
the Russo-Japanese war in 1904

Jakub Mortkowicz during a prison
walk-about at Pawiak prison, 1906

Maksymilian Horwitz, *circa* 1904

Stefania Horwitz, née Heryng,
circa 1904

A family holiday in 1910. Front row, from the left: Stefania Margulies, Lucien, René and Charles Hilsum, Gustaw Beylin. Middle row: Stefania Beylin, Gizella Bychowska, Marta Bychowska, Julia Horwitz, Róża Hilsum, Janina Mortkowicz, Hanna Mortkowicz, Jakub Mortkowicz. Back row: Karolina Beylin, Samuel Beylin, Flora Beylin, Genia Beylin, Mania Beylin, Marysia Margulies, Julian Margulies, Henrietta Margulies.

Genia Beylin, *circa* 1911

Julia Horwitz, *circa* 1910

bunch of violets on the sewing machine of Miss Ludwika, the ugly seamstress whom everyone scorned. He used to visit boring old relatives whom everyone else had forgotten. His family adored him, he had lots of friends, and he was in love with a sweet girl who loved him in return. So why did he do it? Why?

To the end of her days my grandmother felt pangs of conscience about his death. On finishing secondary school Staś had confided in her that he did not want to go away to study. He dreamed of becoming a professional gardener, and he hoped his sister would promote his plans to their mother; but instead of hearing out his arguments, she accused him of lacking higher aspirations and spent such a long time talking him round that finally she dissuaded him from pursuing an occupation that she thought too modest.

Was she really to blame? Or was she too a victim of the iron doctrine in force in their home that intellectual achievements were the most important thing in life? The persistent demands to develop and shape oneself, to blaze an intellectual trail, passed from generation to generation. In youth they were wildly irritating, but later on they proved very positive. However, the ruthlessness of these demands bordered on cruelty. Measuring everyone by the same mark, ignoring other people's individual traits, inabilities and fears, and the pressure of impatient expectations – 'When will you finally show some flair, become famous, show what you can do?' – all that was crippling, produced complexes and could lead to breakdowns and depression.

Is that what happened to Staś? Or was the *Zeitgeist* to blame too, the spirit of the age, which whispered to weaker, more sensitive people that they would not be able to endure the anguish Destiny would bring, and prompted them to withdraw from the game? There were a lot of suicides among young people in those days, so much seemingly irrational pain and terror did they feel. Perhaps they had a sort of presentiment. Maybe Staś lacked the strength to face the approaching century? In 1939 he would have been fifty-eight, and would almost certainly have been murdered by the Nazis, like his older brother Lutek, who was just as gentle and helpless in life, lacking the dynamism that characterised the rest of the family.

Their mother's despair must have been intensified by a sense of failure. She had tried so hard to bring her children up to be strong, psychologically resilient people. She had made such an effort to counteract any signs they showed of spiritual slackness or impotence. They had all accepted her demands in a disciplined manner – all apart from that single one, the youngest. The proof of their devotion and concern shown by her remaining children after this misfortune was some consolation. Their boundless love for their mother was very touching – after all, she was strict and bossy, not inclined to be affectionate.

Now that she had lost all her vigour and optimism following Staś's death, her closest relatives felt responsible for her and started trying their very best to revive her from her torpor. Flora and Gizelka spent every evening with her, Róża invited her to Paris and Henrietta to Vienna. And despite the period of mourning, Janina brought forward her wedding to Jakub Mortkowicz, in the hope that this important event would occupy her mother's thoughts and inspire her to be as energetic as before.

Indeed, the marriage of the daughter who had postponed her choice for so long did draw Julia out of her melancholy mood. She had so many things to think of: preparing the trousseau, organising the wedding, but above all persuading her own brothers that the groom was a suitable match. Bernard and Michał Kleinmann were not happy with their niece's choice. It was they who turned the family capital to profit, and the young ladies' dowries were invested with them. Each girl was getting a large sum of money – 15,000 roubles – so the aspiring husband had to be a person worthy of their trust. They had to be sure he would not waste the money, but increase it. The young man earned seventy-five roubles in silver each month at the Wawelberg Bank. He was a humble office clerk with no property. His parents, who were not wealthy, had not supported him financially for years; on the contrary, it was he who helped his younger siblings. In addition his pedigree placed him much lower than them on the social ladder. So why had an ambitious young lady, the hope of the entire family, refused so many superb marriage proposals, only to make such a modest choice? Yet with her mother's support, Janina stuck to her guns.

Enacted in Warsaw at the chancellery of the 8 Jerusalem Commissariat Registry for Non-Christian Denominations on 27 August (9 September) 1901 at 12 noon. We certify that in the presence of witnesses Mordka Salmon, house administrator, age 37, Warsaw resident number 1062, and Moszek Zelenek, private writer, age 42, Warsaw resident number 1464A, a religious

wedding was concluded on 26 August (8 September) 1901
between Jakób Benjamin Mortkowicz, bachelor, age 26, corre-
spondent at a private bank, permanent citizen of the city of
Radom, born in the town of Opoczno, Warsaw resident number
1395, son of Eliasz and Chudes-Liba née Korman, residents of
the city of Łódź, and Żaneta Horwitz, spinster, age 26, perma-
nent citizen of the city of Warsaw, born in commissariat district
III, daughter of Gustav Horwitz deceased and Julia Kleinmann
living, Warsaw resident number 1062 at the house owned by her
mother. Before the wedding the banns were published three
times in Warsaw on 4, 7 and 11 August of the current year. A
religious ceremony to conclude the marriage was conducted in
Warsaw by a minister of this Commissariat, Motel Klepfisz.
They also registered that they jointly concluded a prenuptial
agreement on 25/8 of the current year before Notary of the city
of Warsaw Henryk Kokoszko, registration number 2098. This
certificate was read to them, acknowledged and signed: Captain
von Zigler, Minister M. Klepfisz, Jakób Benjamin Mortkowicz,
Żaneta Horwitz, A. Salmon, A. Zelenek.

So the wedding did not take place in a synagogue but at the
house on Królewska Street, in the presence of a rabbi. Next day,
the marriage certificate was filled in at the registry in Russian, and
was preserved in the registry archive in Warsaw. In 1935 a copy of
it was made in Polish translation, which survived among my
father's papers. I am quoting that document, because it seems to be
evidence worth preserving of some antediluvian customs that have
been displaced from memory.

It is remarkable that my grandmother did not devote a single
word to the wedding ceremony in her memoirs. After taking such
pains to describe the dresses she wore at each of her sisters' weddings, she did not make the slightest mention of how she was
dressed for her own. Despite being so sensitive to everything relating to herself – all the compliments and expressions of warmth and
esteem – she did not devote a single word in her memoirs to the
most important event in her life. All she wrote was that the
wedding ceremony was modest, and took place in the presence of
her closest relatives. The grief following Staś's death must have
still been too fresh. She only mentioned in passing, half joking,
that contrary to custom her mother's Warsaw family did not give
the newly-weds any presents, because they could not forgive her

misalliance. Their behaviour must have hurt her, although she does not admit it. Fortunately, she could add with satisfaction: 'They soon began to congratulate me on my choice.'

JANINA AND JAKUB

———————— ✳ ————————

In autumn 1901 my future grandmother, now Janina Mortkowicz, set off on honeymoon to Abbazia, a fashionable resort on the Adriatic – with her mother, but without her husband. Although he had completed his sentence, Jakub was now permanently a suspect to the tsarist authorities, and had passport difficulties. Finally, after some delay, he did manage to reach his wife. After that Janina's siblings, Kamilka and Lutek, arrived in Abbazia to keep Julia company, and the newly-weds left for Venice on their own.

How I would love to rewind the tape of time and see them both at the beginning of the century, in the Venetian museums and churches, in Saint Mark's Square, in the Doge's Palace, on the Bridge of Sighs, or in a gondola sailing along the Grand Canal among the Venetian palaces. With her waist tightly corseted, she would be wearing a spotted muslin dress and a broad-brimmed straw hat adorned with artificial flowers. He would be in a light suit and a panama hat. They were young, romantic and in love. Unfortunately my grandmother was not able, or rather did not like, to write about her emotions, and left no comments on the trip.

A photograph has survived that was taken in Warsaw, probably just after the wedding. It shows just how handsome they were. They are not looking at each other, and there is no shadow of a smile on their solemn young faces. Their wide-open eyes are staring ahead with unusual intensity at some faraway horizon that we cannot see, as if trying to get a glimpse of the future. The inscription on the back of the photo reads: *Rembrandt. Photographe de la cour de le Shah de Perse. Honoré des recompenses de S.M. L'Empereur de Russie et de S.A. J. Grand Duc Michel Nicolaevitch. Varsovie. Rue Marszalkowska 151. Téléphone 660.*

The picture was unstuck in a violent hurry, and still has four patches of black cardboard on the back. When she fled from

Warsaw in 1940, my grandmother tore all her most precious photographs out of the family albums. But after the war she kept this one hidden; perhaps it was too painful a reminder of bygone, happier times.

࿇

Before the wedding, Jakub lived in a modest bachelor flat that he shared with a friend, Bernard Shapiro, a Polish Socialist Party activist, the future father of Hanka Sawicka, a communist who was killed by the Nazis during the occupation. After the wedding he did not rent a flat of his own, like his brothers-in-law Samuel Beylin and Zygmunt Bychowski, but moved into Królewska Street, where Julia gave up two rooms for the young couple. Perhaps this was the result of Mortkowicz's less than perfect financial situation, or perhaps Janina did not want to leave her mother on her own. One room was made into a study and was furnished with modern mahogany fittings. In the bookcases stood hundreds of books and albums all about art, including the beautifully bound annuals of the arts periodical *The Studio*, which Jakub had contributed to their joint property. On the desk he placed the photographs of his youthful idols, Eleanora Duse and Karl Marx, which used to hang on the walls of his bachelor room.

In the bedroom there were pieces of ash-wood Biedermeier furniture. On the walls were reproductions of paintings by Fantin-Latour, Puvis de Chavannes and John Singer Sargent. The interior was decorated with vases full of flowers, Secession-style decorative glass, and finely crafted silver and brass ornaments. They also had the drawing room at their disposal, where they received their friends. On a small round table lay an expensive gift from Jakub's bank colleagues, two huge portfolios of heliogravures of pictures by Arnold Böcklin bound in light pigskin, then the height of fashion.

Despite clear differences in their characters, Janina and Jakub were able to adjust to each other extremely harmoniously. He adored her and went into a panic whenever she caught a cold, showered her in presents, and wrote to her daily from every trip he made, confiding: 'I never stop thinking about your virtues.' But he kept total sovereignty in their union. It was he who took the most important decisions, organised their lives and planned the future. Sometimes he grew enthusiastic about some crazy project, and then his wife would try to restrain him; but she always gave way in the end. They never quarrelled, although she liked company, whereas he was a loner, she was impulsive, while he was placid, she was talkative, he was reticent, she was loud, and he was quiet. It is great good fortune when a couple come together who respect each other's differences. It takes rare wisdom to find the sort of *modus vivendi* that allows you to go through life giving each other mutual support, with no fighting for the upper hand. I think they were also a success-ful couple because her inner equilibrium gave him support. He suf-fered badly from a tendency towards neurasthenia and mood swings from euphoria to depression.

Julia passed the running of the house over to her daughter and gave the young couple complete freedom. Free of her duties, she once sighed and said, 'You know, children, if I weren't too ashamed, I'd go to university now. I've always been so interested in history, but I've never had the time to study.' But family life, though calmer now, still did not spare her emotions. One autumn day, all of a sudden and out of the blue Maks appeared in the house. He had escaped from Siberia after a year of exile. One can imagine how upset she was. How had he struggled through the long and difficult journey? What did he intend to do with himself now? From then on he was a fugitive, wanted by the police, one of 'the underground'. For people like him there was no way back to normality, a professional job and a stable existence.

Not at all perturbed by this, Maks threw himself into his con-spiratorial activities with redoubled energy and published a lot in the clandestine press. He changed his Party pseudonym and now signed himself not as 'Piotr' but 'Wit'. He no longer lived in the family home, but spent each night in a different place. One evening he came to Królewska Street to have a proper sleep at last. He must have been followed, because before he had gone to bed there was clattering at the door. He just had time to whisper to his sister, 'On the console table under the mirror,' and bolt down the kitchen stairs. The gendarmes searched the entire flat, including every single room, cupboard and chest of drawers. Janina was in the late stages of pregnancy at the time, and disguised her state by wrapping herself in a large shawl. She leaned against the console table, felt for the roll of papers behind her and hid it under her shawl.

The search ended with a basket full of Maks's notes and books being carried out of the house. The papers she had hidden were saved – it was the manuscript for an article, which was delivered to the editorial office the next morning. But Maks had vanished; not long afterwards he got in touch from Switzerland to say he was alive.

My great-grandmother had nerves of steel, but she fled abroad from Warsaw as Janina's delivery date approached. She later admitted that she felt extremely frightened and did not want to pass on her fear to her daughter. Perhaps it was a good thing she missed that October night in 1902 when my future grandmother lost consciousness, and my future grandfather, insane with worry, ran out of the house and rushed down Królewska Street without his hat and coat calling desperately for a fiacre. During the birth, which according to the custom of the day took place at home, complications arose that the doctor attending Janina could not cope with. In an incredibly short space of time Jakub managed to drag the best gynaecologist in the city from his bed and take him to Janina in his dressing gown. After a difficult and dangerous operation performed under anaesthetic, at one in the morning my mother was born.

Enacted in Warsaw in the chancellery of the 8 Jerusalem Commissariat Registry for Non-Christian Denominations on the 6/19 October 1902 at 12 noon. The father – Jakób Benjamin Mortkowicz, correspondent, age 27, Warsaw resident number 1062, appeared in the presence of Moszek Zelenek, private writer, age 43, Warsaw resident 1464a and Berek Graber, businessman, age 64, Warsaw resident number 2491d, and presented a child of the female sex, declaring that she was born in his flat on 2/15 October of this year at one o'clock a.m. to him and his wife Żanetta née Horwitz, age 28. The child was given the name Marja Hanna. This certificate was read, acknowledged and signed. Captain von Zigler, Jakób Benjamin Mortkowicz, M. Zelenek, B. Graber.

I have a vague sense of guilt about quoting my mother's birth certificate. I felt the same unease about reproducing my grandparents' marriage certificate in the previous chapter. Is it because I am being disloyal? I do not know. After all, my family never hid their ethnic origin, so I am not betraying any secrets, yet I am writing at some length about things they were reluctant to talk about. They were so proud of their Polishness that they preferred not to emphasise what a short distance separated them from the Jewish world they had run away from. My grandmother would certainly have insisted that I cross out the 'Jerusalem Commissariat' and the witnesses' Jewish names. She would have thought it sounded too exotic, like something out of Singer, not suitable for a portrait of the publisher of famous Polish writers such as Maria Dąbrowska and Stefan Żeromski.

Maybe I have pangs of conscience because I am exposing my relatives' carefully concealed emotions to the light of day, as if I were breaking into someone else's locked drawer; but I am simply trying to get closer to the truth about them, and the truth always consists of both light and shade. I am also trying to find out the truth about myself. I feel that by overcoming my own reluctance to quote those documents I am overcoming fear, my own and my inherited fear – during the war quoting them would have meant a death sentence. It is astonishing that my father calmly kept them in a drawer in Warsaw while my mother and grandmother were hiding in the provinces under assumed names. I think they entrusted those papers to him when they had lost all hope of surviving. They must have thought that after the war they would help him to prove my rights to inherit their remaining property.

Luckily it was they that survived and their property that did not, so they never laid claim to the documents. Perhaps they even forgot all about them. The documents reached me after my father's death in the 1980s, and went on lying in a drawer, in Kraków. To be frank, only a few years ago I would not have had the courage to publish them. I would have thought of them as part of the long forgotten past – it has been and gone, there is nothing to go back to, and why bother, anyway? Who knows what might happen next?

But maybe the time has come at last to rid myself of the genetically encoded sense of fear and shame that is hidden deep in my soul. It is high time to uncover the tracks and to resurrect the names of all those people who died so long ago, such as Mordka Salmon, Moszek Zelenek, Rabbi Motel Klepfisz, Berek Graber, and the mysterious Captain von Zigler, who were there with my grandparents at the most important moments in their life.

By including these documents I am committing one unquestionable indiscretion: I am betraying the exact date of my mother's birth. I would not unmask the touching coquetry with which she took three years off her age, if it were not going to cause inaccuracies and chronological absurdities in this account. Was it a common custom, or was it just in our family that women rejuvenated themselves in this way? On her wedding certificate my grandmother reduced her age by two years. During the war all the ladies in hiding altered the dates on their fake documents, taking years off themselves. After the war, when they went back to their real names they did not change the dates back. This could cause terrible confusion if it were suddenly to appear that one of the heroines of this story had a child before her wedding, another began her university studies as a fourteen-year-old and my mother, for example, knew how to read and write when she was two. I would never have managed to battle my way through all that, so I think she would forgive me my treachery.

An adorable, pretty, clever child, love for each other, a modest but adequate income, the same intellectual and artistic interests – it seemed as if the young couple lacked nothing for their happiness; but Jakub was plainly bored by his work at the bank. He was too much of an individualist, with too much energy, too many dreams, too much inventiveness and ambition. So he started looking for another field of activity. His wife supported him in the conviction that he should do what really interested him. And what interested him most of all? Books.

At number 143 Marszałkowska Street there was a well-known bookshop and publishing firm, selling its own publications and those of other publishers, and operating on a sale-or-return basis, founded in 1876 by Gabriel Centnerszwer. His only son, Mieczysław, did not want to take on his father's firm. He had chosen an academic career and later became a chemist, lecturing at the universities in Riga and Warsaw. Old Mr Gabriel had less and less strength, so he was looking for partners.

In 1903 Henryk Lindenfeld, a bank colleague, brought the news that there were shares for sale in Centnerszwer's bookshop for 15,000 roubles, and suggested to Mortkowicz that they acquire them in partnership. Jakub was immediately in favour of the plan, and Janina welcomed it enthusiastically too. They both realised that they could draw the necessary sum from her dowry, invested with her Kleinmann uncles. However, the provident Julia was afraid the money might be wasted and consulted her brother for advice. Evidently, Bernard must have come to like his niece's husband by now. He replied philosophically: 'Why not? Books are not a bad business. Glücksberg, Orgelbrand and Lewental have proved right...' And he paid out 4000 roubles to Jakub on account, giving him another 3500 the next year.

On 13 May 1903 the partnership contract was drawn up, and so Jakub Mortkowicz became co-owner of a publishing firm, which would later belong to him alone. He would have preferred to start his business independently, and his wife's dowry would certainly have been enough to acquire his own small bookshop; but as a 'suspect individual' he could not have obtained a concession to run a publishing firm in his own name. So at 143 Marszałkowska Street there hung a new black sign with a gold inscription in Russian and Polish reading: 'G. Centnerszwer & Co.' That sign was not changed until 1915.

If the plan of our lives is really written in the stars and our happiness depends on how we interpret and implement that plan, my grandparents fulfilled the task with unusual intuition and confidence. Looking back on their fortunes from a distant perspective it is plain to see that they made very careful preparations for their joint path in life. The individual character of the Mortkowicz publishing house arose from their independent youthful passions. Without knowing of each other's existence, they had followed the same paths, visited the same museums, adored the same paintings and brought home the same albums full of reproductions. So it is not surprising that artistic publications, produced to a high standard of graphic design and elegantly bound, became the firm's main aspiration. Their shared love of poetry bore fruit in the well-known 'At the Sign of the Poets' series. My grandmother's educational and social interests found expression in the publication of valuable books for children and younger readers. She also specialised in seeking out and translating formerly unknown works for young readers. Selma Lagerlöf's *The Wonderful Adventures of Nils*, Ferenc Molnár's *The Paul Street Boys* and Ågot Gjems-Selmer's *By a Far Silent Fjord*, and volumes of the adventures of Doctor Dolittle by Hugh Lofting later went into the canon of children's classics.

The dreams that united the newly-wed couple might have got lost later on in everyday life, which usually bids us renounce our youthful ideals and forces us to make compromises; but, with touching persistence, they both preserved their faith in their own convictions that life should be run according to higher than purely material values and should serve the interests of the general public. The only luxury they allowed themselves was foreign travel.

Immediately after acquiring their share in the bookshop they set off for Vienna, Munich and Leipzig, to learn about the bookselling trade and to supply the shop with new publications. *I went with him* – my grandmother recorded – *because our relationship was such that he allowed himself no pleasure without me. And this sort of journey was a pleasure in every sense of the word. We spent two weeks among books, reproductions and works of art – our favourite interests.* My grandfather noted: *I became acquainted with the international bookselling organisation and conceived a plan to make use of this relationship for our aims, not just the commercial but also the cultural ones.*

A few days after they returned to Warsaw crowds began to gather in front of the bookshop on Marszałkowska Street. Never before had such an attractive bookshop display been seen in the city. In one window a huge copy of a bas-relief called 'Diocletian's Throne' had been placed. The original, dating from the Ionian era, was in a museum in Rome, and had so enthralled the young couple with the range and beauty of its details that they had bought a skilfully patinated plaster cast and hauled it back to Warsaw. The bas-relief delighted the Varsovians, and a few years later features from it were used in the design of the logo for the 'At the Sign of the Poets' series. In the other window there were fine reproductions of the most famous masterpieces of classical art, brought back from their travels, and piles of the latest foreign publications, mainly art books. 'Windows onto the world' – that was what the windows of the bookshop's next headquarters on Mazowiecka Street were called, but those 'windows' were first opened on that occasion, on Marszałkowska Street.

The editorial activities began later on. In 1903 only two publications appeared, the second of which was *Where your Little Brother Came from*, a title from Centnerszwer's old collections. There is a story connected with the first publication. To avoid any conflict with the tsarist authorities, until Poland gained its independence my grandfather did not put his name on any of the books he published. Only once, in 1903, did the name Mortkowicz appear on the title page, and that exception was a great source of pride for my grandmother.

She always had a fondness for educational matters, and shortly before their marriage she had become interested in a new trend that had arisen in Germany, called *Kunsterziehung*, which meant 'education through art'. She wrote an authoritative report on the subject, which she delivered to the Educational Circle of Women of the Kingdom of Poland and Lithuania and which was so well received that a well-known publisher, Michał Arct, offered to publish it. In the meantime she got married. However, the publisher insisted that she feature on the cover as Janina Horwitz, because he thought her new surname sounded bad and might put off the readers. Offended, she withdrew the manuscript.

'Mortkowicz, Janina: *On Aesthetic Education*, 8°, 74 pages' – that was the very first item to have been published by the new firm. *Somehow that name was accepted within Polish culture. Somehow it did not put off the readers*, she wrote in her memoirs with ironical satisfaction.

ANULKA

———— ✳ ————

My mother was a year older than the bookselling firm that would later turn into Jakub Mortkowicz's publishing house. She grew up and took her first steps alongside it. In her book about the history of the publishing house, which was published after the Second World War and entitled *At the Sign of the Ear of Corn*, she recalls her earliest childhood memories. She and her parents still lived at the home of her grandmother, Julia Horwitz, on Królewska Street. From there it was not far to Marszałkowska Street, where the bookshop was located. At first she was taken there in a pram, dressed in a little white piqué coat and an embroidered cap. Later on, wearing colourful dresses or a sealskin fur coat, she went there with her mother or nanny holding her by the hand.

When she learned the alphabet, she tried to understand what it said on the bilingual sign above the bookshop door. It was a good opportunity to explain the political situation to the child: we are in captivity and the Russians have ordered all the signs in the city – street names, advertisements, theatre posters and so on – to be written in Russian first of all, and only then in Polish. However, even in Polish the bookshop sign was incomprehensible. She writes: *I knew and loved old Mr Centnerszwer. But what did the mysterious word 'S-ka' mean, that you could read on other Warsaw shop signs too? It was explained to me that it was short for 'spółka', meaning 'company'. Who was the company? Daddy and Mr Lindenfeld. Mr Henryk Lindenfeld was always in the bookshop for as long as I can remember. He didn't sell any books, he just remained somewhere on the sidelines, by the desk. He had a beard and a big son called Kazio, who later grew up to be a prominent physicist.*

The mysterious 'S-ka' that so intrigued her referred to the fact that Centnerszwer's old firm continued to conduct the same activities as before, selling books it had bought or taken on commission from other publishers; but now each of the two new partners also had the right to publish books as 'author-publisher' – in other words, at their own cost and risk. The lame old Mr Centnerszwer no longer interfered in anything. He sometimes came to visit the bookshop on Marszałkowska Street, because he felt happy among the books, and sometimes his wife Regina came with him.

Mr Lindenfeld was fat and jolly with an excellent appetite. My mother remembered that once to her amazement 'at one sitting he ate about half a pound of ham'. He seemed to her the embodiment of happiness and lack of cares, in comparison with her own father, who 'was thin, nervous, ate little and was always hurrying off somewhere'. She was eight years old when in a congratulatory poem for his name-day entitled 'To Mr Jakub' she asked him to follow his partner's example:

> *Why are you so solemn, always toiling with your books?*
> *While your friend Mr Henryk – what a jolly fellow he looks!*
> *And now you've grown so thin that to look at you's a sin,*
> *Take Mr Henryk, your friend, why, his appetite has no end,*
> *But you eat so little food,*
> *Mr Jakub, it's no good.*
> *What a tiny bit of meat you're having for your lunch,*
> *Your friend Mr Henryk will get six that size to munch.*
> *I don't want to spoil your mood,*
> *But Mr Jakub, it doesn't look good.*

She remembered the actual bookshop as *a long, fairly dark interior, where at the so-called 'front', the 'gentlemen' stood behind a wooden counter selling the books, like wonderful wizards who dealt out all manner of favours. It was they who had access to the shelves full of books that reached up to the ceiling, and they used to put me up on the ladder so that I could touch the gilded letters of the titles on the red and blue spines. Sometimes they gave me those books as presents for free 'without a single rouble' – as I used to boast to other children.*

Hania was three years old when her parents moved into a flat at 8 Szkolna Street, with windows looking onto Marszałkowska Street. *From there it was only a couple of steps across the street to the bookshop, which was situated almost directly opposite*

Szkolna Street. Next to it, on the corner of Próżna Street, was Birtümpfel's pharmacy, where there were two glass vases full of bright-green liquid in the window, shining mysteriously and venomously. Further down, on the same odd-numbered side of Marszalkowska Street was the 'Rembrandt' photography studio, where in glass showcases in the gateway there were some pictures of ladies in trailing dresses and enormous hats with ostrich feathers. And finally that much-coveted, enchanted paradise, Malanowski's toyshop on the ground floor of the corner building that housed Jadwiga Sikorska's famous girls' school. From there you only had to cross the street to reach the iron railings, and there beyond the gate the Saxon Gardens lay open before you, ever changing as the years went by, full of criss-crossing avenues, clumps of greenery and allegorical figures with broken noses.

In front of the iron gate stood a caretaker, who measured up the people entering the gardens with his watchful eye. He did not admit Jews dressed in gabardines, pedlars, street urchins, or anyone who was badly or poorly dressed. As in her mother's childhood, elegant ladies with parasols in various colours walked along the well-tended avenues, while well-dressed little girls with bows in their hair ran ahead, rolling colourful hoops or playing a wonderful game called *cerceau*. On gala holidays and Sundays a military orchestra played in the concert band-shell. As in the past, a large fountain refracted the rays of the sun in its spray. The swans that swam on the pond were fed the remains of uneaten rolls. Just as a quarter of a century earlier, children hid panting in the undergrowth as they played the usual childhood games. Time went on standing still, as thick and sweet as honey.

It was not far from Szkolna Street to her grandmother's. My mother could not remember much about the flat on Królewska Street. *Sunlight reflected on a very shiny floor, a flowerpot with sapphire-blue cinerarias standing on the table in the dining room and the dark silhouette of an old uncle sitting in front of the window at table. Was it Uncle Bernard or Uncle Albert?* She had a much clearer memory of her grandmother Julia with the city in the background. Small, stout, active and energetic, she always had lots of business to attend to. Wearing a black hat over her white hair and an old-fashioned mantilla, every day she set off on long outings, tirelessly tripping along the main roads of the city and the narrow little streets of the Old Town. She was happy to take Hania with her. They were very fond of each other.

As my mother writes: *I was the fifteenth of her huge herd of grandchildren, but that did nothing to diminish our friendship or opportunities for frequent meetings. From early childhood I went for walks about Warsaw holding my grandmother's hand. It was Grandma who told me about the popular revels that were held in the spot where Ujazdowski Park later came into being, and about the soap-covered pole that was climbed by a daredevil who wanted to win some clothes and a watch. Grandma was eighteen years old during the 1863 Uprising and wore national mourning. Grandma used to go away on holiday to Agricola Street or Flory Street, which seemed to me hugely funny and entirely improbable* [because the city had grown since then, engulfing these formerly rural places]. *I found all her stories about old, though for her not so old Warsaw just as alluring as the sweet gingerbread she used to buy on Count Berg Street and the* framboise *raspberry toffees from Lourse's café, like fragments of pink glass in pieces of white paper rolled up into a little cone.*

Julia Horwitz had to divide her time and affections between eighteen grandchildren. The Beylins had five children: Gucio, Genia, Mania, Karola and Stefcia, who was known as Funia. The Bychowskis had three: Gustaw, Janek and Marta. The Margulieses had three girls: Stefa, Marysia and Alisia. The Mortkowiczes had Hania. In Paris, Róża Hilsum had three sons: René, Lucien and Charles, who often came to Warsaw. Maks Horwitz's marriage produced three children: Kasia, Staś and Anusia. So my mother had a great many cousins. The huge family could not live without each other, so the Warsaw children were always meeting up. They used to go for walks together in the Saxon Gardens and at Lazienki Park, and on trips to holiday resorts near Warsaw. Every week there was a communal Sunday dinner at a different home, and in the event of any problems, journeys or illness, the aunts would take in their nieces and nephews for weeks on end. The symbiotic tie that linked the parents' generation now passed on to the next one.

As happens in families, relations between the youngest children were sometimes good, sometimes bad. The first cousins were envious that Hania – an only child – was treated like a little princess by her parents. Indeed, they worshipped and pampered her. The lovely little girl with golden curls and sky-blue eyes had a nanny, her own nursery, the most beautiful dresses, books, dolls and toys; but this did not spoil her character at all: she was cheerful and good by nature, though sometimes she felt jealous too. Instead of all those beautiful books and games she would have preferred to have some siblings. She used to sit at a little green table in her nursery and fill dozens of pages with drawings of her imaginary brothers and sisters, writing their names and ages underneath: 'juzefa – 13, antek – 7, wacek – 9, frania – 20, zosia – 105'. Then she would play with them. And her mother, who was so keen on education, would watch these games, make notes and put the drawings away in a drawer.

Once upon a time there was a little girl called Anulka. The day she was born the sun must have been shining very brightly and merrily in the sky. And an invisible, good fairy must have leaned over her cradle and whispered a magic spell. Because otherwise it would be hard to understand why Anulka had such a good life, why she was always laughing and so often skipping about and singing softly to herself, 'How lucky I am, how lucky!' Once the little girl's mother overheard her singing and started thinking about Anulka's good luck. And that made her remember various times in her life, and so she would never ever forget, she wrote it all down in a diary. That was how this little book about the good luck and happy childhood days of little Anulka began.

Anulka, or Eight Years of a Little Girl's Life is the tale of little Hania, illustrated by her childish drawings. Following the fashion of the day, my grandmother used the notes she kept to write a detailed description of the child's development from the first days of her life, including her behaviour, interests and games, her first words, questions and conversations. The result was a very private, very personal book. I do not know if it had many readers, but for me it represents an invaluable source of information about my mother's childhood.

In the book Jakub Mortkowicz appears in the role of a loving father who carries his daughter piggy-back, laughs and jokes, and Janina Mortkowicz is a down-to-earth, not-too-sentimental mother who explains the world and is not sparing with the educational comments. The beloved grandmother is also not one to sentimentalise, but carefully inspects her granddaughter's school exercise books, asks her questions about all the daily events and praises her drawings, latest poems and handiwork. There is a good nanny, the best in the world, who sings her to sleep. 'Over the

Niemen I ride out abroad, my horse and my armour are ready, so hug me and hand me my sword, my darling girl, my lady!' And a faithful old servant called Marcinowa, who is always on the child's side, shows her 'treasures' hidden in a green chest and makes her porridge.

They visit the holiday resorts near Warsaw, Skolimów, Konstancin and Piaseczno, which have a scent of pine and hot sand. Then they go to a small German village at Hel on the Baltic coast, empty and still undiscovered in those days, to Zakopane, which was on the other side of the Russian–Austrian border so you had to have passports to get there, and to the Tatras, on the Hungarian side, where the peculiar name of the town Szmeks – which in Polish sounds like 'laughter' – made them laugh. Those eight years of Anulka's life seem idyllic, although in fact it was a stormy, dramatic period.

On Sunday, 22 February 1904, the newsvendors ran out onto the streets of Warsaw early in the morning shouting, 'Stop Press. Dispatch from Saint Petersburg! Diplomatic relations broken between Russia and Japan! War! War!' Next day posters announcing mobilisation went up on the walls. Soon after, crowds of terrified recruits called up for the Russian army, in huge sheepskin hats, began to make their way to the Saint Petersburg Railway station, from where they departed for the Far East, in the very middle of the dreadful Siberian winter, over the Urals and beyond Lake Baikal. They were seen off by their sobbing wives and mothers. Aunt Gizelka Bychowska was in tears, and so were her two sons, Gucio and Janek. Doctor Zygmunt Bychowski was off to the front, mobilised along with a group of sixty-five Warsaw doctors, which also included Henryk Goldszmidt, the jolly young paediatrician who treated Hania, and who signed his first literary works with the pseudonym Janusz Korczak.

Later, joyfully welcomed news of Russia's defeats began to come through. The exotic names were on everybody's lips: Port Arthur and Harbin, Khabarovsk and Tsushima. Everywhere the waltz 'In the Trenches of Manchuria' resounded, played in the Swiss Valley garden, in cafés, on the streets and in the courtyards. The hope was born that military set-backs would weaken the tsarist empire and lead to a relaxation of its anti-Polish policy. The greatest hotheads claimed that the time for a new uprising was approaching. The Polish Socialist Party, headed by Józef Piłsudski, was inciting active resistance against the Tsar's rule.

It was at this point that twenty-five-year-old Kamilka Horwitz came back from Zurich, where she had completed her medical studies, and started work at the Jewish Hospital in the Warsaw district of Czyste. She was also active in the Warsaw cell of the Polish Socialist Party. On Sunday, 13 November 1904, she took part in a socialist march that formed on Grzybowski Square outside All Saints' Church. As the demonstrators set off for the city carrying their red flag, the police and dragoons started trying to disperse them. Just then fifty revolvers fired a salvo of shots from the demonstrators' side. It was the Battle Organisation Pilsudski had established, using weapons against the Russians for the very first time, which made a huge stir in Warsaw and at least for a while dispelled the general sense of helplessness. The encounter resulted in victims on both sides and a large number of people were detained. A couple of days later Kamilka too ended up under arrest in a women's prison known as 'Serbia'. She was released on bail paid by her mother.

In January 1905 unrest broke out in Russia that led to the start of the revolution. 'Bloody Sunday' – when the police took brutal action to crush people demonstrating against the war outside the Winter Palace in Saint Petersburg – on the one hand sparked new demonstrations and riots, and on the other increased repression. In Warsaw the Polish Socialist Party declared a general strike. Hundreds of thousands of workers took part all over the country. The young people also started a strike in the name of the fight for Polish schools. One of the main organisers of the strike at his school was sixteen-year-old Gucio Beylin.

Jakub Mortkowicz, a Polish Socialist Party sympathiser, was also involved in underground activity. He communicated with independent organisations in Kraków, co-organised the Society of People's Publishers in Warsaw, helped to found educational institutions such as the Polish Cultural Society and the University for All, and imported and distributed books that had been banned by the tsarist censors. *As she walked along the street with her father, at the sight of a Russian policeman Anulka would helplessly try to shield him with her little hands. At the sound of the doorbell she would helplessly wake up in her little bed and whisper: 'Hush! Don't open the door, it's a search!'*

One night in 1906 the tsarist gendarmes banged on the door of the flat on Szkolna Street and, after searching the place thoroughly, took Jakub Mortkowicz away. He was held in custody pending enquiry at Pawiak prison, and was under threat of exile to Vyatka; but by some miracle, maybe in exchange for some cash, or maybe with the help of some acquaintances, after a few months' investigation he was sentenced to a year's exile beyond the borders of the Russian empire. His punishment turned into a delightful, thrilling adventure. Instead of going to Siberia, he went on a trip around Europe, taking his wife and child with him. It was 1907, when Hania was five years old.

His partner, Lindenfeld, and his devoted colleague Marian Sztajnsberg stayed behind in the bookshop [writes my mother]. *Our servant Marcinowa stayed behind in the partly rented-out flat. The route of our travels, which had priceless results – Lehr- und Wanderjahre – took us to Kraków, Vienna, Venice, Florence, Rome, Naples, Sorrento, Paris, Munich and Leipzig. Looking back, I admire my parents for trailing about Europe so enthusiastically, studying art, spending days on end in museums and churches, and relentlessly educating themselves while at the same time caring for a child with no nanny the entire time. According to family legend, I usually slept at the foot of their bed or on two chairs pushed together, spent long hours in the care of museum attendants and knew just how to ask at critical moments, 'Dóve rittirata?'* ['Where's the convenience?']

Despite all the attractions, the journey was often difficult for the five-year-old. In the museums and churches she was made to visit she used to cry: 'This is too boring for little children.' By the time they reached Rome she was so sick of sightseeing that when told to lie on a bench in the Sistine Chapel and fix her gaze on Michelangelo's ceiling, she had a hysterical fit and had to be taken outside, because she was sobbing as loud as she could: 'I can't go on, I can't go on just looking and looking all the time.' So they went to Sorrento, and there it was wonderful, with golden oranges on the trees, a sapphire sea and an azure sky. Then came the magical Blue Grotto on the isle of Capri, where there were extraordinary treasures on the beach – mussel shells, branches of coral and an amazing variety of coloured pebbles.

Some atmospheric sepia photographs of those days have survived, in which the little Hania is dressed up in the style of old-fashioned portraits. In one picture her curly hair is loose, falling on her shoulders. She has a satin band tied round her forehead and is wearing a short dress edged in fine lace. In her arms she is holding an orange branch covered in fruit. In another one she is wearing a muslin dress with a pattern of little roses, a white hat, little white open-work socks and white slippers. Plainly every detail of the outfit was carefully chosen. As she dressed up her daughter, no doubt my grandmother was finding a cure for the grudges she had felt in her own Spartan childhood, when the same dress passed from one sister to the next, reaching her fifth time around in a pitiful state.

They spent the next summer at a French village by the Atlantic. Aunt Róża came to join them from Paris with her three French sons. Then they all went together to Merano, where Julia was taking a cure. After that came Paris, Munich and Vienna. During this journey Jakub Mortkowicz made close contact with the top French, German and Italian publishers, and became familiar with the way in which national and international booksellers' and publishers' associations were organised. He and my grandmother also finally had enough time to draw up a precise plan for their publishing activities on their return.

After more than a year he was given permission to go back to Warsaw, so all three went home together. Anulka's parents went back to work in the bookshop, while she returned to her nursery, which had to be refurnished to accommodate some new arrivals: the elegant Parisian Lili in her pink silk dress, the Italian rag-doll Mimi, and six Parisian dolls, a present from Aunt Róża. In one corner a bedroom was arranged for all the 'children', both foreign and local: Zosia with her blonde plaits, Elżunia with her tin face, Jantosia in her patched trousers, and the twins in their little blue dresses. In another corner stood the dolls' dining room, with a sideboard, table and chairs; in a third there was a kitchen with a fireplace, shelves full of pots and a dinner service, a wash-tub and a mangle. Under the window stood a small green table with a green bench, where Anulka could sit down to draw. By the wall stood a green cupboard, where her favourite books were kept.

I am eager to describe my mother's sunny childhood because I myself have few happy memories of that period in my life. I do not remember the time before the war, and I would prefer to forget what I went through during the occupation. I was parted from my family home so early that I do not even remember what my nursery looked like, what sort of dolls, dresses and toys I had. Only now, as I read *Anulka* again, can I state, with no regret, how very different my mother's childhood experiences were from my own. I always envied her her buoyant nature and psychological resilience, but it never occurred to me that not just genes, but also disparate turns of fate, could have shaped our characters in different ways.

Her childhood was pure bliss; and although the good fairy's spells did not last long, although she had tough, dramatic times ahead of her, perhaps it was those happy days, full of love and a sense of security, that engendered the optimism and joy in life that she never lost, despite all her personal misfortunes, the horrors of the occupation and her difficulties after the war. Overworked, burdened with responsibility for the fate of our entire family, and later seriously ill, she retained something of the child in her to the very end – enthusiasm, delight in the world, spontaneity, a sense of humour and a tendency towards infectious laughter. Kind as she was and helpful to others, everyone adored her. Maybe it was that childlike trust and radiance that allowed her to find so many friends during the occupation, and by that token to save my grandmother, herself and me.

Those grim times are still far away, however. Right now, Anulka is drawing a wasp-waisted lady wearing her hair in a chignon and holding a parasol, and underneath she writes:

How much I love my Mama no wise man could declare,
Even if he used the finest words there are.

Mama keeps the drawing safe in a drawer, and will later put it in the book about Anulka, thanks to which this fragment of the past will not be lost. Meanwhile, Julia Horwitz gazes lovingly at the child and says: 'Golden head, golden heart, golden hands.'

METAMORPHOSIS

―――――――――＊―――――――――

In 1904 Comrade 'Wit' – in other words Maks – asked Comrade 'Wiktor' – alias Józef Piłsudski – to be a witness at his wedding. Nowadays it seems highly improbable. The future co-founder of the Polish Communist Party and the future head of the reborn state on such friendly terms? Even then their paths had started to diverge. A clear division had been drawn in the Polish Socialist Party between two trends: the right and the left.

Piłsudski and his supporters, known as the 'old' or 'pro-independence' faction, believed that the Party's fundamental task was to arouse a fighting spirit in the public and inspire the belief that a national uprising was imminent. They felt they should prepare for it by widening the Party ranks, training military cadres and obtaining weapons and ammunition to be able to take action against the invaders at the right moment. The 'young' or 'internationalist' faction, to which Maks belonged, claimed that a fight between a small group of hotheads and the enormity of Russia was doomed to disaster. They thought hopes should be placed in the outbreak of an international revolution. However, despite the difference of opinions, social contact was still possible, and evidently the old feelings were still alive, because Comrade 'Wiktor' took part in the family celebration. The wedding was held in Kraków, as only there, within the Austro-Hungarian partition, could political émigrés reveal their real names.

Maks had met his future wife, Stefania Heryng, in Switzerland. She was the daughter of Zygmunt Heryng, a famous economist, sociologist and socialist activist, and Helena Cohn. Her uncle was Feliks Kon, a socialist and later a member of the Polish Communist Party, later still a Bolshevik and in 1920, during the Bolshevik attack on Poland, a member of the Polish Revolutionary Provisional Committee. She was born on a ship on the Siberian

River Yenisei, because her mother had accompanied her father into exile. This dramatic start in life was enough to recommend her as the wife of a revolutionary, but in her youth, as a student of economics and law in Geneva, she was also an active socialist volunteer. Her political work brought her into contact with Maks, and later on it developed into love – and a homeless life as émigrés, wandering from country to country and from city to city.

In 1905, when the revolutionary unrest began in Russia and the Congress Kingdom of Poland, Maks came illegally from Kraków to Warsaw as a representative of the Polish Socialist Party's Foreign Committee. Revolutionary fever hastened his left-wing metamorphosis. It was on his initiative that a two-year period of dramatic arguments began within the Polish Socialist Party, ending in its split.

Michał Sokolnicki, a Polish Socialist Party member and Piłsudski's closest collaborator, had got to know Horwitz earlier, in 1899, at a Party conference in Paris. At the time he had even invited him to stay with him. Writing his memoirs thirty-seven years later he characterised him as follows: ... *an acrobatic dialectician and a relentless polemicist, mad with ambition to fight and take charge, he was preparing himself for a great role in the Party.* One can sense that he tried to like Maks: *He was quick-witted, shrewd and full of initiative in his ideas, extremely dogged in his convictions and I would say in the ardour of his convictions. With my youthful intellect, eager for justice and the equalisation of social differences, I idealised him for some time as the heir to the Wohls and Meiselses, as the archetypal Polish–Jewish scapegoat, and even his passion for the Party seemed to me to flow from the depths of human dignity insulted by racial hatred, while I was keen to interpret his frequent doctrinal obduracy as extreme idealism.*

Relations between them later cooled as Horwitz's views grew more radical, while Sokolnicki resisted *the Talmudic observance of principles derived from Marx.* Sokolnicki gives a horrifying description of the successive Party congresses and councils held in the years 1905 to 1907. He relates how it was not ideas that were being expressed at this stage, but a power struggle, mutual enmity and suspicion, ambitions great and small, a vapid juggling of words and demagogy.

In March 1905, at the VII Party Congress, the 'young' faction, headed by Horwitz, forced through a resolution that pushed the demand for Poland's independence into the background. The 'slogan for today' was to support the revolution in Russia and demand greater political and civil autonomy from the tsarist government. The resolution was adopted by a majority of votes, despite protests from Piłsudski and his supporters. In June 1905 at the Polish Socialist Party's Party Council Horwitz was elected to the new left-wing Central Workers' Committee, and the old Party leadership was removed from the administration. Piłsudski still retained management of the Battle Organisation, the underground army he had created, which was preparing spectacular large-scale armed action aimed at tsarist dignitaries, the Russian army and the gendarmerie, and also expropriations, known as 'exes' – in other words, raids on banks and post coaches to swell the Party coffers.

Conflict arose in this context too. The 'young' faction agreed with the idea of attacks aimed at the most hated individuals, such as spies, agents and police superintendents, but they regarded mass actions, in which Russian soldiers were killed, as a lack of solidarity with the Russian proletariat. As it was impossible to come to an agreement, they formed their own paramilitary organisation, which was called the Technical Battle Organisation. It provided security for worker demonstrations and also organised 'exes', thanks to which it obtained money for its own Party aims.

This was when thirteen-year-old Mania Beylin had an extraordinary adventure that she described in her memoirs. In those days she often spent the night at her grandmother's home on Królewska Street. Since the Mortkowiczes had moved out, Julia felt very lonely in her huge flat and the revolutionary atmosphere was always giving her reasons to feel nervous. Despite having been arrested, Kamilka went on with her agitation work and spent all her time off from her job at the hospital at Party meetings. After arriving in Warsaw, in view of his underground status Maks preferred not to live at Królewska Street. In any case, he had immediately been imprisoned yet again and was locked up in the Tenth Pavilion. The old lady was afraid to sleep alone in the empty house. Just as in the past her mother, Miriam, had done, so she too now asked her grandchildren to keep her company.

Mania came to see her most often. The evenings and nights she spent at her grandmother's flat later determined her choice of a path in life. Grandmother Julia was extremely interested in international politics and subscribed to three European daily papers, and every night before going to bed Mania had to read her the most important articles published in the *Journal des Débats*, the *Berliner Tagesblatt* and the *Neue Freie Presse*. That would then start a discussion on current affairs, which was also a lesson in knowledge about the world. The young Miss Beylin very soon became an expert on world politics and a maniacal reader of newspapers, and only a few years later, in France, she herself took up political journalism.

One evening, when they were considering the situation on the Russo-Japanese front, the doorbell rang. The servant very cautiously opened the door without taking off the chain, but, on seeing familiar people, let them in. One of them was Stefania, Maks's wife, who was then working for the Party's Technical Battle Organisation as a distributor, or 'dromedary'. This was the term for women who smuggled underground propaganda and other secret dispatches – sometimes weapons – usually by hiding them under the voluminous dresses of the day. The other lady was Zofia Posner, known as 'Anna', the wife of Szymon Posner, a renowned socialist activist. Both ladies were wearing long black cloaks and huge black hats, and looked very romantic. First they asked for the servant to be sent off to bed. Then they drew all the blinds and door curtains. Next they demanded to be taken to the room furthest from the entrance, where they took off their cloaks and asked for help unfastening their dresses and corsets. Then they undid the canvas belts that were wrapped around their waists. Grandmother and granddaughter went pale. Under the belts countless bundles of Russian banknotes were hidden. As they took them out, the conspirators explained that they had come from a raid by the Party fighting squad on a post train carrying bank cash. They would have to keep the booty for the night, but someone would come for it in the morning. They got dressed, wrapped themselves in their black cloaks, put on their hats and were gone – rather coolly leaving thousands of roubles on the table.

Their hands trembling, Mania and Julia packed the bundles of banknotes into bags and shoved them into a storage space among some old rags and suitcases. Later on the girl went to bed, but she kept being woken by nightmares: gendarmes storming the house, a search, an interrogation, prison and penal servitude. She could hear her grandmother pacing about the flat, looking out of the windows and listening at the door. In the morning a young 'fighter' appeared. He packed the money into a huge suitcase and left. They had swelled the Party coffers. Not long afterwards the money proved extremely necessary.

※

At that point Maks had been in prison for over two months. He had plenty of time for thinking, and from his thoughts arose a brochure entitled 'On the Jewish Question', which was published two years later. His words on such a complex and painful matter deserve some attention – not because of his main thesis, which is that capitalism is to blame for all the misfortunes of the Jews and non-Jews, and that revolution alone can change the downtrodden masses into free and happy people. It would be unfair to sneer at this conviction nowadays, because it has been all too tragically taken to task by history.

However, what is striking is the sincerity with which my grandmother's brother acknowledged the complexes arising from his Jewish origin and the psychological wounds caused by the process of assimilation. One can sense that he knew these problems from dissecting and observing his own immediate surroundings. He was twenty-eight when he wrote this brochure. He had long since ceased to be the romantic boy who fell in love with being Polish and believed that he only had to devote his life to the fight for liberty and justice and Poland would love him like its own native son. By now he knew that he would always be an unwanted stepchild.

In the final decades of the nineteenth century anti-Semitic propaganda was on the rise, and Polish patriotism quite often turned into nationalism guarding against an influx of 'ethnically alien, harmful elements'. All those insulting epithets familiar since childhood, the accusations of prevarication, avidity, hypocrisy, cowardice, ruthlessness and disloyalty, must have cut deep into the soul, especially as they did not come only from implacable anti-Semites or from people who were just mindlessly repeating some platitudes they had overheard. As the great novelist Bolesław Prus himself wrote in *Kroniki Tygodniowe* ('The Weekly Chronicles'): *The Jews do not just represent an ethnic origin and a religion, so much as ignorance, conceit, separatism, idleness and exploitation.*

To the public mind, as Maks put it: *The unassimilated Jew, the Jew who was not yet elevated to the status of a Pole, was a sort of sub-human.* Brought up in the spirit of assimilation, in his early youth he had been able to delude himself that he would avoid the fate of the 'scabs', being insulted, humiliated and suspected of all manner of villainy. The recipe for avoiding being despised had seemed simple: *In order to become human, the Jew must cease to be a Jew, and must become a Pole...* All you had to do was commit a double betrayal – renounce your unassimilated brothers, in other words your own roots, your own history, religion and tradition – and also disown your own self, your own identity as formed over the centuries. You had to make every effort to hide everything that made you psychologically, intellectually and culturally different and pretend to be someone else, *to become completely Polish, to a point of illusion.*

There was no way of coping with this sort of mimicry without still feeling shame. Who was Maks talking about? Himself? Or his family? *They were ashamed of their own origin. Understandably, they never denied it among those who knew about it. But even here, in deed, word and gesture they tried to prove and convince others that they felt themselves to be completely and utterly Polish, and that they were entirely rid of their Jewishness. What a mixture of pride and shame they had on their faces as they accepted the compliments a genuine Pole once paid them as he clapped them on the shoulder in a friendly way and said: 'You're a real Pole, there's not a speck of Jewishness in you. If I didn't know I'd never have been able to tell... if only all Jews were like you! But you've got nothing in common with that foul, swindling, Yiddish-speaking rabble!'*

The more the number of Polonised Jews increased, the more aggressive the anti-Semitism aimed at them became. In his brochure Maks called assimilation *the bankrupt ideology of the Jewish bourgeoisie and intelligentsia.* It was no protection against insults; quite the contrary. As Jan Jeleński, the editor of the anti-Semitic journal *Rola* ('The Scroll'), wrote: *You are a Jew, so be one! We prefer the benighted Orthodox Jew to the civilised nonentity, because the former believes in something, he is something, but the latter gives no guarantees. In his shady dealings he will sell or traffic anything, because he is an advocate of ruthless, base utilitarianism.* Leader of the radical right-wing Endecja ('National Democracy') movement Roman Dmowski, in publishing *Thoughts of the Modern Pole,* argued: *The ranks of Poles of Jewish origin grew vastly, but these were ever more defective Poles. In view of its large numbers, this new Polish-Jewish intelligentsia was quite simply not automatically in a position to enter as deeply into the Polish sphere as had been possible for the small number of individuals who had assimilated earlier. It created its own Jewish sphere, with a separate soul, a separate attitude to life and its problems. In addition it could feel itself growing stronger and stronger, and in the natural course of events, whether consciously or not, increasingly started trying to impose its own notions and aspirations on Polish society.*

In 1904 Horwitz demanded that the Polish Socialist Party put up a fiercer fight against National Democracy's chauvinist agenda. When this produced no response he began to ask questions: Will there be room for Jews and other ethnic minorities too in the jointly regained motherland? What sort of position will they have? Second-class citizens? Intruders, or plain enemies? But still he got no answer. Piłsudski never hid the fact that for him the most important issue was the question of independence. Resolving social conflicts over class, race and nationality was something he put off for later.

Wounded pride engenders helpless regret and anger, aggression, the desire to get even, and dreams of domination. If a person cannot cope with the experience of humiliation, he cannot accept himself, whatever other people say about him, and enmity and resentment will ferment in his soul, poisoning him psychologically.

Limping, Maks paced his cell in search of the words that would define a goal for the humiliated. Was he aware of the paradoxes involved in his mission? He was telling the Jewish proletariat to replace their faith in Yahveh with a belief in socialism. Unlike the religion of their ancestors, it did not demand waiting patiently for the Promised Land. It proclaimed that they should regain their lost dignity right now. No rational proof was needed – assurances were enough: *And yet it is possible to move straight from the Jewry into humanity. The Jewish socialists have brought the torch of class consciousness to the Jewish masses. With a verse from the Talmud on their lips: 'Who will help you if not you yourself? And what will be your strength if you are isolated? And when – if not now?', they went to the Jewish worker and taught him about solidarity and the struggle, they taught him to feel, think and live. The lowered brows were raised, the bowed necks were straightened, the sad, downcast eyes grew bright with a new radiance... The idea of the struggle... has shattered the old, traditional image of the Jew, who only keeps his head above water*

by having a supple neck and a mixture of seeming humility and
persistent cunning. It has counteracted the age-old notions and
prejudices about the 'Jewish soul'... By this very action the new
human-Jew has come to the fore in all his greatness and beauty.

Did he really believe in a socialist 'promised land'? Did he want
to believe in it so very much?

ᴊᴂ

In October 1905, at news of the strike in Moscow and Saint
Petersburg a general strike erupted throughout the Congress
Kingdom of Poland. On 30 October the Tsar capitulated and
announced his famous manifesto, promising Russia the first constitution in its history. This meant an increase in civil liberties,
and in the Russian partition it aroused hopes of full autonomy.
The manifesto also announced an amnesty for political prisoners.
On 1 November crowds gathered outside the Warsaw prisons at
the Town Hall, Pawiak and the Citadel demanding the release of
the detainees. Among those freed that day was Maks.

Mania Beylin wrote about that day. It was unusually warm and
fine for the time of year. In the afternoon the increasing noise of
crowds of people talking and singing began to pour in through the
open windows of their flat. The worried residents ran out onto the
balcony and saw a procession of marching demonstrators, a grey
and black crowd, including men in workers' caps, women in head-
scarves, students and school pupils in their uniforms carrying red
banners and singing the patriotic anthem, 'Warszawianka':

Boldly let us raise our standard on high,
Though a storm of hostile powers rages all about,
Though sombre forces are bleeding us dry,
Though who holds tomorrow is ever yet in doubt.
March on, Warsaw, march on! To a bloody fight,
Holy and right. March on, Warsaw, march on!

'A socialist demonstration!' shouted Gucio and ran for the door,
with his sisters Genia and Mania after him. 'Wait! I'm coming with
you!' cried their mother, Flora Beylin, and ran after her children,
hurriedly seizing her hat from the hat-stand and pinning it on along
the way. They joined the ranks of enthusiastic people and went with
them to the Town Hall on Teatralny Square, where the Russian
police prefecture and prison was situated. There the demonstrators

began to demand that the Tsar's promises be fulfilled and the political prisoners released. The gates of the Town Hall opened. Suddenly the crowd realised that instead of political prisoners they had let out the criminals and cutthroats. As soon as they tried to protest, mounted Cossacks attacked the defenceless crowd, lashing them with whips, slashing them with sabres and trampling on them. It was one of the bloodiest massacres in Warsaw. 'That's how the Tsar keeps his promises,' cried the beaten people.

The Beylins only just managed to get away and reach home without injury. Mania remembered the scene for the rest of her life: pools of blood on the ground, people pouring with blood, the redness of the banners passed from hand to hand by the wounded; and a massive shout: 'Long live freedom!' – and a sense of brotherhood with that whole unfamiliar, yet suddenly intimate crowd.

Michał Sokolnicki has different memories. He writes: *To my incredible surprise I had to ascertain that the crowd was not Polish. What I saw all around me was an improbably large concentration of people from Nalewki, Gęsia and Nowolipki* [streets in the Jewish district], *who as if at a given signal, on a solidary promise, had headed into the centre of Warsaw. In many places I saw a lot of Russians, and all around me I heard Yiddish or Russian being spoken, least of all the Polish language [...]. On 1 November Warsaw saw socialism. For many socialists, myself included, that day remained in our memories as a dark nightmare.*

In a story entitled 'Stacho' my grandmother described that day as joyful and radiant, full of hope despite its tragic end. *People suddenly dropped their everyday concerns and ran outside in crowds... It was as if they were no longer the same people who the day before had pushed past each other as strangers, indifferently, often reluctantly or inimically. Today there were no strangers, no servants and masters, no differences. There were equal rights and equal duties for everyone. And they spoke to one another like brothers, like comrades – they understood each other at once and agreed – immediately – because for once at least they were breathing freely.*

As he falls asleep the eponymous hero, Stacho – based on the ten-year-old Gucio Bychowski – dreams *that now it would be like this for ever; from now on people would be brothers and comrades, no one would ever hurt anyone else again...* And he whispers in his sleep, *Long live liberty.*

THE TEN FROM PAWIAK

———————— ✷ ————————

In December 1905, after a few weeks at liberty Maks Horwitz was arrested again. He was detained at the editorial office of *Kurier Codzienny* ('The Daily Courier'), a newspaper that had been the Polish Socialist Party's organ during the few revolutionary months, and he was under investigative arrest in Pawiak prison. In April 1906, without leaving his cell he succeeded in organising one of the most daring political acts: the famous escape of 'The Ten from Pawiak'.

In the inter-war period a film was produced with this title and numerous publications were issued telling the story of the event. It is generally Jan Gorzechowski who appears as the main hero of the enterprise, known as 'Jur', the future husband of the writer Zofia Nałkowska and one of the most active members of the Polish Socialist Party's Battle Organisation. He really did play the most spectacular role in this event, demanding the greatest courage and sang froid; but the idea was born in the head of 'Wit', as Horwitz was known. He and his cellmate, his Party comrade Paweł Lewinson, worked out the details of the enterprise, and Feliks Kon, who was at liberty, coordinated operations. All three were on the left wing of the Polish Socialist Party, all three were Jews and also future communists.

Despite the growing dissonance within the Party, the left-wingers were still acting in solidarity with the right. Fourteen years later, in 1920, with the help of Bolshevik bayonets Kon would try to turn the reborn Poland into a Soviet republic; Maks would be in prison as a dangerous political criminal, and Gorzechowski would be Commander-in-Chief of the Warsaw City Militia.

Without getting involved in political considerations and without exaggerating or underestimating anyone's merits, I would like to tell this story the way it was recorded in Feliks Kon's auto-biography and in an account of Maks written by his nephew, Dr Jan Kancewicz. The mathematical precision of the plan, the details of the action, the number and clarity of the concrete facts mentioned would make a thrilling film plot – one that might well sound highly improbable:

Maks had already been imprisoned in Pawiak for a few months when the news went round that ten comrades had been brought to the prison who, acting on Party orders, had provided security for the socialist demonstration and had been caught by the police while firing at the Cossacks who were attacking the crowd. A state of emergency was then in force in Warsaw, so after a short trial they were sentenced to death. The sentence had yet to be confirmed by the Governor-General. Then they were to be transferred to the Citadel, where the executions would take place. The situation looked hopeless; but hopeless situations always stirred Maks into action. He and Lewinson thought up a plan to rescue the condemned men, naturally with the help of people on the outside.

In some mysterious way he managed to gain the confidence of the head of the prison, who gave him to understand that he could no longer bear his job and would be happy to slip abroad, if only he had enough money. After some lengthy bargaining it turned out that for 10,000 roubles he would be prepared to cooperate. The liaison between Maks and his comrades from the Warsaw branch of the Polish Socialist Party was his sister Kamilka, who used to visit him with their mother. Julia put up with many eccentricities on the part of her youngest daughter; she had long since come to terms with Kamilka's political involvement, and instead of complaining when she was arrested, came forward with money for bail without any resistance, thanks to which the girl was released from prison. However, Julia still regarded it as unacceptable for a young lady to roam about prison corridors on her own, with no chaperon, amid the coarse comments of the guards. So they used to go and visit Maks together, and that was when he approached Kamilka with a request to summon Comrade 'Bolesław', alias Feliks Kon, to visit him as soon as possible.

Kon does not hide the fact that he was horrified when Wit's sister came to see him at the Central Revolutionary Committee premises, where he was on duty, with this instruction: *I couldn't believe what I was hearing [...] Wit – a veteran Party man who had escaped from Siberia, a member of the Central Committee*

[...] was summoning me, a former convict sentenced to hard labour, living on an illegal footing, wanted by the police, to 'come and visit' him in prison!... In the first instant it seemed incredible. But I was being summoned by Wit, a serious activist who weighed every word and considered every decision precisely.

'Didn't he tell you what it's about?' Wit's sister, who was very like him, replied calmly: *'No. All he said was that you should come and see him as a relative, with his mother.'*

So with his heart in his mouth Kon set off to 'visit', pretending to be Maks's relative, which was not much of a lie, as he was his wife's uncle, after all. He was accompanied by my valiant great-grandmother, who after so many visits to her repeatedly locked-up children, almost felt at home in Pawiak by now. In the visiting room her son summarised his plan through the bars:

'You must send the prison manager an official note signed by Chief Police Superintendent Meyer to inform him that at such and such a time the captain of gendarmes will appear at the prison with an escort for prisoners X, Y and Z who are condemned to death, and that he should have a prison carriage and the arrestees ready at that hour. It won't be hard to pick people for the plan either: they must be brave, determined and most importantly resourceful.'

Kon regarded the plan as a dangerous fantasy. During a state of emergency police vigilance was increased, there were military sentries at every crossroads, and Cossacks went galloping about the streets by day and night.

'You must and you can do it', insisted Wit. *'The tailors' group can prepare the uniforms, the tinsmiths can do the tin for the caps, and the military can train the "policemen" or "gendarmes"... I am convinced it will work.'*

The bewildered Comrade Bolesław promised to cooperate.

Now it was Bolesław's job to convince his Party comrades to adopt the plan, find suitable people to carry it out, and prepare them for their assigned roles. Comrade Anna – alias Zofia Posner, who in the previous chapter had helped Maks's wife Stefania to hide stolen money at my great-grandmother's flat – proved an enthusiastic helper. Jan Gorzechowski agreed to take part as the captain of the tsarist gendarmes. He had nerves of steel and feared nothing, but he spoke Russian very badly. So he became Baron von Budberg, a German from the Baltic coast in the service of Russia. Kon drilled him on the correct way to pronounce a few sentences in Russian that he would have to use when he fetched the prisoners. The most important and hardest word of all was *Poshevielyvayties* – meaning 'Get moving!' – and it was the one that made the greatest impression.

Volunteers were also found to play the roles of 'prison escorts' from the Citadel and their commanding officer. The Party tailors took measurements and sewed the regulation uniforms, caps and greatcoats at lightning speed. A professional instructor taught the future 'policemen' their drill in a private flat: *The instructor and his pupils took off their boots – some were barefoot, others were wearing socks – so that twelve people 'marching' would not make any noise, and did about turns to order, stood in two ranks, goose-stepped one behind the other, and formed twos and fours. They did all that in silence, concentrating hard, and the only sounds to be heard were the half-whispered commands.*

The easiest thing was to falsify an official letter signed by the Chief Police Superintendent and ordering the prison head to hand over the prisoners. The Party printers were immensely skilled at producing all sorts of fake documents, fully equipped with the proper signatures, stamps and seals. It was decided that to be on the safe side the order would not be sent by post; instead Baron von Budberg would simply hand it to the prison head, but an hour earlier Feliks Kon, who spoke superb Russian, would telephone the prison and give orders to prepare the prisoners for the transport.

Every detail was thought of. An orchard was found at the Warsaw toll-gate where the prison carriage would be hidden once the arrestees had been released. At the right moment the prison head was given his money, so that immediately after dispatching the prisoners he could head for the Warsaw–Vienna railway station and flee abroad. I would not be at all surprised to learn that the 10,000 roubles were smuggled in by my great-grandmother – in a plum cake she had baked for her son, for example.

On 23 April 1906 all the preparations were complete. That evening, the 'escort' congregated at a previously located safe house, dressed in their police uniforms. Gorzechowski – as von Budberg – was the perfect image of a German baron, with a broad beard brushed up on either side, gold-rimmed glasses and a blue gendarme's uniform with epaulettes and aiguillettes. Once it was completely dark in the city, Feliks Kon went to another pre-arranged flat, and rang the telephone number. At the prison chancellery someone picked up the receiver and heard a Russian voice saying:

'This is Warsaw City Police Superintendent Meyer. To whom am I speaking?'

'This is the head of the investigative prison [...]. At your service, Your Excellency.'

'In an hour Captain von Budberg will report to you with my orders. By then you must prepare the following prisoners for dispatch to the Tenth Pavilion. Please write down the names carefully [...]. Everything must be prepared for the Captain's arrival. Get a prison carriage ready. No need for a convoy: the Captain will bring his own. Have you got all that?'

'Yes.'

'Make sure it all goes ahead without delay.'

'Yes, Sir, right away, Sir.'

At two in the morning two vehicles drove up to the Pawiak prison. From one emerged the Captain and two policemen, and from the other came four more policemen. In the prison chancellery the Baron handed the prison head a sealed packet containing the Chief Superintendent of Police's orders. The prison carriage and its driver, who was unaware of the conspiracy, were ready and waiting. The prisoners were woken up and informed that they were being taken to the Citadel. They were convinced they were going to their execution. When they appeared in the prison courtyard, on their 'commander's' orders the 'policemen' drew their sabres, and Baron von Budberg began to shout gruffly at the condemned men, 'Poshevielyvayties.' Once they had got into the carriage, two policemen sat on the box beside the unsuspecting driver, and von Budberg and the four others sat inside. The carriage drove out of the Pawiak prison gate.

They turned towards the Citadel. For some time they drove in silence along the empty city streets, but once they were in the suburbs, one of the policemen sitting on the box shouted, 'Stop! There's a wheel loose,' and jumped to the ground. His colleagues hurried to help him. The driver stopped the vehicle and got out to see what had happened. A handkerchief soaked in chloroform was thrust in his face, he was tied up and pushed inside the carriage, while someone took his place on the box and drove the horses on. Only then did the prisoners realise what was happening.

As soon as the carriage drove into the suburban orchard on Żytna Street, near Okopowa Street, everyone felt safe except for the driver. There the prisoners were let out and given detailed instructions. Dressed in civilian coats made ready for them in advance, they were to head for friends' houses, where they could change and shave, and where false passports were waiting for them. Next the Party railway workers were to transport them to the station and send them on the nearest passenger or goods trains to the border. They were also given addresses abroad where people were waiting to take care of them.

The policemen threw off their uniforms, under which they had civilian clothes, handed over their revolvers and disappeared. The prison carriage and its unhappy driver were found in the orchard early in the morning of 24 April. By then the arrested men were already speeding towards the border; and the walls of Warsaw were adorned with proclamations, prepared in advance by the Polish Socialist Party's Revolutionary Central Committee, entitled OUR AMNESTY. They informed the city that the ten prisoners had escaped from Pawiak and gave their names. No one who took part in the action was harmed, and the authorities never guessed that Maks was involved in it. A couple of weeks later he was once again condemned to Siberia, and went on another long journey; but after reaching his destination, he escaped even sooner than before. How Derengowski, the prison head, managed abroad is not known.

FAREWELL TO JULIA

———————— ✳ ————————

In December 1906 the cultural sensation of the season was a concert at the Filharmonia concert hall given by Wanda Landowska, the already world-famous Polish harpsichordist who lived permanently in Paris. Her performances of the classic composers, above all Bach, were unrivalled and she made a great impression on the public not just with her playing but also with her appearance, which was styled according to the modern spirit. She wore her dark hair smoothly combed over her ears, a black dress with no adornments, and her special way of tilting her head made the press compare her to 'the heroines of Maeterlinck or Burne-Jones's maidens'. There were plenty of ladies with similar hairstyles and clothing to be seen among the audience. I can safely assume that the concert-goers included that great theatre and music lover Flora Beylin, and her older daughters, sixteen-year-old Mania and seventeen-year-old Genia, who was a talented pianist. On this occasion Gucio, the secondary-school student, who was also an ardent music lover, did not accompany his mother and sisters.

On 13 January 1907 the French consul Bayard wrote to Paris: *Although it is somewhat safer on the streets of Warsaw than for example at this time a year ago, towards the end of last year, on 15 December, eight bombs were thrown on the streets. One of them was thrown by a seventeen-year-old schoolboy. There are also numerous attempts to attack the gendarmes and police with revolvers [...]. There is no end to the raids on state cash desks, offices and stations, even in the most populated districts. The Warsaw police can do nothing, because the public refuses its help. Lately there have been more and more confiscations of printing presses and books. The ban on all kinds of political gathering is strictly enforced. The prisons are full to bursting. They say that in*

November last year in one month alone there were 23,601 people
on the list of prisoners at the Citadel. Most of those arrested do
not appear before a court but are administratively sentenced to
exile outside the borders of the Congress Kingdom, or even to
death. Since 15 December I have noted 39 executions.

The revolution was being lost, the tsarist repressions were
acute, and four members of the family were in Warsaw prisons.
Kamilka had been arrested for the third time for illegal Party activity, and Lutek was imprisoned for the same offence for the first
time. Jakub Mortkowicz, my grandfather, was there for importing
banned literature from abroad. Gucio Beylin was there for co-
organising a school strike and for belonging to the Polish Socialist
Party's Battle Organisation, which was the most severely punished
crime. The fighters, who conducted armed combat against the
regime, were regarded as terrorists and were tried by a military
court. The boy was more of a sympathiser than an active member
of the organisation, but although he did not have much on his
conscience the mildest penalty he could expect was exile to
Siberia.

By some miracle, Maks, the 'professional revolutionary', was
still at liberty; after his latest escape from Siberia in 1906 he circulated between Vienna, Łódź and Kraków, continuing to conduct
lively agitation activity while dodging the police. As the Russian
Governor-General of Warsaw, Georgi Skalon, told Consul Bayard,
The Poles are bandits who would stop at nothing [...]. They hate
the Russians who are their masters. The only way to restore order
is to use brute force. It should be used without limit [...]. The
Poles must be annihilated. My great-grandmother Julia, a tiny,
rotund old lady, with her black mantilla, black hat and snow-white
hair, and her two daughters Flora Beylin and Janina Mortkowicz
got in a droshky and went to the prisons at the Citadel and at
Pawiak, lugging parcels of food, books and journals. In dingy visiting halls, among crowds of distraught wives and mothers they
waited for their loved ones, putting on a show of good cheer as
they related the news from home in an artificially animated way
and, as they bade farewell, whispering that everything would be all
right, that they were doing everything in their power to get the
sentence commuted.

They really did mobilise every possible influence and acquaintance. My grandmother's close friend Stefania Sempołowska was
summoned to help as co-founder of the renowned Political

Defendants' Group, which provided a legal-aid service for prisoners. The fate of the four 'criminals' was also considered by two now famous Warsaw lawyers who were involved in the Group's activities, namely Stanisław Patek and Leon Berenson. Some 'approaches' were found, some suitable 'doorways'. Samuel Beylin went all the way to Saint Petersburg to help his son's case. Once again, one is tempted to praise the corruption as well as the benevolence of the tsarist era. Gucio was sentenced to exile in Khabarovsk, but was allowed to take his matriculation exams and enrol at Saint Petersburg University to read law. After two years the sentence was changed to 'banishment from the Russian empire', so he went to Paris, where he continued his studies. The other three were also expelled beyond the borders of the empire, so instead of terrible Siberia they went away to safe, peaceful Europe. Kamilka and Lutek went to live in Lausanne, where she took a job as a doctor and he studied geology under a famous specialist, Professor Maurice Lugeon. Jakub Mortkowicz and his family went to Italy, as already mentioned.

When most of the family had gone away, Julia felt very lonely at Królewska Street. Moving in with Flora or Gizella, the daughters who had stayed in Warsaw, did not enter the equation: Julia was too wise for that. She was not used to playing second fiddle and would be unable to come to terms with losing her throne, which in someone else's house seemed inevitable. In any case, she was over sixty and was having trouble with her health, so for the first time in her life she decided to look after herself. So began the final stage in her life story: her travels.

In those days people believed in spas and health resorts, in the salutary effects of fresh air, sunshine, mineral springs and baths. Every self-respecting lady, if of course she could allow herself to, spent some time each year 'taking the waters', being cured of all her more or less well-defined ailments. Karlsbad and Menton, Abbazia, Ostend, Merano and Wiesbaden – from all these renowned nineteenth-century health spas, nowadays known only from novels, postcards and letters embellished with views of fashionable hotels reached Warsaw.

Julia believed in fairness, and is sure to have conferred her correspondence on all her children in equal measure, but only her letters to her oldest daughter, Flora, are extant. All the other family archives were burned in Warsaw during the war, but the Beylins' papers were carefully hidden with friends somewhere in the provinces, and so they survived.

A lot of information has been preserved in Julia's letters, thanks to which I shall attempt to recreate an image of the past and evoke the atmosphere of those years. Only now can I see what a down-to-earth, sober person my great-grandmother was. There is not a trace of any poetical flights of fancy or philosophical reflections in what she writes. She is concerned purely with practicalities and continues to keep an iron hand on the helm of the family vessel. Out of the mist of hints and half-statements her true character finally emerges, and also her talent as a financier – the foundation on which future generations built their destinies.

She knew how to add up, and she loved it. With the skill and ease of a Rothschild she would hold forth about capital and percentage points, stocks and shares, bonds, bills of exchange and stock-exchange rates. With her son-in-law Samuel Beylin as a go-between she ran dozens of transactions from afar, giving him concise instructions: *Sell my 10 Rudzkie shares at the current rate. – Please send me 300 roubles in 100-rouble notes to my address, Payerbach Sudbahn, via Vienna, Villa Composita. – Ask Rosenthal to draw up a statement for me for the month of July 1909. – Have Lichtenberg pay 4000 roubles, and he can have 3000 extended for four months. – Of that 4000 I shall ask Samuel to give Machleid 3000 and Reich 1000. I think it'll be best like that, because it looks as if the shares are already very expensive now. – Have Samuel do as he thinks fit with Lichtenberg's bills of exchange; if he doesn't need the money, let them extend it for four months, because nothing has been lost on it. The Lichtenbergs are decent people and won't cause any problems...*

Most of these instructions were sent on ordinary postcards. For me, brought up during the communist era and accustomed from childhood to all financial transactions being secret and punishable, this is amazing; but even earlier, in my mother's generation, people were reluctant to talk about money and only did so with some embarrassment, making it clear that it was not proper to mention the subject. I think this was the result of various complexes. According to the stereotypes current in Polish society shrewdness, resourcefulness and 'a head for business' were typically Jewish characteristics, and were inevitably associated with avidity and dishonesty. Julia on the other hand never treated material things as taboo. She spoke to her own children openly and without restraint about financial issues.

In 1909 she wrote from Menton to her daughter Kamilka in Lausanne: *As I have already mentioned to you, my estate consists of over 100,000 roubles, of which 10,000 is due to each of you three as an inheritance, that is, you, Lutek and Maks. I have apportioned the legacy left by my Staś, his patrimony of 10,000 roubles, to Róża, by which token your capital jointly totals 40,000, and the remaining 60,000 roubles is my property. To give you what you should have from me compared with what I have endowed on the other children, I have left 45,000 roubles on the mortgage of the house on Królewska Street, so I wish now to write off that sum in four parts to you, i.e. as I have detailed above 10,000 roubles to each of you, but the mortgage total does not give more than 7%, so by that token you will have only 700 roubles annually, that is 58 roubles 33 kopecks monthly. Like this, for the time being I shall be obliged to supplement each of you from my excess income. Meanwhile I have promised to pay Maks 500 roubles annually, so he will have 100 roubles per month, and must try to earn the rest himself. I must pay more to Lutek and his wife too, Róża all the more, so there remain my savings, which somehow will have to be enough for you, my dearest child – please send me your comments on this plan, entirely frankly and openly.*

What did Kamilka, her 'dearest child', reply? She must have agreed to her mother's request. She was the only one of the children to be working and earning a living, and although unmarried she stood firmly on her own feet. Róża Hilsum could not have managed to maintain and educate her three sons in Paris without help from Warsaw. Lutek, the 'eternal student', was doing yet another doctorate. Maks could not have conducted his struggle against capitalist exploitation without money drawn from his capitalist mother's purse. The remaining daughters were not badly off, but they too sometimes had problems requiring financial help. As fate would have it, of all the children it was Kamilka, the youngest girl, the one who had left home earliest and had always demanded the least for herself, who now took the most care of Julia. She had her to stay with her in Lausanne, then in Munich, took her to see eminent doctors and ferried her about the spas, although she could not stand the places. And from Gardone Riviera Julia wrote contentedly to Warsaw: *I am sitting by the lake, in the sunshine, it is as warm as in July, and every day I feel better and better.*

One might think that after spending so many years leading such an active existence in Warsaw, she would feel depressed abroad by inactivity; but her correspondence shows that she continued to bubble with energy and still exercised control over family matters. The most important thing was health. *I am rather worried about Florcia's bad throat. – Is Janina better now? – I'm concerned about Henryka and the child. – Is Gizella over her intestinal problem? – Is Maniusia still in any pain? – Is Stefa's health better? – Is Maks calmer by now? – I am alarmed by Geniusia's cold, the only thing for shooting pains in the back is to rub on turpentine, and she must be sure to wear a thin vest under her dress.*

She also thought about her relatives' financial needs. She was always reminding the kindly Samuel: *Send Lutek 200 francs by postal order. His address is Ludwik Horwitz, route de Montoie 32. Suisse. Lausanne. – Regarding the settlement of Julian's bills everything is and will be in order, as my accounts with my children and sons-in-law usually are. – Please send 500 roubles urgently to Maks's address in Vienna, as I already asked in my previous letter...*

She used to organise joint family holidays. *Perhaps Gutek and Genia will come to stay with me in Merano. Janinka will be there with the little one [...]. As for a summer flat, I have decided for now perhaps to lodge at a boarding house, in Michalin or Konstancin. If we get a flat it should be something good.* A photograph of just this sort of summer expedition has survived, dating from 1910. It includes my great-grandmother, sitting in the middle of the group, my grandmother wearing an enormous hat decorated with flowers, my mother as a little girl and my grandfather. It is the only photograph of its kind to have survived showing an almost complete family gathering.

She also passed on family news: *Janina is better, she will be able to go away at the end of next week, Jakub is already in Kraków, because it is very cold in Zakopane, with alpine winds. They shall probably go to Nervi for two weeks. – I've had a letter from Róża, she is expecting Gucio back on Sunday.* She always kept in touch with Poland: *Subscribe to* Nowa Gazeta ['The New Gazette'] *and* Kurier Poranny ['The Morning Courier'] *for me.* She did not spare herself pleasures: *I bought myself a black dress and a grey silk one... Kamilka and I were at a Mozart concert. Now as for furs I need one very much, because there are winds here like in Warsaw and people are already wearing furs, but just be very careful how you send it, because it could get lost or destroyed.*

She was interested in the doings of the youngest generation: *A plague on those romances of Gutek's... Isn't Manieczka sorry the boys are getting engaged, while she's still on the shelf?... On the matter of Genia's future I might be able to give you some advice, my dear Florcia. I think you should let her stay in Warsaw for another year. The universities are not going to run away.* And later, when the oldest Beylin girl decided to study in Paris, she rejoiced: *I fully felt your upset over Genia's departure, because didn't I have the same experience with Kamilka, but when our life turns out like this, nowadays it seems to me from life's experience that it is no worse than before.*

Once again the ghost of Regina Beylin, known as Genia, emerges from the Land of the Dead, just as pale and unclear as her fading writing on the crumbling pages of letters from almost a hundred years ago. I do not know much about her, yet the letters that have survived reveal such a touching, charming person that I would like to summon her up for a moment and light a candle in her memory, just as we light a candle on someone's dark, abandoned grave on All Saints' Day. She was lovely, as we can see from the photographs, and also good, sensitive and affectionate, as we can tell from her letters. In 1910 she and her brother Gucio went away to study in Paris, when she was twenty. They both lived with their aunt Róża Hilsum on rue Saint Didier 5. *Róziulka is as sweet and pretty as ever and is looking after us. She bought Gucio some woollen socks,* she wrote just after arriving.

What was she studying? She did not yet know what she wanted to do. She was just sure she should break away from Warsaw for a while, take a look at the world outside and find her path in life. Her mother Flora supported her daughters' aspirations. She was very keen for her children to have higher education and climb a rung higher in the social hierarchy. So although Genia was frail and tired easily, she approved of her going, and simply urged her not to overwork. In one of her first letters from Paris Genia told her mother: *Yesterday I was at Mrs [Marie] Curie-Sklodowska's inaugural lecture. Gucio was with me and kept cursing because he was bored – she went on for an hour and a half to a packed hall. I shan't go to see her, as Lutek has advised me to, because I have no intention of taking up chemistry or working in a chemical laboratory.* In her next report she said: *Meanwhile I'm going to geology classes, and will start embryology too, because there are some interesting lectures this year, and I might yet go to geophysics and physics.*

Don't be worried that you're not learning much, God forbid, someone who at your age knows as much as you do..., wrote her mother. *Don't get wrapped up in philosophy, Bergson's lectures are still too hard for you and will be no use at all... As for music, be sure to go and see Landowska. I gave you the address in my last card (rue Jacob 24, Hotel d'Angleterre) and get her advice...*

Genia later wrote to tell her about the visit: *Landowska said that as she is going to be in Paris for the next 3–4 weeks, in that time she would like to give me a lesson twice a week, and after that just from time to time whenever she comes here. Now the most important thing – money. She told me: 'I take 40 francs per hour. From you as Poles I can take half, that is 20 francs.' What could I say in return? Everyone says that for her that's very little, but for me it's an awful lot. You can't imagine how worried I am about that money – I'm glad it's only for the next few weeks, and after that I'll only have a lesson occasionally. But where am I going to get all that money?*

Later on she reported: *I have been to her for lessons twice now – she told me so much about myself and my music... She praised me a lot and says that in one lesson with me she can do as much as with everyone else in three, and that she has great hopes for me... Thanks to the lessons and the things she says, all my old dreams and ambitions have come back... She wants to keep me in style – just classical music for now, and at the same time she wants to teach me theory and harmony. She says she has 'taken me in hand'. And because she thinks I should listen to a lot of good music, every few days we get tickets for all sorts of good concerts in Paris – for free from her and her brother. She claims it's her duty, sends me music books etc. As Gucio rightly claims, it's worth it too – we would have laid out a lot on concerts anyway (two tickets every time) – because the cheapest seats upstairs and standing cost 3 francs – but we're sitting in the 12-franc seats. However, I do know that it's an awful lot of money, so please will you write and tell me frankly what you think about it?*

The money was found, the family ambitions grew, and Genia tried to believe in herself. A year later she wrote: *Landowska wanted to take me off to the countryside this week for a couple of days, but I didn't want to go – she seemed rather offended by that. But she has only just moved there and hasn't got a piano yet, so what would I have done there with them for a few days... She is always telling me I'm so capable and asks me to work, or I'll waste my talent. She says I've got what it takes others months to achieve in my fingers, I should just study more and something will come of it.*

But how can you become a real artist if you lack self-confidence, if you keep so many doubts and fears alive, constantly wondering, 'Can I do it, shouldn't I rather get on with something positive, is it worth spending so much money on me?' – if you haven't a trace of ruthlessness and selfishness, and other people's problems seem more important than your own? What did Genia think about in Paris? Not about her own brilliantly promising career as the favourite pupil of the famous Landowska. Not about her own ambitions and dreams, but about sending some tinned pineapple for Daddy, buying fine-spun knickers and shirts on sale at 6 francs each for her mother – *it's high time you wore something elegant –* or satin hair ribbons and dress material for her little sisters, Karolina and Stefania.

What did Genia get upset about in Paris? That her brother Gucio had run up debts again and that Mama would be angry with him, that he absolutely, really did need a dinner jacket and shoes, that he had fallen unhappily in love again and that he wasn't doing much work; that Aunt Róża had no rent money; that her sister Mania missed her very much, and what could be done about it; that Grandma was ill, so maybe she should leave Paris and take on care of her. She is nothing but a living, beating, sympathetic heart. *I love you all. – I can't live without you. – How I long to be with you at last. – Without you, none of my life here has any meaning. – Ah! if only I could take my entire Paris life home to Warsaw.*

In their youth, Julia's grandchildren and their generation were prone to feeling *Weltschmerz*, being dissatisfied with themselves, and asking existential questions, such as 'How should one live?' It was a serious problem. As the third generation of assimilated Jews they already felt fully Polish, but they knew that to achieve a reasonable degree of social acceptance they had to take the next seven-league step to join the Polish intelligentsia. And that required not just a university degree but also some intellectual achievements. The level of demands was set high. Gucio Beylin wavered in Paris between contradictory ambitions, wondering whether to become a lawyer or a writer, and instead of going to law lectures he would run off to the Orléans Library in search of obscure manuscripts by Norwid. Genia Beylin shuddered at the thought that without a diploma from the Sorbonne she would be a nobody in Warsaw. The psychological pressure was so great that the entire generation of boys and girls, at first scared and unsure of their vocations, found places for themselves in life, in science and literature.

Compared with her children and grandchildren, my great-grandmother Julia seems like a monolith. Apparently she always recognised her own value and never had to prove it to anyone; she knew what she wanted and had no doubts. This sounds fairly terrifying, and fortunately is probably not the whole truth, but that is the image of herself that she left behind in people's memories. In 1910 she made the last of her major decisions in life, which was to sell the tenement building on Królewska Street and wind up her flat, without any sentimental feelings, hesitations or scruples, and with no objections from her children either. The beloved family nest, where so much had happened, was not needed any more. She herself felt she would never go back there now. My heart aches as I write about it, but in Julia's letters there is not a trace of emotion or sadness. There are just sober, matter-of-fact instructions: *Florunia, do you want to hang the mirror from the hall and the round one from the bedroom at your place, and maybe sell the black one? Move my clocks to your flat too, put the one from Danzig in Samuel's study and the bedroom one in the dining room above the black sideboard. As for the furniture, the Mortkowiczes should take the piano and the chest; Maks only wants his library, Kamilka's wardrobe and the mirror with the small cupboards... Once again, please give the piano only to Janinka, not any of the Luksemburgs. It's possible that I might come back in a year's time and take some things, what claim do the Luksemburgs have on the piano?*

After the house was sold Julia's children avoided Królewska Street, because it stirred too many memories. My grandmother went there for the last time in her life with my mother after the capitulation of Warsaw in 1939. In the very first bombardment of the capital that street and the neighbouring ones were badly damaged, and many of the buildings were reduced to ruins. In the places where people had been killed candles were burning in mourning. They both felt as if they were in a graveyard. The tenement building's annexe had burned down, once the home of a very distinguished tenant called Chaim Zelig Słonimski, grandfather of the poet Antoni Słonimski, the white-haired old man who used to watch the children playing in the courtyard all those years ago.

The beloved, legendary little garden, that childhood paradise, had been burned to a crisp, with the black skeletons of trees protruding from it. My grandmother, who was not at all prone to sentimentality, burst into tears.

At the time it seemed as if nothing worse could possibly happen. Later on the Jewish inhabitants of the district were forced to settle in the Ghetto and were then murdered. Finally there was the Uprising, which completed the destruction work. After the war my grandmother never set foot in that area again. She preferred the family home to go on existing unaltered in her memory. And right into her old age that was just how she kept 49 Królewska Street alive in her memory – as a vivacious dreamworld full of love, security and happiness.

Julia Horwitz died in the winter of 1912 at Dr Friedländer's sanatorium in Wiesbaden. For many months she had been ill with some sort of stomach complaint; Kamilka nursed her to the end, and all her children had time to say goodbye to her. She was buried in Warsaw, at the Jewish cemetery on Okopowa Street. In her later memoirs my mother wrote: *I was not taken to Grandma's funeral. It was December, with terrible icily rainy weather and my parents decided that I was too small, even to go by carriage. So my cousin Stefcia Beylin and I were left at home and played with some beautiful modern baby-dolls that our mothers had brought us from Wiesbaden... I wasn't at the funeral of my beloved oldest cousin Genia either. Mama left me in Stolpmünde, nowadays called Ustka* [a resort on the Baltic coast], *when she was summoned to Warsaw by the tragic telegram...*

Genia died six months after Julia, in the summer of 1913, in Warsaw. An apparently innocent appendix operation ended in a fatal infection. Not even her fiancé, the handsome Dr Szper, could save her; like all those who loved her, he went mad with despair. No one could understand why on earth Genia, so charming, so good and so talented, had to depart this life so early. She was undoubtedly the most poetic soul in our entire rather prosaic family, or maybe it just seems like that because she died so young. She was buried beside Julia at the Jewish cemetery. Nowadays hardly any of us knows how to find the grave any more.

A photograph of Julia showing a white-haired, cheerful old lady has survived to the present day in many of our family collections.

Her children and grandchildren were extremely devoted to her. They owed her not only their attachment to Polish culture, but above all the obligation to keep making a constant mental effort, the duty to prove that 'one is not just anyone'.

She loved her family with a wise but demanding love, and after her death she watched over them from the next world – in a rather paradoxical way. During the occupation my grandmother hung a photograph of her own mother above her bed, beside an icon of the Virgin Mary, because Julia, with her 'Aryan' looks, precluded any suspicions of Jewish origin.

LONG LIVE POLAND!

————————✳————————

On Sunday, 28 June 1914 the Austrian heir to the throne, Archduke Franz Ferdinand, was shot at Sarajevo by the Serbian assassin Gavrilo Princip. The summer had begun, and people calmly departed for spas and holidays, to Krynica, to Biarritz, to Piszczany and Nałęczów. No one had any idea what the effects of this tragic event would be. My grandparents and their almost twelve-year-old daughter Hania set off for Stolpmünde on the Baltic. The charms of today's Ustka had been praised in newspaper advertisements: *Sea bathing in the open sea, amid forest. The coast is 500 metres long, with a broad sandy beach. There are new family baths for ladies and gentlemen. There is a modern bathing facility equipped for hot, sea, curative, electric and mud baths. There is a superb orchestra, a theatre, sports and a lively coastal transport system.*

Flora Beylin and her teenage daughters Karolina and Stefa joined them, and so did Gizella Bychowska and her children, little Marta, Janek and Gustaw. My future mother, a patriot, was always reminding her cousins that they were at the Polish seaside, on Polish territory wrongfully appropriated by the Germans. She kept correcting everyone, telling them not to call the nearby town 'Stolp', but Słupsk, and told them to call the stream that ran across the area the Słupia. As a result, the other children nicknamed her 'the Słupia-monster'. It made her cry, but she refused to give up her patriotic efforts.

The holidays did not last long. At first the newspapers made light of the situation, writing: *Clash between Serbia and Austria! Albania in confusion! Russian diplomatic circles are convinced a catastrophe will be avoided!* Then in mournful black lettering the word WAR appeared on the front pages, heading a troubling report: *On 28 July the Austro-Hungarian Monarchy declared war on*

Serbia! Russia has begun mobilisation! On 1 August Germany declared war on Russia!

The German authorities immediately demanded that all Russian subjects leave German territory. So in a crush and a panic, travelling in dreadful discomfort by goods wagon because there were not enough seats in the passenger cars, they had to leave the ancient Polish town of Stolpmünde. It was a good thing they managed to get out of there so soon. Those who failed to take the decree seriously or lingered too long suffered experiences that left them with horrific memories for the rest of their lives. They were evacuated to Stockholm, and only managed to return to Warsaw many weeks later. Lots of families were separated by the front. Every day the newspapers printed long columns listing the names of people looking for one another.

At the start, people thought the war would last a few months at most. No one imagined the conflict between the great powers would have an influence on Poland's situation. Only Józef Piłsudski believed he would succeed in provoking an anti-Russian uprising. On 6 August 1914 he told his Cadre Company to march out from Kraków, cross the border of the Congress Kingdom and incite the citizens of the border towns to join the fight against the Russians. He did in fact encounter some resistance from the civilian population, but his display of aspirations towards independence awoke patriotic hopes in many hearts.

The firm belief that one day the motherland would arise from the dead was familiar to Hania Mortkowicz from childhood onwards. She was brought up on great romantic poetry, and at home they sang songs of rebellion, which said that the time had come to leave your loved ones and go into battle for Poland. As a little girl she was woken at night by the sound of the doorbell and knew that it was the Russian gendarmes, who would search the whole house, and might then take her father away, because he was a rebel who hated the Russians. At private classes she was study-ing Polish history and Polish literature, in other words hearing endless stories of the struggle against captivity, of heroism and bravery. Sometimes she cried in secret. She knew she must die for Poland, because that was how every 'decent' Pole died, but she was terribly afraid of dying on the gallows.

Hanna Mortkowicz later described the four war years, during

which she changed from a child into an adolescent girl, in a story entitled *The Bitterness of Springtime*. In it she described some historical events, and also the experiences and feelings of a teenager growing up in a world that is just starting to collapse in ruins.

At the beginning of the story, the war has been going on for nine months, and the heroine has already had plenty of experience of the evil around her. First, crowds of Polish boys called up from the entire Congress Kingdom to join the tsarist army trail through the streets of Warsaw to the station, with their tearful wives, mothers and children running after them. Then the first reports appear in the newspapers describing battles fought on Polish terrain, and burned and ruined cities. Transports of wounded soldiers pass through Warsaw, and the same boys, crippled and bloodied, are taken on horse-drawn trailers and in vehicles to the city's hospitals. People visit them and take them food and clothing, because most of them come from poor villages and towns far away. Her heart breaks at the thought of the fratricidal fighting, because the enemy armies include compatriots from the Prussian and Austrian partitions.

There are more and more homeless people on the streets, who have come in to Warsaw from areas destroyed by the Russians or the Germans. They have nothing to live on and no homes to go back to. The city shelters are full to bursting. Gifts and money are collected for them, children are advised to give up new dresses or sweets and the money saved is given to the needy. The heroine's cousins whisper about Piłsudski's rifle divisions, who are fighting on the Austrian side against the Russians. Like all the boys at the time they are storing up provisions and discussing plans to run away to the Polish forces. Should she run away with them, if the motherland is to be reborn? Should she fight for Poland? Or rather, like successive generations of Polish women, should she nurse the wounded? Or simply obediently go to school, as her mother says, and study, to develop her mind for the future?

Her oldest cousin has made his way across the border to Piłsudski's headquarters and joined the Polish Legions' Fifth Infantry regiment. The heroine is thrilled by the grey colour of his army jacket and the white eagle on his cap. She thinks regretfully: Why wasn't I born a boy? Her cousin assures her that if she really and truly wants to, she will turn into a boy when she reaches fifteen. She doesn't believe him, but sometimes she thinks to herself, What if...?

That legionary, full of seductive charm, reciting de Musset in

French to the ladies, was a real person: Flora's son Gucio Beylin. In 1915 he was twenty-six and had a doctorate in law from the Sorbonne. As soon as the war broke out he joined the Polish Military Organisation, a secret institution established by Piłsudski. Later on he was in the Legions. I know nothing about his fighting exploits, but Zofia Nałkowska often mentions him in her *Diaries* of those years. Did he have an affair with her? He may have, though Nałkowska used to sigh and say she was not made for ephemeral love.

In 1914–16 Zofia Nałkowska was doubly implicated in my family's life, because at the same time she was having a romantic adventure with Gucio's brother-in-law, Dr Józef Szper. After the death of his fiancée, the sweet and talented Genia Beylin, the handsome surgeon had married her sister, young Mania. Mania was just as lovely. Why was he immediately unfaithful to her? At first Nałkowska felt some moral doubts:... *because that little girl is too defenceless for one to do her harm and I think the kisses stolen from those girlish lips would taste bitter.* But in the end she gave in to Szper's seductions. She recorded that it happened on 1 June 1914. *I know his eyes, smile and voice by heart. The racial difference that divides us merely enriches the emotional atmosphere by adding an exotic element. I shall know him fully... I forgive him everything.*

The affair lasted for over a year. Mania, never guessing a thing, used to come and see Nałkowska with cream-coloured roses, and *subtly and with restraint, childishly even,* she would complain about life and her husband's infidelities. *No one is happy. It's no good being a wife and it's no good being a mistress,* she noted philosophically. In 1915 Mania and Józef Szper's son Konstanty was born, known as Kostuś.

In the summer of 1915 the front came close to Warsaw. The Germans were gaining the upper hand. In the first few days of August the Russians left the capital. German troops had actually invaded the city, but people went mad with joy, because 120 years of tsarist captivity had ended. The Namiestnikowski Palace, a symbol of Muscovite force, was hung with red-and-white flags. On the streets people shouted the phrase that had been banned all that time: 'Long live Poland!' Everyone flung their windows wide open and sang the legions' song at the top of their voices:

Fusiliers, one and all, the White Eagle leads us on to war,
Our deadly foe is ranked against us for the fight!
Soon from our guns the shots will fire with thunderous roar,
Our Saviour God will guide our bullets in their flight!

Despite the hopes of freedom, it was harder and harder to bear
the shocking news from the fronts, fears about the future and desperate poverty all around. First ration cards appeared for bread, then
for other food products. Queues formed outside the shops. At home
people ate gluey, musty wholemeal bread, dried salt fish that had to
be soaked in water for thirty-six hours to become edible, spongy,
pale minced meat made of cows' udders and gingerbread made of
carrots. They drank tea made of apple peel. There were endless
stubborn arguments about ideology, as political factions, parties,
programmes and slogans multiplied like mushrooms after rain.

Right at that time, in the first year of the Great War, as if in defiance of the political chaos and death that were raging all around
him, my grandfather brought his bookselling and publishing world
to life.

He was then forty years old. He was already quite a well-known
publisher, had paid off his partner Henryk Lindenfeld and was now
the sole owner of the firm called 'G. Centnerszwer & Company',
and also had his own small printing press, at a site on Mazowiecka
Street. In the first few months of the war all publishing activity
was at a standstill. Strict censorship was introduced, which made
the job much harder, and because of higher prices people stopped
buying books. Common sense told him not to enlarge the enterprise, but to wait patiently and see what the future would bring;
but Mortkowicz was an impatient man. He realised that, since the
political change that had been anticipated for such a long time had
finally come, he too must make changes in his life without delay.

First of all, the simplest thing to do was to change his accommodation. The Mortkowiczes' new, larger and nicer flat was at 5
Okólnik Street, on the fifth floor of a building on the Vistula
embankment. The windows looked out on the River Vistula, the
old rooftops all around and the bridges linking central Warsaw and
the Praga district. They moved house in July 1915, just before the
Russians abandoned Warsaw, fleeing the approaching German
troops and blowing up the bridges behind them.

Mortkowicz's next step was designed to improve the firm's financial condition. He had plenty of publishing plans, but not enough capital, so he decided to transform his enterprise into a joint-stock company and persuaded Teodor Toeplitz, a friend from his student days in Antwerp, to be a partner. The company's founding capital, fixed at 200,000 roubles, was divided into 2000 shares, each priced at 100 roubles. Mortkowicz bought shares for 100,000 roubles, Toeplitz for 59,000, and Janina Mortkowicz for 10,000. The rest of the shareholders, of whom there were nineteen in all, contributed far smaller sums. A founding deed for the company was drawn up on 2 July 1915 and certified by a notary. Teodor Toeplitz acted as founder because my grandfather was still out of favour with the tsarist authorities and could not figure in a commercial register under his own name. That was also why the new firm was given the enigmatic name 'Publishing Association in Warsaw, Joint Stock Company'.

Thanks to the increased capital, in July 1915 my grandfather bought a building on Warsaw's Old Town Marketplace, No. 11, and moved his printing press and warehouse there. At the same time he opened a new, beautifully fitted-out bookshop at 12 Mazowiecka Street, which soon became Warsaw's cultural salon.

Making investments of this kind during the war might have seemed madness, but Mortkowicz had not graduated from the Commercial Academy in Antwerp and spent several years working at the Wawelberg Bank for nothing. Although he was happy to pass for a romantic dreamer, he must have had some business talents, because lately he had managed to run his firm very well and to invest the money Janina had inherited from Julia profitably.

When the Germans entered Warsaw, marks became the statutory currency, and raging inflation meant that from one day to the next they lost value; but in 1917, after the Bolshevik revolution, the tsarist currency, so scrupulously amassed by my great-grandmother, ceased to exist.

In the summer of 1914 Kamilla Horwitz travelled from Zurich, where she was working as a doctor, to Zakopane for a holiday. On returning from a hike in the mountains, she heard about the outbreak of war. She wanted to reach her family, who were on holiday in Rabka, as quickly as possible, but she only managed to get as far as Poronin. Her friend, Vladimir Ilyich Lenin, who was living there at the time, suggested she take the bicycle – a lady's model – that he was riding. He merely asked her to return it quickly, because he had borrowed it from the neighbours. Kamilka was in such a hurry to get back that she fell into a ditch and damaged the valuable vehicle. Lenin was upset: 'How am I going to look those people in the eye now?' he asked.

In 1915, as Janina Mortkowicz was sorting out her new flat on Okólnik Street and the interior of the bookshop on Mazowiecka Street, Kamilka was bandaging wounded soldiers in the Czech city of Brno. As an unmarried person, she had inherited Austrian citizenship from her father's side, so when the war broke out she was mobilised by the Austrians and sent to a military hospital in Galicia. That was where the most important and most secret event in her life occurred. She never discussed it with any of the family, not even her own son, so I too shall not dwell on the subject. All I know is that one of her patients was a wounded Austrian soldier of Ukrainian nationality called Janko Kancewicz. Once he had recovered, he went back to the front and was killed.

In 1916 Kamilka went from Brno to Zurich, and there in April she gave birth to a son, who was named Janek after his father. A child outside marriage in those days? It was proof of extraordinary courage; that at least was how the matter was regarded within the family, with great respect and no petty bourgeois gripes. Kamilka's two brothers were living in Zurich at the time: Ludwik, now a geologist at the university there, and Maks and his wife and three children, Kasia, Staś and Anusia. They must have given her psychological support, but even so the young doctor's situation was not easy. She did find a job at a psychiatric clinic in the Zurich suburb of Waldau, but her employers insisted that as a single woman she could not have her son living with her, so she had to rent a room for Janek and his Swiss nanny outside the grounds of the institution, and used to visit him after work.

The little boy with golden curls was not yet a year old when in February 1917 the Tsar abdicated, and he was only eighteen months old when in October 1917 at the Congress of Soviets in Petrograd Lenin greeted the coming of 'the worldwide socialist revolution'. Maks Horwitz, editor-in-chief of the communist newspaper *Volksrecht*, issued in Zurich, wrote that it was high time the proletariat took power throughout Europe and overthrew the crumbling capitalist regimes. It was a terrible year. In September two-year-old Kostuś Szper, Mania's son, died of diphtheria, and in December Hania's closest friend, her cousin Janek Bychowski died, who was one year older than her.

He must have been an extraordinary boy. Mature beyond his years, sensitive, intelligent, well-read, he was passionate about social issues, burned with enthusiasm and dreamed of a free Poland, where there would be so much to achieve. The unusual ones always die too young. Or perhaps it is posthumous legend that gives them their unusual quality? In those days medicine knew of no cure for 'galloping consumption'. The front and the borders made it impossible to leave for a sanatorium. His father, though a doctor, could not help him.

Janek died in December 1917, when he was not quite sixteen years old.

In August 1918, a few months before the regaining of independence, the first all-Poland booksellers' congress took place in Lublin. The idea was to demonstrate the national and cultural unity of the state, which did not yet officially exist. Jakub Mortkowicz belonged to the group that initiated and organised the event. He opened the proceedings in the name of the Warsaw-based Union of Polish Booksellers. In the closing words of his speech he said: *[...] Polish booksellers, as the greatest enemy of the partitioning powers, have been the greatest mainstay of our nation, which is now gaining what is due to it – independence and unification [...]. I call on you, the booksellers of Poland, to take up the fight for the Polish cause, for the development of the most essential forces of life and creativity, for the development of Polish culture.*

On 11 November 1918 Józef Piłsudski assumed military power in the state. *It is impossible to describe the rapture, the frenzy of joy that overcame the Polish population at that moment. After 120 years the bonds were broken [...]. Liberty! Independence! Unification! Our own state [...]. Four generations had waited in vain for this moment, and the fifth had lived to see it.*

In December 1918 Maksymilian Horwitz-Walecki joined the Central Committee of the newly founded Polish Workers' Communist Party. It aimed, by means of violent revolution, to smash the apparatus of the bourgeois state, abolish democracy, dissolve parliament and establish in its place the dictatorship of the proletariat, seeking alliance with Soviet Russia, which was at the forefront of 'the titanic contest between the old and new orders'.

And that was when my grandparents said, 'Enough!' Mortkowicz's left-wing tendencies and my grandmother's 'radical progressiveness' were not enough to temper their indignation. They were both fanatical about independence, however imperfect it would be. To destroy the new life that had only just been born seemed to them a base act. In any case, destruction had never been their medium. They had always preferred to build rather than destroy. With two very different world outlooks, two different attitudes to life, there was no question of reaching agreement. From then on relations between them and Maks cooled greatly.

Yet family solidarity continued. At the beginning of 1919 the Warsaw relatives greeted some new arrivals from Zurich at the station.

Kamilka had arrived in Warsaw earlier with three-year-old Janek; his charm and good looks, his golden locks and the comical *schwitzerdeutsch* (Swiss German) he spoke, immediately captured the hearts of all.

This time it was Maks's wife, Stefa, who got off the train with their three children: thirteen-year-old Kasia, eleven-year-old Staś and eight-year-old Anusia. The little Horwitzes were wearing oversized, threadbare coats, clearly bought in a second-hand shop, and were tired and sleepy. They stared in amazement at their strange aunts and elegant cousins, who embraced them and wept as they asked the children if they were glad to be home at last, in the free motherland. But their father had told them that militaristic troublemakers and bourgeois exploiters were in power in Poland; and as for a home, they did not have one.

KASIA, STAŚ AND ANUSIA

———————— ✳ ————————

Maks Horwitz and his wife Stefania, and later their three children too, spent their lives for ever wandering from place to place, with no stability at all, often with nothing to live on and with a constant sense of threat. Stefa was so dedicated to 'the cause' that she meekly put up with this sort of existence, but their involuntary fate as nomads caused the children a lot of trauma. They were born in turbulent times, and their father's status as a revolutionary, hounded by the police of all the countries they stayed in, made their childhood even more complicated. The winds of change were blowing: empires were falling, the map of Europe was changing, subjugated countries were regaining their independence, and ideologies were vying with one another to shape the twentieth century. Meanwhile, in worn-out shoes their little feet toddled over the paving stones of Kraków, Vienna, Switzerland and Berlin, as 'uncles' with names that nowadays cause a shudder of horror pressed pennies into their little hands for sweets.

Maks's older daughter, Kasia, had been born in 1906, in the Finnish town of Kerimäki on Lake Ladoga. This exotic place featured in her biography because after the defeat of the 1905 revolution political activists of all sorts of nationalities and beliefs who preferred to avoid contact with the tsarist police were eager to take refuge there. In June 1906 Maks had escaped from Siberia again, and as he was a wanted man, he hid there with his pregnant wife. From this town, only thirty-five kilometres away from Saint Petersburg, he could easily slip into the Russian capital to take part in the conferences of the Russian revolutionaries – like Lenin, who was also living in Finland at the time.

Later on the Horwitzes and little Kasia spent some time living in Warsaw. Then they emigrated to Kraków, where in 1908 Staś was born. From Kraków they made their way to Vienna, where in 1911 Anusia was born. From Vienna they moved back to Kraków again, and lived there through the outbreak of the war. Then they were deported back to Vienna, from where they moved to Zurich.

So it was a constant carousel of different countries and cities, different languages and customs, different schools, different demands and different friends. Everywhere they had similar, shabby rented flats. Strange furniture, windows with no blinds or curtains, bare bulbs in the lamps, worn-out clothes, endless guests arguing until the early hours over strong tea about incomprehensible things, the fear that at any moment the police would come and there would be another search, that they would arrest someone – that was how Kasia remembered her childhood, which she hated.

Her father was always at Party congresses or in prison. When he did appear, he shouted. He was tyrannical by nature. Her mother was gentle, but did not provide proper support. She did not know how to run a home, how to cook or foster a family atmosphere. She was more interested in social problems than her children's emotional needs. When Kasia was eleven years old she was awoken in Zurich by her parents' voices arguing. Terrified, she pushed their bedroom door ajar. She was amazed to see her mother, who was usually so calm and self-controlled, running about the room in her nightshirt shouting at her father, something that simply never happened. She was trying to convince him that the February 1917 revolution in Russia was already a socialist revolution, and not, as Maks asserted, still only a bourgeois one.

A fundamental question comes to mind: what on earth did they live on? Maksymilian Horwitz, writing under the pseudonym Henryk Walecki, was in those years the editor of numerous socialist journals and published a lot, but the fees from journalism were not enough to maintain a family. Not long after their wedding Julia Horwitz visited her son and daughter-in-law, and then wrote to her daughter, Flora Beylin: *They are having a very sad time in Kraków because her parents and brothers are there with absolutely no money to live on. They have to keep themselves on a very tight rein there too, and on top of that poor Stefa is neither thrifty nor resourceful.* She longed for her son, who had been educated abroad at such expense, who was so intelligent and such a talented mathematician, to get a job that matched his qualifications. From her letters it appears that sometimes he thought of abandoning Party work and wondered what to do next. Conform to the middle-class way of life? Find a job that would guarantee a regular income? Opt for the academic path, *that is, entirely devote himself to mathematics and work in this field heart and soul. For these aims, understandably, he must go to the West more, but for the time being I could not, and it has been impossible, to demand this sacrifice of him, but in a while he will do it, I hope.*

Once he had gone to the West, however, Maks did not devote himself to mathematics *heart and soul*. In Vienna he worked as a clerk at an insurance firm, and in Zurich he taught mathematics at a middle school. They were casual, badly paid jobs, but he reacted neurotically to any attempt to find him better paid work. The same warning keeps appearing in the family letters: *... do not talk to Maks about his job. – You had better not make any special efforts to find him a job without coming to terms with him first. – Don't tell him that Samuel sees some opportunities for him. – Don't put pressure on him. – Don't annoy him.* It is plain to see that he had no intention of giving up his profession as a revolutionary. Julia recognised his right to make his own choices, and she also facilitated his fight against inexorable capitalism by regularly sending him the interest earned on her own capital.

Who financed the (albeit cheap) flats in Vienna, Switzerland and Berlin, the living expenses of five people, the children's education and Maks's endless journeys to international congresses and conventions? It must have been the Party, though it was not very generous, if the 100 roubles sent each month by his mother were such a major support for the family. Sometimes they fared poorly, sometimes quite well. After visiting the Horwitzes in Vienna Julia wrote with satisfaction: *I am really pleased with Maks and the children's appearance. Kasia is beautiful, and the little boy is wonderful, a lively little spark. They are already attached to me, as if we lived together.* The children were lovely – fair-haired, blue-eyed, bright and full of charm. Their grandmother did not have much time to enjoy them. She died when Anusia, the youngest of the siblings, was one year old.

In those émigré years Maksymilian Horwitz-Walecki was extremely politically active. In 1906, at the dissenting, final congress of the Polish Socialist Party in Vienna he definitively broke with his former comrades who supported Piłsudski. The ideological differences between the Polish socialists had become too great to maintain the illusion of unity. From now on the pro-independence Revolutionary Fraction concentrated on preparations for armed combat. The Polish Socialist Party Left Wing aimed for an international socialist revolution. The more likely the prediction of war, the more distinctly radical Maks's views became. As a member of the inner circle of the Party leadership he began to seek an agreement with the representatives of the extreme, anti-independence left: Rosa Luksemburg and Julian Marchlewski, the leaders of the Social-Democratic Party of the Kingdom of Poland and Lithuania.

When war broke out in 1914, bringing hopes of liberty with it, and Piłsudski sent his Cadre Company to help Austria in the fight against Russia, Horwitz was in Kraków preparing an anti-war declaration by the Polish Socialist Party Left Wing, which announced: 'This war, though being fought on Polish lands, is not a war over Poland.' When the Austrians arrested Lenin, who was hiding within Galicia, at Poronin, Maks tried to have him released from prison. Evacuated with his family to Vienna, he at once began to agitate from there against the war in Upper Silesia. Arrested by the Prussian authorities in January 1915, he was brought before a court martial, but managed to get himself off the death penalty and was acquitted. At that point the whole family moved to Zurich, which was the centre for revolutionary ideas during the war. Anusia was then four, Staś was seven and Kasia nine.

In Europe a massacre was raging that would cause the deaths of about ten million soldiers and countless civilians. In Zurich, cut off from the atrocities of war, Lenin wrote an essay entitled 'Imperialism: Highest Stage of Capitalism'. In it he proved that the imperialist war must change into civil war within the quarrelling countries, and then into a joint proletarian revolution. In the cheap socialist soup-kitchen the members of the individual parties sat at separate little tables – at one the Bolsheviks, at another the Mensheviks, at a third the Polish Socialist Party Left Wing and at a fourth the Social-Democratic Party of the Kingdom of Poland and Lithuania. They did not fraternise with one another. The children addressed 'their' people as 'uncle', and avoided 'strangers'.

The Horwitzes' closest friends were the left-wingers: Henryk Lauer, Paweł Lewinson and Feliks Kon, who in 1920 would become a member of the Polish Revolutionary Provisional Committee called into being by the Bolshevik government, but who for now brought the children presents, so they did not think he was a revolutionary, but Santa Claus – incognito.

Lenin lived nearby. Maks used to hold endless political discussions with him, as they accompanied each other to and from home. As she laid the table for dinner their mother would say, 'I thought I saw your father through the window. Would you look outside, Kasia, and see why he isn't here yet?' Kasia would report: 'He's walking up and down the street with that bald uncle with the beard and talking.' 'Well then, let's sit at table.' Stefa would finally give up and say they would eat without him, 'because we can't go on waiting for him'.

It was a period of great ideological disputes, but Kasia was not interested in politics. However, she remembered a lot of small details of everyday life, such as the iron beds and straw mattresses her mother bought when they moved to a strange, furnished flat. She wanted at least these items to be their own. She remembered ration cards for bread, flour, meat and sugar, two days without meat each week and the discipline of the Swiss. The Poles used to ignore the government regulation, but in Swiss homes meat did not appear on the table on those days. She was amazed that Swiss schools were co-educational. She was furious, because her father, although himself not a believer, told them to go to the Evangelical Sunday school so they would not be different from the other children. Afterwards Staś painted some pictures showing his parents in hell and the children in heaven. At home they went hungry, but at school rice and fruit were handed out. When there was no bread, their mother used to bake rice cakes, which they spread with jam, or she made so-called 'Finland soup' out of prunes and potato flour.

At school they spoke in German, and at kindergarten Anusia picked up the Swiss dialect, but at home they had to speak Polish. Their father kept a strict eye on this. He also took care of their manners, no doubt applying the orders and restrictions learned in his own 'bourgeois' home. To the amazement of their schoolmates, they were not allowed to eat in the street, not even the apples they were given for elevenses. Maks believed that little girls should play the piano, so Kasia was given lessons by Zofia Dzierżyńska, the wife of Feliks. Fortunately, she soon perceived her pupil's lack of ability and resigned. Their father was easily annoyed. Once he noticed that Kasia had holes in her shoes, and made a hellish scene to his wife about it. He demanded that she buy wooden sabots for all three of them, because they were cheaper and neater. From then on, winter and summer they went about in clogs – the footwear of the very poorest people – which

infuriated Kasia, who cared about her appearance. She liked everything that was not provided for her at home: comfort, pretty
things, order, regularity, cosy interiors and predictability in life. 'A
typical petty bourgeoise', her father used to shout. She was always
quarrelling with him. She was cheeky and insolent – like him. Staś
was reserved, reticent, quiet and undemanding, like his mother.
The light and joy of the household was little Anusia, who at the
toughest times was always jolly and sunny. She could recite hundreds of little poems and songs in all the languages she knew. She
was always humming a tune or singing softly to herself. She was
crazy about the theatre. She used to make fancy-dress costumes
out of the bedspreads, scarves and curtains and perform in them
each evening in all sorts of different theatrical roles. Sometimes
she was Ophelia, sometimes King Lear. Everyone adored her, but
her father undoubtedly loved her most of all his children.

In 1917 the theoretical debates in the socialist soup-kitchen
came to an end. In April Lenin went back to Russia. In October he
headed the Bolshevik coup d'état. The 'class struggle' – just an
orator's phrase until now – became reality. In Russia the Red
Terror began. Feliks Dzierżyński at once created the Cheka – an
extraordinary committee to combat counter-revolution – 'the
armed wing of the proletarian dictatorship'. In November 1918 he
was sent to Switzerland to save his own physical and mental
health. The number of murders, executions and bloody repressions
that he had directed in the course of the past year was so vast that
in his absence the Bolshevik Party considered how to limit *the
excess of zeal on the part of an organisation interspersed with
criminals, sadists and degenerate elements of the lumpen proletariat.* Lenin, however, came to the defence of this worthy institution, and when Dzierżyński had had a rest, he went back to work.

Was Maks aware of the scale and methods of macabre madness
that had been unleashed in Russia? He was forty-one. Could he
still have withdrawn from the game? Or did he think the game was
only just beginning? That at last the time had come, so long
awaited by humanity, and by him too, after so many humiliations?
*Denounce! Destroy! Combat! Devastate! Overthrow! Annihilate!
Reduce to ashes! Blow up! Drive out! Eliminate without mercy!
Crush! Smash! Grind! Denude! Flog! Nail down! Whip!* The
vocabulary he used in his journalism stirs unambiguous associations. Nor did he spare the invective for his political opponents,
describing them as *puppets, flunkeys, frauds, traitors, parasites,*

and *servants of the putrefaction and odiousness of bourgeois politics*. The clouds of aggression still rise over his long-since-stale texts. In no other profession could he have allowed himself such a violent display of all the hatred he had suppressed for years.

He declared himself to be on the side of the Bolsheviks. In accordance with the Leninist postulate to kindle rebellion in the capitalist countries, he set about organising a general strike among the Swiss railway workers. Wanted by the police, he managed to escape to Poland via Berlin. After his departure the gendarmes arrived at his flat in Zurich. That was the first time Kasia witnessed a real search as the police went through all the cupboards and desks, confiscating books and papers. A couple of days later her mother received an official order to leave Switzerland with the children.

✝

As soon as they arrived in Warsaw they were parcelled off to their relatives: Anusia lived at the Beylins', Kasia at the Bychowskis' and Staś with my grandparents. They had to get used to new faces, a new language and new customs. They were not happy, most probably because they were parted from each other and from their parents. Maks was organising revolutionary strikes and demonstrations against the 'bourgeois regime', and Stefa too was involved in Party activity. They had no time for their children.

The little Horwitzes could see how critical their Warsaw family's attitude was to their parents' 'Bolshevik agitation'. Their relatives belonged to the crumbling social class that was condemned to extermination, but they led very attractive lives. They lived in beautiful, cosy homes and were comfortably off. Kasia compared her own fortune to her cousins'. Her contemporary, Marta Bychowska, had her own room, beautiful dresses, books and toys, was surrounded by love and care, and all her needs were met; and above all she was at home. For the rest of her life Kasia never stopped feeling her old childhood rancour about the Warsaw days. She would talk without any bitterness about the terrible experiences she underwent later, but she always felt like weeping with resentment when she thought about the real or imagined humiliations she encountered in Warsaw. She claimed that her aunts did not show the new arrivals enough affection, patronised them and criticised their manners. Apparently my grandmother once complained about Kasia's 'proletarian appearance'. This reproach was deeply painful for the daughter of the man who eulogised the 'dictatorship of the proletariat'.

There must have been a clash in the end, because after a few months Stefa took the older children away from their aunts and lodged with them in a crowded little flat belonging to a friend of hers, a communist activist called Mita Wleklińska, née Brun. In her memoirs entitled *Scraps of a Family Saga*, Celina Budzyńska, Mita's daughter, describes the stay of 'Wit' Walecki's family on Nowowiejska Street and her brief friendship with Kasia. They used to run about the streets of Warsaw together, deliver underground post, and listen in at political rallies. Sometimes, for a change, they would visit Kasia's family, including my grandparents and my mother, the laughing, curly-haired Hania Mortkowicz.

Fourteen-year-old Kasia thought of her older cousin as a 'princess from the sea foam' who had no idea about life. She herself was by then an experienced conspirator. During a police raid and search, when there was no one else at home, she had managed to warn her father through the window to turn around and flee; and when the policemen left, without having noticed an enormous crate of propaganda publications hidden in a wardrobe, she and Celina spent all day burning piles of paper in the tiled stove in fear of another search.

The adventures of a revolutionary's daughter might have had a romantic aura in the days of the tsarist empire, but here they were happening in the first year of independence, when the newly born state had hardly drawn breath. Regaining liberty did not mean peace or calm. At once internal and external conflicts began, over the form of the political system, over power, and over the country's borders. Dramatic efforts were under way to incorporate the provinces of Wielkopolska, Pomerania and Silesia into Poland, and there was fighting with the Ukrainians for Lwów and with the Russians for Wilno (all places that had belonged to Poland before the partitions; nowadays Lwów is Lviv in Ukraine, and Wilno is Vilnius in Lithuania). Imperceptibly, the Polish–Bolshevik war was beginning; the Polish communist leaders were inciting the workers and peasants to anarchy and rebellion against the state authorities, to seize power, and thus to start a civil war, which the country was very close to in any case.

The post-war poverty, unemployment and social pressures seemed impossible to overcome. Communism looked like a remedy for all misfortunes, and was gaining support not only among the proletariat, but also in intellectual and bourgeois circles. Meanwhile, the state was trying to restrain revolutionary activity. In response to its revolutionary propaganda, the Party journal *The Standard of Socialism* was closed down, and searches and arrests began.

In autumn 1919 Stefa's activities were judged a 'threat to public security and peace', and she was imprisoned. Maks was in hiding, so Kasia and Staś were left alone, while Anusia was still living at the Beylins'. One day they received permission to 'visit', so all three went off to the Pawiak prison. 'Take Anusia to live with you,' their mother asked the older children, and showed them a smuggled message that her youngest daughter had sent her through Gucio Beylin, the lawyer. On the card in childish scrawl was written: *I'm wandering from a. to a. I'm longing to be home now.* Seeing that her mother was crying, the little girl burst into tears too and said: 'Don't be afraid, no one'll guess it's about my aunts because I only wrote the first letters.'

Stefa was still in prison when, in October 1919, Maks was arrested in Kazimierz on the River Vistula, where he was in hiding under a false name. As in tsarist times, he was put in the Tenth Pavilion at the Warsaw Citadel. He then fell seriously ill with dysentery. On one of the first days of his imprisonment, as he was lying on his bunk, semi-conscious, with his face turned to the wall, he heard someone come into the cell. It was Bolesław Wieniawa-Długoszowski, who had been sent by Józef Piłsudski in his name, to offer his former Party comrade a transfer to more comfortable conditions where he would have better care. Maks did not even turn to face Wieniawa, but answered over his shoulder that as far as he was concerned his 'Party comrade' had died in 1906, and any offer from the present Head of State was unacceptable for a Communist Party member.

The children visited their father in the Tenth Pavilion. It was not a suitable place for them to be. Anusia always closed her eyes as they came up to the terrible walls, where executions had taken place until a short time ago. Later on Maks was transferred to a tougher prison in Wronki. After ten months, in summer 1920, when the Polish–Bolshevik war had been going on for a few months, and the Red Army was approaching Warsaw at lightning speed, he was deported to a camp for Soviet prisoners of war at Dąbie near Kraków.

On 2 July 1920, in Smolensk the Red Army commander, General Tukhachevsky, issued decree No. 1423, which was at the same time a dramatic challenge:

Soldiers of the Red Army!

The time of reckoning has come.

The army of the Red Banner and the army of the predatory White Eagle face each other in mortal combat.

Over the dead body of White Poland shines the road to world-wide conflagration.

On our bayonets we shall bring happiness and peace to toiling humanity.

To the West!

The hour of the attack has struck.

On to Vilna, Minsk and Warsaw! March!

The Red Army marched on Poland, took Wilno (in Russian, Vilna) and crossed the Polish border. The country erupted into panic. The Polish communists in Moscow established the Polish Provisional Revolutionary Committee, whose members included Julian Marchlewski, Feliks Dzierżyński, Feliks Kon, Edward Próchniak and Józef Unszlicht.

On 30 July the committee members reached Białystok, which had already been captured by the Bolsheviks, set up their head-quarters there and issued a communiqué, proving their incredible confidence. The committee declared that it was depriving the present Polish government of power, taking it into its own hands, and intended *to lay the foundations of the future Soviet system of the Polish Socialist Republic of Soviets.*

The Polish government began preventative arrests among communists and people suspected of pro-communist sympathies. The arrestees were interned in the same camp at Dąbie to which Maks had been transferred.

By then Stefania was at liberty again, and had taken the children on holiday to Józefów near Warsaw. She had a lot of visitors, which seemed suspicious to the local police, who set up a trap by encircling her flat. Somehow twelve-year-old Staś managed to slip out and ran to the station to warn the comrades arriving for the latest conspiratorial gathering of the danger. He was picked up by the secret police and taken to the commissariat, where he was interrogated for a few hours about the names of their acquaintances, addresses and contact details, but as a seasoned conspirator he either kept quiet or said, 'I don't know.' He only began to cry when his mother found him and had him released.

The Polish–Bolshevik Battle of Warsaw went on for six days, and finished with 'the Miracle on the Vistula', as the Polish victory is known. At the presbytery in Wyszków the Revolutionary Committee representatives were expecting a Bolshevik victory. What they got was a disastrous defeat: *At the sound of the shots ringing out across the River Bug, Dr Julian Marchlewski, his colleague Feliks Dzierżyński who was steeped in human blood from head to foot, and the respected veteran of socialism, Feliks Kohn, bolted from Wyszków. They left behind them a great stench of burned petrol, a little sugar and the memory of debates conducted at table and beneath the apple trees in the shady orchard. Before their departure Dr Julian Marchlewski kept repeating over and over in a melancholy tone:*

'My boy, you had a golden horn
My boy, you had a feathered cap...
All that's left you is a cord...'

As in many other things, so here too, the would-be ruler had made a fundamental error. He had never held the golden horn of Poland in his hand at all. Nor did the Cracovian four-cornered cap ever fit him [...]. That invader did not even have the right to the wretched cord from the Polish golden horn. He who has set the age-long enemy on his motherland, even if it is sinful and evil, he who has trampled it down, trodden it underfoot, plundered, burned and pillaged it at the hands of foreign soldiery – that man has deprived himself of his motherland. It can no longer be a home to him or a place of rest.

I am transcribing this extract from Stefan Żeromski's story, 'At the Presbytery in Wyszków', from a small, navy-blue volume with an ear-of-corn logo and the letters 'JM' on the cover. The book was published by Jakub Mortkowicz on the tenth anniversary of the rebirth of the Polish state.

On 2 November 1920 Adolf Warski, one of the founders of the Polish Workers' Communist Party, sent a very stern letter from Berlin to the Bolshevik Party's Polish Bureau in Moscow, urging his comrades to hasten an exchange of political prisoners between Soviet Russia and Poland. He wrote: *Whether you detain in Russia for a longer or shorter time the Polish idiots who aren't going to save white Poland, neither Russia nor Poland will profit from it [...]. But why, for God's sake, do our best people have to lose out because of it, why do they have to waste their strength and ability? A whole crowd of our people is now going to trial, including Vera, Horwitz, the Lauers [...] etc. Good brains, good publicists, good organisers. All the comrades who have undergone trial so far have received at least four years in prison or prison with an arduous regime. [...] and for some of those in prison such as Truskier, Horwitz, Vera and others, it is equal to either a death sentence or at least the loss of their health and capacity to work, in view of the fact that they are ill.*

By December 1920 Horwitz was already at liberty. He and a couple of his comrades had escaped from the camp at Dąbie by forcing their way through a hole in the rotten fence boards. Maks went first, which caused him some difficulty because of his stiff leg. But once he had climbed through, he showed his usual sang froid; he stood calmly in the road and lit his pipe, pretending to be a citizen of Kraków taking a rest while out for a walk. Only when the sentry patrolling the fence had gone past him did he slowly hobble off towards Kraków. From there he fled to Berlin, and the Ministry of Military Affairs issued a warrant for his arrest.

He was not present at Anusia's death. She died of scarlet fever in Warsaw in January 1921. She had only just turned ten. Staś was then thirteen and Kasia fifteen.

THE INDEPENDENCE YEARS

The new chapter in Poland's history was a new stage in my family's life. The generation of Julia and Gustav's grandchildren had reached maturity. The young people had already finished or were finishing their studies, were achieving financial stability, shining with professional success and building nests of their own. The first great-grandchildren had been born. In the twenty-year inter-war period my mother had fifteen first cousins. The life story of each one of them would make a separate volume in a lengthy psychological and historical saga. I cannot devote as much space to my mother's cousins as I would like, but to keep things in order I shall have to summarise their fortunes in as few words as possible. It might be boring, like any report, but if I lose a single thread of this densely woven tale, nothing will tally in the end.

In 1921 my grandmother's oldest sister, Flora Beylin, was living with her husband Samuel and two daughters, Karolina and Stefania, on Za Żelazną Bramą (meaning 'Behind the Iron Gate') Square. Karola and Stefa were students, one of Polish and the other of German literature. Flora's son, Gustaw, was already gaining a reputation as a good lawyer. A little later on he became legal adviser to ZASP (the Union of Polish Stage Artistes) and a renowned expert on copyrights. A theatre lover, friend of actors, and above all actresses, the author of a couple of light plays performed on the Warsaw stage, he was a charming person, a man of the world, a bit of a snob and a bit of a dandy. In his grandson Marek Beylin's family archive a frivolous photograph has survived, showing Gucio standing fully dressed on a beach by the sea; he is holding a rose, and he is surrounded by young ladies in swimming costumes that are scanty for those days.

After the death of little Kostuś Mania Beylin had divorced her husband, and by 1921 had been living in Paris for two years, where she continued to study mathematics at the Sorbonne, a plan that had been interrupted by the war. She earned a living by giving maths lessons and doing translations from foreign languages. In 1923 she took a step that would determine the course of her entire life. She had always had left-wing tendencies, so when an old friend of the family, Michał Muttermilch – now a writer and publicist who in France had changed his name to Merlé – offered her a job at the newly established Soviet telegraph agency, ROSTA, she agreed, partly out of sympathy for the 'Land of Soviets' and partly for financial reasons.

She thought she would just work there for a couple of months until her final university exams. She passed the exams, but was enjoying her journalistic activities and went on working at the institution, which later changed its name to TASS. In her memoirs she writes: *In this way, without realising what I was doing, and without foreseeing the consequences, I joined the Soviet state apparatus.*

My grandmother's second oldest sister, Róża Hilsum, was bringing up her three sons in Paris on her own. Her unfaithful husband, whom she had tried to leave a couple of times, had finally left himself, in a most mysterious way. The story of this event sounds like the plot of a bad novel, but unfortunately in its broadest outlines it is true. It was familiar in all our homes, and only varied in the topographic details. According to Marta Osnos, it all happened in a shop called Au Bon Marché, but to this day Janek Kancewicz is convinced it was in a bar in the Marais; I shall quote the version my grandmother used to tell.

Just before a festive family meal, perhaps on Christmas Eve, or maybe Hanukah, Jakub Hilsum said he had to nip out for some cigarettes. He left the house and never came back. Apparently someone saw him that evening at the Gare de Lyon with a harlot. Everyone knew he was alive, but he never got in touch again. Róża once found an announcement in the daily paper that said: *Rose! Pardonnez moi. Je t'aime.* It allowed her to believe to the end of her life that her husband would come back one day.

Under the influence of Maks, who was often in Paris, two of Róża's sons, René and Charles Hilsum, became ardent communists. Were they carried away by the ideology, or did material interests play a role? When a bank cooperating with the Soviet

Union was established in Paris, Charles Hilsum became its director. René worked as a publisher of communist literature. Only Lucien kept his independence. He did not want the patronage either of Maks or of his famous cousin, André Citroën, so he remained a worker at the Citroën factory.

The third sister, Gizella Bychowska, lived in spiritual mourning after the death of her beloved son Janek. She had always been prone to depression in any case, whereas her sixteen-year-old daughter, the energetic, self-confident, cheeky Marta, was the epitome of mental health. She was still at school and wanted to study medicine. Gizelka's husband, Zygmunt Bychowski, was a neurologist, who before the war had headed a ward at the Hospital of the Transfiguration in Warsaw's Praga district. Dismissed from his post in 1912 because of his ethnic origin, he now ran a private medical practice. He was passionate about social work, and volunteered for Polish as well as Jewish institutions. He was vice-president of the Warsaw Neurological Society, a board member of the Doctors' Association of the Polish Republic and founder of the periodical *Polish Neurology*, as well as performing the duties of a municipal alderman, belonging to the board of the Jewish local administration, and lecturing on social sciences at the Institute of Judaic Studies.

Gizella and Zygmunt's oldest son, twenty-five-year-old Gustaw, had completed his medical studies in Saint Petersburg, Wrocław and Lausanne. He took his doctorate in 1919 in Zurich. He specialised in psychiatry; his first supervisor was Eugen Bleuler, a famous psychiatrist and psychologist. In 1921 he went to Vienna to deepen his knowledge as a pupil of the founder of psychoanalysis, Dr Sigmund Freud. This experience inspired a life-long commitment in the field.

My grandmother's fourth sister, Henrietta Margulies, spent a lot of time at sanatoria. The mental illness of one of her daughters, Alisia, and Henrietta's own physical as well as nervous complaints meant that this branch of my relatives was somewhat on the sidelines of family life, about which Stefa and Marysia Margulies always had huge and well-justified grievances. Both girls took university degrees in chemistry in the inter-war years. Stefa then got married and left for Kraków, while Marysia got a job at a company that made cosmetics, and after their mother's death took on care of her handicapped sister and ailing father.

Ludwik Horwitz, my grandmother's brother, and his wife Genia had no children. After returning to Poland in 1919, first he worked at the State Meteorological Institute, and later at the State Geological Institute.

After escaping from the camp at Dąbie Maks Horwitz remained an émigré. He belonged to the inner circle of Communist Party leaders abroad. He was a member of the presidium of the Communist International (known as Comintern) and was its permanent representative in Moscow. In 1922, hidden in a peasant cart under some hay, he illegally entered the United States via Mexico as a Comintern emissary to help resolve a split in the local Communist Party. In 1923 he and his family settled in Berlin. Along with Adolf Warski and Maria Koszutska – alias 'Wera' – he was part of a separate group within the Party leadership, known as '3W'.

After returning to Warsaw, my grandmother's youngest sister, Kamilka, became an object of concern for the entire family. As a single mother she was condemned by the legislation of the time and by public opinion to all sorts of difficulties, administrative, professional and social. The letters 'NN', representing 'father unknown' on Janek's birth certificate could have ruined the child's life, so she took a step that to today's way of thinking seems extraordinary. She found a man who was willing to contract a marriage of convenience with her and adopt the boy.

The man was called Herman Horwitz, thanks to which she did not have to change her own or her child's name. He lived in Brody, was over sixty, and the marriage certificate tells us that by profession he was a writer; he was clearly in need of money.

He married Kamilka in 1921 at the Jewish administrative office in Vienna. She divorced him three years later. Gustaw Bychowski was a witness to the marriage and the divorce. So Miss Horwitz became Mrs Horwitz, the child had a legal father and the most important problem was resolved.

She took a job as a doctor at Amelin, an institution for people with nervous illnesses run by Dr Rafał Radziwiłłowicz, who was one of the few Warsaw clinic proprietors to employ Jews. Little Janek lived with relatives, first the Margulieses, then the Beylins, and finally with my grandparents. After some time, thanks to her siblings' help, or perhaps taking advantage of her share of the inheritance left by Julia, Kamilla bought her own flat in the house where Flora lived.

Gustaw Bychowski diligently studied the mysteries of

psychoanalysis under Dr Freud, and in the evenings he went out to eat chocolate cake – the ersatz kind, made with chicory and cinnamon – at run-down post-war Viennese cafés, or to drink a double slivovitz at gloomy variety clubs, where the fall of the monarchy was lamented. At one of these clubs a music-hall dancer, an Austrian Jewess called Ellen, used to perform. What happened next is the stuff of the standard romantic plot: he fell in love with her. Was it because of her beauty? Or the young man's loneliness? The charm of the Viennese spring? Or was their marriage the result of true love? Or necessity? Whatever the reason, in Vienna in 1922 the first representative of the next generation, Jan Ryszard Bychowski, was born.

Once he had gained his psychoanalyst's diploma, Gustaw and his family moved to Warsaw, where he began active professional employment. He worked at a hospital, lectured at the university and ran a private practice at home. Bored by the bourgeois way of life, Ellen fairly soon got involved in an affair – as rumour had it, with a woman – and went back to Vienna, leaving Ryś with his father. She later maintained feeble contact with her son.

In Berlin, Maksymilian Horwitz-Walecki wrote for the organ of the German Communist Party, *Rote Fahne* ('The Red Banner') and was very politically active. After Lenin's death and Stalin's assumption of power the 3W group came into sharp conflict with the ultra-left wing of the Party leadership and began to lose influence. Stefania Horwitz worked at a communist educational establishment. Staś was enrolled at one of the best Berlin boarding schools. The elite school was located in a beautiful park, there were only a small number of pupils in each class, and the teachers put emphasis on learning languages, an all-round education, social polish and physical development. There the timid, introverted boy gained impeccable manners and a familiarity with all the most abstruse principles of *savoir-vivre*.

Kasia circulated between Berlin and Warsaw, where she lived with her aunts and was preparing to take her final matriculation exams. She had grown up to be a pretty girl who liked pleasures and luxury. Seeing that she had no specific interests, her father advised her to become a dentist; it is not clear why, as she had plainly inherited his talent for the exact sciences.

However, she had not inherited her parents' passion for communism. She was not at all interested in politics, but she did not belong to the world of her Warsaw family either. She had been brought up differently and had a different character. She was not attached to anyone in Warsaw and no one there was particularly fond of her, nor did anyone feel responsible for her future. At the age of sixteen a person is greatly in need of authority and guidance in life, but her relatives only bothered about serious family problems. No one was concerned about the whims of young ladies – they all had enough of their own concerns.

Some sort of bad luck kept dogging my mother's cousins. Where did the amorous lawyer Gustaw Beylin meet Rebeka Friedman, a wealthy Dutch girl, daughter of a diamond dealer, known within the family as Rex? Was it at one of the European spas? Nothing is known about this love affair, apart from the fact that it ended in a failed marriage. On 27 July 1926 in Harlem, Holland, the second representative of the youngest generation was born, Paweł Beylin, a future journalist and philosopher. Was his parents' relationship already falling apart by then? One can understand that the spoiled Dutch girl was afraid of the Warsaw clinics and preferred to give birth in her home country; but where was the family to be based? Gucio had already achieved great professional success and did not want to move to Holland to live there on the bounty of his rich father-in-law. His wife was not eager to settle in Warsaw, so from the very start they lived apart.

According to family legend, a couple of months after Pawełek was born Rex went to an Italian resort, taking the child and his nanny with her. There she gave in to the persuasions of a handsome seducer and ran away with him, leaving the nanny and child at the boarding house. Summoned by telegraph, Gustaw took the child to Warsaw. Rex disappeared from the family's life, leaving no memories behind her.

Gustaw was not ideally suited to looking after his abandoned son, so he entrusted the child to his own parents, Flora and Samuel, and his two unmarried sisters, Karolina and Stefania. Pawełek even went on living with them when his father got married for the second time, to an actress named Aleksandra Leszczyńska.

Kasia Horwitz did not, as Maks had suggested, become a dentist. She was very enterprising and keen to see the world, so after gaining her matriculation she went to France, where she rapidly learned the language and began studies in the electrical engineering department at Grenoble Polytechnic. She was the only female student among 300 boys, which pleased her very much. She soon became a modern, worldly person. She loved travel, flirtations and luxury, played tennis, swam at a pool, went dancing and attracted men. She got married, and divorced. She would certainly have soon found another husband and stayed in Europe; she always blamed her father for the fact that things turned out differently.

In 1927, when Staś took his matriculation exams in Berlin, as a result of a Comintern resolution Maks was transferred to Moscow, and the whole family went with him. Kasia did not have the slightest desire to go, but love for her mother, and above all practical reasons – a lack of money to continue her studies abroad – won the day. The only concession she managed to get was that she lived apart from the family, in Leningrad, where she went on studying at the local polytechnic.

Staś was then nineteen. He had always dreamed of becoming a professional pilot, so he was very pleased when he got into the Military Engineering Department of the Pilots' Academy, one of the most prestigious military training establishments in the Soviet Union. Soon his greatest passion was parachute jumping.

On moving to the Soviet Union, like all political immigrants, Stefania, Kasia and Staś changed their surname and from then on were called Bielski. Maks was known as Henryk Walecki, and went on working within the Comintern leadership, although he was gradually falling into disfavour. Removed by Stalin from Polish affairs, he was involved in issues concerning the Balkan parties. Stefania worked in the Polish section at the Red Trade Union International.

In October 1927 Gustaw Beylin carried off a great professional success. He appeared in Kraków as the private counsel for the prosecution in a sensational action, which the celebrated writer Tadeusz Boy-Żeleński brought against Antoni Beaupré, editor-in-chief of the Kraków journal *Czas* ('Time'). Out of concern for 'good taste and decency' Beaupré had arbitrarily removed two paragraphs from an article Żeleński had written, entitled 'From Impressions of Paris – At the Sorbonne and Elsewhere'. One included the word *żdziry*, which means bitches, and the other had the word *dziwka*, which means a whore or prostitute. In another passage he changed *dziwka* to *kobieta*, meaning simply 'woman', and 'pederasts and lesbians' became 'odd characters'.

At the trial 'the elegant representative of the Warsaw bar, lawyer and man of letters, Gustaw Beylin' made the following statement, which is still topical today: *This is the first trial of its* *kind in the Polish Republic, and it will be the first court ruling designed to establish whether the property of an artist, his right to what is most of all <u>his</u>, to the products of his mind, will be recognised in practice – because in theory the law has confirmed it most categorically – as no lesser a right than other property rights. Polish writers are awaiting this verdict on tenterhooks; today's action is one of those literary trials we have seen so many of in the past, and which mark the stages in the artist's struggle for the right to his own thoughts.*

Antoni Beaupré was found guilty and was obliged to pay a fine of 200 zlotys, publish the court verdict in *Czas*, pay the private plaintiff, Żeleński, damages totalling 500 zlotys, and repay him the costs of the court action. The press reported: *From now on in Poland it is an undoubted, irrefutably established fact that an author is the single and absolute master of his own work; a work can be freely accepted or rejected, but no one has the right to lay incompetent hands on it.*

Flora's daughters had no luck with men. Karolina and Stefania did their doctorates at Warsaw University, one in Polish language and literature, the other in German, then both worked as journalists and did literary translations; Karolina translated Dickens, and Stefania translated Andersen's *Fairy Tales*. The one was energetic and resourceful, the other was quiet and shy, neither was bad looking, both were full of charm and gifted with a special, self-ironical sense of humour, so they were able to attract men, and yet they invested their emotional capital badly and their relationships were always failures.

In Paris Mania got married a second time, to a poet, journalist and aesthete called Adolf Pfeffer, who wrote under the pseudonym Artur Prędski. He was an expert on art, and was friendly with lots of artists, so Modigliani, Picasso, Chaim Soutine and Eugeniusz Zak often visited their flat in Montparnasse – Paris's entire bohemian set in those days. They led an interesting life, but there was always a lack of money in their home. Mania was still working for the TASS agency.

In December 1927 Pierre Pfeffer was born, nowadays a renowned French zoologist and traveller. His father was charming company, but not a very responsible family provider. In the 1980s, when I was visiting Paris, Mania, still full of gentle, girlish charm, invited me to the famous Parisian café La Coupole. Rosy-cheeked after a glass of red wine, she confided in me: 'This was where my husband was having fun the night I gave birth to Pierre. This is where he met the ballerina he went to live with, taking all our pictures with him. When I got home from the clinic with the baby I found the flat empty.' She said it without regret; so many calamities had surged through her life since then. A year after her son's birth she and her husband parted for good, and he went back to Poland. That was when she became a member of the French Communist Party.

Marta Bychowska, an energetic, pretty and spirited girl, graduated in biology instead of medicine, then married a very handsome, enterprising engineer called Józef Osnos. They both left for Paris because Józef got a good job there. In 1931 in Paris Robert was born – the fourth member of the youngest generation. He was four years old when his parents went back to Poland. A year after their return to Warsaw, Dr Zygmunt Bychowski died and was buried at the Jewish cemetery. On his tomb there is a bronze sculpture representing an open book, with an inscription in Latin: *Judeus sum, humani nil a me alienum puto* – a travesty of a Latin proverb, meaning, 'I am a Jew, so nothing human is strange to me.'

In 1932 Staś Horwitz, now known as Staś Bielski, graduated with the rank of a Red Army officer as an engineer and specialist in airport construction. A year earlier a fellow student had introduced him to his sister, a draughtswoman by profession, named Vera. They fell in love and before he took his diploma they were married. For a few months he worked as commander of the military airport at Orsha in Byelorussia. Then he took on the post of deputy military attaché at the Soviet embassy in Rome. In September 1932 his daughter Halinka was born in Rome.

In 1932 Mania Beylin went to Moscow, where she started work in the French section at TASS's foreign service. What inspired her to leave Paris? Was it for ideological reasons? Out of curiosity? Or emotion? She was probably in love with a famous Soviet journalist called Sergei Lukianov, who worked at the Paris agency, but was recalled to Russia. There is not a single word about it in her memoirs. Luckily, she left five-year-old Pierre at her parents' house in Warsaw for some time, because her lofty hopes for the radiance of the socialist paradise began to crumble as soon as she arrived at the port in Leningrad. She was subjected to a personal search, her luggage was gone through and a large part of her clothing was confiscated because she had exceeded the permitted norm. She was horrified by the crowd of miserably dressed, resigned-looking men, women and children wandering about the dirty station, waiting for trains that arrived at random. After that it got worse and worse, but Mania's shocking experiences in Moscow are worthy of a whole separate account.

In 1934 I was born, about which I shall say more in a later chapter.

A few years after parting from Ryś's mother Ellen, Gustaw Bychowski got married again, to Maryla Auerbach. Elegant, pretty and well educated, she came from the rich Jewish plutocracy and was certainly a much more suitable wife for a renowned Warsaw psychiatrist than her predecessor. Like Gustaw, she was divorced and had a daughter called Krysia. Maryla and the girl, who was a year younger than Ryś, were immediately accepted by the family, which was not a typical reaction. This large group of relatives, otherwise sympathetic and tolerant people, had very sharp tongues and usually picked their cousins' suitors and sweethearts to pieces. One of my cousins put off her marriage for a long time simply because they all made fun of her long-term, faithful suitor. My father was not accepted either – for all I know this may have had an influence on his fiasco of a relationship with my mother.

In 1936 the youngest representative of my generation was born, Maryla and Gustaw Bychowski's daughter Monika.

The Bychowskis and their three children lived at 47 Wilcza Street, in a beautiful big flat full of books, records and works of art. A pioneer of psychoanalysis in Poland and the author of a book entitled *Slowacki and His Soul*, Gustaw was a man of wide interests and an extremely lively mind. He loved literature and music, adored travel, knew all the European museums, spoke and read several languages fluently, had a very friendly manner and made social contacts easily. His drawing room was a meeting place not only for his professional colleagues, but also for the artists and writers he befriended. In Warsaw they loved to make fun of his Freudian interests and now and then a joke would appear in *Wiadomości Literackie* ('Literary News') featuring Gustaw as its main character.

Gustaw Bychowski is a doctor and the author of a book called Psychoanalysis, *from which I learned that if you dream about a wardrobe, it means a woman's genitalia. I asked if it works the other way around, so if you dream about a woman's genitalia, it means a wardrobe. The Freudians were very cross with me for that innocent question*, wrote Antoni Słonimski, one of the most famous writers of the day, in *An Alphabet of Memories*. But despite the gibes they were happy to spend time together.

Gustaw's son Ryś went to the Stefan Batory High School. In his first year there he made friends with Kocik Jeleński who, years later, as writer and critic Konstanty Jeleński, reminisced about their friendship in a letter to Józef Lewandowski that was published in the periodical *Zeszyty Literackie* ('Literary Notebooks'): *I joined Batory in the third class (I spent the first two at a boarding school in Switzerland) [...]. As a new boy I was immediately taken under the wing of a twelve-year-old (born like me in 1922), lively, like-able blond boy with freckles and a snub nose – Ryszard Bychowski, son of Gustaw, a renowned psychoanalyst and author of a book that was famous for its kind, 'psychoanalysing' Hitler. I remember how on the second day we 'bribed' a fat boy, to whose (two-person) desk I had been assigned, Rysiek sat in his place and from then on we were practically never apart, escorting each other home, seeing each other all the time outside school, sharing reading matter, the cinema, the swimming pool and tennis. Bychowski was a Jew, as he told me himself, but apart from me I don't think anyone in the class knew about it – in any case, it would be hard to imagine anyone less typically Jewish looking – non-Slav moreover – I only discovered this physical type later on, during the war in England, among the Irish. At home my parents greatly approved of this friendship, they were both staunchly opposed to anti-Semitism [...]. During the first year at Batory we didn't join any of the class gangs or make friends with anyone else, but both Rysiek and I were quite 'popular' within the class elite as the owners of good records and books which we were happy to lend, and for having a good balance between academic work and sport (I think we were in the top ten in both areas of activity, out of a class of thirty-plus pupils). Towards the end of the second year (1934–5) the proverbial bolt out of the blue hit us – though we were not really aware of it. It was in a mathematics lesson, taught by Professor Jumborski [...]. He called Rysiek Bychowski to the black-board (both he and I were weakest at maths) and Rysiek got the answer all wrong. Somewhere from the back of the class someone started intoning: 'Zyyt' (not 'Żyd' [the proper Polish word for a Jew], I can remember that 'Zyyt', it's still ringing in my ears), and soon almost the entire class had taken up the chant.*

Never before had we had any unpleasantness because of this! Professor Jumborski (nicknamed Jumbo as he was large, heavy and a bit elephant-like – afterwards we found out that he himself was a Jew) began to shout something like 'You barbarians, you vile barbarians!', then left the classroom, slamming the door, to fetch the headmaster. At that point I threw myself at the boy sitting nearest to me, who was one of the 'choir', Rysiek jumped up too, and a literally bloody fight began, in which only five of our thirty-plus classmates fought on our side.

One of those five classmates was Krzysztof Kamil Baczyński, Ryś's closest friend, who went on to be a legendary poet and hero, dying tragically young in the Warsaw Uprising.

❧

Children were born and the older generation passed on. In the twenty-year period between the wars my grandmother lost four of her siblings. In 1928 Henrietta ended her days in an Austrian sanatorium. More will be said later about Gizella and Maks. In June 1939 the kind, caring Róża died in Paris.

A year earlier she had managed to visit Warsaw. A souvenir of that visit has survived, a photograph taken in a garden, perhaps on a joint holiday. The two sisters – Róża and my grandmother – are sitting in wicker armchairs, smiling cheerfully, and I, a very little girl, am lying on the grass blowing a dandelion clock. There is something metaphysical about this idyllic image – it is a fragment of life, frozen for ever, like in a drop of resin. Time, ever rushing onwards, has stood still for a moment.

It seems as if only yesterday a very young Róża was scrubbing her little brothers' ears and necks in her white wedding dress. Soon she will no longer be alive. Soon the days of peaceful outings to summer resorts and lazy afternoons in wicker armchairs will be at an end. Róża's sons, those three smiling boys, René, Charles and Lucien, with whom only such a short time ago my little mother was collecting mussels on the beaches of the Atlantic Ocean, will change into indifferent strangers. They will cease to keep in touch with the rest of the family, so in the distant future, in other words now, I shall be unable to write about them – I shall not even know how many children and grandchildren they had.

Very soon Fate would drive me from the sunny summer resort into the menacing world outside; but nowadays I am in control of events, and like in a safe microfilm library I can rewind the scroll of time and go back to the era before I was born.

❧

AT THE SIGN OF THE EAR OF CORN

In 1918 my future mother wrote:

> *At sixteen years old your life lies before you,*
> *Your head's full of plans and desires,*
> *Forward you run in joy and delight*
> *On a wonderful sapphire-blue day.*
>
> *At sixteen years old you have sturdy young legs,*
> *And strong hands for toils yet to come,*
> *You run down the footpaths, the byways and tracks*
> *And live free among forests and fields.*
>
> *At sixteen years old you smile and you laugh,*
> *You look on the world and its people with love,*
> *You wake up each morning with joy in your heart,*
> *How fine to be sixteen years old!*

I envied her that poem. I reached the age of sixteen at the apogee of Stalinism and neither the present nor the future stirred any enthusiasm in me. Only now am I aware how very jealous I was in my youth of my mother's and grandmother's past. Pre-war Poland seemed to me an Arcadia, a lost paradise, whose delights I had never sampled. It shone in their reminiscences with the brightness of a thousand lamps, with not a single shadow to darken the heavenly landscape.

For my grandparents independence meant above all the urgent need to get down to work, for the present at last, not the future, and with no fears or political repression. In spring 1919, thanks to special licences and permits, Jakub Mortkowicz travelled to France and England on one of the first express trains used by diplomats and the military to renew the professional contacts that had been cut off by the war. He took samples of his publications with him. In a brochure entitled 'The Polish book as an agent for international relations and propaganda' he later mentioned: *During our discussion the managing director of the Oxford University Press, the famous publisher Sir Humphrey Milford, said to me: 'Show me how you publish your books, and you will win me over to your culture and your country's independence.' I showed him, and I won him over.*

He came home delighted with the proposals for cooperation he had received, and with plenty of plans and ideas. He brought some French and English literary novelties back to Warsaw, including lots of picture albums and reproductions, which he used to decorate the display windows at the bookshop on Mazowiecka Street, and rolls of coloured cloth for bookbinding. With immense difficulty his wife and daughter managed to persuade him to give them a few metres of this wonderful stuff to make summer dresses.

In the lean post-war year of 1919, when inflation was rampant and prices kept changing by the hour, Mortkowicz's publishing firm issued thirty-one titles, including five small books by the poet Leopold Staff, five volumes by the novelist Stefan Żeromski, *How to Love a Child* by Janusz Korczak, *The Bow*, a psychological novel by Juliusz Kaden-Bandrowski, and *Spring and Wine*, the first collection of poems by Kazimierz Wierzyński. Seventeen-year-old Hania used to gaze at the handsome young poet in a lovesick way.

Right next to the bookshop on Mazowiecka Street there was a famous café, the Ziemiańska, where the most popular poets, writers, theatre people and painters used to meet for a small black coffee. That was where all the most interesting creative ideas and the best jokes were born, and amid the atmosphere of a champagne party the social hierarchy was mercilessly established; anyone who was not accepted by the mischievous members of the 'Skamander' group of poets, Julian Tuwim, Antoni Słonimski and Jan Lechoń, was finished in the eyes of society, and a newcomer who was allowed to sit at their little table on the mezzanine felt ennobled.

Hania's girlfriends, pupils at the state Klementyna Hoffman née Tańska Secondary School, used to stare at the famous literati through the café window with schoolgirl reverence, but she knew them all personally. She wanted to belong to that world, not because of her parents, but on her own merits. She wrote poetry and drew beautifully. Should she become a writer? Or maybe a painter? She could not make up her mind.

After her matriculation she began Polish studies at Warsaw University. As an extra subject she chose art history, and also enrolled at the School of Fine Arts, which was later renamed the Academy of Fine Arts. She was taught by famous professors including Konrad Krzyżanowski, Tadeusz Pruszkowski and Stanisław Noakowski, who was well known for his lectures, during which he would conjure up wonderful architectural drawings with chalk on the blackboard. She took her university studies seriously, whereas she remembered her years at the Academy as a time of youthful lack of cares. Fanciful painters' revels, champagne balls, outings to paint *en plein air* at Kazimierz on the River Vistula, and the artists' satirical revues that were popular in the city were an exciting contrast to the solemn atmosphere of the cult of art that prevailed at home.

She led a life worth envying. She had adored and loving parents, with the magical atmosphere of their own publishing firm and bookshop, her academic studies, interesting friendships, foreign travel, museums, society life, balls, the theatre and exhibitions.

She was twenty-two when, on 16 December 1922, she went with her parents to a private view at the Society for the Encouragement of the Fine Arts building on Małachowski Square (better known as the Zachęta Gallery). They were standing in the front row of the audience when a shot was fired and Gabriel Narutowicz, who was opening the exhibition and who a week earlier had been elected President of the Polish Republic, staggered and fell. It was hard to tell what had happened. Someone shouted: 'A doctor! Get a doctor at once!' The poetess Kazimiera Iłłakowicz, who was a qualified nurse, laid the dying president on a plush-covered museum sofa. An ambulance was summoned and the audience were ushered out of the hall. The assassin, Eligiusz Niewiadomski, a painter and art historian as well as a fanatical supporter of the opposition Endecja ('National Democracy') movement, was standing in the corner with a revolver in his hand, waiting for the police.

Narutowicz died in hospital. Niewiadomski was given a summary conviction and condemned to death. The sentence was carried out. For many years his grave at Powązki cemetery was littered in flowers and funerary candles lit by people who regarded him as a hero. Earlier on, the presidential elections had divided society into two hostile camps. The National Democracy radical right wing complained loudly that Narutowicz, who had spent a long time living in Switzerland, was not a 'real Pole', that his election victory had been decided by the ethnic minorities, the Jews, Germans and Ukrainians, and that the national character of the Polish state would suffer as a result of this choice. Yet no one had expected that in the newly reborn motherland it would come to 'regicide' – the murder of the head of state. At the time this crime seemed an incomprehensible source of shame and disgrace, proof of a political and emotional immaturity that would eventually pass. But later on the racist insanity of the right-wing ideologists who had divided the Poles into those 'of Polish blood' and 'the vagabonds', began to grow.

At home I never heard anyone mention trouble with anti-Semitism, which must after all have affected my family in the inter-war years, just as it affected other assimilated Jews; but there were the *numerus clausus* (a ceiling on the number of Jews admitted to institutions), the segregation of Jewish students, who were obliged to sit in a separate area of the university lecture halls, and open insults by colleagues at the university. Attacks by the extreme right wing were always in the same, all-too-familiar tone: The Jews are everywhere. The Jews are a threat to national unity. The Jews are scheming. The Jews are lording it over us. The Jews have taken over the economy, literature and art. They're poisoning Polish souls. They're depraving the nation.

Did my mother never experience any unpleasantness at school? Or at college? How could my grandfather bear the insults that dogged him throughout his life? How did my grandmother feel? Nothing was ever said about it. My relatives preferred to nurture the good memories than remember the bad ones.

After the experiences of the Second World War, in the hopeless gloom of the Communist regime, the years 1918–39, despite their shadows, seemed like a lost paradise. The achievements of the renascent Poland, the exuberance of artistic and literary life, the firm's successes, their friendships with writers – it had all happened so recently and was so irrevocably lost. In her book *A Riot of Memories* my mother describes a conversation she had with Julian Tuwim after the war, at a time when the publishing bureaucracy was expanding monstrously.

Do you remember? said Tuwim. *The sapphire-blue study on Mazowiecka Street, behind the shop. No janitor, no secretary, no waiting room. Mr Mortkowicz would be at his desk under the window chatting to Żeromski or Staff, or Dąbrowska, or me. And the whole time customers would be coming into the room to buy the pictures hanging on the walls. It never bothered anyone. Some beautiful books used to appear in those days. Who published them? Two, or maybe three people… I once brought a manuscript to the bookshop for Mr Mortkowicz. A little exercise book full of poems, do you remember? So then what? Mr Mortkowicz put the exercise book under his arm and took it straight round to the printers in the Old Town, on foot. And there was no planning or editors, no revisers, nothing. The typesetter just took the poems to set, and a few days later the first proofs were ready.*

My mother described the doings of the publishing firm in her book, *At the Sign of the Ear of Corn*, where she exhaustively and expertly recounts Mortkowicz's multifarious activities, supported by his wife's cooperation. She describes the authors and the graphic artists, the process involved in producing a book, the employees, including the printers, bookbinders, salesmen and caretakers, contacts with foreign firms, successes and failures, and also endless financial difficulties.

Despite its achievements, the twenty-year inter-war period was not favourable to the book business. First inflation, then financial reform, and finally an economic crisis, general impoverishment and rising production costs all caused a drop in sales. The headlines cried out about: 'The agony of the Polish book business!' They reckoned young people did not read books because they were distracted by the cinema, sport, the radio and illustrated weeklies. Mortkowicz wrote articles in the professional press and in literary journals about the importance of books in public life, and thought up ways of attracting readers into the bookshops. In 1918 he and some other well-known booksellers founded 'Ruch', the Polish Society of Railway Bookshops, which was involved in the distribution of magazines, books and literary works throughout the country, and became the Ruch kiosk chain that still exists today. In 1929 he suggested to his fellow booksellers that they should have a colourful, mass exodus onto the streets: a great big book fair with stalls in Teatralny Square. A 'Book of the Month' competition and 'Good Book Days' were all ideas of his that are still practised today.

But he spent the whole time hovering on the brink of bankruptcy. There was a constant fear that income would not cover expenditure, and that there would not be enough money for the employees' pay, authors' fees, paper, print and living expenses. He had never made a fortune, so he used bank credits to pay for new titles, and paid them off afterwards from the money they brought in. Sometimes he got his sums wrong: a book did not sell and he was forced to run up more debts. Yet he did have a talent for business, and for a long time good fortune smiled on him. Whenever things got very bad he would hit upon a new, superb idea and a period of prosperity would set in again. However, he refused to succumb to the rules of the market and only published the books that genuinely interested him.

It is hard to identify the publishing firm's speciality. Poetry, perhaps? In 1910 the famous poetry series 'At the Sign of the Poets' was born: small, slim volumes of poetry with a beautiful graphic design, bound in chamois-leather and coloured cloth. The name was not original. It was what Michał Gröll, a typographer from the era of King Stanisław August, had called his printing house. However, the vignette that appeared on the covers was Mortkowicz's idea: a gilded drawing in the shape of a circle, inside which two Greek maidens sat facing a smoking censer; one was playing the flute, and the other was making a sacrifice to the gods – a motif from a Roman bas-relief.

In 1928, when on the tenth anniversary of Poland's rebirth the tenement houses on the Old Town Marketplace were adorned with brightly coloured paintings, Mortkowicz suggested naming tenement house No.11 'At the Sign of the Poets' according to the mediaeval custom, and decorating it with a sculpted emblem on the façade. The sculpture, topped with some book volumes with the names of the authors carved on them, was designed by Stanisław Ostrowski.

Or maybe the house speciality was belles-lettres? It was Mortkowicz who persuaded the novelist Maria Dąbrowska to leave her state job and offered her a monthly stipend against future earnings, thanks to which she could concentrate on writing her family saga *Nights and Days*. Having signed a contract with Stefan Żeromski in 1914 to publish his collected works, he regularly paid him a set amount as an advance, enabling the writer to have a peaceful existence. During the First World War, when the postal service was not functioning, he used to slip out of Warsaw and over the border to Zakopane, where Żeromski was living at the time, to deliver his money. In 1915 Żeromski wrote to him and said: *I received the contract and thank you most sincerely for it, and for all the kindness that you have so constantly and systematically shown me. In a life as tough as mine I have rarely had such a friendly and kindly helping hand as yours, which I warmly press.*

Or perhaps it was children's books? This department was run by my grandmother, who oversaw their literary and graphic standards. Under the slogan 'Let's give children the best we've got' Mortkowicz's publishing house issued Janusz Korczak's successive works, Julian Tuwim's poems for children, Bolesław Leśmian's *Sesame Tales* and *The Adventures of Sindbad the Sailor*, and translations of children's classics such as Andersen's *Fairy Tales*, J. M. Barrie's *Peter Pan* and Thackeray's *The Rose and the Ring*.

Or inexpensive books for anyone? Żeromski for All Poland at an exceptionally low price; collected editions of poets Cyprian Norwid, Leopold Staff and novelist Andrzej Strug; the Serialised History of Art in Poland; Good Books for Young People – a zloty a volume; Polish Painting Serialised for All – I could go on listing titles ad infinitum.

But my grandfather's greatest love was art publications. Here he could put his ideas into action, choose the fonts, graphic materials and cover colours. He produced luxury editions printed on hand-woven paper, richly illustrated and bound in leather with gilded decorations and lettering stamped on the covers. These included *Ashes* by Stefan Żeromski; *Polish Folk Woodcuts* by Władysław Skoczylas; folders with pictures by Józef Pankiewicz, Eugeniusz Zak and Moïse Kisling, reproduced so faithfully that they were no different from the originals; dozens of other elegant albums illustrated by the best graphic artists including Franciszek Siedlecki, Władysław Skoczylas and Edmund Bartłomiejczyk, which are masterpieces of the arts of publishing, graphic design and bookbinding to this day.

Mortkowicz also performed some responsible social functions. He was an active board member of the Union of Polish Booksellers. He belonged to the Polish Book Publishers' Society. He went to international booksellers' conferences and congresses as the Polish delegate. He issued a periodical called *Myśl Polska* ('Polish Thought') and later *Świat Książki* ('The World of the Book'). He wrote a lot himself.

I do not know how he found time for it all, and it is hard for me to believe that this colourful, abundant period in his life, the richest in terms of achievement, lasted barely thirteen years.

I never knew my grandfather. He died before I was born, but his legend has accompanied me throughout my life. My grandmother and mother endlessly adored him, and I never heard them criticise him; but he must have had some shortcomings and oddities. From other people's accounts it appears that sometimes he was unfair, and he often let himself be carried away by over-extravagant ambitions. He had no sense of restraint in his expenditures. It is not impossible that he was a snob. He did not always play the role of a philanthropist towards the writers, and often made a good income out of them – after all, the money needed to keep the firm going did not fall from the sky. Antoni Słonimski portrayed him critically in his satirical comedy *The Negro of Warsaw*, and Bolesław Leśmian's letters are full of complaints about Mortkowicz's meanness and conceit.

Relations between writers and publishers are usually full of irritations and mutual grievances. Each side feels as if it is being used; but luckily I am not writing an academic work and I do not have to try to be objective. I would simply like to understand him better.

He seems like a character out of a romantic tragedy. He had a sense of mission and he achieved success, but he was never happy with himself. He lived in a constant state of dissatisfaction and longing. Was it because of an illness? Over-extravagant ambitions? The complexes of someone from the provinces? Or his unrequited love for Poland? He enlisted in the service of Polish culture like a knight errant. In exchange he heard and read that he was just a Jewish tradesman who should know his place, not play the artist – and that hurt.

In periods of euphoria he was not bothered by such unpleasantness; he had thousands of plans and projects, infected everyone with his enthusiasm and, driven by a sense of omnipotence, he would take on the boldest of enterprises. But then months of depression and apathy would set in. My mother and grandmother did not like to talk about it, though they blossomed whenever they started to recall the intensity of all the flavours and colours that made their lives sparkle when he was on good form.

He adored travel: the distant journeys, such as to Italy, and also the short ones, to the fair at Białystok. It gave him sensual pleasure to shop for cheeses and wine, holy images and clay pots, flowers and coloured chintz – he used to bring all these goods home in wholesale quantities. He enjoyed tirelessly running about museums and lazily lounging on beaches. When on holiday he liked to play the role of a painter, took paints and an easel outside with him and sat for hours by the sea in a straw boater and a blue artist's smock; but he never had the courage to touch the canvas with a brush dipped in paint. He knew his limitations.

He was an artist *manqué*. He was extremely talented at dressing the display windows of the bookshop on Mazowiecka Street. He would be overcome with joy at the sight of a large space to be organised in an artistic way. At exhibitions and the International Book Fairs held in Florence, Vienna, Leipzig and Paris, where he used to appear as Poland's permanent representative, he took charge of designing the Polish exhibits himself. He organised the first Polish book show, at the Fiera di Libro held in Florence in 1922, in partnership with Karol Frycz, a well-known set designer. They carried off a great success.

In 1925, at the next Florence exhibition, Poland did not have the money to pay a professional, so he worked on his own, with the help of an Italian assistant assigned to him on behalf of the consulate. When someone had to climb a ladder to hang tapestries high on the wall, with the portraits of three writers, Henryk Sienkiewicz, Władysław Reymont and Stefan Żeromski under them, the assistant refused because he was afraid he would fall. So my grandfather, though not the youngest of men by then, climbed up to the ceiling, banged in the nails and positioned the exhibits himself. He barely had time to change out of his worker's overalls into his dress coat to take part in the exhibition's opening ceremony. From a platform decked in flowers and flags in the Palazzo Vecchio he made a speech as the Polish representative before the Italian royal family, state dignitaries and people from the entire world of European culture. Later on he showed the Italian king around the Polish stand, which delighted the press with its charms.

From then on he was entrusted with preparing the Polish stands at all the international shows. He found all the decorative features within Poland, selected books and reproductions and paid for the transportation costs out of his own pocket. Once on the spot he would design the space, arrange the tables and bookshelves, hang up the pictures, lay out the publications and even change the water in the flower vases himself. During one major exhibition, the Salon International de Livre d'Art held at the Petit Palais in Paris, he ran to the market at dawn for fresh flowers, choosing the right shade of violet to match the grey glaze of the jugs.

He enjoyed the beauty of the world. He had a successful family. He led a happy life. He did what he liked, and achieved what he wanted to. But the whole time despair was lurking in the background. I do not know how my grandmother – an out-and-out optimist – coped with it. My mother admitted that the constant anxiety poisoned her youth.

❧

During the thirteen years of Mortkowicz's feverish activity, the little girl with curly pigtails turned into a mature woman. Sometimes it felt as if her parents had not noticed. They treated Hania as their successor and thought it quite natural that their only child, despite her own occupations, should devote some of her time to the firm's concerns. In the intensive pre-holiday period she used to help pack books, run to the printer's with manuscripts, take the authors their galley proofs to correct, and at international exhibitions she helped to cover the pedestals in canvas and arrange the books artistically among vases of flowers. The older she was, the more responsible tasks were entrusted to her. Gentle and sensitive, she did not know how, or did not want, to tear herself away from their world to discover one of her own.

She was twenty-two when her father published her first collection of poetry, *Rowanberries*. Would any other publisher have been willing to publish her poems? He published her successive works, including her novel, *The Bitterness of Springtime*, and some journalistic sketches entitled *On Both Sides of the Highway* and *On the Roads of Poland*. Was she entitled to consider herself a writer by now? She did not know.

Her love for her parents was so unlimited that she was unable to exchange it for emotion towards a man. Time was passing, and no one had appeared who was important enough for her to give up her current life for him. At the next Painter's Revue a puppet representing Hania Mortkowicz sang:

> *I am almost like a mum*
> *To Stefan Żeromski and Miriam,**
> *Everyone in Poland's heard of me,*
> *Bookselling's future good fairy…*
>
> *I'm the pride of both higher academies*
> *But who will call me 'my sweetie'*
> *When my tender heart lies buried deep*
> *Beneath that literary rubbish heap!*

* Translator's note: The pseudonym of poet and critic Zenon Przesmycki.

I do not know if she found that song particularly amusing.

She was twenty-five when she gained her D. Phil at Warsaw University on the basis of a thesis entitled 'The Legend of Wanda – The History of the Literary Plot'; but she did not take up academic work – she was needed at the publishing firm. She also graduated from the Painting and Graphics Faculty at the Academy of Fine Arts, but she did not have enough courage or maybe talent to try her strengths as a painter. Her contemporaries there, Feliks Topolski, Eliasz Kanarek and Antoni Michałak, all achieved fame. She did illustrate her own children's books. A second volume of her poetry, entitled *A Redundant Heart*, came out when she was twenty-six. There is a lot of sadness and resignation in the poems, as well as allusions to unreciprocated emotions and unfulfilled hopes.

Then love made its appearance. A handsome, talented young painter – a colleague from the Academy – became a very important person in her life. He started spending time at the family home and gained her parents' acceptance. There were some serious conversations about the future. The boy was extremely interested in publishing, knew about art and seemed the ideal candidate for a husband as well as a son-in-law. My future mother was happy.

In spring 1931 she went to Paris with her parents for the Salon International de Livre d'Art. A chauffeur in grey livery drove their car, a fabulous Chrysler 75. The exhibits had been sent ahead in advance by train. As commissioner in charge of the Polish section, Mortkowicz spent a long time designing the stand before the opening. He chose the most beautiful books issued by the best Polish publishers, reproduced the most interesting illustrations, selected frames for colourful posters, and collected Hucuł tapestries from the East Carpathians, colourful ceramics and folk sculptures.

It was the time of a major economic crisis. The book market was in a state of stagnation, and publishing firms were crashing. Seriously in debt to the banks, the printers and the authors by then, as usual Mortkowicz was not being very careful about money. For the exhibition he designed and issued a promotional album at his own cost, *Le livre d'art en Pologne 1900–1930*. This fat, beautifully bound volume was a review of Polish publishing in the first thirty years of the twentieth century. Colourful insets depicting the achievements of the Polish publishers, book illustrations by famous Polish graphic artists, elegant rag paper and a special font all came together to produce a refined and costly whole. The book was not destined for sale, but was generously distributed to exhibition participants as a gift from a Polish publisher to publishers from all over the world.

The trip was one long stream of successes and pleasures. The French press wrote: ... *none of us will ever forget the fine contribution of M. Mortkowicz in organising the Polish section. It was one of the most attractive at the exhibition and made an enormous impression on all the visitors.* The International Congress of Publishers was being held in Paris at the same time. At the opening ceremony my grandfather said: *It is with great emotion that I address you on behalf of Polish booksellers and publishers. Twenty-one years ago at the Congress held in Amsterdam in 1910 I gave a report on the need to grant representation at the Congress to Poland, a country that was then divided between three powerful monarchies. My motive for that report was that although physically divided by three borders, Poland was still a single nation with a single, united culture, and that Polish books had never recognised those borders. The report was received favourably and a seat on the International Committee was conferred on the Polish nation. Today I have the honour and – I would say – the good fortune to stand before this gathering a second time, and in the name of the publishers and booksellers of a free, united Poland to express to the Congress here in Paris our appreciation and gratitude for the prophetic resolution of 1910.*

The Jewish boy from Radom had risen high. He was warmly applauded and honoured, and he and his family took part in a celebratory *déjeuner* hosted by the French President. *And*, wrote my mother, *as I listened to the proceedings and attended the receptions, I felt like a citizen of the entire world, the representative of my nation's great culture, more firmly and happily than ever before or after.*

On 4 July 1931 they left for Poland. Mortkowicz left his trunk at the Hotel Cayres on Boulevard Raspail where they had been staying, with his dress coat and folding top hat in it, the obligatory costume for his official appearances and receptions, because he planned to return to Paris in the autumn for the closing of the exhibition. As the car drove away, the hotel manager and the porter stood outside and called after it: *A bientôt, Monsieur Mortkowicz, à bientôt!*

In Warsaw there were reprimands and warnings waiting for him from the banks where he had drawn credit. Taciturn and secretive, he never admitted to his family how heavily he felt the burden of his endless financial difficulties. He was unable to limit himself or abandon his artistic ideas, to save or make a profit. He refused to live with a constant sense of threat.

On 9 August 1931, at the flat on Okólnik Street, in a state of total nervous collapse he shot himself with a revolver. He was immediately taken to an infirmary on Zgoda Street, but died at twelve o'clock. He was fifty-six years old. In the letter he left for his wife and daughter he wrote: *I have never been a tradesman and I shall not die like one.*

The funeral took place on 11 August 1931 at the Jewish cemetery. Stanisław Arct spoke at the graveside on behalf of Polish publishers, and Jan Parandowski spoke in the name of Polish writers. A copy of *Le livre d'art en Pologne* was placed in his grave.

Gustaw Beylin in the
Polish Legions, 1915

Mania Szper, née Beylin

Józef Szper, 1916

Ministerstwo Spraw Wojskowych
Oddział II Sztabu
Sekcja 2 Defenzywy
Liczba 16250/2) Def.

Warszawa, dn. 11 grudnia 1920 r.

W nocy z 8-go na 9-go grudnia b. r. zbiegł z obozu dla jeńców i internowanych w Dąbiu pod Krakowem:

Maksymiljan Horwitz

jeden z przywódców Komunistycznej Partji Robotniczej Polski, aresztowany 14.X 1919 roku, za fałszywym paszportem na nazwisko inż. Stanisława Hildta, w Kazimierzu nad Wisłą, gdzie zamieszkiwał z dwoma innymi wybitnymi działaczami K. P. R. P. Wróblewskim i Landauem, którzy równocześnie zostali aresztowani, w odosobnionej willi pod miastem, specjalnie na ten cel wynajętej.

Stamtąd wspomniana trójka kierowała całym ruchem komunistycznym w Polsce, redagując odezwy i artykuły, oraz podtrzymując kontakt z komunistami w kraju i z Rosją Sowiecką, za pośrednictwem emisarjuszy, którzy do Horwitza co jakiś czas przyjeżdżali po informacje i instrukcje.

Horwitz jest jednym z najbardziej niebezpiecznych prowodyrów komunistycznych, osobistym przyjacielem i współpracownikiem Trockiego, oraz krewnym głośnego komunisty Feliksa Kona.

GENERALJA: Maksymiljan Horwitz (pseud. lit. i partyjny Walecki), syn nieżyjącego Gustawa, dra filozofji, i nieżyjącej Julji, z domu Kleinmann; urodzony w r. 1877 w Warszawie, wyznania mojżeszowego (podaje się za bezwyznaniowca); żonaty z Stefanją z Heryngów, zamieszkałą w Warszawie przy ul. Nowowiejskiej 25; z zawodu nauczyciel matematyki i literat; włada językami: polskim, rosyjskim, francuskim i niemieckim. Przed wyjazdem do Kazimierza był zameldowany w Warszawie na podstawie fałszywego paszportu na imię Leona Brandta, inżyniera, w domu przy ul. Siennej 32, następnie przy ul. Nowolipie 49.

RYSOPIS: Wzrost średni, twarz owalna z zapadłemi policzkami, czoło wysokie, nos długi, semicki, oczy szare (wybitnie krótkowzroczny, nosi binokle albo okulary), włosy ciemne (szpakowate), przerzedzone (łysawy), wąsy krótko przystrzyżone, silny zarost. Wygląd chorowity, ponad wiek; cera żółto-ziemista. Nogi kabłąkowate.

ZNAK SZCZEGÓLNY: Utyka na lewą nogę.

Jako szczegół charakterystyczny podaje się, że Horwitz w chwilach wolnych zajmuje się nałogowo matematyką.

Wobec tego, że przebywanie na wolności Maksymiljana Horwitza może przynieść nieobliczalne szkody dla Państwa Polskiego, należy wytężyć całą energję w kierunku unieszkodliwienia go.

W razie schwytania Horwitza, należy go pod silną i pewną eskortą odstawić do dyspozycji Prokuratora przy Sądzie Okręgowym w Warszawie, zawiadamiając równocześnie o tem Sekcję Defenzywy Oddziału II Szt. M. S. Wojsk. z powołaniem się na Licz. 16250-20 Def.

Fotografja w trzech pozach przedstawia Horwitza, zdjętego w październiku 1919 r. po aresztowaniu.

Z. r. Szefa Oddziału II Szt.
(—) WITECKI
Rtm. i p. o. Szefa Sekcji Def.

Maks Horwitz's arrest warrant

Ministry of Military Affairs   Warsaw, 11 December 1920
Division II HQ
Defence Section 2
Number 16250/29 Def.

On the night of 8-9 December this year there escaped from a camp for prisoners of war and internees in Dąbie near Kraków: Maksymiljan Horwitz, one of the leaders of the Polish Workers' Communist Party, arrested on 14.X.1919 on a false passport in the name of engineer Stanisław Hildt, in Kazimierz on the Vistula, where he was residing with two other leading PWCP activists, Wróblewski and Landau, who were also arrested, in a secluded villa on the edge of town, specially rented for this purpose.

From there the above-mentioned three were running the entire communist movement in Poland, editing proclamations and articles, and maintaining contact with communists within Poland and in Soviet Russia, through the intermediacy of emissaries who came to see Horwitz now and then for information and instructions.

Horwitz is one of the most dangerous communist ringleaders, a personal friend and collaborator of Trotsky and a relative of the renowned communist Feliks Kon.

GENERAL DETAILS: Maksymiljan Horwitz (literary and party pseudonym Walecki), son of Gustaw (doctor of philosophy) deceased and Julia née Kleinmann deceased; born 1877 in Warsaw, of the Jewish denomination (he claims to have no denomination); married to Stefanie née Heryng, resident in Warsaw at 25 Nowowiejska Street; by profession a teacher of mathematics and a writer; fluent in Polish, Russian, French and German. Before leaving for Kazimierz he was registered in Warsaw on the basis of a false passport in the name of Leon Brandt, engineer, at 32 Sienna Street, then at 49 Nowolipie Street.

DESCRIPTION: Medium height, face oval with hollow cheeks, brow high, nose long and Semitic, eyes grey (highly short-sighted, he wears pince-nez or glasses), hair dark (going grey) and thinning (baldish), moustache cut short, heavy stubble. Looks sickly and past his age; skin sallow yellow. Bow-legged.

DISTINGUISHING FEATURE: Limps on the left leg.

A typical feature is that in his free time Horwitz habitually works as a mathematician.

In view of the fact that Maksymiljan Horwitz remaining at liberty could cause incalculable harm to the Polish State, all possible energy must be exerted to neutralise him.

If caught he is to be delivered under strong and secure escort into the custody of the Prosecutor at the District Court in Warsaw, and at the same time the Defence Section at Division II HQ of the Ministry of Military Affairs is to be informed with reference to Number 16250-20 Def.

The photograph shows Horwitz in three poses, taken in October 1919 after his arrest.

Head of Division II HQ
(–) WITECKI
Capt. and Acting Head of Def. Section

Julian Margulies and his daughters Stefania, Marysia and Alisia

Gizella Bychowska, née Horwitz, and her grandson Ryszard Bychowski, 1930

Karolina Beylin

Stefania Beylin

Gustaw's wife
Maryla Bychowska

Jakub Mortkowicz

POD ZNAKIEM POETÓW

SERJA NOWA

WYDAWNICTWA J. MORTKOWICZA

The frontispiece to the 'At the
Sign of the Poets' series

Jakub Mortkowicz's company emblems

Jakub Mortkowicz at an
exhibition stand

Hanna Mortkowicz

Professor Tadeusz Olczak

Joanna Olczak

Robert Osnos, Joanna Olczak and Ryszard Bychowski, 1939

WHITE LILAC

———————————— ✳ ————————————

Naturally, the entire family was at my grandfather's funeral, as well as all Warsaw's intellectuals, including the booksellers, writers, painters and graphic artists who were his friends, and crowds of readers. The tragic death of a well-known publisher caused a commotion in Poland and abroad. The posthumous memoirs listed his merits, and one can sense that the universal grief was genuine: everyone realised that no one would ever again serve Polish books and their authors with such disinterested love.

Janusz Korczak wrote: *It was not melancholy that put the revolver in his hand. It was an act of protest about the fact that life demanded him to be different from the man he was. No one is allowed to follow their own path without paying the price.*

Maria Dąbrowska: *He was a wanderer from another world, lost in the sphere of commerce. He was from a world whose passion is not to have, but to be, not to accumulate, but to create ... If he had any personal ambition, it could only have been a desire to distinguish himself by what he did, never by what he possessed.*

The booksellers, writers and artists set about commemorating his life with incredible commitment. A special issue of *Przegląd Księgarski* ('The Booksellers' Review') was dedicated to Mortkowicz, and featured remembrances of him by authors including Leopold Staff, Bolesław Leśmian and Janusz Korczak, graphic artists including Władysław Skoczylas and Franciszek Siedlecki, and colleagues such as Gustaw Wolff and Wacław Anczyc. Recollections of him by Maria Dąbrowska and art historian Mieczysław Sterling were published in a special section in *Wiadomości Literackie* ('Literary News'), along with a poem 'To Jakub Mortkowicz' by Or-Ot (whose real name was Artur Oppman).

In October 1931, at the Arts Club in the Polonia Hotel building, an exhibition opened of 'Publications by Jakub Mortkowicz, the prematurely deceased promoter of literature and art in Poland', organised by the president of the club, Władysław Skoczylas.

The Board of the Union of Polish Booksellers announced a nationwide 'Jakub Mortkowicz Publications Week'. Posters were sent to all the bookselling firms with his photograph and the following appeal: *Our public commemoration of the great publisher will also be an appreciation of valuable books and their role in the national culture. If the history of bookselling is to assign Jakub Mortkowicz the place due to him among its most worthy representatives, his contemporaries must pay homage to his very real contribution. This duty to the memory of Jakub Mortkowicz is the duty of the Polish bookselling world.*

Bookshops in Warsaw and the provinces were invited to take part in a competition for the most beautiful shop display dedicated to Mortkowicz's memory. First prize was won by Arct's bookshop on Nowy Świat Street in central Warsaw. There were silver leaves against a black mourning background, and on either side of the photo-poster lamps draped in crepe were burning. *There were a lot of bookshops on Nowy Świat Street [...]. As you walked along the noisy street, at almost every step you came across a window with beautifully arranged, multi-coloured books and a sad, pensive face – 'the artist's publisher', as the poster called him – looming out of a black background*, wrote my mother.

A few lines further on she recalls her visit to Arct's bookshop, eight years later, in October 1939 when Warsaw had been bombarded by the Germans: *I ran there to see Mr Stanislaw Arct, to tell him that to protect them from the Nazis Mrs Żeromska had taken over our bookshop and publishing firm, that Mr Henryk Nikodemski was still the manager, but we were moving into the shadows, probably going away to the provinces.*

When I entered the shop, Mr Arct was just sweeping the floor, which was covered in rubble. As soon as he saw me he set aside his great broom and asked me to sit down. He solemnly heard me out, and once he knew why I had come, he pressed my hand warmly and said: 'Please rest assured, Miss Hanka. Please be certain of one thing – no one in Polish bookselling will ever betray you.'

The exceptional, spontaneous tribute paid to my grandfather by artistic and bookselling circles was of course some comfort in their mourning, but it did not allay his family's despair. I do not wish to dwell on my grandmother's feelings. She was always proud of her self-control and inner strength. This catastrophe not only took away the person she loved most, but with his departure the whole of their previous life died too. She might not have survived her husband's death if not for her nearest relatives. Her three sisters, Flora Beylin, Gizella Bychowska and Róża Hilsum, who had come from Paris, watched over her day and night, preventing her from taking any drastic steps. The two family doctors, the neurologist Zygmunt Bychowski and the psychiatrist Gustaw Bychowski were also an enormous help. Their psychological support and medicines helped Janina to return to some sort of equilibrium.

Everyone around her was waiting patiently for her to recover her wits and take a decision on what should happen next. According to the legal regulations, his wife and daughter were Mortkowicz's sole heirs. They could forgo the inheritance, and its future fate would then be in the hands of the appropriate authorities. The firm would be declared bankrupt, its assets would be auctioned, and the major debts would be paid out of the resulting income. The rest of the liabilities would be frozen. The family would not be responsible for the debt, but could calmly watch as the publishing kingdom was wound up, say goodbye to their long-term employees, and then look for something else to do.

They could also accept the inheritance 'with reservations', in other words, take upon themselves the burden of the collapsing firm and all its obligations to the banks and private individuals, and try to save the sinking ship. This would allow them to keep a clean conscience towards those employees who could count on their claims being paid off, and those who would not lose their jobs; and above all they would save Mortkowicz's honour, because the old-fashioned commercial morality regarded bankruptcy as shameful.

Neither Janina nor Hania had a clue about financial matters. Bookkeeping, commercial records, balance sheets, settlement of accounts, assets and liabilities – it was all black magic to them. The boss had always taken care of those things. Now they spent hours sitting with the company's accountant and lawyer, reviewing the registers of debtors and creditors, renewed bills of exchange, reminders from banks withdrawing lines of credit, and letters reprimanding, urging and threatening. It was clear that Janina Mortkowicz would never be able to cope with it all on her own.

At the time her daughter felt caught in a trap by Fate, like in a Greek tragedy. By encouraging her mother to renounce the inheritance she would take away the meaning of her life and would be putting her father's work to death. By accepting the legacy along with her, she would be making a sacrifice of herself. She had never wanted to devote herself to the publishing profession. She was tempted by so many different paths. She dreamed of becoming independent. She had an eye on her own home and her own family, on her literary work being taken seriously. Now she would have to say goodbye to all her own dreams and devote herself to laborious, thankless rescue work, amid financial statements, constant cares and humiliating appeals for help. Finally she took the hardest decision in her life. She and her mother jointly accepted the inheritance 'with reservations'.

A few days later the young artist paid her an official visit and informed her that he was breaking off their engagement. He politely and mercilessly explained that he had been counting on co-ownership of a prosperous publishing firm. In view of the new situation he was backing out. He was an artist, and must think of himself. He could not take on responsibility for a family in such difficult financial circumstances. He had imagined their future together differently, he said, and left. Afterwards, one of Hanka's cousins heard her weeping in despair. This breach of promise was never mentioned at home. My family was morbidly discreet.

Years followed spent patiently overcoming some dramatic difficulties. The two women would never have managed on their own without outside help. Their mainstay was a friend of the family, Jerzy Kuncewicz, the husband of the writer Maria Kuncewicz. He was a legal advisor and a very resourceful man. Thanks to him, they managed to establish an order of priorities for their affairs and gradually began to disentangle their complicated problems.

The creditors behaved extremely well. The ones who were friends, such as Anna Żeromska (the widow of Stefan Żeromski), showed goodwill by waiting patiently for the fees overdue to them. The authors hurried to help. Maria Dąbrowska had already had the first volume of her epic novel ready for a year, but did not want to publish it until she had finished the whole thing. She did not even know what she would call it. The news of Mortkowicz's death shocked her greatly. *I did not know how I could help Janina, I just wanted to hurry to her aid, so I grabbed the manuscript and ran to the bookshop on Mazowiecka Street. It turned out to be a help.*

The provisional title, *Nights and Days*, was received splendidly and that first volume, published immediately, was a huge success; the author soon finished the next ones.

Wacław Fajans, Chairman of the General Union Bank, performed some incredible financial manipulations, quite beyond my understanding, to enable them to pay off their bank debts on particularly favourable terms. When it appeared that despite their greatest efforts and renunciations the firm was still under threat of bankruptcy and could only avoid insolvency on condition that it be subject to court supervision, the supervisor appointed by the court, Juliusz Kloss, at once became their best advisor and friend.

He and Jerzy Kuncewicz kept the progress of the firm's commercial activities on an even keel, and thanks to them it gradually began to pick up again. The debts were paid off, and the bookshop and publishing firm continued to function. Of course they had to give up the expensive editions and lower the price of the books and albums already in print, but new titles also went on appearing. Not quite two and a half years after Mortkowicz's death their Christmas list included, among many other titles, a complete edition of the collected works of Leopold Staff in twenty volumes, two volumes of Maria Dąbrowska's *Nights and Days*, with a third under preparation, and two new collections of poetry: *The Gypsy Bible* by Julian Tuwim and *Fir-Tree Lullaby* by Jerzy Liebert. The crisis had been averted.

≈

How and where did my future mother meet my future father? A young geophysicist, with a junior post at Warsaw University's Geology Faculty, he was a friend of Tadeusz Przypkowski, an art historian and renowned eccentric who was desperately in love with Stefan Żeromski's daughter, Monika. So perhaps they met through Przypkowski? Tadeusz Olczak was very handsome, with dazzlingly blue eyes, a charming smile and a difficult character – or at least that is what was said about him within the family. They fell in love, but it was not a good relationship. They came from different social spheres, they had different temperaments and different needs. Pampered by her parents, she was cheerful and smiling, and sought affection and protection in him. He, severe, dry and principled, did not know how to show his feelings, maybe because he had grown up without his father, who had left the family early on. She longed for a partnership in marriage, like the one the

Mortkowiczes had created. He, an ambitious scientist, wanted a submissive wife who would take care of the home and not have any business of her own. He was highly talented and later achieved serious academic success, but perhaps he had an inferiority complex. He was irritated by Hanka's artistic friendships and a certain tone of exalted snobbery that prevailed in her home, whereas she could not bear his patent contempt for everything that she valued.

He was the first and only non-Jew to marry into the family. Did this have any significance? He himself had no anti-Semitic prejudices at all, but in the pre-war era mixed marriages of this kind did arouse antipathy. The wedding took place in 1933, at the Evangelical-Augsburg parish church in Warsaw. My mother was the first in the family to change her denomination, which did not provoke any particular reaction among her relatives. Apart from the pious Samuel Beylin, none of them was religious. They remained members of the Jewish faith out of a sense of independence. They refused to renounce it just to make their lives easier.

My father certainly made a terrible mistake by moving in with his wife on Okólnik Street. At once two very bossy natures collided – those of mother-in-law and son-in-law. My poor mother was already pregnant, felt ill and was in tears again, while they conducted a stubborn battle for leadership. In November 1934 when she came back from the clinic with me in swaddling clothes, Julian Tuwim sent her as a present a white lilac bush in an enormous flowerpot, with a note saying: *To poetry and geodesy in beautiful harmony.* For some reason this infuriated my father so much that he threw the lilac, pot and all, out of the fifth-floor window. Not long after he himself moved out. He managed to take part in my christening celebrations, but got irritated again. He regarded the choice of my godparents, Anna Żeromska and Leopold Staff, as flaunting one's literary connections.

The care he took to keep my birth certificate and other documents, photographs and volumes of my mother's poetry all his life is evidence that we did matter to him, but he never showed it. I do not know who thought up the idiotic theory that after the divorce he should not see me any more, 'to avoid complicating my life'. As a result I only got to know him during the war, because of one of the many dangers that threatened me. It was not the best time to come together. Our contact after the war was rare, formal and devoid of the slightest hint of intimacy. As I think about it now, I feel sorry for him and for myself. But most of all I feel sorry for my mother.

So my family home was a crippled home, deprived of any male element, and controlled by women, because our servant, dear Anielcia, and my nanny Halinka lived with us too, and later so did my tutor, the unappealing Miss Anna. My grandfather's unmarried sister, Aunt Edzia, who worked in the bookshop, also ate with us and spent all her spare time at our house; but despite the lack of a man's influence this small female statelet was superbly organised and functioned extremely efficiently. The two big personal tragedies – my grandfather's suicide and my mother's divorce – had left wounds in the heart, but did not disturb the order of life. They were rescued from despair and resignation by inner discipline and the sense of mission provided by the publishing firm.

At the same time the atmosphere at home was far from ascetic. Both my grandmother and my mother loved the joys and pleasures the world had to offer in a childishly avid, sensual way – beautiful objects, elegant dresses, fur coats, hats, fashion magazines, the theatre, exhibitions, restaurants, cafés, parties and pleasant company. They were both highly sensitive to the beauty of their surroundings, so our five rooms *en suite* – my grandmother used to stress this phrase (which I found incomprehensible) with pride after the war – were composed like a work of art, with great care taken to ensure that the colours of the walls, furniture and pictures were in harmony.

Of course there were library shelves with books in beautiful bindings everywhere. There was ash-wood Biedermeier furniture against the green dining-room walls and a colourful frieze below the ceiling, made up of portraits of the Piast kings by Zofia Stryeńska. 'It makes my stomach churn whenever those twenty fellows stare daggers at me,' the old servant Marcinowa, whom I never knew, used to complain. A wine-red colour in the drawing room harmonised with the shining mahogany furniture. Leon Kaufman's portrait of my grandmother in her red cloak shone with Secession-style charm. On the walls hung pictures by Eugeniusz Zak, Bolesław Cybis and Leopold Gottlieb, and also my likeness, painted by Eliasz Kanarek, a friend of the family.

On the tables, chests of drawers and bureaux stood the Secession-style objects my grandmother so adored: patterned vases full of fresh flowers, intricate little baskets made of silver, plates and platters made of Meissen porcelain. My grandmother was thrilled if anyone expressed their appreciation of her taste. One day she invited Zofia Stryjeńska to dinner, who before the war was extremely popular as a painter of folklore pictures that appeared in albums published by Mortkowicz, and who was famous for her eccentricity. Before dinner my grandmother showed Mrs Stryjeńska around the house, boasting about her latest artistic acquisitions and showing her, as a connoisseur, the company trademarks and stamps on all her valuable objects. Then everyone sat down to a carefully laid table. When the tomato soup had been ladled out of its tureen, the artist lifted her full plate and turned it upside down. Amid the general consternation she politely explained: 'I just wanted to check what make it is.'

Our home – that mythical land of first delights, thrills, fears and primary experiences – evidently disappeared from my life too early, because I have retained no memory of it. I do not remember my nursery or my toys, or what the other rooms looked like. Everything I know, I learned from stories. I cannot recall anything that happened at home, neither the ordinary things nor the extraordinary. Janusz Korczak was my doctor – apparently I did not like him very much. Julian Tuwim brought me a copy of his children's book *Trunkson the Elephant* with a dedication that rhymes in Polish, reading: *For darling Joasia from dearest Juleczek*. I do not think it made any special impression on me. Not a trace of the colours, flavours or smells of my childhood has remained in my memory.

Nor do I remember the bookshop. I must have been there lots of times, but however hard I strain my eyes I cannot see a little girl with a then fashionable quiff of hair on the top of her head, running about among the ash-wood shelves and looking at the illustrated albums. I can only imagine those visits. Both my grandmother and my mother had an immensely solemn attitude to everything to do with the publishing firm. They certainly tried to attract the little heiress to the throne, the sole inheritor of the firm and the tradition, to the beauty of her surroundings, and teach her to respect and love books.

That must be why the only things I can clearly remember from my pre-war childhood are some brightly coloured books full of wonderful illustrations, poems and fairy tales. First I was read to aloud, and later I learned how to spell out the phrases on my own. The books were big and heavy, so I used to spread them out on the fluffy carpet, waving my legs in the air as I floated away into magical lands – into the enchanted world of Peter Pan with

pictures by Arthur Rackham, into the mists and snows of Hans
Christian Andersen's tales, illustrated by Eduard Dulac's ethereal
drawings, into a more real world, where Marcelianek the
Handyman, *with his bundle full of everything, even one hundred
and forty tools*, took out his hammers, nails, saws and chisels and
repaired broken tables, chairs and even his own sandals; his crafts-
manship was depicted so precisely in Stefan Themerson's illustrations. I cried when the unfortunate Kasia died in Lucjan Rydel's
story *Kasia and the Prince*. I split my sides laughing when the fat
people drawn by Lewitt and Him ate greasy sausages in the
carriage pulled by Tuwim's *Locomotive*.

Somewhere up in heaven there is a glass-fronted cabinet with all
those books, read and lost so long ago, just waiting for me. I think I
owe them my peace of mind and psychological salvation during the
war years. The adventures of Doctor Dolittle, Nils Holgerson's
wanderings about Switzerland on the backs of wild geese, sad little
Nemecsek from *The Paul Street Boys* – that was the reality I took
notice of in those days. Everything else was like a nightmare to me.

I also remember my cousins well. In 1939 there were five of us
in Warsaw, the pampered and cosseted youngest generation of the
family – two-year-old Monika and seventeen-year-old Ryś
Bychowski, thirteen-year-old Paweł Beylin, eight-year-old Robert
Osnos and I, not quite five years old. Our grandmothers were sym-
biotically linked throughout their lives, and our mothers and
fathers were always together in childhood and continued to keep
in touch with each other as adults. Therefore we children were
very close to one another.

Nursed by an attentive nanny, Monika was still too little to play
with me, and Ryś, a high-school boy, was too grown up, but I had a
great friendship with Pawełek and Robert. I treated them like older
brothers, and they behaved most chivalrously to me and even let
themselves be ordered about. At least that was the impression I
had.

The Bychowskis' house was refined and run, as they used to say
in those days, 'to a high standard'. Perhaps Gustaw's position
demanded this, or maybe it was determined by his wife, Maryla,
who loved luxury and living in fashion. I used to compare their
way of life and ours with some envy. At our house there were only
two servants, while they had as many as five: apart from the maid,
there was a cook and a housemaid, Monika's nanny and a non-
resident *Fräulein* who taught Ryś and his stepsister Krysia

languages. On walks in Lazienki Park with my little cousin, her nanny used to dazzle my tutor with the prosperity of the Bychowski household, and drove me wild with her stories of how much the parents adored and pampered their little girl. Whenever I complained at home about some injustice or other, or was fussy about my food, I would hear Miss Anna's sarcastic comments: 'So move to the doctor's house, they'll dance to your tune there.'

In the spring of 1939 Ryś Bychowski took his matriculation exams at the Stefan Batory High School. He and Krzyś Baczyński studied loathsome mathematics in the same class, and fooled around after their exams. They danced a waltz together, with Krzyś, who was smaller, as the lady, the length of Myśliwiecka Street, and Ryś walked on his hands outside the National Museum. In the summer he dropped in at Skolimów, where Robert and I were spending our last holiday before the war. A photograph has survived, showing the three of us sitting on the wooden steps in front of the house.

Pawełek Beylin, a dark, curly-haired thirteen-year-old with brown eyes, had an incredible sense of humour and a love of playful hoaxes. I could never work out if he was telling the truth, or making fun of me and his audience. His talent for grasping the satirical side of reality and his love of surreal jokes always fascinated me. Now I wonder if he used jokes to help him cope with his fate, which was so complicated in his childhood. He must undoubtedly have suffered from having his grandparents and two aunts as substitutes for a mother and father. He must have encountered some malice from his schoolmates, who made cruel remarks about this unusual situation. The future philosopher and art-college professor, adored by several post-war generations of students, was already able to disarm everyone with his intelligence, charm and sense of humour.

In the *Gazeta Wyborcza* magazine dated 21 October 1999, Andrzej Seweryn, describing March 1968 (when active opposition to the communist regime first erupted in Poland), recalls how the 'red' rector of the Theatre School of the time urged the students to calm down, advising them: 'Don't lose your heads.' 'Then our much-loved philosophy lecturer, Professor Paweł Beylin, stood up. "Yes, yes," he said, "you mustn't lose your heads, but you mustn't lose face either."'

I spent most time with Robert. His parents, Marta and Józef Osnos, were very active professionally. Józef worked at an electrical engineering firm called Kaloryt, and Marta at a pharmaceuticals company called Magister Klawe. They did not have much time for their only son. The boy, quite lonely perhaps, was extremely fond of his grandmother, my grandmother's sister Gizella, who showed him great affection. She died in 1937 when he was six. Nowadays he says that was probably the last time he cried in his life.

But my memories of Robert are only connected with happy things, echoing with carefree, children's laughter that smacks of the sweet, nose-tickling coloured froth on a glass of fruit juice and soda. Our nannies sometimes used to buy us that sort of drink at Lazienki Park. We spent a great deal of time together. We used to run about the Lazienki avenues until we were out of breath. We used to go to summer resorts on the outskirts of Warsaw, and in photographs from that era we look like siblings – a couple of dark, pretty, laughing children.

Once we were taken to the circus. I was dazzled as I watched a miracle I found hard to comprehend. The circus arena began to fill up with real water, reaching almost to the floor of the box in the stalls where we were sitting. Then the lights went out, and a golden moon and stars appeared in a navy-blue sky. Onto the water sailed gondolas, illuminated with Chinese lanterns. Now I know that that pre-war, magical performance was at the Staniewski Brothers Circus, in an enormous amphitheatre-shaped building on Ordynacka Street, right by my home. The building was bombed flat on 13 September 1939.

In June 1999 Robert took me to the ballet of *A Midsummer Night's Dream* in New York. I gazed in wonder at the virtual reality of the Athenian Wood, conjured up by computers and lasers. The wonderfully nimble dancers moved about in it like airy spirits. And that was when I remembered that we had already sat like this beside each other in the darkness once before, immersed in a fairy-tale world; and although *The Venetian Night* in Warsaw was naïve and very old-fashioned in comparison with what I was now watching, I was suddenly overcome by a Proustian sense of happiness coming back to me from the faraway land of our common childhood.

❧

The 1939 catalogue for the Mortkowicz publishing house recommended the following new titles: poetry by Jan Kasprowicz, Leopold Staff, Kazimierz Wierzyński, Julian Tuwim, Bolesław

Leśmian and Maria Pawlikowska-Jasnorzewska; foreign literature including Cervantes's *Don Quixote*, *The Red Lily* by Anatole France, and *When the Mountain Fell* by C. F. Ramuz; and Polish literature including stories and articles by Maria Dąbrowska, and *Pillars of Fire* by Pola Gojawiczyńska. It also included *The Roman Empire* by Tadeusz Zieliński, three volumes of reproductions: *Italian Art*, *Italian Sculpture* and *Polish Dances* by Zofia Stryjeńska, and for children *The Stubborn Boy* by Janusz Korczak, *Doctor Dolittle's Caravan* and *Doctor Dolittle's Post Office* by Hugh Lofting, translated by my grandmother. Not bad. And I have not listed all the titles.

On the next page, after the list of new books, a facsimile of a letter from Józef Piłsudski was reprinted, and also a letter dated November 1937, in which the Commissariat of the Polish Section at the Paris World Exhibition announced that by resolution of the international jury the publishing firm had been awarded the Grand Prix for art books.

In August 1939 eight years had passed since Mortkowicz's death. My grandmother and my mother could be proud of themselves. They had risen to the task. I do not know if the division of roles was fair. My grandmother took on the spiritual side of the enterprise: the inspiration, ideas, conversations with authors, correspondence and representation. She did not learn bookkeeping or deal with commercial matters. All the donkey work landed on my mother: battling with financial problems, negotiating with creditors, supervising the printing work, and responsibility for the artistic standard of the publications, as well as for the continued existence of the firm and family survival.

The first of August 1939 was a fine, sunny day. My mother went out to the bank, where she paid in the final instalment of the firm's debt, and then to the Ziemiańska café for a coffee. Maybe even before that she bought herself a new hat. She deserved a reward. All the debts had been paid off. Thirty thousand zlotys lay set aside at the savings bank for the autumn season. For the first time since her father's death she felt free. She was only just thirty-six, with a failed marriage behind her, and a future before her in which, as she deluded herself, she would finally be able to think about her own life. A month later the war broke out.

JANEK

―――――――✳―――――――

In 1929 Janek Horwitz was thirteen years old and was in the fifth class at secondary school in Warsaw. His mother was working as a school psychiatric doctor. She and her son were living at 6 Za Żelazną Bramą ('Behind the Iron Gate') Square.

Until recently Kamilla Horwitz, alias 'Comrade Julia', had still been an active member of the Polish Communist Party, editing the periodical *Robotnica* ('Worker Woman'), attending international conferences and congresses and running the women's section of the Party's Central Committee; but now she no longer performed any significant duties.

In 1926 the Party definitively split into two factions. Adolf Warski, Maria Koszutska – alias 'Wera' – and Maksymilian Horwitz-Walecki, the so-called 'majority' who were demanding some independence from the Kremlin, as a result of Stalinist manipulations were branded 'the right-wing deviation', removed from the Party leadership and deprived of influence. Power was assumed by the 'minority' – the extreme left wing, who were blindly subordinate to Stalin.

That was why Kamilla, who held 'majority' views, was dismissed from her post as head of the women's section and debarred from the more responsible tasks.

Chance, as we all know, can completely change people's fortunes. On 22 November 1929 she was on her way home from work. As she was nearing the house, she heard a man's footsteps running behind her. She turned around and saw a Party colleague, clearly fleeing from someone. 'Hide this! Perhaps you'll escape,' he whispered when he reached her, thrust a roll of papers into her hand and disappeared into the nearest gateway. She instinctively threw it into her handbag, quickened her pace and rushed home. Seeing how upset she was, Janek immediately understood that something had happened. In a flash he raised the lid of the desk at which he was doing his homework, and she threw in the handbag; but there was already a plain-clothes policeman standing in the room. He had been following the man who was running away, had seen what happened in the street, and come after Kamilla. Now he calmly took her handbag out of its hiding place and pulled out the bundle of banned propaganda material. It was so damning that he took her to the police station straight away.

She was placed under investigative arrest at the women's prison known as 'Serbia'. The situation did not look good. The penal code from the pre-independence era was still in force in Poland, and so in each of the former partitions different sentences applied to the same offences. The severest were stipulated by the tsarist code, and thus it was that in Warsaw a person would receive five years in prison for something for which in Kraków he would be acquitted. Kamilla was accused under Article 102, which concerned 'subversive activity'. She was in danger of receiving a six- to ten-year sentence. Her defence was undertaken by her nephew, Gustaw Beylin. He was a good lawyer, and as a rule, whenever one of the family ended up in hot water, the relatives rushed to his or her aid.

The investigating magistrate, Jan Demant, had superb knowledge of current relations within the Polish Communist Party. He knew that 'Comrade Julia' had been side-tracked by the leadership and no longer played an important political role in Poland. So he agreed to Gustaw's suggestion, in view of her state of health, to release her from custody on bail until the time of the trial. The prison doctor, suitably prepared, had no trouble in diagnosing the fifty-year-old arrestee with complaints that justified her release. Now they had to obtain the money for bail, which came to 3000 zlotys. It was a large sum, far exceeding the financial limitations of Kamilla, who earned 250 zlotys a month. So she decided to sell her flat, but even with the money from the sale she could not afford the bail. At that point her sisters and their husbands jointly contributed to making up the required amount.

On 21 January 1930 she was released from preventive arrest. Now discussions began on whether she should stay in Warsaw and wait for the hearing, risking at least a six-year sentence, maybe more, or whether she should escape abroad; and if she were to escape, where to? She did not decide on Switzerland, where she had completed her studies and worked for many years. Instead, she preferred to go to the Soviet Union, as she reckoned it would be easier to find a job there. Her choice must also have been influenced by her ideological commitment and her emotional ties to her brother, Maks Horwitz-Walecki, who had been living in Moscow for a few years now, working on the Executive Committee of Comintern.

Emigrating to the USSR was no simple matter. First Kamilla had to gain permission to depart from her Party superiors in Poland. It was they who arranged immigration papers with the relevant organs in the Soviet Union; but the factional fighting and mutual animosities were so strong that the minority powers were in no hurry to help a majority member, although they knew that if she did not leave Poland she would be sentenced to long-term imprisonment. She became quite embittered as she had to wait three months for a decision. In the end, maybe thanks to pressure from her brother, she obtained the crucial permission and a promise that her travel documents would be waiting for her in Berlin, where the Party leadership was based, and that the comrades there would organise her journey from Germany to Leningrad, on condition that she made her own way across to Berlin.

That was not easy either. She was due for trial, so she could not cross the Polish border legally. The passport inspection on the trains was very strict. So she hit upon the idea of flying by plane to Danzig, which as a 'free city' did not belong to the territory of Poland. Aeroplanes were a comparatively new and still risky form of transport. People rarely flew in them and travellers' documents were rather superficially checked at the airports.

In March 1930 she flew across the border without any hindrance. From Danzig she sailed by ship to the then German port of Stettin (nowadays Szczecin in Poland). After that she took the train to Berlin, and there she waited for the promised documents for herself and her son.

She was most anxious that Janek should not interrupt his education because of their departure, so he stayed on in Warsaw until the end of the school year. First he moved to his aunt Flora Beylin's, who lived in the same building. Flora kept a tight rein on the entire family and at once decided to bring her nephew into line. With Kamilla, the boy was used to a partnership arrangement based on mutual respect and trust. So when his aunt began to impose too much control on him, he wrote to his mother about it. One day, when he came home from school, he found a letter from her on the chest of drawers. It gave a reassuring answer, but had clearly been opened and read. The entire Beylin family was already waiting for him in the drawing room. They glared at him reproachfully and demanded an explanation. Deeply hurt by their indiscretion, he objected to them opening his letters. His aunt in her turn accused him of ingratitude and disloyalty. It ended in him packing up his belongings and moving to 'Aunt Janina's' – to my grandmother's house.

My grandfather, Jakub Mortkowicz, was still alive then. My mother was twenty-seven and not yet married. The little guest became very important to the three-person family; it seems he satisfied some unfulfilled dreams of having a son and a brother. In my childhood I was fed endless stories about Janek, in which he featured as a sensitive, intelligent and headstrong boy. Somehow he managed to get on well with my grandmother. She was more liberal than her sister Flora and offered him far more attractions, from albums full of reproductions and volumes of poetry to long walks in the woods. There were clashes here too, but fortunately they were trivial. Perhaps he felt more sympathy from 'Uncle Kuba', 'Aunt Janina' and 'Hanka'. The then fourteen-year-old, now a serious, grey-haired professor at Warsaw University, still uses those childhood nicknames when he talks about my relatives. I was not yet born when he left Poland. I only got to know him in 1945, when he came back from Russia. Nowadays he is my only source of information about times I cannot remember.

The Mortkowicz family's life, everything they did and talked about revolved around literature and art. My grandparents treated their work like an extremely sacred vocation and took it deadly seriously, without any distance, which Janek sometimes found annoying. Boasting of their achievements for culture and childishly showing off about their friendships with famous writers were rather snobbish characteristics. Yet nowadays Janek remembers his almost year-long stay in their home as a time of exciting cultural experiences that sank into his mind for ever and helped him through tough times in the years that followed. He does not like to exaggerate or gush, so he would be sure to ask me not to use any over-literary expressions, but just to record literally what he says: 'What I read of Tuwim's and Wierzyński's poetry at your house in those days, and what I saw of the reproductions in the bookshop, those Turners, Monets, Pankiewiczes and Zaks – that's mine.'

Two of the stories told about him used to raise my spirits whenever I heard complaints that there was never such a difficult child in the family as I was. A passionate devourer of books, he had a constant battle with 'Aunt Janina', who claimed that he read too much, and used to turn out the light in his room every evening. As soon as she left he would turn it on again, so she started unscrewing the bulb from the lamp, but then he bought himself a torch and used it to read under the eiderdown. She confiscated the torch, so then he stood at the window with his book and read by the light of the street lamp. Apparently that is how he ruined his eyesight.

The other incident happened earlier, when he was about eight years old and went with my relatives to visit Mr and Mrs Żeromski. He was to meet a great writer, so I can imagine how many times he was reminded in advance that he must try very hard not to bring shame on the family. He wore a spotless white shirt and well-polished shoes, and his hair was smoothed down at the last moment by Hanka – that is, my mother. He cut a dash when he was introduced to Mr Żeromski and his wife. When asked what he wanted to be in the future, he boldly replied that he would be a writer, and that he planned to write serious books, 'not just for servants'. Where such scorn for the lower orders came from in a boy from a communist home, no one could tell. Then the adults sat down to tea, while the children, in other words Janek, the lovely little Monika Żeromska and her friend Marysia Skoczylas, were sent out into the garden, where they were supposed to play together. After a while a piercing shriek was heard from Monika, who ran onto the terrace a moment later sobbing: 'He's smashed my rib cage! He's smashed my rib cage!' Mr Żeromski, who adored his daughter, was horrified. He caught her up in his arms and began to kiss and comfort her, and asked her what had happened, but she was unable to stammer out a single word. The atmosphere became rather unpleasant. Aunt Janina tried to relieve the tension, while Hanka ran off to look for Janek in the garden. He was sitting in a fury under a tree. 'I tried as hard as I could,' he muttered, 'but those idiots wouldn't take any notice of me and just talked to each other. I wanted to show them how strong I am. I pushed one of them over and kneeled on her. How was I to know she'd start squealing like a stuck pig?' They came home from that visit in a dismal mood.

In June 1930 Janek received his certificate for completion of the fifth class at secondary school. His mother thought this document very important. On the strength of it, as she reckoned, he would be able to continue his education in Moscow. So he treated the certificate with great reverence, placed it in a separate folder and made sure it would not get damaged during his long journey. His whole future was to depend on it.

His Warsaw relatives escorted him to the station. No one in their worst nightmares could have foreseen what the future would bring for the family members who left for the east and for those who stayed behind. It is astonishing that both the former and the latter came out of the oppression of two totalitarian states alive. Did they owe their lives to good fortune? Or accident? Above all they owed it to people's help and kindness. Because People – with a capital 'P' – are to be found everywhere.

A few sentences from my mother's account of this farewell scene have stuck in my mind with striking clarity. Before he got into the train Janek asked her anxiously: 'Hanka! Is my tie knotted properly?' And she adjusted his tie for him with sisterly affection. Once he was in the compartment, as the train was moving off, he called to her through the open window: 'Remember to send me *Wiadomości Literackie* every week. And every new book by Tuwim. And Wierzyński. Promise! Don't forget.' And she ran after the train shouting: 'I promise! I won't forget!' It soon turned out that parcels from bourgeois Poland could only do him harm.

The Party comrades in Berlin had delayed providing the Soviet documents, so Janek and his mother went on holiday to a boarding house. It was almost as if the capitalist world was still trying to seduce them, warn them and stop them from going. Finally they received the crucial papers, which were handed over by Alfred Lampe, a well-known communist activist, who during the war co-founded the Kościuszko Army (Soviet-controlled Polish detachments) in the Soviet Union. His wife, the lovely Krysia Jurkowska, was tortured in 1937 at Moscow's notorious Butyrki prison. Lampe only escaped death during the Stalinist purges because he was in a Polish prison at the time. Weren't the signs fairly unambiguous? Couldn't they have foreseen what would happen? Janek says that in those days, in 1930, it was impossible to tell, or at any rate, not when viewed from a distant, foreign perspective.

From Berlin they travelled by train to Stettin, and from there they sailed on a Soviet ship to Leningrad, then reached Moscow by train. It was a blazing hot day in June 1930 when they alighted at the station in Moscow. They still had the rich and colourful streets of Berlin in mind, so they were all the more struck by the greyness and poverty of Moscow. It was the first time Janek had ever seen endless queues of people in front of the shops. He could not understand why the customers were standing meekly outside instead of going in and buying whatever they needed. He only understood when he saw how empty the shops were.

They reached the Hotel Lux, where his aunt and uncle lived, Maks and Stefania Horwitz (now Henryk Walecki and Stefania Bielska). Before the revolution the Lux was one of the best hotels in Moscow. Later, when it became the headquarters of the top Comintern officials, it lost much of its former splendour. Maks and Stefa's rooms were not big. In one of them, his uncle's room, a camp bed had been set up for Janek, and in the other, her sister-in-law's, Kamilla was given an equally improvised bed. Sometimes guests came to visit Maks and Stefa. More camp beds were set up for them, with not much space to squeeze one's way between them. Maks's room was full of books and periodicals that did not fit on the shelves, so he kept them in the bathtub, which was never used because the bathroom had no hot-water supply. They washed in a communal bathroom shared by everyone on the entire floor. During his first stay there the fourteen-year-old Janek was rather disconcerted because there were no separate areas for men and women in the bathroom. Later on he became used to the sight of naked people of both sexes bathing together. His biggest shock was the incredibly large number of bedbugs, which they could not cope with at all.

Life in the Lux was very modest. The Comintern members received a monthly salary of 300 roubles, the so-called 'Party maximum'. It was an established rule that not even the most high-up Party functionary could earn more than a qualified industrial worker. This amount was barely enough to live on, especially as industrial workers were only entitled to the lowest category of food-ration card. That was also when Janek saw ration cards for the first time in his life – the monthly allowances of bread, buckwheat, fats and meat were not large. The meat-ration cards were handed in at the Lux canteen, where they ate rather miserable dinners.

Maks was already in a difficult situation by then. Stalin had not forgotten that Walecki had dared to speak against him in the past, and he never forgave his opponents. The stronger Stalin's authority grew, the worse Maks was rated within the Party apparatus, and the lesser the role he played in the public forum, the more unbearable and despotic he became within the family circle. Kamilla's attitude to her brother was somewhat ambivalent. She respected his knowledge and authority, and was extremely fond of him, but with time they differed in their views more and more frequently. She resented his political disloyalties, and also the disorder in his personal life.

For he was leading a double life. Although he had been living with his wife Stefania for twenty-six years, in Moscow he had taken up with a girl almost a quarter of a century younger than himself. Józefina Swarowska, known as Josza, was an Austrian, the daughter of a famous Viennese prima ballerina. She was brought up in Vienna, in a wealthy home and a refined atmosphere. Her brother gained a higher education in music and became a well-known violinist, leader of the Vienna Philharmonic Orchestra, but she had other ambitions. Very early on in life she became involved in communist activities; she met Maks at an international congress, and they fell in love.

She followed him to Moscow, and in 1932 she bore him a son, who was named Piotr after his father's tsarist-era pseudonym. Maks helped Josza to find work at the Comintern Secretariat, and put her up in a nice, two-room flat on Gorky Street, but he never had the courage to legalise the relationship. He went on living with his wife, who eventually found out all about it and demanded a divorce, mainly for the sake of little Petya.* But Maks refused to give his consent. His grown-up children, Kasia and Staś, bore immense grudges against him. In their view he was making himself and his relatives miserable. The down-to-earth Kamilla shared the view that her brother was acting dishonestly, and she did not hide her disapproval; but Maks refused, or was unable to take criticism.

Once in the Soviet Union, Kamilla and Janek changed their names. He was now called Jan Kancewicz, like his father, and she was Leonia Kancewicz. Not long after arriving they encountered their first disappointment. It turned out that 'Comrade Leonia', a medical doctor with twenty-five years' practical experience, could not count on either a job or a flat in Moscow. Belonging to the

---

* Translator's note: The Russian diminutive for Piotr.

Polish Communist Party's opposition faction was very harmful in the USSR. Being related to the not-too-well-regarded Walecki did not help either. In any case, Kamilla did not want to solicit anyone's patronage.

Only after two months of fruitless effort did she finally find a job, in the village of Troitskoye, seventy kilometres from Moscow, and fifteen kilometres from the railway station, where a former army barracks now housed a hospital for the incurably insane. They only needed nursing care, because the specialists could no longer give them much help. For an ambitious psychiatrist this sort of institution was a form of exile. Brilliant experts, superbly educated at European universities, were often sent to such places simply because they were politically 'unreliable'. In this godforsaken backwater Janek had to hide away his Warsaw secondary-school certificate in a drawer. There was nothing there but a primitive village school, so he began his education all over again. He soon learned Russian, and the teachers and his classmates were very kind to him. He was never aware of the slightest antipathy towards him for being a foreigner; but the short trousers he wore in summer, out of Polish habit, made his new friends laugh a lot. The village boys, who wore out their fathers' and brothers' old clothes, had never seen such an oddity, so he asked his mother to buy him some long denim trousers as soon as possible.

Meanwhile Kamilla was starting a new chapter in her life. None of the medical personnel belonged to the Party, so authority at the hospital was held by a five-person Party 'cell' consisting of manual workers – 'true proletarians', whose main occupation in any case was drinking, and who did not care about hospital matters. A former cavalryman from Budyonny's army (victorious in the Russian Civil War but beaten by the Poles in 1920) held sway among them. He regarded all the white-collar employees as a 'harmful element' and as counter-revolutionaries; when he was drunk he used to threaten to deal with them right away. So the doctors were very pleased that Kamilla, who was appointed assistant head, belonged to the Party. Finally at meetings of the omnipotent cell someone would be able to bring up the problems that troubled all of them. They complained of low pay, the worst category of ration cards for the nurses, and a lack of medicines and basic sanitary equipment.

At the next Party meeting Kamilla presented the staff's grievances and suggested sending a delegation to the relevant ministry in Moscow to report on the institution's difficulties and ask for help. The next day a report was sent to the regional Party committee stating that Comrade Kancewicz was openly inciting the hospital staff to rebellion. At once the regional committee excluded her from the Party. She would have been thrown out of the hospital, but Maks rescued her from her predicament by explaining that she had come from capitalist Poland and was simply defending the hired workers. However, there was no more talk of any attempts at reform.

In 1931 Kamilla got a job that was less far away, only forty kilometres from Moscow and only three kilometres from the railway station, at a sanatorium for the mentally ill in Golitsyn. As he packed, once again Janek carefully put his school certificate into his folder for the most important documents. And once again it proved useless. Under the terms of the latest educational reform the secondary schools and lycées had been abolished in the USSR, and the intermediary link between schools and institutes of higher education was professional schools that were supposed to prepare one for work in industry, and to 'boil' the future white-collar workers 'in the factory boiler', as they put it in those days. So, in order to study history later on, he went to the professional school attached to the famous Amo car factory, later known as ZIS, then ZIL, and spent two years there learning to be a metal turner.

He lived with his mother in Golitsyn and travelled from there to school in Moscow every day. It took him half an hour to reach the station on foot, an hour and a half to travel by train, and then fifty minutes by tram – almost three hours in total – and afterwards it took three more hours to get home. Sometimes, when Maks was away for any length of time, he stayed overnight at the Lux. The school was organised in such a way that for one week they had practical lessons in the factory, and the next week theoretical lectures on mathematics, physics, chemistry and Marxism–Leninism. He gradually forgot that once upon a time he had studied Latin and modern languages. Many of the thousand or more pupils were from intelligentsia families and belonged to the Moscow elite. Just like him, they wanted to study, so they had to go through this school, which at least was of a high standard. Supported by the regime, the prestigious factory employed excellent teachers, often with university degrees, who were lured there by high salaries and good supplies of food, which in an era of universal scarcity was crucial.

On the first day of his studies Janek and a group of his new classmates went into the professional school's huge hall. They were told to stand at the workbenches, fix a piece of iron in a vice, take a metal chisel in one hand and a hammer in the other, and keep hitting the iron with the chisel until it reached the required shape. At the same time two nurses entered the hall and laid out their kit: cotton wool, iodine, plasters and bandages. Once he had hit his own hand with all his might instead of the bit of iron a couple of times, he guessed what they were there for. They dressed his bleeding wound, and when he went up to the foreman with his bandaged hand to ask to be exempted, he was told to return to his workbench. So he did. Next came further stages in the training: the forge, the furnace, red-hot iron that had to be moulded with a hammer, and some painful burns. Here too the nurses were very helpful. Later on came the turning and grinding workshops, where tooling the polished parts required precision to one hundredth of a millimetre.

He was then fifteen years old, and had to work in three shifts. During the nights he had to press his fingernails into his neck to avoid falling asleep at the workbench. Fortunately, the worker women at the factory were very kind to him. The foremen were also decent people. Only one of them teased him – a bad worker, but a Party activist; and it was this man to whom he most wanted to prove that although he was an 'intellectual weed' he could manage.

Once again a tie features in this story. As a boy Janek must have cared about his appearance, if on leaving Warsaw he had asked my mother to check if his tie was knotted properly. On his arrival in Moscow, his Uncle Maks donated his wardrobe to him. Maks lived very modestly, but he bought his clothes abroad, because he often travelled to the West on political missions, and as he did so incognito, posing as a tradesman or a banker, he had to be suitably dressed. In shabby, Soviet clothing he would have been unmasked immediately. So Janek was given his elegant European suits, waistcoats and ties as hand-me-downs. One day he confided to a schoolmate that he wanted to join the commune organised by the Komsomol (the Communist Youth League). Its members were supposed to live together, pool the money they earned in a common kitty, prepare meals, study and play together. His friend warned him: 'Don't take offence, but the lads won't let you join.' 'Why not?' 'Because you're a "pigeon".' In the slang of those days that meant a fop or a dandy. In the Soviet Union a strict proletarian style was de rigueur. Party activists, following Stalin's example, wore army greatcoats and jackets or black Russian shirts – so-called *kosovorotki* – that fastened below the neck. In his waist-coats and ties that came from the 'putrid West', Janek was a suspicious 'bourgeois'. So he stopped caring about his clothes, and only then was he accepted.

In 1933 he finished the metalworkers' school. He was then seventeen. He was still thinking of studying history, so he enrolled for the so-called Rabfak ('Workers' Faculty'), a preparatory course for workers who planned to study. It was not entirely easy; to get a place on the course you had to have four years of factory experience behind you, but Janek had only just completed two years of profes-sional school. He was helped by Henryk Lauer, a mathematician who used to be a lecturer in Zurich and knew Kamilla from there. Lauer was a long-term communist connected with the majority group, and thus after 1929 he was frowned upon in Russia. Debarred from political matters, he worked on the Planning Committee, and although he no longer had much influence, in this sort of case he could still be effective. Four years later he was arrest-ed and, after a brutal interrogation, murdered – like all the leading activists in the Polish Communist Party.

Janek's colleagues on the course no longer included anyone from an intelligentsia background. The young people, from peasant and workers' families, came not just from the Moscow area but from the most far-flung parts of Russia and were very poorly prepared for further education. Some of them, like a trio of North Ossetians, for example, could hardly speak Russian, so they were taught the most elementary things: how to read and write, and correct pro-nunciation. They were supposed to be future representatives of the new intellectual elite of the Soviet Union.

Towards the end of 1933 Janek was thrown out of the Komsomol for the first time. In a conversation with a classmate he repeated a nasty comment made by Lenin about Stalin that he had heard somewhere. The classmate at once ran off to the Rabfak Komsomol authorities asking them to explain this blasphemy. A meeting was called, at which Janek was accused of disseminating counter-revolutionary views. It would not have taken much more for him to be expelled from the school. Luckily, somehow he managed to exonerate himself, and later on the Komsomol took him back again.

On 1 December 1934 Sergei Kirov, a member of the Politburo of the All-Union Communist Party (Bolshevik), regarded as Stalin's chief rival in the struggle for power, was assassinated. As rumour had it, Stalin had ordered him to be purged, but officially 'Trotskyite terrorists' were blamed for the killing. Among the initiated no one had any doubts that the murder of Kirov would be used as an excuse for settling accounts with the anti-Stalinist opposition; indeed, arrests began at once on the most absurd charges, and immediate death sentences were passed. A psychosis of fear gripped the entire country.

In 1934 Janek finished the Rabfak, took competitive exams to enter university and finally started to study his long-desired history. Meanwhile, History itself was busy making life more and more of a misery. 'Traitors to the nation' were being branded at public rallies, and at the university the more zealous students were attacking the professors, reproaching them with all sorts of political sins; the accused were contritely confessing and being self-critical, and everywhere people to blame were being sought and found without much difficulty. But young people have greater psychological resilience, so Janek kept trying to lead a normal life. He went on studying and going to the cinema and theatre, on dates and walks, to museums and 'university of culture' classes, where lectures were given on the history of literature and art. He had a lot of spare time in the evenings, because for the first few years of his studies he was homeless, and would try to arrive wherever he was staying the night as late as possible, to avoid disturbing the residents more than necessary.

By then Kamilla had moved from Golitsyn to Moscow, where she was employed at the Institute of Neuropsychiatry. But the idea of obtaining a flat was beyond her wildest dreams. The Institute had its own outpatients' clinic, consisting of two rooms, a waiting room and a doctor's office. She lived in the office, and because there were two couches there, meant for the patients, Janek sometimes slept on one of them. He simply had to leave before the patients arrived.

He often stayed the night at Maks's place, because his uncle was away a lot. At other times Maks's daughter Kasia took him in. She was now the wife of a respected engineer called Viktor Taner, whom Dzierżyński had brought in from Switzerland to set up the Soviet power industry. They were very well off, because in their communal flat, known as a *komunalka*, they had two whole rooms, and even a servant. For some time he lived at Mania

Beylin's. She had brought her little son from Warsaw and was earning quite a good living at the TASS agency, so she could afford to rent two rooms in a *komunalka*. Sometimes he spent the night with some friends who did not have an inch of spare space in their crowded rooms, so he used to spread a mattress under the table and disappear in the morning before his hosts got up.

He was happy when he was assigned a place in a student hostel, i.e. a bed in a room where thirty other students slept too. Finally he could gather up all his things – papers, letters, documents, some pieces of clothing, and at least a dozen cardboard boxes full of books that he kept maniacally buying and had stored at his friends' and relatives' places. There was no room for the books in the dormitory, so he kept them in the hostel storeroom.

The year 1936 marked an intensification of the Great Terror. There were mass repressions and show trials. Among the Polish communists more and more of the apparently most faithful comrades were being arrested, and terrified people held endless dramatic discussions that could be summed up in one word: 'Why?' Some believed in the treachery of those arrested, others questioned it; while people consoled each other that it was a mistake that would be sorted out immediately, at the same time mutual mistrust and suspicions grew. 'There's no smoke without a fire,' they kept repeating; 'there are evidently some reasons.' 'The Party knows what it is doing' – and so on.

At this point Janek was thrown out of the Komsomol for the second time. In a private conversation he had dared to criticise one of the trials and the general tone of the press for brutally attacking the defendants. As the witnesses later attested, he had claimed that the press was lying, and cast doubt on the reliability of the statements it had published. On top of that he had stood up for the daughter of a faculty dean who had been imprisoned. The girl had been refused admission to study at the university because her father had proved to be an 'enemy of the people' by daring to say that he did not recognise collective responsibility. Someone had immediately informed on him. In the prevalent atmosphere of fear and suspicion the matter might have ended in disaster. Somehow this time too Janek came out of it intact. The decision to exclude him was changed into a reprimand and a warning, with his young age as justification for commuting the sentence. He was nineteen at the time.

ঙ

The Hotel Lux was gradually being depopulated. At night cars would drive into the courtyard. In their rooms people listened intently to hear which way the NKVD* men's footsteps were heading. Sometimes a scream rang out, sometimes a woman or a child was heard crying; and then came footsteps on the stairs again, as the arrestees were brutally hustled away.

Mania Beylin was no longer working at the TASS agency, but at the editorial office of a propaganda magazine, *Journal de Moscou*. Worried about the family, every day at dusk she ran to the hotel. Years later in Paris she told me that before entering the gate she used to look up at Maks and Stefa's windows. The light would be on, and a stone would fall from her heart. For the rest of her life she never forgot that ghastly sight: from day to day there were fewer and fewer lighted rectangles in the wall of the building.

On the evening of 21 June 1937 the light was on in the familiar windows; but the hotel seemed dead. There was no one on the stairs, and the corridors were silent and empty. Mania knocked at Stefa's door, entered and found her lying in bed. She was having some sort of heart trouble and was desperately sad. Soon after Maks came into her room, changed beyond recognition. Usually full of energy and life, he looked like an old man now. His face was sunken, his lips compressed and his eyes dead. He sat on his wife's bed and said nothing. Feeling at a loss in this atmosphere of hopelessness, but in an effort to help somehow, Mania went into the kitchen and made some tea. They gratefully accepted the glasses of hot tea, but could not swallow a drop of it. She tried to talk to them, but all her words died in mid-air. It was as if they were in another reality, another dimension, where she could not reach them. Time was passing, and midnight was approaching. She did not want to leave them alone, but finally Maks said, 'Go now. It's getting late!' and he hugged her goodbye.

Downstairs in the hall she saw an NKVD detachment coming through the hotel doors. 'Who will be the unlucky one tonight?' she thought. First thing next morning she called Maks. His son Staś picked up the phone. 'How's your mother feeling?' she asked. 'Don't come here,' he replied, and hung up.

* Translator's note: The People's Commissariat for Internal Affairs – the secret police.

'ENEMIES OF THE PEOPLE'

───────────✳───────────

They came for Maks on 22 June 1937 at about two in the morning. Stefa, who could not sleep, decided to look in on her husband. She could hear men's voices on the other side of his door. She tried to enter his room, but was not allowed inside. Instead she was brutally ordered back to her own room. According to the neighbours, Maks was taken away first, and then Stefa. Next a thorough search was conducted in both rooms. The books were thrown from the shelves, papers from the drawers and clothes from the wardrobes, as usual in such cases. Early next morning, worried that neither his mother nor his father was answering the phone, Staś ran to the hotel. When he saw what had happened, he tried to get some information about their fate, but no one was willing to tell him which prison they had been taken to, what sort of danger they were in, or what could be done for them. Neither influence nor personal connections were of any use. At that time people were disappearing without trace, as if they had never existed. As they were taking old Adolf Warski away, the NKVD men smashed his glasses, although he could not see without them. Next day his daughter ran to the Lubyanka with a spare pair, but she was refused admission; all she heard was: 'He won't be needing them now.'

In the memoirs she wrote many years later, Maks's niece Mania Beylin mentions that she found out from a reliable source in Paris why he had been in such despair that evening when she saw him for the last time. By then he had no doubt what was in store for him. He had already been 'thoroughly investigated' earlier by the Special Control Commission attached to the Comintern. His closest collaborators and friends had interrogated him, including leading Italian communist Palmiro Togliatti, the Finnish communist Otto Kuusinen and the then president of Comintern, the

Bulgarian Georgi Dimitrov – the man who in 1933 was accused of setting fire to the Reichstag. On that occasion he had had enough courage to denounce Nazi provocation to the court, but now he did not dare to contradict Stalin's orders and did not even attempt to defend his colleague. His faithful comrades of many years' standing presented Maks with the most absurd accusations: belonging to an 'anti-Soviet Trotskyite group', 'counter-revolutionary activity', 'spying for fascist Poland', and other European countries as well. For three days he tried to prove his innocence, but the sentence had already been passed a long time ago, and at a much higher level.

He was told that he had been dismissed from the Party and was ordered to hand back his Party membership card. For a dedicated communist losing this document meant annihilation, civil death and spiritual bankruptcy. He had lost faith in the meaning of his entire life, and he must have sensed that he would soon lose his life as well. After all, he could see what was happening all around him. While the Committee's verdict was being read out, his old friend Dimitrov, whom Maks had often rescued from all sorts of political troubles, turned his back on him and gazed out of the window.

Mania Beylin's memoirs include another upsetting scene, which took place after Maks's arrest. When on the morning of 22 June she called the Hotel Lux and heard Staś's voice at the other end, she immediately understood what had happened. There was no way she could help. She had no influential acquaintances. Next day, she and her small son left for France, because it was impossible to defer her departure any longer. For a year now she had been in a desperate situation. *The Journal de Moscou*, the French-language magazine where she worked, had been closed down. The editor-in-chief, Sergei Lukianov, had been arrested. Since losing her job she had been giving maths lessons, but then the Soviet authorities had withdrawn her residency permit. She would have to leave the USSR as soon as possible, but she could not go to Poland, as the Polish embassy had taken away her Polish passport because she was a communist. Thanks to the fact that her son Pierre had been born in Paris she managed to obtain a French visa, drawn up on a scrap of paper because she had no travel document. All around her the situation was growing more and more dangerous. Leaving Russia was her final chance of salvation.

She did still manage to seek out her uncle's young girlfriend,

Josza, however. She was afraid someone uncaring or malevolent would pass on the tragic news, and preferred to do it herself. She wanted to leave her some money, because she could tell that the girl would be in a difficult situation. Unknown to the rest of the family, who refused to tolerate the relationship, she had been to see Josza before, and was very fond of her. She could see how much Maks loved her and how affectionate he was towards his little son, Petya. She knew he must be worrying about their fate.

Josza and Petya were now living in a Comintern dacha at Serebryany Bor in the Moscow suburbs. That evening Mania went there by suburban train and got out at the small station. There were dozens of identical summer-holiday cottages, with the same sort of curtains in all the windows and the same verandas in front, with little tables set out on them. On each table stood a samovar, around which the holidaymakers were gathered, eating their supper. The air smelled of pine forest. From a distance she could hear the sound of an accordion and someone singing. It was a peaceful idyll, an atmosphere out of Chekhov, as if the echoes of all the dramas being enacted so nearby did not reach this far; but the carefree mood was just superficial. When Mania tried to find out where the Communist International house was, at the sound of her foreign accent fear appeared on the faces of the people she asked, and they fell silent. No one knew a thing, and no one was willing to talk to her. She was foreign, and that made her suspicious – she could bring the all-pervading misfortune down on them. Finally, someone very bravely whispered, 'It's over there,' and showed her the way.

She opened the gate. She could see people's silhouettes in the illuminated windows of the villa. On the lawn there was a motionless white shape, like an elongated bundle. When she had gone a few steps forward, the shape began to move, and someone raised their head. It was Josza; she was lying on the grass, on a straw mattress. Beside her, wrapped in a blanket, little Petya was sleeping. She threw herself into Mania's arms, sobbing, 'It's impossible! It's not true! It's a terrible mistake!' She already knew what had happened. Mania tried to comfort her, saying, 'Of course it's a misunderstanding! He'll be back. He's sure to be back.' Then she asked in amazement, 'Why are you sleeping here on the damp grass and not in the house?'

It turned out that the Comintern authorities had acted very efficiently. They had instantly removed their former comrade's rights to a flat in the service dacha and had assigned it to the family of another top official who was still in favour. The new tenants had arrived that afternoon, brought the news of Maks's arrest and told Josza to get out at once. Trembling all over, she had not had the strength to organise the move and did not even have the money for a ticket to Moscow. So they had agreed that she could stay until morning, but outside, not in the house. She and her son had spent the whole evening on the lawn, and then she had covered him up and cuddled him until he fell asleep. 'The worst thing', she cried, 'was that they wouldn't let their children play with Petya. And he couldn't understand why.'

Mania had to go home. The only thing she could do was wish the broken-hearted woman courage and offer her the money she had brought. Then she left them both on the lawn. Next day she and Pierre departed for Paris, and Josza and Petya returned to Moscow.

Josza never saw Maks again. None of the family ever saw him again either. The Polish Communist Party leaders were not given big show trials, and their sentences were not announced publicly. Instead they were liquidated on the quiet. Their relatives deluded themselves for years with the idea that they were still alive. However, they could not make any proper efforts to find out the truth, because they themselves were in prisons and camps under long-term sentences. They belonged to a special group of victims that bore the official title 'members of families of traitors to the fatherland'. By some miracle Josza escaped repression, though fate still had some trials in store for her and Petya too. But that is another story.

Staś Bielski, Maks's son, was then thirty. For a year he had been working at Red Army General Staff in Moscow. When he found out about his father's arrest, he was in no doubt that his turn would not be long in coming. He was immediately dismissed from his post, transferred to the reserves and thrown out of the Party. He was already divorced from his wife Vera and was not in contact with her or with his then five-year-old daughter Halinka. He had nothing to do, nowhere to hide, and did not want to see his friends and relatives for fear of contaminating them, so he sat at home and waited – for five months.

Meanwhile, life had to continue. Kamilla was working at two jobs and by a miracle had managed to get a small sub-let room in a communal flat, so Janek, although still living at the hostel, finally had a substitute home. In the summer of 1937 his mother took a holiday at a rest home outside Moscow, while he went to the seaside, to Crimea. On the final day before going home he bought her a box of beautiful grapes as a present. He had two roubles left in his pocket for his train ticket and a loaf of bread. The journey took two days. Throughout the journey he fed himself on nothing but bread, grapes and water, so on the way he came down with some terrible stomach pains. He had just enough strength to lug the box of fruit to Kamilla's flat, where he left her a card saying that he had arrived and was going to the student hostel. There he went to see the doctor, who told him to go to bed. Without realising that his mother might misinterpret his words he sent her a telegraph saying, 'I'm ill. Come and have some grapes.' In the prevalent atmosphere of threat she read this message as if it were coded, informing her of some catastrophe. She rushed back to Moscow, stopping first at her flat, where the grapes and the card were waiting for her. Reassured, she ran to the hostel to find out about her son's health. They chatted, then said goodbye. It was almost eight years before they saw each other again.

Kamilla was arrested on 10 August 1937. When she got home, the NKVD men were waiting for her. They had already been there a few days earlier, in her absence, and had told the neighbours to let them know when she appeared, so the neighbours had informed on her, not out of ill will but out of terror. They were afraid that if they did not inform on her, someone would inform on them for not having done so. No one warned Janek, who was lying in the student sick bay, that they had taken his mother away. When he finally recovered and, surprised that she had not put in an appearance, went to her room, he found the door sealed. At the commissariat he asked to be let inside to fetch his things. He was allowed to enter with a police escort. He was hoping he would find a letter or a sign of life, but there was nothing. Nor were the grapes there any more. He was given all the books, two thousand of them, and some personal things. He deposited it all in the student hostel storeroom and began to wonder what to do next.

First he reported at the University and told them what had happened. The secretary of the Komsomol organisation immediately demanded that he return his membership card. Then he was called into the rector's office. Rather confused, the rector informed him that he would have to leave the history faculty. He could move to another one – natural science or physics and mathematics – but he should understand that the son of an 'enemy of the people' could not study a humanities subject. Trying to find the most bearable solution for himself, he chose geography. Later he was summoned to a session of the Komsomol Central Committee, which turned out to be an interrogation. They did not ask him about his own views, just about his relationship with his mother. He replied that she was his personal and political authority. At this point he was excluded from the Komsomol for the third time, this time for good and all – which, as he now supposes, ultimately saved him from a much worse fate than the one he endured.

A void soon developed around the relatives of the victims. People were afraid of contacts that might bring misfortune down on them as well. There were no institutions or individuals that could help, and it was hard to obtain any sort of information at all. In the end he found out in which prison Kamilla was awaiting trial. Although visits and correspondence were out of the question, he had the right to send her fifty roubles a month. The second payment was not accepted. That could have meant the worst, but news came from her very soon, from near Krasnoyarsk in Siberia.

On 10 September 1937 she was sentenced to ten years at a 'corrective labour camp'. One of the main accusations on her charge sheet was that she had known Józef Piłsudski personally. The final line of the sentence read: 'She fought against the Party line and Comintern.' She only escaped the death penalty because she had not been politically active in the USSR.

In November 1937 the NKVD men came for Staś Bielski. *He underwent the hell of the toughest interrogation in that notorious torture chamber, Lefortovo prison, from where he ended up at a camp with broken ribs, almost no teeth left and deaf in one ear,* wrote Witold Leder in an article published in 1988 in the Polish newspaper *Polityka*. Lefortovo was the military prison. Staś was accused of counter-revolutionary activity, 'Trotskyism', 'spying' and 'operating as an enemy agent on behalf of fascist Poland'. Thanks to his physical and mental resilience he survived the interrogation. He refused to confess or to sign anything. He was not sentenced to death, just ten years' hard labour in the mines of Vorkuta, from where few people came back alive.

Janek Kancewicz was taken from the student hostel not quite a year after his mother, on 30 April 1938 at four in the morning. Someone knocked at the door of his room and asked for him to go down to the doorkeeper's lodge with his identity card. Apparently there was something that needed an urgent explanation. As he had been woken up, he quickly put on the clothes he wore indoors and ran downstairs, and that was how they took him away, in summer trousers and a pair of boots that were too tight. He was not allowed to go upstairs to fetch his things. As a result, later on, in December, when he had to work in the forest in those boots, his toes were frostbitten.

The first prison he ended up in was the Lubyanka. First came the usual prison ritual: a personal search, removal of watches, shoelaces, belts, braces, notebooks and pencils. Then came the cell, which was crowded and stuffy. There was no contact with the outside world. A week later he and a group of more than a dozen people were taken to Butyrki in a prison van with the word 'Bread' painted on the side as camouflage. In the van one of his fellow prisoners, a former NKVD employee, and until recently head of the district secret-police office, told how he had been tortured to force him to make the right statements, and how he had tried unsuccessfully to commit suicide. Only then did Janek feel truly terrified.

In Butyrki, an old tsarist prison, about a hundred people were crammed into a cell designed for twenty. There was no room on the wooden bunks that ran from wall to wall, so some of them had to sleep on the stone floor. To fit in, they lay on their sides and turned over on command. The food was bearable, but they suffered from the terrible heat and the lack of air. Twice a day the prisoners were taken out to the latrine. Those for whom that was not enough could make use of the *parasha* – a barrel standing in a corner of the cell. For understandable reasons, anyone who used it was greatly resented by his cellmates, but this was often unavoidable. The *parasha* was to be the cause of a tragi-comical incident.

All the prisoners had sharp objects taken away from them, such as needles, pins and safety pins. Whenever they had to sew or darn something, at the cell foreman's request the guard would lend the man in need a needle and thread, which had to be returned afterwards. One time the needle disappeared. The guard announced that if it was not found, the whole cell would be deprived of their only chance of a bit of air and movement, i.e. their daily walk about the inner prison courtyard. Every inch of the cell was searched, and every scrap of clothing was inspected, but all in vain.

The prisoners came to the conclusion that the only place where the needle might be was in the *parasha*. Someone who had used it must have dropped that priceless treasure into it. There was nothing for it: the cell foreman ordained that they would have to carry the barrel to the communal lavatory, pour its contents out onto the floor and search until the lost item was found. Four people volunteered for this task, the strongest and least exhausted by their interrogation; Janek was one of them. For three hours they sifted through the excrement with their bare hands, until amazingly they did find the needle in the shit barrel – which gives the old proverb a new twist.

As a reward they received an extra visit to the bathhouse, and the undying gratitude of their cellmates, for whom they had rescued the privilege of a daily fifteen-minute walk.

Only a sense of community and solidarity saved people from breaking down. Most of the prisoners had already been interrogated and were awaiting sentence. Those who were summoned for interrogation came back physically and mentally battered, with their legs swollen from standing up for over a dozen hours, which was a special form of torture.

Fortunately, Janek was spared the worst – that is, a brutal interrogation. He reckons there were three contributing factors. Firstly, towards the end of 1938 the wave of repression was already on the wane and there were no more injunctions from on high to force confessions at any cost and apply the highest sentences. Secondly, he happened to encounter a fairly good-natured investigating magistrate, who did not have sadistic tendencies and, as it seemed, performed his duties in a routine way, without greater involvement. Thirdly, in a paradoxical way his repeated and finally definitive expulsion from the Komsomol was a good thing. He had already been categorised as a counter-revolutionary agitator, so there was no need to prove his guilt, and he was too unimportant to be implicated in some imaginary political affair.

However, this mild treatment might also have been sheer accident, an oversight, a caprice or a lucky coincidence. No one ever knew fully why his or her fortunes turned out as they did, and not differently. Sometimes a mistake in the evidence or in the name or date of birth saved people's lives. Sometimes someone survived because his papers got lost. Often the date of arrest had a decisive effect on the sentence, or it could be the investigator's tedium or zeal. The magistrate dealing with Janek was lazy. He called him for investigation a couple of times. The witnesses, his fellow students in the same year, confirmed his guilt. 'Did he hold counter-revolutionary conversations?' 'Yes, he did.' 'Did he conduct anti-Soviet propaganda?' 'Yes, he did.' And that was the end of it.

He spent almost six months in Butyrki, from the beginning of May until October 1938. One day in October he was told to come out of the cell with his things. He was given a document to read and sign, which informed him that he was charged under paragraph 58, point 10, for 'counter-revolutionary propaganda', and sentenced to five years at a 'corrective labour camp'.

Once sentenced, the prisoners were given forms to fill in, on which they wrote down their family addresses with a request to provide warm clothes. Those who had relatives were equipped with sheepskin coats and felt boots. Janek had no one to ask for help. In Moscow only Maks's daughter Kasia was still at liberty, but he did not want to remind the NKVD of her existence. So he set off on the journey in his ill-fitting summer boots.

They were taken away at night, under guard, to a suburban station. The prison carriages they were put in – eight people in one compartment – came from the era of tsarist Premier Stolypin, and seemed extremely decent in comparison with the goods wagons or cattle trucks used to transport prisoners during the war. In the same compartment as Janek there were people from very varied backgrounds: some students, a painter, a political activist, a prosecutor, and a poet who spent the whole journey reciting his verses. They talked about everything, except politics. Twice a day they were given salt fish and some water. They were very thirsty. They travelled for five days, without knowing where they were going.

They were let out of the carriages at the town of Solikamsk, in the northern Urals, on the River Kama. It was there that the headquarters of 'Forestry Camp Usollag 10' was based. All around the town, in the vast Ural forests, 'sub-camps' had been set up, known as *lagpunkty*. The prisoners spent a few months there, cutting down trees over a range of about a dozen kilometres. As soon as it took too much time to reach the work site, the camp authorities closed down the sub-camp and set up a new one, deeper into the forest.

Immediately after arriving in Solikamsk they set off on a long march, until that night they reached a huge barracks at the distribution point. Inside, three or four hundred people of both sexes were already encamped on three storeys of wooden bunks, mainly criminals and prostitutes. The criminals immediately attacked the better-dressed newcomers, tore off their fur coats and felt boots, took away their trunks and suitcases and threw them some torn rags in exchange.

The bunks on which the 'new' people were told to settle down were swarming with lice. The things that went on in the barracks were horrifying: brawls, mob law, rape and sex conducted publicly, with no restraint. The food rations, consisting of 400 grams of black bread and hot food twice a day, were not enough to satisfy one's hunger. Ten days later a 100-person group (known as an *etap*) was assembled and sent on further under a convoy of guards. It was the beginning of November and the temperature was already below freezing, and would stay there until the end of April. They walked from dawn to dusk, up to their knees in snow. Twice they spent the night in deserted wooden shacks in a temperature of minus ten degrees centigrade. Finally they reached their goal, a freezing cold barracks in a vast, desolate clearing. It was to be their home for the next half year.

They had to create their own living conditions from absolutely zero: fence off the area, build latrines, a kitchen and a bathhouse, bring in water and dig poles into the ground for the electricity supply, while at the same time working in the forest from dawn to dusk. They were divided into brigades, jointly responsible for a defined portion of the work, and then into smaller gangs tasked with cutting down individual trees. Two sawed, while the rest cut the branches off the felled tree. Most of them did not have a clue about this sort of work, and at the start they came close to killing one another. They did not know that a sawn tree loses its flexibility at minus fifteen degrees and can topple sooner. When it happened earlier than expected, a branch of the tree hit one of the gang members, a Polish cobbler, without actually crushing him. In a paradoxical way this accident saved the injured man's life. He was taken by sledge to the camp and given medical exemption, and when the authorities found out about his professional skill, which was invaluable because of a universal lack of footwear, he was told to open a cobbler's workshop at the camp. After that he sat in the warm and was given better food, and everyone envied him.

In the early days a large number of prisoners fell ill and died of hunger, cold and exhaustion. They could not work, which reduced the production of wood. The authorities became worried and organised medical clinics that were not subordinate to the camp management, but to the health service. Although they lacked basic medical resources, most of the staff were decent people and tried as best they could to help their patients.

Janek can thank his lucky stars for the fact that his toes were so quickly frostbitten and he ended up in the sick bay. A medical exemption, a few weeks' stay in a warm place and a slightly better food supply determined whether or not a person would at least partly regain the strength to go on living, or else change into a *dokhodyaga* – someone about to breathe their last. The doctor's assistant at the sick bay did not in fact have any suitable medicines and cauterised the frostbite with iodine, but he did save Janek's toes – and his life too, for sure.

The hardest thing to bear was the hunger. The food rations depended on performing the daily work norm. The lowest ration – a bowl of watery liquid called soup twice a day and 400 grams of bread – was apportioned to those who did not complete the norm, which soon reduced the body to irreversible emaciation; but even the top ration was not enough to fill one's stomach. In summer and autumn they were saved by berries – bilberries, cranberries, wild rosehips – and mushrooms they picked in the woods. In winter it was much worse. The temperature went down to minus forty degrees and lower. They had no warm clothing. After some time they were given padded jackets and trousers, but there were no felt boots. Instead, they were sent thick socks made of felt that came up to the knees. The prisoners fitted moccasins made of woven birch bark onto them, and thus a special kind of footwear, known as *paypaki*, came into being. They proved invaluable in freezing temperatures, but they did not keep out the damp – on the contrary, they soaked up water and simply added to the pain of marching many kilometres to work and back again.

That journey was yet another tribulation. They went out at dawn and came back after sunset. In spring and autumn they spent hours wading through boggy, wet ground. In winter they walked in snow up to their knees, in strong winds and blizzards. During one of these nightmare winter journeys back to camp, at dusk, after ten hours of murderous toil in the forest, Janek realised that he could not see anything. He had lost his sight. To avoid getting lost in the forest, he seized the comrade in front of him by the coat-tail and managed to get 'home'. In the morning he was all right, but that evening he could not see again. He was suffering from night-blindness, an ailment that was widespread among the prisoners, caused by vitamin deficiency. Once again the medical orderly saved him. A spoonful of raw, minced liver made the symptoms of the illness go away.

How can I fit the story of those five years into a few sheets of paper? How can I cover all the anguish he experienced, in a sort of telegram shorthand? 'There's nothing worth dwelling on,' says Janek. 'Everything there ever was to say on the subject has already been written by Alexander Solzhenitsyn, Gustaw Herling-Grudziński and others...'

It was a great blessing that both he and Kamilla had the right to correspond. Once a month they could write to each other, and luckily the letter in which she gave him the address of her prison camp had reached him when he was still at liberty. Once in prison he would no longer have received it, because prisoners awaiting sentence could not receive postal deliveries, and for the next few years they would have been ignorant of each other's fate. He was less worried about her ever since she had written to say that she was working as a doctor in the camp clinic – thanks to this alone she managed to survive, but she never told anyone what she had experienced.

When four years had passed, Janek began to hope that he would live to see the end of his sentence and started wondering what he would do on leaving the camp. Former prisoners were not allowed to settle in the forty biggest cities of the Soviet Union or in the front-line zone. He had no relatives in the entire country, so he wrote to his mother to ask her advice. She mentioned his problems to one of her patients, an old peasant woman from a collective farm in western Siberia whom she had befriended. Before dying, the old woman provided a solution: 'You have looked after me like a daughter,' she said, 'so tell your son to go to my family, the Gulayevs, in Tomsk province. I shall write and ask them to take care of him.'

On 30 April 1943 Janek's five-year sentence was up. As bad luck would have it, the next day was the First of May holiday. To celebrate it, there were two days off work and the camp's administrative office in Solikamsk, which was in charge of the essential formalities involved in being released, was closed; but he still had to observe the regulations in force, under which a prisoner who had completed his sentence could not remain on camp terrain an hour longer, so he was told to go away and come back on 3 May. He was ill, so he asked to be allowed to spend those two days in the sick bay, but the authorities were more concerned about law and order, so he was given a loaf of bread and pushed out of the gate.

So it was he spent the first two days of his long-desired freedom without a roof over his head. He walked about the streets, dreaming of a bowl of hot soup, but he could not summon up the nerve to ask anyone for help. He slept in the porch of the 'house of culture' (as Soviet cultural centres were called); he waited until the final film show ended, and once the people had come out he bedded down there. On 3 May he reported at the camp again. The farewell ritual included a medical examination. By then he weighed only forty-six kilos. The doctor examining him asked in surprise: 'How did you get into such a state?'

Finally he set off for Tomsk province, to the Gulayev family. Former prisoners attracted attention because of their impoverished appearance and prison-camp clothing, and were exposed to many difficulties and dangers. They could not travel alone, but had to wait until there was a group of newly released men travelling in the same direction. The station police shut them all in the same compartment and only let them out at their final stop. While changing trains in Kurgan, Janek had a lot of time until his next train departed, so he decided to visit the city. He was immediately stopped by the police and escorted to a lock-up for homeless people. It took a long time for him to explain who he was and where he was going. Finally he reached his destination, Tatarskaya station, and found the address written on the card: 105 Zakriyevsky Street.

The Gulayevs fed and clothed him, but after that he had to look after himself. Over the next two years he took on all sorts of jobs. He had completed four years of higher education, so in the distant Siberian province he was a very welcome employee. He worked at the abattoir, which was grandly called the meat *kombinat*, then at the construction site for a power plant in Tomsk, and later on he was evacuated to the northern Caucasus, where he worked as a procurement manager for construction gangs. In autumn 1944 Kamilla was set free.

❧

Towards the end of 1944 leading Polish communist Bolesław Bierut (then President of the self-appointed 'National Homeland Council'), trying to strengthen his power in Poland, persuaded Stalin to pass a decree on the early release of Polish communists and their families from the camps. The leading activists had died long ago, and the NKVD was in no hurry to seek out the handful of remaining prisoners who were scattered about the entire 'Gulag archipelago'. They claimed that they did not feature in their files. The only ones to be released were those for whom someone spoke up officially, by giving the victim's surname and place of residence. As the arrests made in the 1930s included all their relatives, most of the prisoners had no one to speak up for them, and so regaining one's liberty depended on a lucky coincidence: someone heard about someone else, someone met someone else in prison or on a journey, someone passed their name to someone else, then it carried on from mouth to mouth. Some people came out at once, others were imprisoned until 1956, and others were never found again.

News about the release of Poles appeared in the Soviet press, and although camp prisoners had no access to any sources of information, Janek's mother came across a scrap of newspaper with a photograph of an activist from the Union of Polish Patriots and the name Bolesław Drobner, whom she knew from her student days in Zurich. She immediately wrote to him, and he intervened in her case. And so after eight years she was freed.

Such was the bureaucratic order in force during the terror that she was given back out of the camp depository all the things that had been taken from her in prison and sent to the camp after her, including a Swiss watch that she had bought in Zurich before Janek was born. After her release, while she was on the week-long train journey from Krasnoyarsk to the Caucasus to join him, all her newly recovered possessions were stolen from her little cardboard case; but the watch, which she was wearing, survived – and only stopped working recently.

In a world where so many people had been lost without trace, any sort of permanence was astounding. Before his arrest Janek had a savings-bank book with about a thousand roubles recorded in it. When, after arriving in Moscow in July 1945, he asked about his account, more for a joke than seriously, he found out that it still existed and that in seven years the statutory interest had built up on it. Encouraged by this success, he applied to the student hostel for the books he had left in the storeroom, but discovered that he had come a few weeks too late. In May 1945 the hostel management had accepted that students who had not yet applied for their belongings must have died on the front. The possibility of emerging from the Gulag had evidently not been taken into consideration, and Janek's books were now enriching the local library.

In 1995 he was in Moscow to lecture at the university, and paid a visit to the 'Memorial' institute ('Memorial' is an organisation that provides information on past human-rights abuses and supports present-day human rights in Russia) to ask if he could see the interrogation documents relating to his own and his mother's cases. A friendly lady, a Romance philologist by profession, first asked him not to call her 'Comrade' in the Soviet fashion, and then advised him to apply to the archive of the Federal Security Service (formerly the NKVD) with a request for access to the documents. A few days later he received permission to see them.

When he arrived at that institution, still a terrifying place until so recently, two folders full of papers were ready and waiting for him. 'How much time do I have to look through all this?' he asked the clerk. 'As much as you need,' she politely answered. He realised that he was in a different era now. It turned out that he could also make photocopies of the documents, and on top of that he was given back the documents confiscated on his mother's arrest, all of which had been carefully preserved. Among them he found his own Warsaw secondary-school certificate, in which he had once placed such hopes.

The pedantic, bureaucratic order that accompanied the insane years of the Great Terror is astounding. A grey folder that Janek keeps in his desk contains an impressive dossier, comprising a short history of the sixteen years from 1929 to 1945. In July 2000 I examined those yellowed papers at his flat in Warsaw. They included:

- Kamilla's certificate of employment at the 'Closed Institute for the Mentally Ill at Amelin, run by Dr Bornstein, later Radziwiłłowicz', 1929.
- A declaration signed by my grandmother Janina Mortkowicz stating that in her own name she guarantees payment of the court bail, on the basis of which her sister Kamilla Horwitz was to be released from prison. Warsaw, 1930.
- Kamilla Horwitz's release, on bail of 3000 zlotys, from preventive arrest in Warsaw. It is signed by 'substitute investigating magistrate' Jan Demant, 1930.

– A warrant for the arrest of citizeness Leonia Kancewicz. Moscow, 22 November 1937.
– The minutes of her interrogation: 'While living in "former Poland" she personally knew Piłsudski, was closely connected with his agents and with members of the Polish Military Organisation: Horwitz-Walecki, Sochacki, Żarski.' 'While residing within the territory of the USSR she maintained contact with members of the Communist Party who were accused of treason.' 'While residing within the territory of the USSR she showed an interest in arms factories.' (This charge arose from the fact that she worked part-time at a medical clinic within the terrain of one of the factories.)
– The witness statements: 'She was secretive. She never talked about herself.'
– The sentence condemning her for all these 'crimes' to ten years at a corrective labour camp. Moscow, 12 September 1937.
– Applications written by Kamilla from the camp to the NKVD appealing for a review of her sentence and complaining of unjust charges, addressed personally to NKVD head Lavrenty Beria's deputy, Comrade Merkulov. There is a short note written on the applications reading: 'To be left unsettled'. (When Janek asked her why she had referred the matter to the authorities when she knew nothing would come of it, she replied: 'In order to leave at least some trace of myself.')

There are also documents concerning Janek in the folder – his arrest warrant, the minutes of his interrogation, his sentence, the decree ending his punishment, and finally documents dating from 1956, rehabilitating both mother and son. The most private document of all makes a strong impression: 'List of items requisitioned at the flat of citizeness Leonia Kancewicz. Moscow. 9 XII 1937'. They had gone through every corner of her room, ransacked the wardrobes and drawers, rummaged in her clothes and papers, and then taken away this pitiful collection, to be delivered to the 'state treasury'. The list includes 260 items in alphabetical order, the number of units and their value. For example:

– fleecy towel, used (1) – 2 roubles
– yellow bathing costume (1) – 3 roubles
– glasses in a case (1) – 50 kopecks
– various lady's collars (5) – 7 roubles
– lady's silk combinations, used (1) – 2 roubles

- lady's skirt (2) – 40 roubles
- aluminium frying pan (3) – 1 rouble
- small glass salt cellar (1) – 50 kopecks
- money of Soviet nominal value – 48 kopecks
- teaspoon (3) – 3 roubles
- mirror (20 × 40) – 3 roubles
- quilted dressing gown, used (1) – 10 roubles
- metal tin opener (1) – 50 kopecks
- woollen overcoat, used (1) – 20 roubles
- leather travelling bag, used (1) – 8 roubles

And so on, and so on.

Manuscripts don't burn, as the saying goes. A yellowed postcard has also survived dated 2 September 1945, in which Kamilla wrote from Warsaw to my grandmother and my mother in Kraków to say:

Dearest Janinka and Hania!
I'm writing to you soon after arriving and I'm sorry I can't see you at once. Today I'm in the countryside at Flora's – she's v.v. weak... I'm negotiating for a job here, but still don't know any- thing definite, or where I'll be. There's talk of the western districts, but I don't fancy that. Janek will study and work.

Commenting on the years gone by, Janek added philosophically: 'Man is the toughest, liveliest creature of all.'

In December 1945 they came to Kraków for the Christmas holi- days. Kamilka had asked in advance: *Don't make any prepara- tions. We shall bring some provisions with us, including flour and sugar.* What was the meeting of the sisters like after sixteen years apart, and after so many terrible experiences? Flora had died a few months earlier; of the nine siblings they were the only ones still alive. Did they tell each other what they had been through? Did they bemoan their fate? I doubt it. They were made of very strong stuff.

Kamilla asked me to accompany her to the National Museum in the Sukiennice (Kraków's famous Cloth Hall). In those days I was a know-it-all ten-year-old, and regarded the patriotic historical paintings on display there with some scorn. I was amazed to see how emotionally she looked at one after the other. She stood longest in front of Jacek Malczewski's 1883 painting, *The Death of*

Elenai (which portrays the death of a Polish woman in exile in Siberia; Elenai was the heroine of an epic poem by Juliusz Słowacki). A tiny old lady in a worn-out coat and a woollen beret, gazing at that rather kitsch, rampant beauty, dying in the snowy Siberian wasteland. Did I imagine it, or did she really wipe away a tear? ...

In July 1946 Kamilla reported: *We have found Staś and we are making efforts to get him here. I've also found out about Maks's little boy, who is being brought up in a children's home, although his mother is alive.* But the fortunes of the half-siblings, Petya, Staś and Kasia, demand their own separate account.

MAKS'S CHILDREN

———————✗———————

Petya has retained almost no memory of his father; after all, they never lived together. But he does remember the festive atmosphere that filled the house whenever he came to visit. His mother would radiate joy, Petya would inspect the foreign gifts he had brought, guests would arrive, and rare delicacies would appear on the table. Once he tried to lift a huge bottle of brandy brought back from a journey. It was almost as big as he was.

When his father was arrested in June 1937 he was five years old. He does not remember living at the Comintern dacha, or the dramatic night spent on the lawn. All he knows is that once they were back in Moscow, the children from the house on Gorky Street, where they lived, refused to play with him any more and ran away at the sight of him, but he did not know why. His mother told him what happened later on. Soon after Maks's arrest the NKVD came for her. Little Petya was seriously ill at the time with a lung infection and had a high temperature. Maybe he had caught cold that tragic night? A doctor who worked for Comintern's medical service was looking after him. He was a Czech, a good doctor and a brave man. He threatened the NKVD men with the fact that responsibility for the child's death would fall on them, saying he would die if they took away his mother. So they went away, and never came back again. It was a time when the authorities were drawing up a new list of thousands of people to be arrested on a daily basis, and even if they had not yet reached their limit, the next day a new list was already in force, which must explain why Josza was forgotten about.

Quite soon, about a month after Maks's arrest, mother and son were removed from their comfortable, private accommodation on Gorky Street into a communal flat in a house that was now the headquarters of an international publishing firm, but had formerly been a tenement building. Each room in the large pre-war apartments housed a different family. The publishing firm's translators, authors and workers were each assigned a separate room. Everyone used a communal kitchen and lavatory, and on the ground floor there was a single bathroom. A detailed timetable apportioned each family two hours once a week for their ablutions. Josza, who was still accustomed to European standards of living, made a pact with her neighbour, a single mother with a little girl, to bathe together, which meant they could do so twice a week.

Despite the personal tragedy of Maks's arrest, despite the lack of any news about his fate and the all-pervading atmosphere of imminent death, somehow she went on living and coping. She was still working at the Comintern Secretariat. In 1939 Petya started going to school. Then suddenly yet another misfortune came down on her. She fell seriously ill with the Spanish flu that was epidemic at the time. Complications set in, causing meningitis and, as a consequence, Parkinson's disease. She was only just thirty-eight when she became an invalid, with her mobility and speech badly enough impaired to prevent her from working. She was given a small pension, on which she had a hard time keeping herself and her son. There was no one she could count on for help; as a foreigner she had no family in Moscow. And then even worse things started to happen.

In June 1941 the Germans attacked the USSR and moved towards Leningrad, Moscow and the Ukraine. The Soviet–Nazi war had begun. In August all foreigners were ordered to evacuate Moscow and go beyond the Urals. This also applied to Josza and Petya, who was then nine years old. Before they left, they were sought out by Kasia, Maks's daughter. Earlier on she had not had any contact with her father's girlfriend and had been hostile towards her; but now, after all the disasters that had befallen her in the past four years, she had no one left in Moscow. Her father and mother, arrested in 1937, had vanished without trace. Her brother was in a labour camp in Vorkuta, her aunt Kamilla was in Siberia, her cousin Janek was in the Urals, and her husband, the great and influential engineer Viktor Taner, had been arrested as a saboteur as soon as the war began. She had lost her flat and her job, she was thirty years old and had not a single friendly soul in sight; and because she was Polish, she too had to leave Moscow. In her general sense of yet another threat, her old hostility towards her father's loved ones had vanished. She wanted to travel with them, and the gentle Josza willingly agreed.

Within a huge herd of evacuees, Kasia, Josza and Petya were deported in a goods wagon to the far side of the Urals. They travelled for ten days in a crowd of people, all sleeping on the floor. Before the war these wagons were used to transport grain, and Petya can still remember that the bane of their journey was the seed husks that crept under their clothes. They were made to get out at the station in the town of Kamyshlov on the River Pyshma. This place had been a halt for prisoners making their way on foot to Siberia in tsarist times. There was a huge prison by the river, and the riverbank was covered in rushes, the Russian word for which is *kamysh*. If one of the exiled prisoners ran away, he could hide in the rushes, hence the name of the city, which means 'a hiding place in the rushes'. From there they went to a nearby village, where they settled in an old babushka's cottage. She gave them a friendly welcome, because she lived a lonely life. Her husband was in a camp, sentenced to eight years for slaughtering his own cow without permission. The new arrivals and their hostess slept in a single room. Then one night the old woman died, and Petya was the first to realise it. He can still remember the ghastly impression it made on him.

Their only source of income was Josza's monthly pension of 200 roubles, but it was not enough for even their basic needs. Before she died, the old woman had let them cultivate her plot near the cottage. They had planted potatoes and vegetables, which the next summer was their only source of food. Petya did most of the physical work. Josza was disabled, and Kasia, an electrical engineer by profession, quite soon found a job as a teacher at a school six kilometres away, which did patch up the household budget, but meant that all the domestic work now fell to the boy.

When winter came the nine-year-old Petya had to fetch fuel to heat the cottage and make a hot meal. This basic duty of his was the most burdensome. Everything in the neighbourhood that could be burned had long since been cut down: trees, bushes, even the fences. Just to get a few dry branches or twigs he had to walk several kilometres, though they had no warm clothing or suitable footwear.

In 1942 Kasia's husband was released from prison and evacuated from Moscow to their region, to Sverdlovsk. She went to join him at once, but the vicissitudes of prison life had left their mark on him and taken away his strength to live. A month after being freed he fell seriously ill and died. However, Kasia stayed on in

Sverdlovsk, where she had found a better job. It is hardly surprising that she did not return to the village, because the situation there was getting worse and worse. Food became more expensive from day to day, and Josza's pension was not even enough to buy bread. At first she sold the things she had brought from Moscow, but soon there was nothing left to sell. She and Petya were starving, and he was losing strength. The frost was becoming unbearable, and the terrible cold, day and night, was driving them to despair. That was when he developed the rheumatism that caused him a serious heart disease later in life.

Somehow they muddled through the summer and autumn of 1943, but Josza was afraid Petya would not survive the approaching winter, and decided that he would have to go back to Moscow. There were still some things he could sell in their abandoned Moscow flat, and he would find neighbours and friends to help him. Whatever happened, he would have a better life than in the countryside. She would manage somehow. However, he would not be able to cope with the long journey on his own, nor would he get permission to travel from the authorities, so she hit upon the idea that someone who was on their way to Moscow should fictionally adopt the boy and take him with them.

Nowadays the idea of sending an eleven-year-old off to such an uncertain fate with instructions to start living independently amid the terrible conditions of war seems absurd. But clearly it was dictated by some extraordinary maternal instinct, like a modern version of an ancient fairy-tale plot where a mother saves her little son from a deadly danger by sending him off alone into the big, bad world.

Was he afraid? Or downhearted? He says he was not, and that children are incredibly flexible, easily adapt and regard everything as an adventure. He knew he would manage, so he took the keys to the flat and left.

It was December 1943. For the first few days in Moscow he was very happy. He took some items from the flat to the bazaar and sold them. He bought a lot of food, and for the first time in ages he ate his fill. He ran about the city, exploring and wondering what to do next. A few days later the house caretaker came to see him and told him he must report his arrival to the militia – then he would be registered, receive ration cards for food and a fuel ration. The caretaker offered to help the boy complete all the formalities, so Petya trustingly followed him to the militia post; but when they got there, he whispered something to the militiaman on duty, then vanished. The militiaman seized the boy by the scruff of the neck and pushed him into a huge, barred room, where there was already a crowd of homeless children milling about.

A few days later the juvenile prisoners were transferred from the militia post to an old monastery, where there was a refuge for homeless children. There they took down their details. Those who had parents or relatives were sent off to their families, and the orphans were sent to children's homes. They wanted to take Petya back to his mother, but he refused to go. He explained why, and asked to be placed in some sort of educational institute near to her. Astonishingly, his requests were heeded, and he was sent to the children's home in Sverdlovsk.

It took three months for a large enough group of homeless children to accumulate who were all travelling in the same direction. Finally, in February 1944, the young people were taken to their destination under escort. Once in Sverdlovsk, he had to fight the next battle to decide his fate. The people running the children's home did not want to take him in because he was not an orphan. Once again he was told to go back to his mother, but he insisted on staying put with such determination that finally he got his way. He spent the next five and a half years at 'Dyetsky Dom (Children's Home) No. 1' in Sverdlovsk. To this day he reckons it was the greatest bit of luck he ever had.

The home was very well run. Most importantly, no one ever went hungry there. Nearby, on the river, there was a farm run by the foster-children, where they cultivated potatoes, grain and vegetables. They had their own horses, cows and poultry. Thanks to this they ate their fill, which in those days was not often the case. Although boys generally used to escape from this sort of institution, Petya cannot remember anything like that ever happening – the best possible proof that they had a rather good life there.

The home was run by a decent, wise principal, whom he remembers with great gratitude. She was very kind to him. At school in Sverdlovsk it was possible for a pupil to take his general matriculation exams and go straight on to university, as long as he had not only excellent academic results, but also special permission from the educational and political authorities. Not many pupils achieved this – just one or two in an entire class.

Petya was a very good student, and had clearly inherited his father's talents for the exact sciences. He was very keen to go on to higher education, but his family situation had deprived him of any such chance. His mother was an Austrian from the 'putrid West'. His father was a 'Trotskyite', 'an enemy of the international revolution'; he himself was. a Pole, his half-brother was in a labour camp – and so by now was his half-sister too.

Maks's daughter, the apolitical, elegant Kasia, pampered by her husband, comfort- and luxury-loving, was arrested in 1944 when the end of the war was already in sight. She was with a group of friends, talking about a defeat suffered by the Germans, and when someone expressed the view that perhaps people would have a better life after the war, she had the nerve to say sceptically: 'Who knows what that Georgian will come up with next?' As the result of an immediate denunciation she was sentenced to ten years in the camps.

Ordinarily someone like Petya, who had nothing but 'enemies of the system' in his family, did not merit any consideration, but the principal of the children's home was stubborn and won him the right to go on studying at secondary school. As a fourteen-year-old, he was invited to perform on Radio Moscow with the school choir. He took the opportunity to visit his mother, who had returned from the Urals to Moscow after the war, and there he met his thirty-eight-year-old half-brother.

In 1946 Staś Bielski was released from the labour camp two and a half years ahead of time. After returning to Poland his aunt Kamilla had been able to apply for his release, thanks to the fact that Josza knew his camp's postal code.

Before his arrest Staś had been ill-disposed towards his father's girlfriend, just as Kasia had; but when, after five years in the labour camp, he gained the right to correspond, he realised that she was all he had left of the entire family circle. His father and mother had disappeared without trace, his aunt and cousin were in labour camps, and the war had swept his sister out of Moscow; terrified by her husband's arrest, she had not left anyone her address. Staś's ex-wife, Vera, had died, and their daughter Halinka's sole guardian, her Russian grandmother, thought only about how to save the child from starvation. So he wrote to Josza. When she was evacuated she had kept her Moscow flat, so the post sent his letter on to her at the village in the Urals. She immediately wrote back, and thus became his contact with the outside world, and with the rest of the family who were scattered about the camps.

As soon as he was released he turned up at her flat, and then often came to visit. At that point he spent almost a year in Moscow waiting for permission to leave for Poland, which Kamilka was trying to obtain for him in Warsaw. He sought out his daughter, Halinka, because he had decided to take her with him when he left. At first the little girl did not want to hear of it. She did not know her father, and she loved her grandmother, who looked after her. After all he had been through, Staś was in bad shape, physically and mentally; his personal problems were an additional torment, and Josza was the only person he could talk to. One day at her flat he met Petya, who had just arrived from Sverdlovsk.

Petya remembers their meeting well, and the next few too. Staś very laconically told him about his experiences. He had survived because the camp's medical unit was looking for an orderly, and he had applied for the job, although he knew nothing about medicine. However, he could remember some general facts about emergency first aid, and not much more than that was needed. He soon began to do quite well and was promoted to doctor's assistant. He had survived seven and a half years of hell, though apparently only by a miracle. Once in Poland he tried to put it all behind him, but was unable to.

In Moscow, he tried to find out what had happened to his parents, but was provided with some evasive, false information, such as the claim that they were both still alive somewhere in Siberia, that a search had been instigated and that he would have to wait. He could not be too insistent, or he might endanger himself again. So although he must have guessed the truth, he never actually discovered it.

In 1947 he and Halinka left for Poland, which should be the subject of another long and sad tale. Meanwhile, in Sverdlovsk Petya passed his exams with a distinction, thanks to which he immediately won a place at the Mendeleyev Institute of Chemistry and Technology in Moscow. The principal of the children's home seems to have determined his entire future. When he reached the age of eighteen and had to fill in a questionnaire to obtain an identity card, she advised him not to mention his Polish origin, as it would only make his life more complicated. So he wrote 'citizen of the USSR', and became a Russian. After graduating he spent two years in East Germany, at the Institute of Organic Chemistry, where he took his doctorate. In 1955 he was summoned to the Central Committee of the All-Union Communist Party (Bolshevik).

At the sight of him, the senior official stood up from his desk and said, 'Congratulations, Comrade! Your father, Comrade Maksymilian Horwitz-Walecki, has been posthumously rehabilitated as a victim of a period of errors and distortions. His Party membership has also been restored to him. You can be proud of him.' Staś had died almost three years earlier; if only he had lived until the 'thaw', perhaps he would not have committed suicide.

At that point Josza was given a better flat and a higher pension; but there was still no information on the circumstances surrounding Maks's death. After 1989, as an employee of the Institute of Organic Chemistry in Moscow, Petya applied to the 'Memorial' institute for help obtaining the documents from the interrogation and trial. Everything had been preserved in the NKVD archives: the minutes of the interrogations, the sentence report, even some photographs taken in prison. He did not have the least trouble gaining access to these documents.

The minutes of the interrogations were horrifying. At the end of every single session, as dawn was breaking Walecki had signed his name beneath the forced confessions. Sometimes the letters are so illegible that it looks as if he could not write himself and someone was guiding his hand. And the next day he always retracted his confession, writing: *I do not confess my guilt. I declare that my signature was forced from me by torture.* He repeated the same thing in his final statement before the sentence was pronounced by the Military Tribunal, but it no longer had any significance.

In May 2000 'Dr Piotr M. Valetsky, Deputy Director of the A. N. Nesmeyanov Institute of Organo-element Compounds', alias Petya, told me everything that I have written here. While we were having our conversation my daughter Kasia was showing his younger son, Sergei, around Kraków. We were all meeting for the first time and were feeling very emotional. I had been aware of Petya's existence, but he had not known of mine. My mother had met him in Moscow in 1964, but he does not remember that. I think the communist era caused a sort of emotional paralysis; in those days he was not in touch with his American, French and Polish relatives, and his only close tie was with his cousin, Janek Kancewicz, and his family. Thanks to Janek we found each other and met.

In May 2000 Petya went to an international conference in

Gdańsk and decided to take the opportunity to visit Kraków. He knew I was writing a book about our family, and agreed to talk to me about it. I noted down the facts. I would gladly have discussed emotions with him, but how could I ask a man I had just met for the first time questions about such painful matters? Wouldn't I be touching a raw nerve, or overstepping the mark?

'No! Talking about the past doesn't cause me pain,' replied Petya. 'Silence is far more distressing. None of the things that happened then should be forgotten.'

So how can this be? How come he doesn't complain about the fate that befell him? Doesn't he blame his father for ruining his mother's life? Or for his homeless, hungry childhood?

'My father? I owe him my existence,' he says. 'He paid the highest possible price for his convictions. My mother loved him very much. Did she regret going to the Soviet Union after him? Perhaps later on, in 1964, when she visited her native Vienna for the first time in thirty years, she began to wonder what she had lost. And me? All those experiences made me very strong. No one ever made it any easier for me or led me by the hand. I never belonged to the Party, I was not an opportunist, and I never wronged anyone. Everything I have achieved I owe to myself alone; but I consider myself a lucky man. I have led, and continue to lead, a successful life.'

Since 1959 Petya has worked at the Institute of Organic Chemistry in Moscow. He is a worker of the Russian Academy of Sciences, a renowned and highly regarded expert in his field. He travels all over the world, writes academic papers and is doing very well. He has three children: Lena and Maxim from his first marriage, and Sergei from his second.

Maxim Valetsky is named after his grandfather. Maksymilian Horwitz-Walecki must be scowling in the world beyond, because his grandson is a businessman on a grand scale. He produces furniture in Russia to American designs, and is always on the move between Moscow and San Francisco, where he lives permanently with his wife and daughter Tania. We exchanged our first e-mails in 1999, when he wrote from California: *Thanks to the collapse of communism, since 1989 I have been making a profit, which in our family full of scientists, doctors and writers might seem strange.*

To me, Maxim's success is like the happy ending to a cruel story – the breaking of an evil spell, like in a fairy tale; and at the same time it is the ironical smile of history.

And yet? Is the image of the typical English gentleman, as presented by Piotr – reserve, lack of passion, self-control – just a mask, or his true nature? What happened along the way? What were all those bygone years really like? He must have rebelled, felt fear, anger and despair, like everyone; but gentlemen do not talk about their emotions.

'There's only one thing I can't understand,' he said, standing up, when I had switched off the tape recorder. 'Why didn't my father just quietly teach maths, instead of getting involved in that hopeless cause that ruined millions of people's lives? Was he so limited? Or so blind? Did he only see what he wanted to? Why did he bring so many misfortunes down on his own family?'

At once he recovered his self-control. Both he and I know well that there is no answer to those questions. It is not our place to evaluate the choices made so many years ago. It is not our place to make judgements.

Not long ago in Gdańsk there was an exhibition about the victims of communism, comprising photographs from the KGB archives, including a picture of Maks, with a caption below it that seems to me the most apt conclusion to the story of my grandmother's brother:

Maksymilian Horwitz-Walecki (1877–1937)
asks to be remembered.

ESCAPE

——————————✗——————————

July 1939 was sunny and carefree. The young secondary-school graduates, Ryś Bykowski and Krzyś Baczyński, were spending the summer at the village of Bukowina Tatrzańska near Zakopane. Cheerful and suntanned, they were enjoying the flowering meadows and mountain views, going on hikes with the young ladies and working out their plans for the future. Suddenly news came that Krzyś's father had died, so he went straight back to Warsaw. A few days later Ryś was called up to join the Young Men's Labour Brigade and sent to a camp outside Zakopane, where the young labourers had to dig defensive ditches. War was getting closer and closer.

Maryla and Gustaw Bychowski spent August 1939 with little Monika by the sea at Jurata. Maryla was very upset by the rumours of war. Gustaw, an optimist, tried to calm her down: 'After all, Mr Beck, the Minister of Foreign Affairs, is spending his August holiday by the sea with his family. He's the best-informed person of all. Would he go off on holiday if the Germans were about to attack the country?' But on 25 August all the state officials were recalled from their holidays, so the Bychowskis returned to Warsaw too, and on 30 August the general mobilisation was announced. On 31 August Maryla, who had an extremely well-developed self-preservation instinct, said to her husband: 'Let's get out of here.' Gustaw defended himself: 'I'm a doctor. If war really does break out, I'll be needed.' The war broke out on 1 September, at five in the morning.

I spent the summer of 1939 at Piaseczno, a small place just outside Warsaw, with my cousin Robert Osnos, who was three years older than me, in the care of my tutor, Miss Anna. On 2 September, as every Saturday, my mother and grandmother came to Piaseczno, and also Robert's mother, Marta. It was the second day of the war. For two days the Germans had been bombarding the capital. Every few hours on the radio the announcer's voice kept repeating: 'This is an alert for the city of Warsaw!' No one had any idea how the situation would develop. The German aeroplanes had started firing on trains full of passengers and people on the roads, but my mother and grandmother, dressed for a day out in summery straw hats and flowery dresses, did not seem perturbed. They sank into wicker armchairs on the veranda and called for something cold to drink, as if the journey in the heat had tired them, but not the imminent danger. Perhaps they were actually hiding their own fear to avoid frightening us children.

The adults' conversation must have been similar to conversations going on in every home. 'How long can it last? How will it end? What safety measures should we take? What supplies should we gather in? Where do we get gas masks from? Should we stay put or get out? And if we get out, where do we go to?' We did not take part in these conversations. We were made to cut newspapers into long strips and coat them in 'dextrin', a paste made of water and yellow powder. Then the strips were glued to the window panes crosswise, 'so they won't fly out during the bombing'. It never entered anyone's heads that in a few days' time they would fall right out of the buildings, frames, walls and all. We were thrilled by this previously unknown game. We went into the bathroom to wash our hands, where for a couple of days the bathtub had been full to the brim with water. 'A reserve supply. Just in case.' I was forbidden to go near it, but the temptation was too great. We dropped all my sand moulds into it and had a sea battle. 'She's got an excuse to be silly because she's still little! But as for you, don't you know what war means?' Miss Anna screamed at Robert hysterically. He stared at her in amazement – no, he didn't know. How was he supposed to know? That was when we realised for the first time that something terrible was happening, because no one had ever shouted at us like that before.

On Sunday, 3 September the Warsaw suburbs were bombed as well, and as a result, on Monday, the fourth day of the war, we were taken back to the city. I cannot remember the return journey on the suburban railway, full of terrified people, or the roads through the city, so changed by those past few days, its streets a whirl of disoriented crowds and its houses on fire. Nor can I remember the piercing wail of the air-raid sirens in the middle of the night, or running in the darkness down to the cellar, full of strange, hysterical people, or the crash of the bombs, or the shudders of fear: will they hit us or not?

On that fourth day of the war Robert went off to his home and I went to mine, and we were parted for many years. In fact we must have seen each other again a few times before he left Poland, but I have no recollection of those meetings or of saying goodbye.

In June 1999, at the Osnos family's country house outside New York I asked Robert about his memories of those wartime days, and found out that, just like me, he can hardly remember a thing – just a few facts, but no feelings. But he must have been frightened, when in the first week of the bombing they fled from their own flat in a district near the airport and moved to the centre of town, into a flat on Twarda Street that belonged to his paternal uncle who had been drafted into the army. He must have felt rejected and betrayed when his father left them alone and abandoned Warsaw, obedient to an appeal by Colonel Umiastowski, who ordered all young men to leave the city and head east, beyond the line of the River Vistula. He remembers the air raids and someone suddenly shouting that a bomb had hit the house and they must get out at once. They ran outside. The whole of Twarda Street was on fire. Through the flames and smoke they could not see if Grandma Osnos' house on the other side of the street was still standing, but they ran blindly towards it. It was still intact, so they found their next refuge there. He can remember the darkness, the wounded and the dead, the lack of water, and distressed people all around, but he cannot remember his own reactions to what was happening. Clearly his child's brain, just like mine, had a healthy self-defence mechanism and, treating the reality like a nightmare, wiped out all the emotions associated with it.

On 1 September Maryla and Gustaw Bychowski, two-year-old Monika and fifteen-year-old Krysia left Warsaw, and in a small Hillman car set off to join an endless caravan of cars, motorcycles, horse-drawn carts and pedestrians crossing Poniatowski Bridge and heading eastwards, beyond the River Vistula. The German troops were advancing at lightning speed, and the Polish cities of Bydgoszcz, Toruń and Grudziądz had already been captured; fear was growing and the eastward evacuation of the government and central authorities had begun. A huge number of people were escaping, so Maryla too had finally managed to convince her husband to leave. They did not wait for Ryś; he was not back from his youth camp yet, and they were not in touch with him, but true to his optimistic nature Gustaw reckoned the war would only last a few weeks at most, and that soon everyone would be back at home on Wilcza Street again.

Meanwhile Ryś was battling his way back from the Zakopane area to Warsaw with a group of friends. In the first days of the war the Germans, attacking from the direction of Slovakia, had occupied Podhale (the Tatra foothills), so the youth brigade was disbanded and the boys were instructed to make their own way home. At first they swaggered along the highway, the entire company singing, but the first German air attack scattered them and forced them to run for their lives. After that they slipped along in the dark more cautiously, taking the field roads. Meanwhile Ryś's family was getting further away from Warsaw, driving by night without lights amid endless air raids, and hiding by day in ditches amid the wailing of terrified, lost and helpless refugees.

When they reached Lublin they ran out of petrol. There was nowhere left in the city to stay the night, so they slept beneath the stars. As bombs fell from the sky, little Monika cried out, 'Tell them to stop it!' In Lublin by an astonishing coincidence they ran into Józef Osnos, Robert's father, who had also left Warsaw by car a day later. He promised to get them some fuel. They planned to meet that evening and travel onwards together, but in the darkness, amid the panic-stricken crowds, they failed to find each other. Next day the Bychowskis found some means of transport and travelled towards Wilno, while Józef headed for Romania.

On 6 September, when the Germans were already near, Pawełek's father, Gustaw Beylin, fled from Warsaw with his wife Aleksandra, leaving his son in the care of his parents. He had reasons to be anxious; just before the war he had appeared in Berlin as the defence barrister for a famous Polish actress, accused by the Nazis of spying for Poland. His participation in the trial had not been forgotten – three days after the Germans invaded Warsaw the Gestapo turned up at his flat on Ujazdowskie Avenue. Fortunately by then he was already in Lwów.

Pawełek remained with his grandparents and aunts. Fearing that the Gestapo would come looking for Gustaw's relatives, as soon as the Germans entered Warsaw they all went into hiding at Milanówek, not far from Warsaw, under assumed names.

In the first week of the war, when the bombing raids had intensified we left our flat in the tall building on the Vistula embankment. It was too dangerous there. *Aeroplanes were circling above the house on Okólnik Street. Once in a while there was a crash and a shell exploded, blowing up a great fountain of splinters, bricks and stones. Already hit by bombs many times, the circus lay at our feet like the ruins of the Colosseum in Rome. In our flat on the fifth floor everything lay flung about on the ground and we stood there amid the shelves and books, helpless and deafened, not knowing what to pick and what to leave,* wrote my mother in her memoirs. Did I take anything with me apart from my beloved celluloid doll, Michał? Did I cry? I don't think so. After all, I did not know I was saying goodbye to the house for ever.

We moved into the Bychowskis' abandoned flat on Wilcza Street. At the time people were constantly wandering from district to district, from place to place, out of the irrational feeling that it would be safer somewhere else. At Wilcza Street my grandmother felt ill at ease. She was determined to get to the bookshop at any cost, because she was more worried about the books that had been left unprotected than about her own fate. Two porters, Michał and Jan, packed some of our cases onto a wooden cart and helped us to battle our way across to Mazowiecka Street through an obstacle course of barricades and beneath the fire of anti-aircraft guns. There we stayed for the next few weeks of terrible bombardments, going down into the cellar at night and camping in the ground-floor rooms during the day.

I remember being shocked by the look of the bookshop interior. Piles of books and albums were lying about everywhere, thrown from the shelves by the shockwaves caused by the bombing. Beautiful colour reproductions torn from their frames were knocking about on the floor among splinters of glass, ripped and soiled with ash and dust. This defied all the principles of harmony and order I had been imbued with all my life, and made a horrifying impression. However, at the same time the new situation was full of wonderful attractions that I had never encountered before. I was thrilled with the camp beds set up in the 'sapphire office'. I remember a turquoise tiled stove with a pipe in the corner and a pot of buckwheat cooking on it, and the divine taste of condensed milk from a tube. There was no glass in the display windows, so I could jump outside through them, which was a nice surprise. There were army horses neighing in the courtyard where the Ziemiańska café's garden used to be. And there, on Mazowiecka Street, was where Ryś found us.

When he finally reached Warsaw he found his family house

empty, with smouldering ruins all around it. A seventeen-year-old in a besieged, devastated city, abandoned by his family, facing the incomprehensible catastrophe of war alone – not an easy situation to cope with. But Ryś had great strength of spirit – he had quite quickly shaken off his despair and begun to find tasks for himself. He proved very helpful. Somewhere he got hold of some plywood and used it to secure the windows that had no glass, fetched water in buckets because the water supply was not working, stood in queues at the baker's for bread, and despite the dangers that were imminent at every step of the way he ran about the city on his own mysterious, underground business. He already knew that his family had reached Wilno safely, so he was not worried about them. He raised everyone's spirits with his optimism and faith that not a hair would fall from any of our heads.

It is astonishing how in accounts of those days shock is mixed with courage, anger with euphoria, mourning with enthusiasm, despair with the madcap light-heartedness so characteristic of Varsovians in times of danger. The German artillery kept endlessly firing on the city, bombs were falling from the sky, houses were on fire, walls were caving in, yet on the streets there was the same traffic as before the war: the shops were open and the cafés full of people. Film shows were still on at the Napoleon cinema on Trzech Krzyży ('Three Crosses') Square. People still paid calls and exchanged the latest news: 'The Castle's on fire! The Cathedral's been hit! The houses have been destroyed on Krakowskie Przedmieście... on Piłsudski Square... on Królewska Street.' People even told jokes.

Every day Janusz Korczak came to visit us. He used to run up from the orphanage on distant Krochmalna Street, all full of life in the officer's uniform he had bought himself on the eve of war in the hope that he would be called up for active service. Despite the apocalypse, he was convinced that 'the times we are living through are wonderful and creative, and in their fire and blood the truth of a beautiful new life is being prepared'. 'Only the weak and despicable are breaking down and having doubts,' he used to say. In the cellars people sobbed and recited the Hail Mary aloud. Only from a collection of poems by my mother, entitled *The Unforgettable September*, have I found out how close to death we came during those weeks of siege.

The capitulation too has left nothing but a few flashes in my memory: being amazed that it is all so quiet, going outside to find the street strewn in rubble and glass, and seeing ruins all around. The house opposite is standing as before, except that instead of doors and windows it has black, burned-out holes. The fire has not yet gone out. A feeble wisp of flame creeps along the walls, and as soon as it finds a morsel of food it leaps into life and soars upwards. This image clearly gave me such a shock that I can still see it. I remember the empty little courtyard, where only so recently the Polish soldiers had been making fun of me, finding an eagle from a soldier's cap on the ground, and a feeling of joy, that somewhere high up in the burned-out house a pane of glass had survived intact in its window frame. I also remember the Germans in their gloomy helmets, and being warned not to accept sweets from them, because they were sure to be poisoned.

After the capitulation we never went home again. The bombs had ripped the roof off the building on Okólnik Street and damaged the walls. Fortunately, the house 'At the Sign of the Poets' at 11 Old Town Marketplace, where the publishing firm's printing press and warehouse were located, had survived intact. It was clear that under German occupation there would be no question of any publishing activity, so the medieval chambers were converted back into living quarters. The effort everyone made at the time to build a new nest and restore a semblance of normality, a decent standard of living and some civilisation amid such endless destruction and chaos seems astounding, but it helped us to keep our dignity.

My grandmother, who was already sixty-five by then, put a lot of work and youthful energy into preparing our new home. She had a bathroom installed and the stoves refitted, then she had the walls painted her favourite sapphire blue, and took trouble positioning the furniture and hanging the paintings brought over from Okólnik Street. Behind all this effort there was a subconscious plea to fate to allow us to enjoy the beauty of our home for as long as possible. Since November rumours had been going round about German plans to establish a ghetto, and that people of Jewish origin would be forced to move there. My family did not take this on board, but just went on trying to rebuild their ruined life. They opened the bookshop and people came crowding into it, especially those who had lost their own libraries and were unable to live without books.

Ryś proved very helpful as a salesman. He hit upon the

innovative idea of placing a small table outside the shop and recommending the publications set out on it with great success. He also used to cycle out into the countryside to get food, bringing back veal and hares from the area surrounding Warsaw. He looked after Marta, Robert's mother, who had fallen seriously ill with a kidney complaint just after the capitulation. And he used to play with me. I no longer had to envy Monika, because suddenly I had an older brother.

In November 1939 Maryla came to fetch him from Wilno, which by that time had been transferred to Lithuania under the terms of the Soviet–Nazi pact. This was an act of immense courage on her part. She did not look like a Jew and spoke German superbly, so somehow she had managed to cross the borders. She brought the news that the American Psychoanalytic Association had begun efforts to have the top psychoanalysts from the occupied countries brought to America. One of the highest on the list was Gustaw. He and his family just had to get across to Sweden, where American visas and money for the journey would be waiting for them. They would have to hurry, because life in Wilno was dismal. They were living in a single room with no money to support them, the winter was approaching, there was no fuel, and imprisoned between the German occupiers and Russia they felt trapped.

Ryś was very reluctant to leave. He was in love with a certain young lady in Warsaw, and as he was involved with the underground resistance, he viewed leaving as a form of desertion. He kneeled before my grandmother, put his fair head on her knees and begged her: 'I'm going to stay here with you.' But eventually he gave in to Maryla's persuasions – and vanished from my life, for ever.

On 30 November 1939 an order was issued obliging all Jews and people of Jewish origin to wear an armband with a star of David on it, regardless of their denomination, including children over the age of twelve. On seeing the armbands for the first time at our house, the publishing firm's old porter, Wincenty, threw them on the floor, spat and stamped on them, shouting that he would never allow his ladies to obey the orders of those swine. Yet my mother and my grandmother did obey them because they did not want to tempt fate. What did they feel at the time? What did they think? It was more convenient not to understand anything. Meanwhile, I obliviously ran about the Old Town Marketplace with the local urchins, joining in as they shouted a jaunty, incomprehensible little rhyme that went:

Jude!
Crawl under your *buda* [shack]!
Now the *buda*'s creaking!
Now the *Jude*'s shrieking!

Once Wincenty had seized me by the ear and marched me home, I found out the real, macabre meaning of those words – and that they applied to us too. It was a shock. To this day I can remember screaming wildly: 'It's not true! I'm not a Jew! I don't want to be a Jew!' My fury was underlined with a terrible sense of humiliation – I must already have been quite well indoctrinated with anti-Semitic feeling. 'What's so awful about it?' said my grandmother calmly. 'Better think how fortunate you are. You will have to seek your friends among decent people only.' She did not yet know that in a short while the modest, old-fashioned word 'decency' would change its meaning and start to signify heroism.

In January 1940 the deadline passed for reporting Jewish property to the Germans. This meant that it would undoubtedly be confiscated. There was more and more talk of plans to move the Jews into a ghetto. After consulting with friends including Anna and Monika Żeromska, Miriam (the pseudonym of Zenon Przesmycki), Maria Dąbrowska and Jan Lorentowicz, a decision was made that the bookshop and publishing firm should be saved, in order to guarantee a living for the owners, authors and employees. So a fictional legal document was drawn up, backdated by three years, signing over the publishing firm's entire assets, fixed and movable, to Anna Żeromska, as if to cover the publisher's debts to the writer's widow. The bookshop on Mazowiecka Street was now given a new official name: 'A. Żeromska. Buchhandlung und Antiquariat – Blumenstrasse 12'. Janina and Hania could no longer show their faces there. I could not get my head round it all. 'Why do the Nazis like Mrs Żeromska better than my granny?' I screamed, and threatened: 'As soon as the war ends I'll stand in Mazowiecka Street and shout, "It's our bookshop. It's ours. Ours!"'

In spring 1940 they began to put up walls dividing off the part of the city centre that was inhabited by Jewish people. Persecution and repression of the Jews increased. Fear of the future was

Janek Kancewicz

Dr Kamilla Kancewicz

Stanisław Bielski

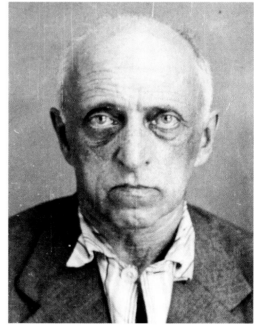

The final picture of Maksymilian
Horwitz-Walecki from the
KGB archives

Robert Osnos and Joanna Olczak, Piaseczno, summer 1939

Dr Gustaw Bychowski

Józef Osnos

Joanna Olczak and a friend, 1940

Anna Żeromska

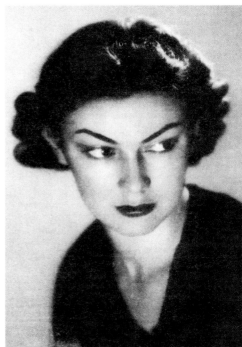

Monika Żeromska

Maria Jahns

War-time First Communion at the Order of the Immaculate Conception –
Joanna Olczak is first on the right

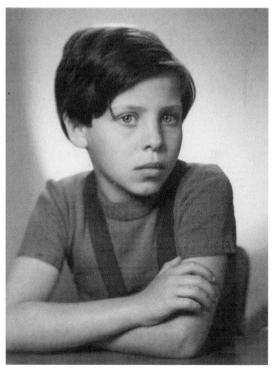

Joanna Olczak, 1945

Ryszard Bychowski, Wilno, 1940

Peter and Robert Osnos in New York

Paweł Beylin in the uniform of
Anders' army

Hanna Mortkowicz-Olczak and Janina Mortkowicz in Kraków after the war

Front row from the left: Sergei Valetsky, Maria Weymayr, Michał Ronikier.
Middle row: Katarzyna Zimmerer, Joanna Olczak-Ronikier, Monika Bychowska-Holmes.
Back row: Petya Valetsky, Jan Kancewicz, Robert Osnos.

From the left: Pamela Holmes, Tania Valetsky, Asia Sokołowska,
Maria Weymayr and Marta Hoffman

growing. It was just then that a little boy from the orphanage brought my grandmother a bouquet of scented spring lilac from Janusz Korczak with a little note saying: *When the forests are burning, we must think of the roses.*

In June 1940 Robert Osnos and his mother left Poland and went to join his father in Bucharest, via Berlin. Very few people managed to get out of occupied Warsaw so late in the day; it is a miracle that they succeeded. To bring it off, two superhuman powers combined forces: his father's and his mother's. In mid-September 1939 Józef Osnos had crossed the Romanian border and reached Bucharest. There, thanks to his extraordinary initiative and know-how he immediately managed to find a job with a company that dealt in used cars. After his first successful deal, he used all the money he had earned to buy an elegant suit, an overcoat and a dozen shirts from the best tailor in town. Clothing and manners always make an impression on officials. When he appeared at the still function-ing Polish Embassy and explained that he wanted to fetch his wife and son from Poland, the secretaries fell under his spell and put him in touch with the visa department at the Romanian Ministry of Foreign Affairs. There too he so enchanted the Minister himself with his impeccable French that he was given a promissory note for Romanian visas for his family. That promissory note – an amazing piece of treasure – reached Warsaw in February 1940.

As the name itself implies, it was only an official promise that they would be given visas, which would have to be stamped into their passports in Berlin. So now they had to get passports, to which Jews no longer had the right. The efforts to resolve this matter took four months. First of all Marta had to erase all trace of her origin. She found a priest who agreed to christen her and Robert and to draw up backdated church certificates. Then she went to Kraków several times, because it was the only place where documents authorising departure were issued. The journeys were dangerous; Jews were no longer allowed to travel, and her appear-ance clearly betrayed her ethnic origin. Once on the spot, she had to overcome countless problems – finding friends in a strange city, finding out to whom to give what sort of bribes, pretending to be confident and unruffled when everything inside her was trembling with fear, not giving up when seemingly reliable people let her down at the final hour, and listening to her instincts, which told her when she should shout and demand that promises be fulfilled, and when to ask humbly and put up with an insult. Thanks to her iron determination, but also some incredible luck, she finally acquired the by then unobtainable passports.

On Sunday, 9 June she and nine-year-old Robert got on the train to Berlin, with two suitcases and ten marks to their name. On Monday morning they got out at the station. The whole city was adorned with fascist flags to celebrate the fact that the Italians had joined the war. In Berlin she again had to overcome dozens of difficulties, especially financial ones. She did not have the money to pay for the visas and for their onward journey. Somehow she got the money and the visas, and finally they got into the train and settled down in their compartment. Robert was very calm and quiet. Only when they had crossed the Yugoslav border did he start to vomit. At last he felt safe. At the station in Bucharest Józef was waiting for them with a bouquet of roses.

PEOPLE

———————— ✳ ————————

In August 1940 the Gestapo burst into the house 'At the Sign of the Poets' on the Old Town Marketplace. They searched the whole interior, from the cellars right up to the attic, threatening and cursing, but without saying what they were looking for. Failing to find anything, they went away. A few days later my grandmother was summoned by the Gestapo. Just in case, she took a toothbrush and towel with her, called a droshky and went to Gestapo headquarters on Szuch Avenue. Luckily, she came home a few hours later. The inquiry was about a fairly absurd matter. Some piles of socialist brochures for workers by Marx, Bebel, Kautsky and Lassalle, published by my grandfather in 1905, had been lying in our attic for years. No one had bought any of them for ages, and they were regarded as troublesome waste paper. While we were tidying up during the move to the Old Town, they were thrown out into the yard without a second thought. A Jewish book dealer had loaded them all onto a cart and gone to stand at the corner of Długa Street and Miodowa Street, where he began to shout out the names of the authors – all banned by the occupying Germans. Of course he was immediately arrested, and when asked where he had got his goods from, had given my grandmother's name and address.

The whole affair might have ended in tragedy, but maybe thanks to her perfect German, her authoritative air, or maybe her lucky star, my grandmother emerged unscathed – or almost unscathed. As she was entering Gestapo headquarters, the doorman insulted her with some anti-Semitic abuse. Remembering the family motto, '*Kopf hoch!*', she began her conversation with the officer by complaining about this behaviour. She was then told that Jews did not deserve better treatment, whereupon she stood up and loudly declared that she was proud of her origins, that her father was a native of Vienna, a doctor of philosophy and a student of the humanities. She saw no reason to be ashamed of her ancestors, who deserved the highest respect. Evidently she had come across someone who reacted humanely, because they did not shoot her on the spot, and despite being accused of 'disseminating communist propaganda on the streets of Warsaw', she was acquitted, 'for reasons of age'. Indeed, two months later, in October 1940, she would reach the age of sixty-six.

*

On 12 October 1940, the Day of Atonement, a decree was issued establishing three districts in Warsaw: a German one, a Polish one and the Jewish ghetto. It was compulsory for the Jews to move into the ghetto by 15 November. Only hand luggage and bed linen was allowed. This decree affected twelve people in our family. In the oldest generation they were my grandmother, her sister Flora Beylin and her husband Samuel, and her brother Ludwik and his wife Genia. In the middle generation they were my mother, Karolina and Stefania Beylin, and Marysia and Alisia Margulies, Henrietta's daughters. In the youngest they were Pawełek Beylin and me. I do not know if there were any family discussions or meetings about it, but the decision was unanimous. Everyone would stay on the 'Aryan' side.

Ludwik and Genia were the bravest. They did not change either their address or their name. Marysia and Alisia moved out of their flat but remained in Warsaw, having obtained false papers for themselves. The Beylins had changed their name and had been living in Milanówek for a year. At this point we moved to a place just outside Warsaw too, near enough to visit each other. But Pawełek was no longer the same sunny boy from before the war. He was not amused by my jokes and tomfoolery – he knew and understood much more than I did.

I never talked to my relatives about the occupation era, neither about the years when we were still together, nor about the years that followed, which we spent apart. I did not want to know about their experiences, and I never told them about my own. I avoided family gatherings where relatives who had miraculously survived swapped stories about their fortunes. Whenever one of our wartime benefactors came to call I fled the house or shut myself in my room. Evidently, the emotions connected with the recent past were still too raw, and yet compared with what might have befallen me, nothing really awful ever happened. Yet what did happen was days, weeks and months of constant danger, and it is not surprising that I avoided reminders, but as a consequence nowadays I have a very foggy memory of the occupation. I have forgotten lots of things that happened, or can only remember the facts but cannot evoke the atmosphere that surrounded them.

I would not attempt to resurrect events that are buried in oblivion if I did not feel the need to write about the people who saved our lives. I have put it off for too long as it is. Anna Żeromska, Henryk Nikodemski, Maria Jahns, Irena Grabowska, Sister Wanda Garczyńska and Maria and Antoni Żurkowski are no longer alive. Not long ago it seemed there was no one left to answer any of my questions. When I tried to get some information out of Monika Żeromska, she said, 'You should have talked to my mother about it. She was the one who looked after you and visited you in all those suburban places. I just stood behind the counter in the bookshop.' She understates her own contribution, but luckily she has included a few comments about our fortunes in her memoirs. My mother's account of the war years has also survived and was published in her books, and there are some photographs too. All this enabled me to fill in at least some of the blanks in my memory.

When I finally got down to writing, however, miracles started happening. Helpful people appeared whose existence I was unaware of. Letters arrived from people who had disappeared from my life long ago. Among stacks of dusty family papers I discovered some extracts from my mother's memoirs, some published after the war, others started and abandoned halfway through. The most incredible surprise was a faded sheet of graph paper that fell out of an old black notebook of my grandmother's, in which she pedantically used to note down her expenditures. It was a precise record, with dates, of all the places where we had hidden during the occupation, together or separately. I saw it as a sign that I should not neglect the details. Now I could faithfully reconstruct the events of our occupation history, find on the map the places where the action took place, and recreate the heroic roles played in this drama by our friends, but also by people who had been complete strangers before the war.

First of all come Anna and Monika Żeromska. Thanks to them the publishing firm and the bookshop were saved from German confiscation, and the bookshop went on functioning throughout the whole occupation – not badly either, because it supported not only the people who worked there, but also provided the money for my family and the Beylin family to live on. 'The money to live on' takes on a whole new, macabre meaning when one considers that it also meant large sums paid out now and then to blackmailers hot on our heels. Once they had collected the money they had extorted from us and gone away, we knew that in a few days they would be back, so we had to find a new hiding place immediately. It was chiefly Monika who used to find them, first of all through her then husband, Bronisław Zieliński, and later through her own contacts in the Home Army (the Polish army that functioned as an underground resistance force during the occupation).

Both Anna and Monika Żeromska were connected with the Mortkowiczes before the war by publishing affairs and a long-term friendship, so it is easier to understand their devotion to them; but Henryk Nikodemski, a bookseller from Katowice, who in September 1939 had escaped with his family from Silesia to Warsaw and found a job in the bookshop on Mazowiecka Street, first met my mother and grandmother when they were already threatened by misfortune and could bring it down on others. He had no obligations of friendship towards them, yet throughout the entire occupation he took care of us, visited us, brought money and acted as an intermediary in finding each new place to live.

According to the yellowed sheet of paper, the first place was Podkowa Leśna, from October to December 1940. I was then six years old. Further down Żbików near Pruszków appears, the small estate of Monika Żeromska's then father-in-law, Dr Zieliński, who in 1940 had rented his villa to the Sisters of the Order of the Immaculate Conception. It was they who provided our next refuge, where we lived from December 1940 to March 1942. I do have some memories of living there: daredevil sledge rides down the surrounding hills, running about marshy meadows in the spring among wild flowers that grew higher than my head, going to mass at the nearby church and people ardently singing hymns begging for mercy: 'Beloved Mother, Guardian of our nation, Hear the orphans weep in supplication. We are Eve's out-casts, unto You we pray, Have mercy, have mercy, Lest homeless we stray.' The words were so appropriate to our situation that I sang them with unusual fervour, so much so that people looked round at us. Clearly, living somewhere off the beaten track more than a dozen kilometres from Warsaw felt so safe that I had not yet been warned not to draw attention to myself. I remember an old park that had gone wild, with dark ponds that I was not allowed to go near. I also remember people bringing in hay from the fields on a wagon, and then jumping about on the hay in an enormous barn.

I was mortally afraid of Mr Glaser, who performed the function of estate farmer. I was reminded every day that I was to be extremely polite to him and take care not to annoy him in any way. But he was often angry with me, especially when I peeped into the barn or hung about in the attic. I often used to play with his daughter, Cinka, who was the same age as me. She was a nice little girl, but she liked to tease me. One day I couldn't stand it, and some sort of devil got into me. As soon as she started teasing me again I seized her hand and bit her finger as hard as I could. She began to howl at the top of her voice. There was a terrible fuss. First Mr Glaser shouted at me, then at my mother and grandmother, who had come running, terrified. I realised that the end of the world had come – we would be driven out, and if we were killed it would all be my fault.

In my next memory we are wading through the mud at night in a headlong panic, God knows where to. That was when my celluloid doll Michał fell from my arms, my favourite doll, whom I had taken with me. I wanted to stop and look for him, but there was no time for that. Dragged along by the hand, I kept running. I knew we had to hurry, or else they would catch up with us. So without any tears I left Michał behind in a puddle, and with him my childhood.

For years on end I used to wonder: 'How did it happen? Did that Mr Glaser drive us out at night, as prey for the Nazis because of Cinka's bitten finger? Isn't that a bit excessive?' It must have been explained to me more than once that our nocturnal rambling had nothing to do with my escapade. In fact it happened much later on, and was the result of a warning that someone had informed the Gestapo that we were living at Żbikówek, that they would be there instantly and we must flee immediately; but in spite of these explanations my sense of guilt remained, and so did my irrational grudge against Mr Glaser, though sometimes it seemed as if he never existed at all, and I had invented the entire story.

My reason for writing about that incident in such detail is that not long ago, to my surprise, Żbikówek – a hazy phantom, like something from a forgotten dream – materialised, took on colour and shone forth with patriotism and the spirit of the resistance; and that was because one day Sister Ena from the Order of the

Immaculate Conception based at the convent in Jarosław called me and said, 'Do you remember me?' I did not, but she remembers everything. During the occupation she was a very young postulant at the order's Warsaw headquarters on Kazimierzowska Street. Nowadays she is a living chronicle of its history, collecting information and writing memoirs. Her most recent publication is characteristically entitled *Where Love Matured into Heroism*, whose heroine, in the literal sense of the word, is Sister Wanda Garczyńska, the Mother Superior at the Warsaw convent. It was thanks to her courage that over a dozen Jewish girls found refuge at the convent boarding school.

Sister Ena knows the names of all the alumnae by heart, corresponds with them and makes sure they keep in touch with one another. I owe her a great deal of priceless information. It was she who sent me a copy of a letter addressed to her from a Mr Józef Kiljański of Duchnice, describing the fortunes of Żbikówek during the occupation.

It is hard to believe that so many dramatic, extremely dangerous things could be happening in one place at the same time. For what was going on in the villa alone the nuns were risking the death penalty many times over. For hiding us – three people of Jewish origin; for running secret secondary-school courses for the local youth behind the guise of a home economics school; for allowing sessions of the Foreign Affairs Department of the government's underground civilian authorities to be held there, and for keeping the organisation's archive there. The Germans never got wind of it, but in communist Poland after the war Bronisław Zieliński, the son of Dr Zieliński who owned Żbikówek, paid for his involvement with the Department with a long-term sentence. Arrested in 1947, he came out of prison on the strength of an amnesty in 1956 during 'the thaw'. After that, as 'an enemy of the People's Poland', he had no hope of finding a job, and as a result became a top translator of American literature, including the works of Hemingway, Faulkner and Steinbeck.

The terrifying Mr Glaser was not a dream at all. He was the tenant farmer, his first name was Tadeusz and his underground pseudonym was 'Żbik'. He worked with the sabotage department, run by General Fieldorf, alias 'Nil'. The barn he used to chase me out of was where he had organised a hiding place with underground tunnels leading to it. Conspirators whose cover had been blown, undercover agents and saboteurs carrying out various special tasks were kept hidden in there. So it is not surprising that he sometimes got angry when I jumped about on their heads or when I romped about in the attic, where he kept underground propaganda material hidden. There was a huge weapons cache in the church tower, which was to supply the local Home Army divisions in the event of an uprising. Towards the end of the occupation Stanisław Lorentz, Director of the National Museum and head of the underground state's cultural department, stored the treasures of Warsaw's libraries in the same church, including Norwid's manuscripts. Not bad for a single occupation-era safehouse.

Someone informing on the nuns for keeping a Jewish family could have had tragic consequences, not just for them and us. A Gestapo raid meant the danger that the underground activities revolving around the estate would be discovered, spelling disaster for everyone involved in them. Incidentally, it would be interesting to know if the person who informed on us was aware of that. And why did they inform? Was it for the money? Out of servile loyalty to the occupiers? Out of ideological anti-Semitism? Or mindless cruelty? It makes no difference – we just had to vanish before they got there, which is why we fled in such panic. How long was our journey? I cannot remember.

In my hazy version of events we knocked at the lighted window of a cottage we chanced upon in a side road and someone invited us inside without any questions or doubts, but that is impossible. After all, the good sisters would not have driven us out into the dark night without anyone to look after us. They must have sorted out a place for us to go, our arrival must have been pre-arranged, someone must have agreed on that address with someone in case of misfortune, and someone must have escorted us and shown us the way. The whole district of Pruszków, Piastów, Żbików and the surrounding area was encircled by a network of Home Army connections. The terrifying Mr Glaser may have been our go-between for that hiding place, and maybe one of his liaison officers escorted us through the muddy darkness.

It was April 1942. In the Warsaw Ghetto about a thousand people were dying of hunger, disease and emaciation each week. Jews hiding outside the Ghetto were being more and more ruthlessly hunted down. It was quite by accident that my mother came across Mrs Grabowska, owner of a five-storey house on Rej Street in Piastów, and her daughter Irena, who would be our most loving protector. She just walked in straight off the street. The place where we ended up after fleeing from Żbikówek was clearly unsuitable for a long stay, and our friends could not help, so my mother wandered about Piastów, carefully concealing her despair behind a smile, and directly asking people for a room to let. In the local shop she was given Mrs Grabowska's address. She knocked at the door and was asked to come inside. Did the lady of the house – a nice, civilised person – realise that she was dealing with a Jew? I do not know. She treated my mother just as one should treat any respectable potential lodger, showed her the empty rooms on the ground floor and told her how much the rent was. A pretty young lady listened to the conversation in silence. She too inspired confidence. We moved in there at dusk.

Upstairs in the same house lived Mrs Grabowska's other daughter and her husband and small daughter Hania. After a while the whole family knew whom they had taken under their roof, yet they never showed a shadow of fear or antipathy; on the contrary, they offered us even greater kindness. At first we found the heavy traffic that passed through the house on Rej Street worrying. There was a never-ending stream of young people dropping in and out, delivering secret messages, bringing in and taking out all sorts of packages and sometimes staying overnight. Miss Irena often vanished for a few days, then came back, bringing strange, quite evidently frightened people to stay the night. Sometimes they stayed longer, and sometimes she found them another hiding place. It was not hard to guess that they were wanted by the Gestapo, and that Miss Grabowska was working for the resistance.

None of us ever spoke about our secrets, but a mutual trust developed between us, which in time grew into a friendship.

After the war my mother wrote: *If Irena ran off somewhere with a bag stuffed with packages, she was sure to be taking supplies or clothing to someone in dire need. If she was heading off to the station at Piastów at an unusual time of day with her eyes red from crying, she was sure to be hurrying to save someone who was in trouble or help an arrested person's family. Flats that had had their cover blown and accommodation for those who had to flee them, false documents, looking after parentless children lost in the chaos of war, or for the ageing parents of once carefree friends, getting hold of money – not for oneself, sudden alarms, going into hiding, and between one and another danger rare moments of light-hearted respite.*

Unfortunately my mother's memoir of Irena is generalised, full of hints and allusions, because in the years when it was published, it was dangerous to mention that she had belonged to the Home Army. Revealing the details of her underground activities was impossible, so along with the people who took part in occupation-era events some of the truth about those times died too. No proper portrait of Irena, known as Nena, was ever written, which is a pity. She was the epitome of the legendary Polish womanhood, full of charm and courage. Outwardly easy-going, she had a serious regard for the old-fashioned moral code, in which loving thy neighbour really meant something. She combined features that would seem contradictory: girlish coquetry, a carefree manner and joy at life, as well as sensitivity to other people's misfortunes, a sense of responsibility, and defiance of the dangers to which she exposed herself. *She was like the breath of life, like a wave of hope, fragrant, dashing and fair against the black of her glossy fur coat, beneath the velvet shadow of her felt hat,* wrote my mother.

I remember Nena well. It was she who took me, on the advice of the Sisters of the Order of the Immaculate Conception, from Piastów to the boarding school they ran on Kazimierzowska Street in Warsaw.

I can clearly see my first encounter with that place. I am standing on the threshold of a huge gymnasium, holding Irena's hand tightly. The shining floor smells of fresh polish. By the wall a large group of girls are sitting cross-legged, all staring curiously at the new girl. I am dying of embarrassment and fear. For the first time in my life I must remain alone in a new place, with strange people. I want to tear away from Irena and run home crying, but I know it is not possible. There is no home, and if I 'make a scene' here – my grandmother's most abusive definition of hysterical behaviour – I shall compromise myself in the eyes of these girls for ever, and that will not help me at all. So I take the first conscious decision of my entire life: I let go of Irena's hand and, on that shining floor, in defiance of fate, I do a somersault, then a second, and a third, and keep on rolling until I end up at the other end of the room. The girls clap and the nuns laugh. I know I have won their hearts; I feel accepted, and thus safe.

That was when I found a way of coping with life by hiding my true emotions behind a jester's mask. I put a lot of effort into pretending to be a resourceful, cheerful child and into amusing everyone around me. It was the special skill of many occupation-era children. None of the dozen or so Jewish girls hidden at the convent, some of whom already had terrible experiences behind them, ever despaired or showed their sadness or fear about the fate of their loved ones. The crying was done at night. The day went by as normally as could be, like before the war, criss-crossed with all sorts of activities. The nuns were gentle and smiling. Nowadays I cannot understand how on earth such extraordinary calm and cheerfulness prevailed in that ark sailing on the oceans of the occupation nightmare, when absolutely everything going on inside the convent carried the risk of death. They were not just hiding Jewish children, but also teaching subjects banned by the Nazis. There were secret study groups for secondary-school pupils, secret university lectures, a priesthood for Home Army soldiers, contacts with the underground, help for prisoners and people deprived of a living, and food for malnourished Jews who had escaped from the Ghetto. Courageous and composed, the nuns were only people, after all, and must sometimes have been terrified at the thought of what would happen if the Germans discovered just one of those crimes. Everyone knows how easily adults' worries are passed on to children. How did they manage to protect us from fear? They did not hide the danger from us. Frequent alarm practices prepared the schoolchildren for surprise raids by the Germans. When an internal bell rang during lessons, we gathered the pre-war books for Polish and history from our desks double-quick and shoved them into a special storage space – a sort of cloakroom – among our shoe bags and gym kits, where we always put them away after school anyway. Sometimes the alarm was real – then the nuns hid the endangered children in the infirmary, behind the altar in the chapel or in the enclosure. I am told that I once sat inside the altar for a few hours during one such search, but I cannot remember. By then I was already thoroughly versed in conspiracy. I knew by heart all the new facts in each successive fake identity card. This time my mother was called Maria Olczak, née Maliszewska, and my grandmother had become her own daughter's mother-in-law, borrowing the name Julia Olczak, née Wagner, from my father's late mother. My grandmother's sister Flora, alias Emilia Babicka, née Płońska, daughter of a carpenter born in Lunińsk in Byelorussia, was no longer her sister, but just a chance acquaintance. Flora's husband Samuel was called Stanisław. Luckily he was still her husband, which made his life much easier, because his daughters, Karolina and Stefania, who had two different surnames and were not apparently related to each other or to their parents, were always making blunders and were incapable of hiding their family connections. It was all very complicated.

What did I tell my schoolmates at the boarding school about myself? I do not think anyone ever asked me any questions, which is amazing, because everyone knows how full of curiosity little girls can be. Evidently the nuns issued a strict ban on talking about personal matters. That must be why I had no idea about the situation and origin of the other pupils. How many secrets those little heads must have been hiding. How many lies they must have contained. How much information as seemingly basic as one's first name, surname and family address they had to bury as deep as possible in their memories to avoid revealing them accidentally and causing a disaster. The challenge to 'be yourself!' – that basic condition for mental sanity – had been replaced with the categorical order: 'Forget who you are and become someone else!' – which was a life-saver, but later on, after the war, made life immensely complicated, because it was hard to recover one's lost identity.

Once every two weeks I visited my family, who were still living in Piastów. Irena used to collect me from the convent and take me home. One day she arrived at Kazimierzowska Street with a strange look on her face; apparently we were not going anywhere. Finally I wormed it out of her that my mother and grandmother had had to run, because the blackmailers had found them again. She swore they were alive and had already found another refuge. She promised to take me there soon, and indeed she kept her word. First we travelled by suburban railway, then waded through a snowy forest, until at last a solitary house appeared on a hill, buried in a copse. They were both waiting for us there, somehow very changed, with ashen faces. Nena had been there earlier, bringing new identity cards, money and warm clothing. Sometimes she stayed the night, but this time she went back to Warsaw and the three of us were left alone. It was Christmas 1942. I had a Christmas tree and some colourful decorations my mother made for it. With extraordinary skill she managed to conjure up a Chinaman, a Pierrot and a Columbine from some blown eggshells, some little baskets and little books made out of matchboxes, and endless chains of shiny coloured paper. As a present she gave me a poem she had written and some fairy tales she had illustrated herself, including 'Little Red Riding Hood' and 'Puss in Boots'. I still have them to this day. That evening, like a good girl I pretended to be asleep and that I could not hear their feverish whispers and occasionally my mother's sudden, violent sobs, interrupted by my grandmother impatiently rebuking her: 'Hush! You'll wake the child!'

I remembered Choszczówka well, but for many long years I had no idea who the owners were and what they were called. Not long ago a pleasant male voice said into the telephone receiver: 'This is Jerzy Żurkowski. We last saw each other during the war. Monika Żeromska asked me to call you. Apparently you are looking for information about those years.' I was being called from Poznań by the son of the people who had owned the house at Choszczówka. At the time of our stay there he was eighteen, and he remembers both ladies and me perfectly. Both he and his sister Krystyna were in the Home Army. Their father, Antoni Żurkowski, then going under the name of Ilnicki, had a high-up post in the underground formations active in that area. Hidden in a large clump of trees in an isolated spot far from the road, the house was ideally suited for an underground hiding place. The Germans overlooked such places, so not only weapons and secret publications were hidden there, but also illicit tenants. Antoni's wife, Maria Żurkowska, took care of them, because the rest of the family was active in the field. 'Who sent my relatives to you? Some mutual friends?' I asked. 'No one ever exchanged names in those days, no questions were asked, and the reasons why people were in hiding were never revealed. They reached us through Home Army contacts. That was enough of a recommendation,' says Jerzy. Perhaps they ended up there as a result of Irena Grabowska's underground connections? Or did Mieczysław Cziherin, a high-up Home Army officer and close friend of Monika Żeromska, find this place?

In January 1943 my grandmother's brother, Ludwik Horwitz, and his wife Genia were arrested. In February they were both shot. Gentle, absent-minded, always as if slightly distracted, Lutek worked at the State Geological Institute in Warsaw. He spoke excellent German and was not afraid of the Nazis. He took no notice of the anti-Jewish orders, never wore an armband and did not try to hide behind an assumed name. He went on functioning like that for three years. The occupation authorities at the Institute, which had been renamed the *Amt für Bodenforschung*, knew about his ethnic origins, but let him continue the research he was conducting in the Pieniny range. In December 1942 he finished his work and handed his superiors his report, written in German. At that point he was dismissed from his job and evicted from his flat. A few days later the Gestapo came for him and Genia. He was sixty-eight years old when he died. Of my grandmother's eight siblings only two sisters were left: the oldest, Flora, in hiding in Milanówek, and the youngest, Kamilka, in a Siberian labour camp.

On 18 January 1943 the German police began the action to evacuate the Ghetto. The staff of the Jewish Battle Organisation issued an appeal to the population: *Jews! The occupiers have started on the second act of your extermination. Do not go to your death without resisting! Defend yourselves! Pick up an axe or a knife! Barricade your home! [...] Fight!* The resulting resistance forced the Germans to interrupt the action and to limit the deportations to Treblinka to about 6000 people, instead of well over 10,000, as planned. From the woods surrounding Choszczówka shots could be heard. With the help of Polish informers, the German military police were looking for Jews who had run away during the liquidation of the ghetto at Jabłonna. At this point Antoni Żurkowski, alias Ilnicki, took my mother to the town of Pruszków, to stay with his cousin Maria Jahns, while my grandmother hid at Milanówek.

The convent refectory smelled of ersatz coffee and slightly burned porridge, while little girls chased up and down the corridors laughing. The whole boarding school was absorbed in preparing a Nativity play for Shrovetide. The play was entirely written and composed by Miss Zosia Orłowska – nowadays Zofia Rostworowska, wife of Poland's first Minister of Culture after independence was regained in 1989 – who rehearsed our roles with us. The show was to be performed before an audience from the city: relatives and friends of the pupils. The little girls of Jewish origin were also eager to take part, so the good Miss Zosia came up with the idea that they would appear as courtiers of the exotic Three Kings. Coloured turbans and make-up would disguise their Semitic looks. I was a Negro page and, all blacked-up, I could freely show off my gymnastic skills. Nowadays the first-hand accounts that Sister Ena has collected in her book remind me of other, less amusing adventures. Anna Kaliska writes:

One day three Volksdeutsch appeared in the parlour with a demand to hand over the little Olczak girl, whose mother was a Jew. They demanded an inspection of all the children, and had come with precise instructions. Sister Wanda locked the little girl and a few others whose origin can easily be guessed behind the enclosure on the second floor, and the rest had to file into the parlour. Then they began to inspect the house, first the ground floor, then the first floor. Sister Wanda showed them round. Her explanation that the enclosure was on the second floor and that access there was forbidden by the rules of the Order was passed over in silence, and the three Germans started to go up the stairs. We remained on the first floor. I can still hear their heavy footsteps today – I can remember the appalling fear – we knew all too well what would happen to her and the children. Some sisters were praying in the chapel as the footsteps approached the door of the enclosure. Then there was a moment's silence, and we heard Sister Wanda calmly say: 'I shall once again remind you that this is the enclosure.' And again there was a silence, in which it felt as if everything around us and inside us had died and gone still. And then footsteps coming down the stairs, and they were gone.

At that point, at the nuns' request Irena Grabowska took me away from the convent to live with Maria Jahns in Pruszków.

My family's friendship with the Jahns family lasted throughout the war years and afterwards we kept up almost family contact, full of immeasurable gratitude on the part of my relatives, because Maria's heroism, and perhaps also her scornful contempt for the dangers she courted, seem incomprehensible. Her story, so typical for those times, shows once again what immense depths of courage came to light in the women whose lives had been ruined by the war and who, though completely unprepared for it, had to take on a lonely fight for their family's survival. This lovely young woman, known as Muszka, was then already a widow and mother of three children. Before the war, her husband, Artur Jahns, was an engineer with a top job at the 'Königshütte' steelworks in Chorzów. He had a German name but he did not want to be counted as a citizen of the German Reich. To escape the pressure, he had fled with Muszka and their small daughter Krysia to Warsaw, where their second daughter, Asia, was born. In 1941 he fell ill with meningitis and died. A couple of months after his death their son Józio was born. It was not entirely clear what a woman should do who had no profession, was not used to working and was alone with three small children. At that point some relatives who lived in the area helped her to open the shop in Pruszków – a miserable little grocery with rationed jam and lard, occupation-era bread the consistency of clay, vinegar, carbide and kindling wood. At the request of her cousin from Choszczówka she found room for my mother at the back of the little shop, and later took me in for a few weeks too.

She took small payments for board and lodging, which helped her modest budget, but the money was of no great significance. If our presence were to have come to light, she would have paid for the deal with her own and her children's lives. To this day I cannot understand how she had the nerve to take on such a risk. The little shop was full of people from morning to evening. In Pruszków they all knew each other. The extended stay of a stranger with a child at the shopkeeper's home must have seemed suspicious, but for quite a long time nobody noticed us there. Naturally, we never stuck our noses outside the four walls of the room that was cleverly hidden at the back of the house. All we had to do was keep our ears open. An unexpected noise, a raised voice or too insistent a ring at the shop doorbell could mean an unwelcome visitor. Then we had to move like lightning to shift the box of kindling wood that disguised the entrance to the cellar in the kitchen floor, lift a trapdoor, go down a ladder and hide among the sacks of coal and potatoes. The householders had superbly mastered the art of opening and closing the trapdoor in a flash, because there was also a weapons cache in the cellar and some underground propaganda material that was distributed locally. Every few days an 'uncle' came by car from Choszczówka and carried mysterious packages down there.

I have no idea how many times we sought refuge there, nor can I remember the feeling of danger at all. Krysia Jahns, now a doctor living in Canada, with whom I restored contact many years later, reminded me how every time the uncle came her mother used to spend hours scrubbing the floor around the trapdoor, because the sacks he brought contained rounds of ammunition. The biggest worry was the silvery dust that rose from the sacks and settled in cracks on the wooden floor. It was hard to get it out of there.

Krysia also reminded me of a rather terrifying incident. Her mother was very attractive, and as a single woman, alongside the many anxieties of everyday life, she also had to contend with the persistent attentions of unwelcome admirers. One evening, after the shop had closed, two German officers rang the doorbell, announcing that they had come to pay a visit for a bit of distraction in the company of a beautiful woman. If we had not been in the house, she would have slammed the door in their faces at once; but she was afraid they would make a fuss, so she tried explaining that it was late, she had to get up early, and the children were asleep. Indeed, Krysia and I were already in the same bed together, because that was warmest and nicest. Hearing what was going on, my mother immediately ran down to the cellar; but I did not have time, because the Germans had overcome Muszka's resistance and gone into the kitchen. Afraid they would look into the bedroom, the resourceful Krysia shoved me under the mattress in her bed, lay down on top of me and pretended to be asleep.

Without knowing if we had managed to hide or not, poor Muszka decided to humour the Germans now that they had invaded the house. She opened a bottle of hooch and treated them to scrambled eggs in pork fat from the stores set aside for the business. They ate, drank and talked about the tough time they were having. Muszka spoke excellent German, so the evening went on and on above my mother's head. Meanwhile, I was being smothered by the mattress, and Krysia, as she tells it, was praying she could withstand the temptation to run into the kitchen and throw herself on the scrambled eggs, the smell of which was driving her mad. The food situation was worse and worse – on ration cards one could get one egg per month, pork fat cost a fortune, and her mother had not made this heavenly dish since time immemorial.

I am most impressed by the discipline of the Jahns children. Józio was still too small to understand anything, but Krysia was already going to school and Asia was at kindergarten. Both had friends and played outside, but neither of them ever squeaked a word to anyone about the guests at their house. They both behaved as normally as could be, as if they were not hiding a deadly secret all the time. After all, they were sworn to secrecy with a rather terrifying warning: 'You don't want the Germans to kill us all, do you?' What a mental effort they must have had to make to take this warning on board, and at the same time not to hate the people whose presence in the house could cause such terrifying results. I never experienced the slightest unkindness, hint of ill-feeling or complaint from them; and not long ago, when I found them both again, we could feel how strongly those years united us.

On Good Friday, 19 April 1943, at dawn, SS divisions invaded the Ghetto shielded by a tank and two armoured cars. No one had any doubt that the final action to liquidate the Ghetto and its residents had begun. The relentless resistance of the Jewish Battle Organisation changed into an uprising. The Germans sent storm troops, Wehrmacht units, flame-throwers and anti-aircraft guns into the battle.

On 25 April Ludwik Landau wrote in his diary: *If yesterday evening the moon went a bit pale, during the day dense clouds of smoke began to rise over the ghetto again – and right now it looks as if the whole ghetto is on fire. Whether last night's strong wind played a part, or one of the two sides set fire to the houses is not yet clear; suffice it to say that the fire has taken on fantastic dimensions – and the final residents of the ghetto, condemned to extermination by the Germans, may be dying there in the flames and smoke.*

According to the list, my mother and grandmother spent that terrible Easter at Tworki, where they lived from March to June 1943. Within the grounds of the mental hospital? Or in the town? I do not know. I can only guess that in both Milanówek and Pruszków life had become too dangerous. The nuns had taken me back in again. The girls in my class were getting ready for their First Communion, including those of Jewish origin, with their parents' consent, if they were still alive, or that of their guardians if they had any. My secular family approved of the Catholic education that was instilled into me at the convent, besides which I had been christened before the war.

Yet the nuns did not force any of the girls in their charge to change their religion. Dr Zofia Szymańska-Rosenblum, who in September 1942 saved her little niece from the Ghetto and brought her to Kazimierzowska Street, writes in her memoirs: *With the greatest subtlety Sister Wanda asked me if I would agree to Jasia being christened and taking Holy Communion, assuring me that it was the child's ardent wish and would be desirable in terms of safety. 'But if you have any objections, please rest assured that my attitude to Jasia will not be changed and that I shall save the person.'*

Jasia's mother had been deported from the Ghetto earlier, probably to Treblinka; her father fought in the Ghetto to the last moment and must have been killed there. I had no idea about my schoolfriend's experiences. She did not talk about them, and if she cried, it was only when no one could see. We were both very excited about our First Communion. We wrote down our sins on cards, so that, God forbid, we would not forget them during confession. We were dying of worry that the Host would stick in our throats and we would have to push it down with our fingers, in other words commit sacrilege. We spent hours at our prayers in the chapel, and now and then we ran to one of the nuns with the happy news that we felt a 'vocation'. Two jolly, lively little girls, enjoying life, as if they hadn't a care.

Not long ago I met up with Jasia in New York. Seeing each other again after so many years was very moving, but I did not dare to ask her too insistently what she felt and thought at the time. To this day she cannot or does not wish to talk about those days.

On 3 June 1943 the day of our First Communion came. Some photographs of the ceremony have survived. In one of them seven little girls in white sacramental vestments are posing for the camera – it is the classic souvenir picture, taken by a professional photographer. Five of the girls in the photograph are Jewish. I am astounded by the courage, and at the same time the sensitivity, of the nuns. They heroically regarded hiding these children as their Christian duty. They treated the inevitable threat of death as a consequence of their decision. But where did they get the motherly sensibility that prompted them, amid the all-surrounding danger, to give us a little joy? Not just spiritual but also secular, the kind little girls should have – somehow they knew we had to look pretty in our white dresses, made to measure and decorated with embroidery, that we had to have little white garlands on our heads, our hair twisted into curls, and that we must have a souvenir of that memorable day. Those photographs, and I have several at home, always move me with their festivity and solemnity, absurd, it would seem, in those awful times. Or maybe the photos had some other, hidden aim? Perhaps they were supposed to save us in the event of danger, to convince the people who came for us that as ardent Catholics we did not deserve to die? If that was what the provident nuns intended, I feel even greater emotion as I gaze at our earnest little faces. We all survived. Thank God.

In June 1943, on Whit Sunday, Irena Grabowska took me to visit my mother and grandmother. On the suburban railway a fellow latched on to us, making jokes and trying to draw us into conversation. Accustomed to men accosting her and well able to deal with such pests, Irena sent him packing quite sharply; but I let myself be taken in by his cajolery. 'Joasia!' he said to me. 'Why don't you want to talk to me? I know your mama very well, and your grandma. Your grandma's called Janina Mortkowicz, right? And now she's living with your mama. And you're going to see them, aren't you?' He managed to get near enough to extract a confirmation, or maybe just elicit an affirmative smile or a nod. Where did he come from? Had he discovered my presence at the convent? Had he been following Irena, and sat behind us in the train in pursuit of her? When we got out, he waved to us and disappeared, and we went on our way. I had only just had time to call from the threshold, 'We're here!', I had only just thrown my arms round my mother's neck, when he appeared in the doorway. He had followed us along the country lanes – we had led him to his goal.

Where did I go while he was negotiating with them? I think I was told to go and play outside. How did I feel, knowing that I had brought ruin on them through my own stupidity? What was established during that conversation? How much money and what deadline were agreed on? I refused to go back to Warsaw with Irena. I wanted to stay with them, to wait with them for the money that she promised to get. But they persuaded me to be sensible, and as I was being tortured by my sense of guilt, I gave way, only making them promise me one thing: that they would not take poison when I left, for that was always my greatest fear. Then I went back to the convent like a good girl, to my French and grammar lessons. Nowadays I find it hard to understand how I lived in that double world, in two realities at once, playing two roles at the same time.

The whole matter came to a reasonable end. The blackmailer waited patiently for the money without reporting to the Gestapo, and my mother and grandmother did not have to break the promise they made me. But we did not see each other again until two years later.

THE LEGACY OF JOANNA O

———————— ✳ ————————

The Warsaw suburbs could no longer guarantee safety, so our friends found a new refuge for my mother and grandmother. In July 1943 they went to live in the Warsaw Polytechnic professor's block at 75 Koszykowa Street, in a little room at the back of the building. The entrance was hidden behind some heavy book-shelves. A caretaker who was in the know brought them food and was their only link with the outside world. They did not emerge from there for fourteen months.

They could not go near the windows; they had to talk in a whisper and move about without making a sound. How did they pass the time? To avoid getting out of practice, one day they would speak in French, the next in German, the third in Russian and the fourth in English. They remembered poems, books they had read, pictures they had once seen and journeys they had made together. They turned their minds to the past, and made plans for the future. My mother wrote a novel entitled *Chiaroscuro*, the story of an artist's outing to paint in the open air at Kazimierz on the River Vistula. My grandmother translated another book by Hugh Lofting, *Dr Dolittle's Return*. They did not come to hate each other, they did not go mad, nor did they commit suicide. They still had lots of energy, without which they would not have survived what lay in store for them.

Despite their inner discipline, they did gradually begin to lose hope. My grandmother was then sixty-eight, and my mother was forty-one. It was their seventh hiding place. For four years death had been treading on their heels. The Nazis were hunting down the few remaining Jews ever more relentlessly. So many people had already been killed. Why should their lives be saved?

They could at least be certain of one thing: the child would live. So age-old providence bid them put their worldly affairs in order and make me the sole heiress to the firm and the tradition. A yellowed sheet of foolscap paper, both sides covered in my mother's pleasant, rounded handwriting, is perhaps the most moving memento to have survived among the family papers.

LAST WILL AND TESTAMENT

I leave my entire estate and that of my mother, Janina M., in shares and assets to my daughter Joanna. [...] I beseech my associates and friends to ensure that from the shares in the enterprise due to us my daughter should have the means to be supported and educated, and I ask them to watch over her estate and look after it with the great goodwill I have known from them. I ask and authorise them to watch over the proper utilisation of the income due to my daughter, both current expenses connected with her upkeep and schooling, and to provide for her future. I also authorise them, jointly with someone from my family: Edwarda M., Karolina B., or Dr Gustaw B., to supervise and consult in my name with her father Tadeusz O. on matters concerning my daughter and to keep an eye on the course of her education.

Until my daughter Joanna comes of age, I bequeath representation of the shares due to us, me and my mother, and the corresponding vote within the company, to my aunt Edwarda M. together with the right to work for the firm and to lifelong maintenance. If the above-mentioned person does not return to Poland, I bequeath representation of our share in the management of the company to Dr Karolina B. Please liquidate my and my mother's estate in fixed assets, furniture, pictures and other objects for the benefit of my daughter. Some of the heirlooms are to be kept, as far as possible, for her in the future. The wardrobe is to be partly adapted and utilised for her future, then liquidated for her benefit or distributed for the benefit of our friends and relatives. I ask my friend Irena G., Karola B. and Stefania B., and also Edwarda M., if she returns to Poland, to take care of this.

The confiscated presses that, according to Mr Henryk N. are my and my mother's property, once recovered (which I beg to be done) are to be liquidated for Joanna's benefit. My manuscripts: 1. A Song About Warsaw Under Siege *(72 poems),* 2. Chiaroscuro *(a novel), dramatisations of three fairy tales for children (*Cinderella, Little Red Riding-Hood, Puss in Boots*) and my* *mother's:* 1. Tereska, 2. *translations of Hugh Lofting's Dr Dolittle books I leave to the firm for publication [...]. Depending on post-war conditions and in consultation with qualified persons I would also ask for some of my books and some of my mother, Janina M.'s books and translations to be re-issued. I personally consider suitable for reissue in first place* 30 Friends from All Over Poland *and* Krysia's Day. *These books, endorsed and approved by the Ministry, might prove profitable. I bequeath all income from my and my mother's books and translations to my daughter Joanna.*

Please provide financial help for my family until the war ends. I beseech all my friends to be kind to my child and to look after her. I ask that my daughter Joanna should learn from the lips of my friends and the Polish writers, first and foremost Maria D. and Leopold S., about her grandparents' and mother's activities and work for Polish culture and the Polish national identity. As we do not know even the approximate size of the legacy that my mother and I are leaving to our daughter and granddaughter Joanna O., we cannot define the financial equivalent of the debts of gratitude that we owe to some people, above all Miss Irena G. We leave these matters to the discretion of Mr Henryk N. For the time being we leave only expressions of our warmest gratitude to the friends thanks to whom we are still alive now: our associates Irena G. and Maria J. and all the others who in these difficult times have shown us their kindness and given us help.

Hanna Olczak
Warsaw, 18/IX 1943

For security reasons the surnames of all those mentioned in the will were given by their initial letters only. Edwarda M. was my grandfather's sister, the rosy-cheeked, radiant Aunt Edzia, who worked in the bookshop before the war, and who in the summer of 1939, to her great good fortune, went to visit her family in the United States and remained there. Gustaw B. – i.e. Gustaw Bychowski, my grandmother's nephew – was already in America with his family and did not return to Poland. Karolina and Stefania B. – the Beylin sisters – were in hiding, one in Biała Podlaska, the other in Milanówek, and it was not clear if they would survive. The Polish writers who were supposed to tell me about my grandparents' and mother's activities were Maria Dąbrowska and

Leopold Staff. The friends to whom they left their expressions of warmest gratitude were Maria Jahns, Henryk Nikodemski and Irena Grabowska.

A striking feature of this document is the unwavering certainty that once the cataclysm of war is over, life will return to its old orbit. After all, that was how history had carried on for centuries – people died, and their property passed from generation to generation. They believed the firm would survive, the estate would recover its value, the printing presses confiscated by the Germans would be retrieved, the firm would start printing books again, the relevant ministries would recommend them to the readers, and the profits would guarantee a living and education for the orphaned child. In making me their heiress, they wanted nothing in exchange but remembrance. It is very moving to discover that though condemned to death for being Jewish, they asked for me to be told about their services to Polish culture and the Polish national identity.

By the spring of 1944 the defeat of Germany seemed inevitable, despite, or maybe because of which German repressions in Warsaw intensified, including round-ups, arrests and public executions. People were hoping for a Soviet invasion and an uprising. The nuns took us away on holiday earlier than usual. They reckoned we would be safer outside the city, so we went to stay at the idyllic resort of Skolimów, just outside Warsaw. One night at our villa all the windowpanes flew out and the garden was showered with shrapnel. German anti-aircraft artillery exercises had started in the neighbourhood. We were evacuated to Mironowskie Górki on the right bank of the River Vistula, not far from Wołomin. A few days later the Warsaw Uprising broke out.

We spent the next few weeks in the open country, in a bunker on the front line. Once the Russians had ousted the Germans, we finally emerged, barely alive from hunger and exhaustion. The nuns got hold of some form of transport and tried to get the children out of the war zone. As they passed through Siedlce, they left me with my uncle Stefan Olczak, who was living there. They hoped it would be easier for me to get in touch with my family through him. I spent ten months in Siedlce, while my uncle and his wife gently tried to accustom me to the idea that my mother and grandmother were no longer alive.

But they had survived in the little room on Koszykowa Street until the Uprising broke out, then spent the first few weeks of the fighting in the building's cellars. When, on 19 August 1944, German detachments captured the Polytechnic area, they managed to reach Mokotowska Street via underground passages, and there, in more cellars, they lived through to the capitulation of Warsaw. That October, in a crowd of refugees they managed to reach a camp at Pruszków. Evacuated to the village of Leszczyna near Kraków, they spent over six months trying to keep body and soul together in appalling conditions. Once the war was over they made their way to Kraków and found a place to live at the Writers' House, 22 Krupnicza Street.

Only then could my mother start to look for me. Travelling by goods train and lorry, or taking lifts she chanced upon, she went from town to town, finally turning up in Siedlce in June 1945. She did not know the way to my uncle's house, so she asked the passers-by about him and about me. Worried and agitated, she must have told everyone the story of her lost child, because a whole string of gawpers came trailing after her, eager to witness our dramatic reunion. They were in for a disappointment, because I failed to recognise her. To me she looked like a stranger. She stared at me in amazement too; she had thought a tearful little girl with long plaits would fall into her arms, but instead she found a short-cropped, self-possessed, resolute person. I refused to go back to my grandmother with her immediately – I had a whole lot of obligations here. I had to dig up potatoes in my aunt and uncle's field, take care of little Jaś and scrub the floor on Sunday. I also had to recite a patriotic poem at the school's end-of-term celebration.

Won over with ice cream, I rather half-heartedly agreed to go with her. 'You'll see, from now on life will be back to normal,' she promised me on the way. I listened sceptically; I did not know what normal life was like.

In Kraków I soon, too soon, recovered my lack of concern. 'That child is completely devoid of feelings,' my grandmother used to say to my mother in a resounding whisper. I never cried, I never complained, and whenever they tried to cuddle me I turned to stone. I was not interested in their tales of what had happened to them during the occupation. I was not surprised we were alive, and I did not care that my would-be inheritance had been blown to the four winds in burned-down Warsaw. The war had sharply sheared through time, which now refused to be stuck together again; it had separated me from my relatives emotionally and destroyed the space I might have moved back into.

The house 'At the Sign of the Poets' on the Old Town Marketplace had been toppled by a German bomb during the Uprising. Fortunately, no one was killed, but all the property we had transferred there in 1939 from the flat on Okólnik Street was buried under the rubble, including the family archives, letters, photographs, valuable objects, furniture and pictures, as well as the firm's property: the printing plates, colour reproductions, stocks of paper, printed folios not yet cut and bound, and book-binding materials such as leather, cardboard, canvas, tissue paper and silks.

The building at 12 Mazowiecka Street that housed the bookshop had also become a ruin. All one could see through the holes that used to be the display windows, once called 'windows onto the world', was scorched bricks, twisted metal and the ashes of smoul-dering paper instead of books and colourful albums. Among the rubble sat the tiled stove, gleaming with a turquoise sheen.

On 26 June 1945 in her first post-war letter to New York my mother tried to sum up what had happened:

My dearest Edzia,
I cannot believe how lucky I am to be alive and well and writing to you. I have lived through this moment so many times, but only in my dreams... Five and a half years of torment – having to hide, drifting like beggars about villages and subur-ban settlements, being blackmailed, running for our lives, two years without my child... The bookshop and the Old Town are a pile of ashes and rubble. Not a single book was saved... Warsaw no longer exists... Of our family on Mama's side only Lutek and Genia were murdered... Your balance is more tragic: Hela, Oleś and his wife were killed in the Łódź ghetto, Kasia in Warsaw, Michal, Helka and Lola in the eastern lands... I have yet to find out about Józio and Maryla's family in Warsaw, but there's little chance that they survived. We are the exceptions...

I had my mind on other things. Once I had tricked them out of a few pennies for another scoop of ice cream and run to the magical ice-cream shop, the 'Gelateria Italiana' on Floriańska Street, my happiness was complete. It never entered my head that we were only alive thanks to a large number of good-hearted people who had risked their own lives to save us. It was a very long time before the idea of gratitude crossed my mind. Recently Jerzy Żurkowski, son of the owners of the house at Choszczówka, came to visit me in Kraków. The meeting was very moving, but Jerzy was distinctly embarrassed when I started to ask him questions that he thought quite unnecessary. He does not regard his parents' behaviour as anything out of the ordinary. He answered me with restraint, not letting himself be drawn into any sentimental feelings.

'Of course we were informed of your ethnic origin. Yes, my father also warned my aunt, Mrs Jahns. After all, she had to make that decision consciously. Yes, Mama knew we were all risking the death penalty for hiding Jews. But my parents also knew that one doesn't refuse people help. Fear? No one thought about fear at the time. We were risking the death penalty for everything going on at home, and for what we were doing away from home. Any one of us could have been killed at any moment. Is that a reason to forget that one is a human being? Heroism? No, just common decency.'

Maria Jahns, Antoni Żurkowski, his children Krystyna and Jerzy were all arrested immediately after the war for belonging to the Home Army. Muszka came out after a few months. The Żurkowskis were in prison for longer. Irena Grabowska was arrested on 7 March 1944 as a courier for 'Zagroda' ['The Croft'] – the Foreign Liaison Department of Home Army Chief Command. After a very tough interrogation she was shot on 26 April 1944 at Pawiak prison. Years later she was posthumously awarded a medal for being 'Righteous among the Nations'.

CHILDREN ON THE MOVE

———————✴———————

While describing my own wanderings during the occupation I broke off my account of the fate of my four Warsaw cousins, Monika and Ryś Bychowski, Robert Osnos and Pawełek Beylin. Following the outbreak of war they gradually disappeared from my life. Now it is time to go back to them.

✍

In early September 1939 Gustaw and Maryla Bychowski, two-year-old Monika and fifteen-year-old Krysia reached Wilno and breathed a sigh of relief. The beautiful, prosperous city, set far behind the front line, was almost untouched by the war. Despite an influx of refugees it was still possible to find a place to stay, eat at one of the many elegant restaurants, relax and think about what to do next. Unfortunately, despite Gustaw's expectations, their hopes of a speedy return home were fading. Troubling messages came pouring from the megaphones installed in the city. The Germans were advancing into the depths of Poland. From 8 September the siege of Warsaw was on, and the loudspeakers emitted the hoarse voice of the Mayor of Warsaw, Stefan Starzyński, calling on the Varsovians to put up resistance.

On 17 September 1939, when the Germans had already occupied most of Poland, the Red Army invaded from the east. During the night the Polish Republic's government members left the country, crossing the Romanian border, and next morning Russian tanks appeared in the suburbs of Wilno. The first Soviet occupation lasted barely forty days, but the city immediately ceased to function normally. The famished Soviet soldiers stripped the shops and stores of all food. There began to be shortages of flour, meat, salt, sugar, fat and matches. People stood in bread queues a kilometre long, taking up position outside the bakeries from five in the morning. A few hours later they would get a small loaf of clay-like black bread. There was also a lack of toiletries, medicines, clothing and footwear. There was no fuel, so people started cutting down trees and fences. Gustaw spent hours standing in queues to get a small bucket of coal, a little milk and a little buckwheat for his family.

On 5 October Hitler was saluted by his victorious troops on Warsaw's Ujazdowskie Avenue. All Poland was in captivity, partly German, partly Soviet. People of Jewish origin knew that for them returning to territory occupied by the Nazis could only end in tragedy. Remaining in Bolshevik Wilno was also dangerous. Executions, arrests and deportation to prison camps in the depths of Russia immediately began. The repression affected Poles and Jews, aristocrats and communists, the intelligentsia and ordinary people, civilians and military alike.

On 10 October, under the terms of the Soviet–Nazi pact Wilno and part of the surrounding district were transferred to Lithuania. When on 27 October the Soviet troops left the city, the citizens sighed with relief. The terror and famine were over. The shops filled up again, and life became normal, although from time to time anti-Lithuanian or anti-Polish atrocities were committed, and as usual at times of social upheaval, anti-Semitic ones too. At first the Lithuanian authorities were benevolent towards the Poles. Polish schools and the Stefan Batory University went on functioning, Polish periodicals went on appearing, and all sorts of Polish institutions continued to operate without any obstruction. Admittedly, the Polish consulate in Kaunas (formerly the Polish city of Kowno) was closed down, but the welfare of refugees was taken over by the British Embassy, which made it easier for Poles to leave the country.

Gustaw got in touch with the American Psychoanalytic Association, which insisted on getting him and his family over to America. They only had to reach Stockholm, where their travel documents and money for the journey would be waiting for them, but they did not want to leave without Ryś.

Maryla came to Warsaw to fetch him, but he could not leave by train with her because he did not have the relevant documents.

Ryś managed to reach Wilno by smuggling himself over the border. Thousands of people were escaping this way from territory occupied by the Germans, especially Jews, hoping from Lithuania to make their way across to the West. Later on he described the route:

Hunted like animals, people from Warsaw and from both occu-pied areas walked along it by night in a temperature of minus forty degrees, wading waist-deep in snow. Men and women carrying children slipped through this way while under fire from the border guards. Many of them did not make it. Beaten, tortured and held under the open sky for days on end by the Germans, arrested and repeatedly driven from one side of the border to the other by the Lithuanian and Soviet sentries, they gave up and went back to starving Białystok or Lwów, or if they had enough strength, to ter-rorised Warsaw or Łódź [...] From among the thousands who trod this path and whom it led to Wilno, the route demanded sacrificial offerings. Sometimes it was a person's entire property, including their last hundred-zloty or hundred-rouble note that was taken away... Sometimes it was their frostbitten fingers, hands and feet, ears or faces... Dozens of small children died of hunger in the wretched 'neutral zone', in the no-man's land between the German and Soviet lines. Many people froze to death in the forest or died of lung infections after reaching Wilno. That's what that costly route was like. When I travelled it in December 1939, it was illuminated by the moon and a starlit sky was smiling down on it. The clear path winding between the mighty black pine trees looked like a man who had lost his way in the dark.

When he reached Wilno, it turned out there was no longer any way of getting across from there to Stockholm. The sea route was controlled by the Germans, who were firing on and searching Latvian and Estonian ships, removing from them all the men aged between eighteen and fifty. There were no seats left on the aero-planes from Riga in Latvia, so they decided to stay put for the winter. To avoid wasting time, Ryś started studying economics and sociology at the university. But meanwhile the Lithuanians had tightened their anti-Polish policy. Hasty efforts began to make the schools and public institutions Lithuanian, Polish shop signs and inscriptions disappeared, the names of the streets were changed to Lithuanian ones and the Polish crests and emblems were removed from public buildings. The closed-down college went on functioning in secret, so the boy still went to lectures and tried to carry on as usual. Despite the anti-Polish restrictions, life in Wilno continued almost normally. There was no lack of food, the restaurants and cafés were open, people traded currency and fake documents, and everyone kept saying that any moment now the situation would change for the better.

In early spring 1940 the Bychowskis managed to fly out of Riga to Stockholm, but there once again they found themselves in a trap. By now the war had engulfed the whole of Europe and it was impossible to leave Sweden for America either by land or sea. The Germans and British were fighting in the North Sea and the Baltic. German raids on the British Isles made air communications with the United States impossible. At the same time as the air raids the Battle of the Atlantic had begun, and the Germans were attacking all the ships and battleships sailing across the ocean.

By now there was a widespread belief that after their European victories the Germans would attack the Soviet Union. There was a well-founded fear that the main victim of the attack would be the Jews living in the eastern territory of Poland that had been seized by the Russians. At this point the idea arose of evacuating people whose lives were in danger via Siberia and Japan, and onward into the world at large. Too little is known about the originators of this idea or those who put it into action. The whole plan was apparently designed by Polish intelligence in cooperation with two consuls in Kaunas, the Dutch and the Japanese. The Dutchman, Jan Zwertendijk, issued certificates authorising the holder to enter the Dutch Antilles without a visa. On the basis of these certificates the Japanese consul, Chiune Sugihara, stamped Japanese transit visas into people's passports.

The Japanese consulate in Kaunas operated during the war as an intelligence post, keeping an eye on unclear German–Soviet relations and cooperating with Polish intelligence. In exchange for passing on information the Japanese helped the Poles with their problems, enabled them to use the Japanese diplomatic post and smuggled Polish intelligence officers to their outposts in Europe. So the Japanese Ministry of Foreign Affairs agreed to issue six hundred visas to Polish nationals. The news spread like wildfire and crowds began to gather outside the Japanese consulate in Kaunas – among them the Bychowskis, who had flown in from Stockholm at the last moment.

On 15 June 1940 the Soviet tanks entered Wilno again, and the second Soviet occupation began – this time lasting a year – and so did everything that went with it: robberies, famine, arrests and mass deportations of Poles, Lithuanians and Latvians into the depths of Russia. Even more people now laid siege to the Japanese consulate, and Sugihara hurried up. At first he had written out the visas by hand, but later on he made a special stamp, which the

Poles who worked at the consulate at once forged and used to stamp passport documents. An estimated six thousand visas were then issued (of which two thousand were official), mainly to Jews.

Two months after the annexation of Lithuania to the Soviet Union the Japanese consulate in Kaunas was closed down, and Sugihara was transferred to Prague. Apparently he was still writing out Japanese visas in the train. The Bychowskis, meanwhile, having obtained exit documents from Russia and train tickets with the greatest difficulty, set off in winter by the Trans-Siberian Railway from Moscow to Vladivostok. The journey took twelve days. Just before they left little Monika fell ill with whooping cough. She spent the entire train journey coughing very badly and being sick. The Russians had a panic-stricken fear of infectious diseases, so if they had found the sick child, the entire family would have been disembarked from the train at a desolate Siberian railway halt. So, during the frequent ticket inspections, her parents hid her, head and all, under some fur coats and rugs so no one could hear her wheezing, which almost made her suffocate.

On 5 February 1941, after the final thorough check, they disembarked in freezing, grey Vladivostok, in the very middle of the Siberian winter. From there, on a dilapidated old fishing boat built to take twenty people, onto which a hundred were crowded, they sailed for half a day to the small port of Tsuruga in Japan. They were lucky: on its very next voyage the boat gave way and sank.

In Tokyo the new arrivals were very warmly received by the Polish ambassador, Tadeusz Romer. He secured them a hotel room for the duration of their stay in Japan and helped them to obtain tickets for a ship sailing to California. This was not easy, because the ships were packed full, and they had to wait a long time for places. Two days before their departure Maryla noticed that she was entirely covered in red spots. Gustaw immediately realised that it was chickenpox, and that the strict American health inspectors at the port would not let her on board in that state. It would be impossible to get tickets for another voyage.

He told Maryla to go to bed and not let the hotel staff enter the room, then ran into town and bought vast quantities of thin, black material. He wrapped his wife in it from head to foot, and explained to the astounded chambermaid that Madam had sunk into a deep depression after losing her motherland and only thanks to complete mourning dress could she more or less maintain her mental equilibrium. Two days later he escorted her on board the ship with a black veil over her face, shrouded in her pall, showed the medical staff their official invitations and explained that as a renowned psychiatrist he would take responsibility for his wife's state of mind. She spent the long journey across the ocean shut in her cabin. In April 1941 they sailed into San Francisco.

*

After the capitulation of France, guided by a self-preservation instinct, Józef Osnos insisted on the need to escape from Europe – to America, Brazil, India, or most readily Palestine; but it was just as difficult as getting out of Warsaw. Above all they had no money. Secondly it was only possible to leave Romania for the Near East via Turkey, while Turkey, allied with Germany, had no desire to help Jewish refugees to escape and would not grant them transit visas. In the end, with immense difficulty they managed to obtain destination visas to the Dutch East Indies, and spent the next half-year trying to find an approach to the Turkish embassy.

It is astonishing how far the entire world conspired to obstruct the salvation of Jewish refugees – as if it were impossible to institute a special system that would have allowed dead-tired and desperate people to find safe asylum and a roof over their heads. The deluge was inundating country after country, yet in every place the system of exit and entry, transit and destination visas and God knows what else went on working with mechanical pedantry. Overcoming all these difficulties, obtaining money for the relevant payments and surmounting the bureaucratic soullessness of the officials became an overwhelming task that people could only manage because death was so hot on their heels.

In November 1940 Providence took pity on them, by inflicting a serious earthquake on Bucharest. To this day Robert reckons this event was his most dangerous war experience – yet it saved their lives. In the shelter to which the terrified inhabitants of the neighbouring houses had run, Józef befriended the Turkish ambassador, who turned out to live nearby and had fled with his family to the very same cellar. Charmed by Józef's perfect French and his courtly manners, he took him for a French diplomat and promised to help with his visa problems. Two days later they had the long-desired stamps in their passports, thanks to which they could also arrange visas to Iraq, from where it was only a short hop to Palestine.

In December 1940 they reached Constanţa, from where they sailed for twenty-four hours to Istanbul in a ship packed full of refugees, including a large number of Poles. In the port the Turkish police boarded the ship, checked documents and warned that those who had transit visas could only stay in the city for a period of forty-eight hours.

Leaving little Robert in the care of friends from the ship, Józef and Marta spent two days and nights running about the city, looking for a way to obtain visas to Palestine. They tried the Polish consulate, the Jewish community, and dozens of restaurants, hotels and cafés where the 'fixers' gathered – people who knew how to arrange the impossible in exchange for money. But this particular problem proved unsolvable. The British did not want friction with the Arabs so they were not admitting Jews to the Promised Land. Meanwhile, their time allowance was running out. As they ran across Istanbul for the umpteenth time that night in search of some influential people recommended to them, they passed the hotel where they had left Robert, and did not even notice that their little son, unable to sleep, was sitting in his pyjamas in his usual way on the steps of the building. They only realised when they heard the patter of small feet behind them and the heart-breaking cry of: 'Mama!'

After many complicated to-ings and fro-ings, hassle with the Turkish police, the threat of arrest and expulsion from the country, as it was impossible to obtain Palestinian visas they decided to travel on to Iraq. At the French consulate, thanks to the fact that Robert had been born in Paris, they got transit visas via Syria, a French colony that was still under the control of the Vichy government. Finally, they left Istanbul on the Taurus Express train, and travelled through an exotic desert landscape to reach Baghdad, the capital of Iraq, in January 1941.

The magical, fairy-tale city of Baghdad seemed to them a dirty, neglected and stinking dump, where, apart from eggs, which they furtively boiled in the hotel on an electric appliance brought from Poland, they could not swallow a single morsel of the oriental food; but in fact the powers of magic were still working here. They had the address of a modest, cheap hotel, meaningfully named the 'Semiramis'. When in a state of total exhaustion they finally reached it, the Arab owner shook his head negatively: he had no spare rooms. In desperation they tried to communicate with him in all the languages they knew, including Romanian, but he could not understand them. They wanted him to realise what a dramatic situation they were in, so they shoved their Polish passports under his nose. At this point he immediately became less stern, indicated that they should wait, disappeared and came back with a tall, thin man who asked in perfect Polish: 'How can I help you?' Then he whispered something in Arabic to the hotelier, and at once a spare room was found. As soon as they had put the sleepy Robert to bed he invited them to lunch and asked what else he could do for them.

And so Mr Jan Miś came into their lives, first as their saviour and protector, later as their life-long friend. He might have seemed like an omnipotent, benevolent genie, who appears at the right moment to provide help, then vanishes; but he turned out to be as real a man as could be, though highly enigmatic. A Pole from Warsaw and an unusually talented linguist, he knew twenty-four languages fluently, including some oriental ones. How had he ended up in Baghdad? Why did he live here modestly as a German teacher? How on earth had they stumbled across him? Why did he take such great care of them?

First he convinced them that above all they must be inoculated against cholera, yellow fever, typhus and some other tropical diseases. Later he put Józef in touch with the British consul. It turned out that the visas to the Dutch East Indies that they had obtained with such difficulty were of no use at all, because the Germans had already conquered Holland. The consul suggested giving them visas to British India. They could settle in Bombay and live out the war there peacefully, while at the same time trying to get visas to America, which each year admitted a fixed number of refugees. They listened to his advice, and after spending two weeks in Baghdad they set off on their next journey.

First they went to Basra, the most attractive feature of which was endless groves of date palms. From there they sailed out to the Indian Ocean on a ship belonging to an Anglo-Indian shipping company. The weeks spent on board, in a crowd of Indians, most intriguing and very friendly, was a truly fairy-tale adventure. They passed Persian and Arab islets, as the waters of the ocean turned all possible shades of green and blue, and at night the navy-blue sky shone with stars they had never seen before. A stop at the Sultanate of Muscat was a fabulous experience, where the ship was invaded by crowds of hawkers offering unfamiliar delicacies and fruits, and little Arab boys dived in search of gigantic mussels which they sold for pennies. Robert was given one of these mussels and regarded it as his greatest treasure.

In February 1941 they landed in Bombay. With the help of some compatriots they met there they rented a room and bought a few of the most essential items at a second-hand market. That was when Robert placed his mussel in the middle of the table and said: 'This is our new home.'

But the boy's anguish was by no means over. Before me lie three pages of yellowed lined paper headed:

EUROPEAN BOYS HIGH SCHOOL, PANCHGANI, Dist. *SATARA*
Dearest Mummy and Daddy
Now I'll describe my journey from start to finish and my first impressions of school. So when the train set off the teacher introduced me to a few boys, in spite of this I didn't talk to them at all just looked out of the window, mountains began and tunnels. All the nicer because our train was electric and you could look out of the window in the tunnel. A bit later I got to know one of the boys who I chatted to. We arrived at Puna at 12.30. We ate lunch there and waited maybe an hour for a bus when it came (it was so huge it had room for 17 boys and when I stood up I hit my head on the ceiling) some of our things were packed onto the roof (mine stayed behind to go in another bus). After five minutes travelling they spent half an hour cleaning the bus then finally we set off. I thought my insides would fly out it shook so much because of the awful road. On top of that it twisted along hundreds of hairpin bends in the mountains. At 6 we arrived at Panchkani, which is quite high in the mountains. There I stood like a madman (the teacher was meant to come in the other bus). At last one of the ladies took care of me. The boys took me to the house. When I got there I had to go back because my things had arrived by then, and after washing and getting changed we ate supper and went to bed. Next day all the boys asked my name and mangled it as much as possible. Our form master is an Indian, Mr R. The man who teaches us Urdu is the one Daddy saw at the station. Mr D., an Englishman, teaches us nature. Unfortunately I've only got half friends. There's one who hates me and tries to make people not like me. The school consists of four houses and a few school houses. I sleep in the smallest, 'Maycroft', it has only just 12 beds. There are 11 boys in the same form as me. I'm in the fourth form. I'm doing quite well in class. Although I messed up a dictation badly because I didn't understand anything, Mummy look:... [at this point there is a line

of mysterious symbols] *that's the Urdu alphabet, I wrote it out by heart, it reads back to front. Show it to Mr Miś to see if he can read it. The food here is puke-making, when we wake up in the morning we go to school and drink tea without sugar. At eight there's breakfast, dry bread tea without sugar of course, porridge (which I don't touch) and bananas. At 1 there's lunch meat (spicy as hell) curry (which I don't touch) pudding (sweet rice). At 4 there's tea: dry bread and tea without sugar. At 8 there's supper soup (cold water with peelings) stew (meat and vegetables, I feel sick when I look at it) bananas, or mango in spicy sauce, and also bread and warm water. Today for breakfast there was a big thing: eggs. That's what our food is like. There's a big problem with washing in Panchkani there's very little water. A lady has my clothes and gives them to me as needed. Regards to all. Goodbye. 100000000000000000000000000 kisses.
Robert.*

A couple of months after arriving in Bombay he was sent to Panchgani, a Catholic school for European boys. He was unhappy there. What hurt him most was that he had to pretend to be a Catholic, though he did not have a clue about the basic principles of that religion. Yet he survived his time at the school, learned English and went 'home' to Bombay. He was fourteen when in October 1943 his brother Peter was born.

In December 1943 the Osnos family received their American visas, after a two-year wait. With Robert and their two-month-old baby son they boarded a ship and sailed across the Pacific to San Pedro in California, from where they set off for New York to start a new life. As he disembarked from the ship, Robert saw that all his American contemporaries were wearing long trousers and he alone, according to European-Indian habit, was in shorts. He found this terribly humiliating and made his parents promise that one of the first items they bought in America would be long trousers for him. When he put them on he realised that he was grown up now, but the most important thing he felt was that never again would he have to pretend to be someone else.

In June 1943 sixteen-year-old Paweł Beylin assumed a new identity. He became Paweł Kurnatowski, the eighteen-year-old son of a peasant from a village outside Warsaw. He used his false identity card to leave Warsaw by goods train to be a labourer in Germany, because this was clearly his only hope of salvation. In Milanówek, the village just outside Warsaw where he had been living with his grandparents and aunts 'on Aryan papers', the dark-haired boy's appearance was starting to arouse suspicions. Someone from the town had informed the Gestapo that he was hiding his origins. Luckily, someone else, a well-wisher, had warned him not to go home on the day of the Gestapo's visit. Indeed, the Gestapo did call at 24 Cicha Street, where he lived with his family, and, not finding him at home, announced that they would be back the next day. One of his aunts immediately took him to Warsaw and placed him with friends.

The lively, high-spirited boy refused to take on board the mortal danger he was facing. He could not bear to stay indoors, so he started running about the city, visiting his pre-war friends and living a normal life, to which he no longer had any right. One day he aroused the suspicion of the Polish police, who stopped him and took him to the police station. By some miracle, perhaps thanks to money delivered by people he had befriended, he was released.

On the advice of friends in the Home Army, his desperate aunts then persuaded him to volunteer for labour in Germany. They reckoned it would be easier for him to hide his origins there. Thanks to their underground contacts new documents were forged for him, which he used to apply to the *Arbeitsamt* (or labour exchange) and was accepted. Travelling by goods train in a crowd of comrades in adversity, most of whom had been caught during round-ups, he reached Wilhelmshagen outside Berlin, the main distribution point for forced labourers, who were brought there from all over Europe. There he spent three days in wooden barracks surrounded by barbed wire, waiting for a work assignment.

As a 'country lad', luckily he was sent to a village in the Rheinland. Factory work was much tougher, and the minimal food rations were barely enough to live on. Underfed and unaccustomed to physical work, he could not have survived those conditions.

He was assigned to work as a farmhand for the wife of a farmer who had been called up to fight. It must have been hard work, but whenever he spoke of those days after the war, Paweł never sounded sorry for himself. Instead, he readily used to amuse his audience with tragi-comic stories of the advances made to him by his hostess, a war widow, at a rather advanced age, so he said. She tried to win him over with copious amounts of food, which in times of universal famine was a much greater temptation than her charms. He put up with torture, because he refused to submit to her. His sense of honour would not let him touch her tasty sausages and cabbage, but his stomach abused him to the utmost for being so stupid. Finally he could not bear the inner struggle any longer, and ran away. He found another job elsewhere, but there he aroused some suspicions and had to run away again. He ran away many times, and spent the final months of the war wandering about in the woods. Once the Americans had invaded the Rheinland he reported to them and was evacuated to France, from where he went to join the Polish army commanded by General Anders.

When he returned to Poland we saw each other often, though he lived in Warsaw and I lived in Kraków. I was very fond of him. He was one of the cleverest, most enchanting people I have ever known, yet I would never go so far as to say we were close friends. We never had a frank or serious conversation with each other. We just used to swap jokes, funny stories and banter, playing the fool together, just like before the war, even at times when laughter was not in the least appropriate.

After his premature death in 1971 I was immensely sorry that I had never known how to get close to him. I think we were both running away from undue intimacy. What did we have to talk about so frankly and seriously? Things that cannot be expressed in words, perhaps? Nowadays I do not regret never having heard a word of complaint from Paweł about his wartime and post-war fate. He lives on in my memory not as a victim, but as a slightly arrogant, very witty man who had a nonchalant air of detachment towards himself and towards reality. I think this sort of image suits him better. In our family no one likes the role of a victim. That is why Janek Kancewicz never complains about his terrible experiences, Petya Valetsky does not weep over his stolen childhood, and nor does Robert Osnos. I too am not particularly bothered about my experiences during the occupation.

Being aware that tragedy and comedy are inseparable elements of life, and that they are not mutually exclusive – on the contrary, they are two sides of the same coin – believing that through laughter one can deal with fear, keep one's dignity and have a sense of victory over Fate seem to me very positive ideas. Perhaps it is part of my Jewish nature. After all, it was Rebbe Nachman of Bratslav who taught that man should only discuss his despair with God, and only for a quarter of an hour a day, not longer. For the rest of the day he is to rejoice and be happy, showing the world a smiling face.

On 8 June 1945 Flora Beylin, still posing as Emilia Babicka, wrote from Milanówek to my grandmother in Kraków in crabbed, feeble handwriting:

My dear Janinka!
Has Hanka found her Joasia? Here I have no news of either Pawełek or Mania. I'm in despair. I miss them terribly. I still don't feel very well, I haven't recovered at all. So please don't forget your sister, write to me as soon as you can.

She did not live to hear news of Pawełek. She died a couple of weeks later and was buried in the cemetery at Milanówek, under her occupation name, beside her husband Samuel, who had died a year earlier and was laid to rest as Stanisław Babicki.

THE BOY FROM HEAVEN

———————✳———————

On 10 April 1941 my grandmother's nephew Gustaw Bychowski, his wife Maryla and their children, four-year-old Monika, eighteen-year-old Krysia and nineteen-year-old Ryś, sailed to the coast of California. On Tuesday, 15 April 1941, just before the Easter holiday, Ryś wrote from San Francisco to his friend Krzysztof Kamil Baczyński in Warsaw:

Dearest Krzyś
It's my fifth day here. The journey was perfect, sunshine almost all day, Honolulu on the way – though I won't describe it here – mainly it's of no significance, and secondly in view of the problems facing us here and the new life we have to start, there's no time to think about it. In a nutshell, our situation is like this: there are lots of opportunities for my father, but he can't get on with anything because we haven't got immigrant visas, just ordinary, tourist visas. So he has to get an appointment at one of the universities or other educational institutes, which isn't hard to do, because even a non-paid one would be enough, then we all have to go away to Cuba or Mexico, and get immigrant visas there outside the quota, on the basis of the appointment. All this can be done – unfortunately it's bound to take 2–3 months, and meanwhile we'd like to get on with things, and we quite simply haven't any loot. But when we re-enter as one-hundred-percent immigrants, I'm sure we'll soon get set up somehow. There's great demand for psychoanalysts, of whom there are still very few, and they earn superbly. I'm not thinking about studying for the time being, why should I? – maybe by a fluke I might get a grant, but meanwhile I should get down to some work [...]. I'll certainly make use of my scribblings too, which have piled up a bit...

In 1999 I fetched those 'scribblings' from New York, where they had been safely kept by Monika Bychowska-Holmes. They include a cycle of short poems, or rather succinct reports in verse, entitled *September 1939*. There are some impressive poems, written in Wilno and later on, that speak of nostalgia for one's native land, city and home. There is a story entitled 'The Return', in which the narrator, like Ryś, escapes from the Germans to Wilno by the illegal route, but then gives up the opportunity to leave for the free world and goes back to Warsaw, by the illegal route again, to work for the resistance. He must have been very upset by his father's enforced, or rather entreated decision to leave Poland. After all, like each successive generation of Poles, he was brought up in a spirit of patriotism and loyalty to his motherland. As for centuries, the fight for freedom was a matter of honour and conscience, so he felt like a traitor.

In April 1941, while taking cover from the threat of Nazi atrocities for a few days in a hospital, Krzysztof Baczyński had a dream about his own funeral; but Ryś, with his usual optimistic drive, was busy organising his new life. He had inherited his father's gift of making immediate, genuine contact with people, and dozens of individuals loom out of his letters who bestowed friendship on him, so important for a young boy alone in a foreign country – because he was alone, of his own choice. Although in a letter to a friend he had said he would go to New York with his family, he decided to take up his studies in California.

On 22 April 1941 he wrote to his father: *On Monday I went to Berkeley to the University. I won't write down all the details, but I liked it so much there that I thought I should do something to be there. A student whom I asked the way got a car out of the garage and took me right to Professor Neyman's house. I went in and told them everything: that I want to study, but the first step would have to be finding somewhere to live in Berkeley, that not having a visa I cannot look for a job through the University etc. In short, as they are alone and I can see that his wife works very hard, I suggested to them that I would live there like the other students, and in exchange for my room and board I would clean, wash up and baby-sit. They were very kind – mainly he was pleased that I don't have any prejudices and don't think of washing the dishes as a negative. They said they'd think about it, have a chat and see if they could borrow a bed etc. And the next evening, that is yesterday, I was to call for the verdict. Yesterday I rang up – and from*

Monday my address will be c/o Professor Neyman, 954 Euclid Ave., Berkeley, California.

He coped with the knotty problems of getting a residency visa for the United States, without which there was no question of being able to study. He had money worries: *fee for one semester – 102 dollars and 50 cents, semesters per year – two, plus administrative costs, books and personal expenses.* But he managed. He found a summer job on a building site as a bricklayer and proudly reported that he had not yet broke into the twenty-dollar bill his father had given him for the road, because he was always being invited out for lunch or supper.

He gave a talk at the Polish Club about the situation at home, he was asked to do some work for the Polish newspapers, and he met a lot of interesting people. Professor and Mrs Neyman looked after him like a son, gave him a room with a view of the garden and the sea, and took him with them on visits and picnics. He passed all his tests with flying colours and was accepted as a student at the University of California in the Department of Sociology and Political Science. While studying he also worked for some Polish organisations collecting money to provide financial aid for the underground in Poland, fund parcels for Polish academics, ransom prisoners and support those in hiding.

In spring 1942 he passed his end-of-first-year exams with excellent results. Amid the insanity of war that had gripped the whole world he was safe, and life was offering him a straight path to peace and success, but he was finding this comfortable situation harder and harder to bear. Immediately after passing his exams he volunteered for the Polish Army.

The Polish Armed Forces organised by General Władysław Sikorski on British territory also recruited soldiers from among Poles living in America. Volunteers who had no military training at all were given instruction in Canada, first at a preparatory camp in Windsor, Ontario, and then, at a more advanced level, at Owen Sound, also in the province of Ontario. They could choose which branch they wanted to serve in: the land army, the navy or the air force. The toughest demands were those required of future airmen: age – 18–24; status – single; superb physical, mental and intellectual fitness. After the successes of the Polish squadrons in the Battle of Britain every one of the boys dreamed of becoming an airman. Ryś possessed all the qualifying criteria, and in spring 1942 he ended up in Canada.

His poem entitled 'First Evening in Windsor' is not poetry of the highest standard, but it gives us some insight into the soul of a twenty-year-old starting a new stage in his life, and trying to sum up his entire experience to date. In yet another foreign place, once again among strangers, he gazed at the starry Canadian night sky, where he would soon be flying. He found comfort in the moon – the only fixed element in his three-year odyssey.

not melted away by the fires of September
it shone on the rubble that once was a city
it came out in hours when the curfew was on
and lighted your way as you stole across the border

and you saw it again on the corner in Wilno
it never once froze in the wastes of Siberia
when it hid behind mountains in distant Japan,
did you know you would find it again over here

the dry wind is blowing a white storm of snow
on the first army evening you're spending in Windsor
you know that the same moon is shining in Warsaw,
you know that from here we'll be going to Poland!

What sort of news was reaching him from Poland? What did he know about the fate of his relatives and friends? About the round-ups, transports to Auschwitz, executions and persecution of the Jews? His stepmother Maryla was trying in vain to get in touch with her mother, who was shut inside the Warsaw Ghetto, but her letters addressed to Helena Auerbach, 24 Grzybowska Street, Warsaw, Poland, were returned to New York unopened, with a message printed on them in French: *On ne peut pas remettre des letters avec avis de réception addressés aux juifs. Bureau de poste à Varsovie.* ['Registered letters addressed to Jews cannot be delivered. Post Office, Warsaw.'] No one ever found out how she perished.

In July 1942 the Germans began the action to liquidate the Warsaw Ghetto. Thousands of people were sent to their deaths on a daily basis. On 5 August 1942 the children from the Jewish orphanage were transported to an unknown place, most likely to Treblinka. Janusz Korczak and his deputy, Stefania Wilczyńska, went with them.

Years later Stefan Korboński, a member of the military under-ground in Warsaw, wrote in his memoirs: *I sent several telegrams to London, one after another, informing them about the liquidation of the ghetto that started on 22 VII 1942. About 7,000 people were loaded onto goods wagons on Stawki Street and transported eastwards, to Majdanek, where they were all gassed. I was greatly surprised that in spite of the BBC's practice to date no use was made of these telegrams and not a single word of this news was mentioned. [...] Only a month later did the BBC issue news based on our information, and many months later a government emissary who had been dropped into the country by parachute explained the whole matter to me: 'Your telegrams weren't believed. The government did not believe it, nor did the British. They said you were taking your anti-German propaganda a bit too far. Only when the British received confirmation from their own sources did consternation set in.'*

In November 1942 the Polish underground authorities informed London that the Germans were exterminating the few surviving members of the Jewish population. From the distance of North America one might well have supposed that all one's friends and relatives had perished; but those who were alive had to go on living. In New York Gustaw Bychowski was learning English to be able to have his medical diploma admitted to the same status as its American equivalent. Little Monika was at kindergarten, and Maryla was running the house. Gustaw's stepdaughter Krysia very soon found herself a boyfriend, got married and left for Virginia.

On official letter paper with two seals: ROYAL CANADIAN AIR FORCE – PER ARDUA AD ASTRA and KNIGHTS COLUMBUS – WAR SERVICES, Ryś reported to New York that he was studying celestial navigation and cartography, meteorology and how to use a sextant, ground orientation, reconnaissance, aerial photography, knowledge of navigational instruments and of course flying itself. *Never in my life have I seen such a colourful sight as the Canadian forest at this time of year – it's a mosaic of purest rust, violet, gold, flecks of orange and every shade of green...* He described fog and rain, and snowstorms in which he sometimes lost his bearings and landed somewhere other than intended. He was pleased to have one of the highest marks in the class for work in the air. He had a new, sky-blue uniform made of thick material and a fabulous Longines navigator's watch that told the time precisely to one third of a second and had a special movable dial for navigation measurements. He was getting a suntan, celebrating his successes, and taking local girls out to dances. There were skiers out on the slopes; *student boys and girls from the university here. I even envied them a bit for being carefree and merry, as if nothing were wrong.*

He was reading a lot, including Józef Wittlin's latest poetry about the Jews, and Arthur Koestler's *Darkness at Noon.* He longingly looked forward to his relatives' rare visits. He followed the political situation carefully, but it was getting more and more confused and more and more desperate. *People are saying that it was the Jews who put out the hideous, incredible rumour about the ghetto.* Flying became his escape from reality: *Up in the air there's such perfect peace and quiet that you don't want to return to earthly matters.*

In December 1942 he passed all his exams and completed his Canadian training with distinction, at the rank of airman observer. After that he waited for orders to leave for Britain, where the next stage of the pilots' training would take place. During the Christmas and New Year holidays he was still in Canada, in a gloomy mood – he wanted to 'fly away to war' as soon as possible, and could not bear the waiting.

In January 1943, within a group of recruits who had already been through basic training, he landed in Harrogate, Yorkshire, six hours by railway from London. As soon as he arrived he fell ill with measles and spent three weeks in hospital. Was it bad luck? Or a warning? He was allowed to spend his convalescence leave in London, where good news was waiting for him: *Mrs Maria Kuncewicz called me, overjoyed that the parcels sent to Janina and Hanka by the Culture Fund (to Mrs Żeromska's address) were confirmed – the one for Janina by Mrs Żeromska, and the one for Hanka by Monika. It looks like an outward sign that they're alive (otherwise Mrs Ż. would have let it be known on the same receipt card).* This news concerned my mother and grandmother, who at that time were hiding in Pruszków near Warsaw.

In London Ryś tried to familiarise himself with the political situation and the complexities of the émigré ideological factions. In the most general terms, everyone was at odds with everyone else, and they were all equally helpless in the face of each successive Polish tragedy. The Soviet Union had already established the future borders of Poland, laying claim to the eastern territory that it had annexed. Roosevelt and Churchill had agreed to the Soviet claims. In April news was broadcast about the discovery of the mass graves of Polish officers at Katyń.

In April 1943 the final act in the annihilation of the Warsaw Ghetto began. Before leaving Warsaw, Jan Karski, the Polish underground authorities' envoy to London, had a meeting with two representatives of the Jewish underground. They had prepared a detailed report on the situation, which was to be publicised in the West. Karski later described the meeting:

Their eyes were the picture of despair, pain and hopelessness, which they were not fully capable of expressing. They spoke quietly, or rather whispered, [...] and yet I felt as if they were shouting [...]. 'Surely it is impossible for the democracies calmly to ignore the statement that there is no way of saving the Jewish population in Europe. If it is possible to save American or British citizens, why is it not possible to organise the large-scale evacuation of at least the Jewish children, Jewish women, old and sick people? Offer the Germans a swap. Offer them money. Why can't the allies buy the lives of a few thousand Polish Jews? [...] Why is the world letting us die? Haven't we made our contribution to culture and civilisation? Haven't we worked, fought and shed blood? [...] Please tell the Jewish leaders that this is not a matter for any political or tactical games. Please tell them they must shake the earth to its foundations, they must wake up the world. [...] Please tell them they must find in themselves the strength and courage to make a sacrifice just as painful and just as unique as the fate of my dying people...'

In London Karski met with Szmul Zygielbojm, the Bund's representative on the National Council attached to the Polish government. For two years Zygielbojm had been trying in vain to interest the Allied governments in the fate of the Polish Jews. Now too he was running from door to door of all possible offices, showing them the telegrams he had received:

Warsaw, 20 April 1943.
V. urgent. On 19 IV SS divisions with tanks and artillery started murdering the remains of the Warsaw ghetto. The ghetto is putting up heroic armed resistance. The defence is being run by the Jewish Battle Organisation, a concentration of just about all the groupings. Constant gunfire and powerful explosions can be heard from the ghetto. There is a glow of fires over the district. Aeroplanes are circling over the site of the massacre. The result

of the fighting is a foregone conclusion. In the evening a flag flies over the positions of the ghetto defenders inscribed with the message: 'We'll fight to the last man' [...]. We are calling for immediate retaliation. Insist that the International Red Cross must visit the ghetto as well as the death camps at Auschwitz, Treblinka, Belżec, Sobibór, Majdanek and the other concentration camps in Poland.

Warsaw, 28 April 1943.
For the ninth day the Warsaw ghetto is fighting heroically. The SS and the Wehrmacht are besieging it. They are bombing it continuously. Against 40,000 Jews they are using artillery, flame-throwers and incendiary bombs dropped from aeroplanes. They are blowing up the most recalcitrant blocks with mines. The ghetto is on fire. The city is wreathed in clouds of smoke. Women and children are losing their lives. [...] The might of the allies can provide immediate, effective help right now. In the name of millions of Jews already murdered, in the name of those presently being burned and massacred, in the name of those fighting heroically and in the name of all of us who are condemned to death we call upon the entire world: Now is the time, not in the distant future, for the Allies to bring mighty vengeance on the bloodthirsty enemy...

Warsaw, 11 May 1943.
The heroic battle of the Warsaw ghetto still has a few points of resistance. Noble dedication and courage of the Jewish Battle Organisation [...] Shocking Nazi atrocities. Many Jews burned alive. Thousands shot or deported to camps. [...] But the world of liberty and justice is silent and inactive. Astonishing. This telegram is the third in the past two weeks. Send an immediate reply reporting what you have achieved.

On 13 May 1943 in London Zygielbojm wrote his last letter:

To President Wladyslaw Raczkiewicz
To Chairman of the Council of Ministers Wladyslaw Sikorski
[...] I cannot live while the remnants of the Jewish people in Poland, whose representative I am, are being exterminated. [...] By my death I wish to make the strongest possible protest against the passivity with which the world is standing by and

*allowing the annihilation of the Jewish people to happen. I
know how little human life is worth, especially today, but as I
was unable to do anything during my life, perhaps by my death
I shall help to break down the indifference of those who have
the possibility now, at the final hour, to save those Polish Jews
who are still alive. [...]*

After writing this letter, he turned on the gas tap in his flat. His
funeral was held on 21 May at Golders Green Crematorium.

On 3 June 1943 Ryś Bychowski reported to New York from the
air base at Blackpool:

My dearest family,
*[...] I was in London until the evening of Friday 21 May, that is
until Z.'s funeral. The funeral, or rather the memorial event held
at the crematorium was staggering. The crowds were so huge
that there was not enough room and dozens of people had to
stand in the garden and on the lawns outside the crematorium.
There were lots of people in uniform, senior army officers and
airmen, not just Polish. Lots of people were in tears (me included). The whole ceremony was all the more tragic in that his
letter to the President and the Premier was not even read out –
British law would not allow it until the inquest was complete
(the letter was only published in the press yesterday).*

*Most of the speakers even refrained from using the words
'suicide', 'protest', etc. for the same legal reasons, and instead of
an ardent protest demonstration, such as he must have wished
for, there was just an atmosphere of tragic hopelessness in the
air, the impression of a heroic, but pointless sacrificial death, a
'breakdown', rather than a great deed.*

*Indeed, only the final speaker disturbed that atmosphere, the
representative of the youth Bund, Oler. He struck the chords
that should have been struck, crying out that this was just the
continuation of the fight, the same fight that is going on in
Warsaw, and that in his letter to his comrades Zygielbojm asks
them not to bother with a funeral ceremony but to exploit his
sacrifice as widely as possible for propaganda purposes.*

Of the newspapers only the Daily Herald *(the Labour Party
organ) and the* News Chronicle *(a liberal, pro-Soviet daily) and
among the weeklies* Tribune *wrote about it. The others apparently prefer to keep silent. The last* Tribune *carried the full text*

*of two telegrams received from the battleground in the Warsaw
ghetto, which reached London on 21 and 22 May, thus 10 days
after Z.'s death.*

*[...] I'm keeping v. active, I'm trying not to think about what's
happening in Poland too much and to live without a care in the
world, otherwise every one of us would have to follow in
Zygielbojm's footsteps.*

The number of tragic events brought by the year 1943 was
beyond imagination. From the letters that have survived it appears
that it was then, in England, that Ryś crossed over the 'shadow
line', as Conrad called it, the magic line that divides youth from
adulthood, the bright realm of hopes and illusions from the gloomy
expanse of experience. His bitterness gradually grew. He was only
twenty-one; in breaks between practice flights he went out on
dates and to dances. He fell in love, and it was requited: *You
should be pleased, because she isn't anyone's wife, no
Norwegian's going to hit me in the face and there's no question of
any matrimony.* He read *The Silence of the Sea* by Vercors, new
poems by Karol Baliński and Louis Aragon, and nineteenth-
century English and American literature including Thomas Hardy,
D. H. Lawrence and Henry James. At Irenka Tuwim's house he
heard extracts from a long poem entitled *Polish Flowers*, forwarded
by its author – her brother, Julian Tuwim. He was pleased when
his father had his diploma validated. He congratulated him on his
success with all his heart, and with a faint note of envy: *Life is full
of paradoxes: you've passed an exam that is supposed to 'verify'
your ability to do medical work, to help people and save them,
while your son is passing exams to verify his ability to destroy
and bombard.*

However, he did hope that he would not become demoralised or
lose the desire for *positive work, building a new, free world.* He
wrote to friends in New York: *I am trying as much as possible to
work not only at military things. I have enrolled as an external
student at the University of London: since the spring I've been
studying more or less regularly. In November I have to take a half-
diploma in economics and political sciences. I'm busy with a
fairly detailed study of the British constitution and parliamentary
system of government.*

In London he bumped into a friend from the Stefan Batory High
School in the street: *I ran into Kocik Jeleński, on superb form. He*

has just finished university (which thanks to connections he attended while on detachment from the army – he only went back to his regiment in the summer) and was going 'into the field'. He was unusually engaging, and spoke with tears in his eyes about the Jewish tragedy…

He made requests for chocolate and sweets. He complained that his stepmother had sent him green socks to wear with his blue uniform. In the hope of a rapid end to the war he wanted to buy himself some civilian clothes: *I've grown out of the things I brought from Warsaw like anything.* His British friends called him 'the boy from heaven'. They later said that *something bright, better and radiant lit up the gloomy, discordant London atmosphere, so full of alarm and bitterness, whenever he appeared there for a short holiday and came into the room in his sky-blue airman's uniform with his sky-blue eyes shining and smiling.*

Towards the end of September 1943 Ryś passed his next, final exams and gained the rank of senior sergeant navigator; and Fate tried to save him for the second time. The day before his first combat flight, his plane crash-landed during exercises. As a result of bruising he had to spend a couple of weeks in hospital, and then wait almost half a year for the complete assembly of his bomber's new crew. The accident and his enforced inactivity did not have a positive effect on his state of mind. The prevailing atmosphere was also depressing. At the Teheran conference the three Allied powers, the Soviet Union, America and Great Britain, had reached agreement on changing the borders of Poland. The Polish government was not admitted to the negotiations.

The Polish Jews had been slaughtered, yet antagonism between Poles and Jews was growing. It seemed incomprehensible. Rumours were going round about how badly the Jews who had volunteered for General Anders' army in the Soviet Union were treated by the Polish military authorities, and about how after the Russian invasion Jews in the eastern part of Poland had denounced the local Polish landowners and military to the NKVD. There was talk of the persecution of soldiers of Jewish origin by their fellow soldiers and commanders in Anders' army, and about the mass desertion of soldiers of Jewish origin from Anders' army. The Jews were claiming that it was Polish indifference that had made the Holocaust possible. The Poles felt mortally wounded by this charge and responded by enumerating their own losses, grievances and credits due. A whole forest of mutual accusations sprang up, a tangled web of grudges that to this day has never been resolved. What hurt most of all was that some people entirely failed to take any notice of the Jewish tragedy, as if it did not affect them at all and had not changed them.

Władysław Kisielewski, author of a book entitled *Lancaster Squadron*, who met Ryś at the air base at Blackpool, tells how one evening a Pole from the local staff sat at their table and started expressing his undisguised satisfaction at the destruction of the Warsaw Ghetto and the killing of the Jews. He shut up when Ryś showed him his RAF dog tag, which besides name and number also featured religious denomination. He was not religious, but he had not changed his Jewish denomination to any other. His Polish-Jewish identity had always seemed something quite natural to him, yet in view of this and similar episodes he came to the conclusion that he had to make a choice.

On 5 December 1943 he wrote the following letter to his father, which has often been published since then. In it he touches on many painful topics; this is not the place to discuss them more broadly, but what I find crucial to mention is his personal reflections that give a dramatic point to our family's lengthy journey towards having a Polish identity.

Bircotes, nr Doncaster

Dearest Daddy,
This is the second letter on the same theme I haven't sent. I wrote the first one in June and it's lying at Max's. I'm writing this one today because there are things I must talk to you about. I want you to know my point of view on certain basic questions. On the night of 2–3 October I had a serious crash, which I only came out of by a miracle, and now I've gone back to flying again. This letter is to guarantee – in case of another accident, with a less fortunate outcome – that you'll know what I would have wanted to tell you if we could have a chat today. [...]

I know it's hard to wipe out twenty years of anti-Semitic propaganda in a short space of time, but I thought that even if the war against Hitler couldn't do it, even if common misfortune couldn't either, then the colossal tragedy of the Jews in 1942 and 43 should have led to a revolution in Polish views. Nothing of the kind. [...]

Today after a year of systematic slaughter in the capital and the provinces, Jewish society in Poland has practically ceased to exist. How did the Polish nation react to this unprecedented crime committed by their common enemy?

My colleagues in the air force and the army were either indifferent, or openly pleased about it. For weeks on end I have seen boys smiling scornfully at the sight of headlines in the Polish Daily *about the murder of the Jews. They didn't want to buy the* Daily *because it kept going on about nothing but the Jews. I'm sure you understand how painful it was, but I can assure you that I realised it was partly affectation, partly ignorance of the true state of affairs, and also great distance, both physical and psychological, from the place where it was all happening. I cheered up again at the thought that in Poland it's not like that, and fed myself propaganda stories that someone was hiding someone else there at the risk of their own life. [...]*

But now I can see that there was nothing but indifference surrounding the Jewish people as they went to their death, and contempt that they were not fighting; satisfaction that 'it's not us'; I can sense that the atmosphere was not the same there as every shot-down allied airman finds today in France, Belgium or Holland – an atmosphere that guarantees help for a Jew fleeing the ghetto. The Jews could not escape en masse because they had nowhere to go. Outside the ghetto walls there was an alien country, an alien population, and that seems to be the terrible truth. [...]

I hope I shall come out of the war safe and sound. I am already determined not to return to Poland. I do not want to be a second-class citizen ever again and I do not want my son not to have the same chance as others. But above all I'm afraid of knowing the whole truth about the reaction of Polish society to the extermination of the Jews. I cannot live with or talk to, I am not able to work with people who found it possible to ignore their destruction, occupy their homes and denounce or blackmail the survivors.

That's all I wanted to tell you, dearest Daddy.

Maybe one day, years from now, I'll go back there to gather material for a book about the Jewish tragedy that I would like to write.

With affectionate kisses,
Your son

When he wrote that letter he had five more months to live. His relatives value every scrap of his existence that has survived in the correspondence he left behind; but the historical record and the authentic atmosphere of the past that are preserved in his letters are also valuable, a mood that is generally falsified by the saccharine optimism of popular airmen's memoirs. The tragic lot of Polish soldiers in Britain in the final years of the war was familiar to Jan Nowak-Jeziorański, the 'courier from Warsaw', who visited the military units in early 1944 and later wrote: *Of all the Poles on the British Isles our airmen lived in the most difficult psychological conditions. The closer the end of the war came the more their hopes died out. On returning from flights over Germany the 'bad' British press would be waiting for them, full of disturbing political news mixed with rumours from London. How the airmen must have felt on reading the first line of Churchill's speech on 22 February, especially those who came from Wilno or Lwów! How many of them must have asked themselves whether dying or being crippled, which could happen to them the very next night, still made any sense! Yet they did not rebel, but performed their soldierly duty without a murmur to the end.*

On a piece of paper headed R.A.F. POLISH DEPOT BLACKPOOL. LANCS. Ryś gives his own testimony to the feelings common among the airmen.

14.1.44

My dearest, beloved family,
[...] It is hard to describe the prevailing atmosphere – sometimes depression, then cynicism or powerless resentment – I'm not surprised by anything or anyone. Most of the people in the air force come from the Eastern Lands and feel as if the ground has been ripped from under their feet. They have been through an awful lot, they have been knocked around the world, they risk their lives several times a week – and now many of them are asking: what's it all for! What is there to go back to! What will happen to our families!

In his case the questions 'What are we fighting for?' and 'What is there to go back to?' took on a doubly dramatic dimension. As a Pole he felt betrayed by the world, and as a Jew he felt betrayed by the Poles. The Polish–Jewish conflict had grown even more intense. Two hundred soldiers of Jewish origin had deserted from the Polish army in Scotland because of anti-Semitic pranks committed by their fellow soldiers as personal retaliation for the pro-Russian behaviour of the Jews in the eastern borderlands. The issue caused a stir and was discussed in the British press in a tone that was aggressive towards Poland, bringing up severe, sometimes true, sometimes exaggerated examples of Polish excesses. As usual when examples of Polish anti-Semitism come to light, the Poles kept asking themselves the single pitiful question: 'What will the world think of us?'

In April 1944 Ryś reached the age of twenty-two. He spent his birthday getting ready for a nocturnal exercise, and the night flying; but even in the clouds he could not escape from the problem tormenting him:

[...] The desertion of the Jews from the Polish army had wide repercussions here. I found out about it long after the fact – it didn't surprise me, though how and when it was settled are worthy of condemnation. My commander summoned me in connection with this matter, and gave me the orders of the Commander-in-Chief and the Minister of National Defence to read – the latter is most specific, threatening among other things repression after the war against the families of deserters (poor families, they can't possibly be alive anyway). Of course I was very upset, because I had not come around the world and volunteered only to desert.

However, what scared me most was the repression the mighty London authorities would be bound to inflict on my parents and sisters. But all this is not worth the paper and ink. In a long conversation I told one of my best colleagues here that I sometimes wonder if I made a fundamental blunder by coming here, but I came to the conclusion that it wasn't a mistake. It was worth coming if only to hear from his lips that he is grateful to Hitler for solving the Jewish question. I think that seriously, not ironically – it was worth it to have my eyes opened for once and for all, finally and utterly. Besides which the time hasn't been wasted, because apart from the vitally crucial moral lesson I've learned, we are busy bombarding Germany...

I would not wish you to get the impression from the superficial, generalised arguments above that I am unhappy, sad or having a bad time... Nothing could be further from the truth. I really am in great shape, I'm in an excellent mood, and my personal relationships are more than good. It might have been enough for my entire life only a couple of years ago...

The whole time Gustaw Bychowski was having the worst possible presentiments. After the first crash he begged his son not to go back on active service, and tried to intervene on the quiet, sending requests to the General Inspectorate of the Armed Forces and to the relevant ministries. In the last few months he was insane with worry. His father's growing fear is recorded in his son's replies.

Father, my dear! I'm sorry you're losing your peace of mind and sense of reality... Try to understand! I am not a separate individual, just a small cog in the terrible machine of war, just another registration number in the card-index of world catastrophe... I am subject to regulations and laws, I have taken on some serious obligations... My training took a long time and was very expensive... What do you imagine? That now at the crowning moment of the war I should back out? Go back to my studies?...

Daddy! Stop interfering! Try to understand that I am one of millions of people taking part in this war. Even so we have had more luck than others. At the Pen Club meeting [Olgierd] Terlecki reported a rumour from Poland that Hanka has been murdered... Our whole nation has been annihilated...

Daddy, dear! The war is ending. Have faith in me...

❧

On 18 April 300 Squadron 'Ziemia Mazowiecka' began its combat flights. Ryś was the navigator on one of the Lancasters. His last surviving letter home was written a month later, on 17 May:

As you know from the press, this month has seen the mightiest airborne operations in history. Every night we've broken the previous night's record, dropping astronomical loads of bombs. I must say, the satisfaction is crazy when you see a German city in flames below. I'd like to write you a bit more about it, but I ought not to, I'm not allowed. In any case the impressions are so unusual, the sights are so unreal and fantastic that sometimes you feel as if it's a sort of great big theatre of madmen, and you ask yourself in amazement what you're really doing here. I've got into the swing of this job and so far I have some of the best results in the entire division – 'Exceptionally good' for the last two flights. I'm the first or second best navigator here. My crew are perfect. The defence is weakening and getting tired out just as quickly as the cumulative strength of our offensive is increasing. I'm convinced that not long from now our supremacy in the air will be complete, just like theirs in September 1939. And then the war will be over. Of the known targets, which you've read about in the papers, I've been over Cologne, Düsseldorf and Karlsruhe. When I was in London I got both parcels, for which many thanks. By the way, please may I have a couple of pairs of summer briefs, because I've worn all mine out and only have warm ones.

That May night, at a height of 5000 metres, a terrible blizzard was raging. While the Lancaster squadron was on its way back from a flight to Dortmund, Ryś's bomber ran into a barrage of German anti-aircraft fire over the Friesian Islands. Under fire, the plane took a few hits and one of the engines stopped working. The crew had a choice between landing and being captured or trying to reach England. They chose the second option. Ryś had to guide the pilot blindfold because the navigation instruments had been damaged. After circling the airfield they came straight down onto the runway, but as they lowered the undercarriage another engine stopped working. The plane went into a skid. Despite a great effort the pilot could not hold it back and they crashed onto the rifle range. The plane broke in half, and soon after there was an explosion. Four people managed to jump out and were saved. Three were burned to death, including Ryś, who was apparently still trying to save the aeroplane documents.

The official communiqué from the RAF read: *F/Sgt Ryszard Bychowski killed in action May 22, 1944.* Ryś was buried at the Polish airmen's cemetery at Newark alongside his two fellow crew members. The field rabbi for the Polish forces spoke at his graveside. The Catholic army chaplain who took part in the funeral ceremony also paid tribute to him.

The Representation of Polish Jewry in America sent the following letter of condolence to Professor Gustaw Bychowski in New York:

Highly esteemed Professor Bychowski,
We send you our sincerest expressions of sympathy at the devastating news of the loss of your son, Ryszard Jan Bychowski, R.I.P., who died an airman's death.

The death of your son, a heroic, fearless Polish Army airman, who waged battle high in the sky against the enemies of mankind and civilisation, the executioners of our martyred Nation, plunges all the Polish Jewry into mourning. His memory will be immortalised in the history of our Nation, among the brilliant names of those heroic sons of the Polish Jewry who took up arms against our oppressors and avenged the death of innocent martyrs.

Your son, a noble warrior, personified all the noblest features of the Polish Jewry: a love of liberty, dedication, honour and heroism. He gave his young life for the liberation of humanity, Poland and the Polish Jewry from the yoke of slavery, for the sacred cause of democracy.

May awareness of the great mission that he fulfilled and the greatness of his heroic deeds bring you relief in the boundless torment of a father's heart.

EPILOGUE

———— ✳ ————

$\mathbf{M}$y mother and grandmother never went back to Warsaw
again. To the end of their lives they lived at the Writers'
House in Kraków, where they rebuilt their existence from scratch.
Their achievements were such that out of the ashes, like the
phoenix, the Mortkowicz publishing house was revived again for a
couple of years. The 'At the Sign of the Poets' series reappeared,
including a coarse grey cloth-covered volume of poems by Leopold
Staff entitled *Dead Calm*, and also *The Age of Defeat* by Antoni
Słonimski. There were some children's books too, a few postcards
in the Polish Painting series, printed from some plates that had
survived, and a couple of other titles. After that the communist
authorities of the People's Poland started stamping out private
activity, and the company was closed down. From then on my
grandmother occupied herself with translation work, and my
mother with writing.

In the collective flat on Krupnicza Street our home was reborn
once again. Instead of original pictures reproductions hung on the
walls. To the bland furniture inherited by the Writers' Union from
a German hotel they added a couple of Biedermeier pieces bought
at an antique shop owned by the silver-haired Zosia Krudowska.
On the bookcases full of Mortkowicz publications bought at
second-hand bookshops stood some of my grandmother's favourite
cobalt-blue glass. It was hard to recreate the atmosphere of refined
aestheticism so typical of pre-war interiors in these gloomy rooms,
but they managed to do it.

Old and new friends buzzed round their home like bees round a
honey pot. It was open house, and according to his needs each
person was listened to, fed, comforted, amused and, if need be,
helped financially. Here, in the home of these two single women,
people who had not yet recovered from the nightmares of the war,

but were already entangled in the madness of the new system, could rediscover their sense of security, an atmosphere of disinterested benevolence, a world removed from everyday reality, and 'quality' conversation – as my grandmother liked to say – instead of grievances.

I do not know how they found the time for all their occupations. They both did a lot of professional work, went to theatre premières, art exhibitions, museums and the cinema, read all the new publications and literary journals, led a lively social life and made frugal suppers for their friends. They regularly went to the hairdresser, manicurist and tailor, and regarded these appointments as a duty that not even illness gave them an excuse to miss; but what still impresses me most of all is that they managed to keep up an immense correspondence with their friends, who were always increasing in number, and above all with their family, who were scattered about the world. Not a day went by without a letter arriving from Paris, New York or Warsaw – and long replies being sent from Kraków.

First of all came some desperate cries: *Where is Joasia? Where is Pawełek?* My grandmother replied: *Joasia's been found! Gucio! We are weeping with you over the loss of Ryś!* Mania Beylin wrote from Paris to say Pawełek was alive. He was in an army hospital in Alessano, Italy, where he had been sent because of his poor state of health. My mother informed our American relatives about the Warsaw family's fortunes during the occupation: *Karola was caught, arrested and imprisoned for a few months. Miraculously she escaped on the first day of the ghetto liquidation, when everyone was transported to the gas chambers.*

An impressive multi-voice choir was soon resounding across borders:

Marta Osnos from New York: *We are weeping with joy that you are alive. How can we help you? We all send huge kisses to Joasia, Robert most of all.*

My grandmother from Kraków: *My dearest Marta! [...] If you can help us, then the main thing is clothes. We haven't got any warm things at all, no sweaters or woollens. We need underwear, stockings, gloves, hats and handbags... Shoes and warm things for Joasia are essential. P.S. Joasia still believes Robert's going to marry her.*

Mania Beylin from Paris: *Pawełek is going to school in Alessano. The boys have the British officers' food, as well as a bar of chocolate and 60 lira a day for small expenses… They do a class in six months, he had only taken his junior matriculation when he was deported to Germany, so he'll do the first high-school one by the end of February.*

Gustaw Bychowski from New York: *Monisia is sweet and clever. If it weren't for her I'd never have survived losing Ryś.*

My mother from Kraków: *I don't know if I have Marta or Maryla to thank for the grey checked suit and the black knitted top… everything fits me now because I weigh just under fifty kilos.*

⁂

Kamilla Kancewicz and Janek came back to Warsaw from Russia, followed by Staś Bielski and Halinka. Paweł Beylin arrived from Paris. Life began to stabilise. Now the letters brought detailed accounts of both everyday and unusual events. In Paris Mania was worrying about her son Pierre. He had been through so much – childhood in Russia and the war in France; he had been in the resistance and the Maquis, and now he was rather strange and introverted, preferring animals to people. Marta wrote from New York complaining about Peter: he refused to study, and read nothing but comics; he was naughty and God knows what he would grow up into. Time went by. Paweł studied at the Academic Personnel Training Institute. Janek Kancewicz graduated from the history faculty at Warsaw University and got married to Bella. Robert Osnos was a medical student at Columbia University, and Pierre Pfeffer studied at the natural history faculty of the Sorbonne. Peter Osnos passed his entrance exam to the exclusive High School of Music and Art with flying colours. Monika graduated from Harvard College and began to study psychology at a university in New York. Every letter gave assurances that they loved and missed each other as much as ever, asked for news and said they must meet.

I did not write to anyone. I felt excluded from this community. I had no access to the land of memory, from which my mother and grandmother drew the strength to live. As I now understand, my unwilling rejection of all attempts to include me in the family circle was hiding envy and resentment. Who cares about someone else's lost paradise?

Robert finished his medical studies and married Naomi. Monika, a doctor of psychology, married a fellow student called Douglas

Holmes. Pawel Beylin, an acclaimed journalist, met a medical
student called Agnieszka in Gdynia, and their wedding was held in
Warsaw. Halinka Bielska, a student at the Warsaw Polytechnic,
married a fellow student called Staszek Lewandowski. Children
began to be born. For many years photographs of each new descendant were sent to Kraków. By then I was leading my own life in
Warsaw, not taking much interest in all this. Racing along ever
faster, time increased the geographical distance not only between
Kraków and New York or Paris, but also between Kraków and
Warsaw. My relatives more and more rarely came to visit. My
grandmother stopped going out at all. Nowadays I cannot help
admiring the continuous effort she put into spinning the torn web
of her old connections.

My grandmother died in 1960, and my mother in 1968. After her
death I had to clear out the flat on Krupnicza Street. There was not
much of value, but from every drawer of the ash-wood chest and
the writing desk came an endless stream of letters, postcards,
wedding announcements, children's drawings, photographs and
newspaper cuttings about the family. Pierre Pfeffer had started
work at the Natural History Institute in Paris, made trips to the
wildest countries and had two books about his scientific expedi-
tions published by Flammarion, *Bivouacs à Bornéo* and *Aux îles
du dragon*. Mania had sent French reviews of his work. Peter
Osnos had gone to the Soviet Union as the correspondent for the
Washington Post. Marta Osnos had sent his articles. Nothing had
been thrown away – neither Karola Beylin's theatre reviews, or
Stefa Beylin's film reviews, or Pawel Beylin's editorials.

I bought two large wicker baskets and packed it all into them
without sorting or even looking at any of it. My home had died all
over again, and I could not afford to be sentimental about a lot of
old scraps of paper.

For years the baskets were a faithful companion through my
nomadic life, every once in a while changing address along with
me. They were always in the way, being a nuisance and taking up
space, and I never so much as took a peep at them. I did not feel
like the rightful heiress to this particular legacy, consisting as it
did of other people's affections, regrets and nostalgia. After my
mother's death my encounters with my relatives became rarer and
rarer. Whenever we did meet, it was said that someone should
write the history of our family, but nothing ever came of it.

Now I think we were still a bit too close to the Holocaust,

which cast a long shadow over bygone days. Compared with what had happened since, memories from before the deluge seemed rather trivial. In any case, those years gone by were not exactly one long stream of bright events, but consisted first and foremost of tough experiences and painful tragedies. Yet evidently it was hard to be objective about the past. Shortly before her death my grandmother started writing her memoirs, taking them only as far as the year of her marriage. My mother left behind extracts from a book of memoirs she was planning to write, but never managed to finish. Even the oldest members of the family who remembered the most had postponed this task until later, while the present day kept forcing other, more immediate obligations on them and coming up with new, often dramatic twists. The communist era forced one to exercise self-censorship, and one's self-preservation instinct told one not to stop and summon up the memories, but to keep going forward without looking back.

My mother and grandmother must certainly have been prevented from completing their memories by their ill-defined attitude to their own ethnic origins. Throughout their lives they had emphasised their Polishness and they refused, or were unable, or did not know how, to identify the practical and psychological problems that resulted from their Jewish heritage. They must have had to confront this issue when writing about the past, but clearly the time for that had not yet come. During the occupation the fear of death probably affected them less than the humiliations they suffered; they were not yet able to talk about it.

After my father's death his widow, Maria Olczak, gave me a folder she found in his archives. One of the documents it included was my mother's occupation-era will, gone yellow with age. It was like a message from the other world; only then was I struck by the Talmudic challenge: 'Who, if not you? When, if not now?'

Janek Kancewicz, who has a photographic memory, told me about the fortunes of the family members who went to the Soviet Union in the twenty-year inter-war period. Marek Beylin, Paweł's son, gave me access to the family archives kept by his aunts, Karolina and Stefania, and I also had Mania Beylin's memoirs at my disposal. But there were so many plotlines missing. We had lost touch with our American cousins. I could write to them, but would they reply?

In autumn 1998 Monika Bychowska-Holmes called me in Kraków. She was passing through London and told me she was coming to Warsaw for two days. Would I like to see her? She was like a gift from heaven. We met in the lobby of the Hotel Europejski, and during our meeting I felt as if years and years of ice were melting inside me. We could not tear ourselves apart. Monika's friend, Lisa Apignanesi, watched dumbfounded as we sat in the hotel bar for hours and hours, jabbering away one after the other, shouting out the exotic names: 'Gizella', 'Flora' and 'Henrietta', scrawling our family tree on scraps of paper, laughing and crying. It was a surprise to find out how much we had in common – similar interests, a love of the same books and films, an identical sense of humour, and a recently discovered curiosity about our family history. After this meeting in Warsaw we knew we could no longer live without each other.

Just as our grandmothers used to send a constant stream of post-cards and letters to and fro, now e-mail became an invaluable intermediary between us. Almost every day we reported the most important and the most trivial events to each other – about the progress of redecorating in my kitchen in Kraków and in her country house in Connecticut, about her daughter Pamela's engagement to Borys, about my daughter Kasia's plans for her life, about theatre premières in London, Warsaw and Kraków, and also about the family history that I was writing. On account of it we came to an important decision: Robert and Peter Osnos offered to finance my travel to New York, and Monika invited me to stay with her. There they would tell me what they remembered and show me their letters, documents and photographs.

In June 1999 I landed at JFK airport, and then had an amazing few weeks. Beneath the rich, colourful, incredibly lively present-day existence of my American relatives lay the dwindling, hazy past of our parents and grandparents. As we walked about the city, visited museums and chatted over a glass of wine, we kept crossing the borders between the most varied times and spaces, moving between this world and the other, between Manhattan and Hades.

For me, the most striking story I discovered during this trip was the fate of Ryś Bychowski. The enormous archive that Monika sacredly keeps contains an invaluable record of the three years he lived in the West. Unfortunately I have only made use of a small part of it.

Only then did I learn from Monika what she had experienced during their escape from the bombardment of Warsaw. She was two years old when they left, so she would not have remembered much at all, apart from a few vague images, if not for conversations with her parents in which they kept coming back to the subject of that nightmare journey.

At Robert Osnos' country house outside New York the birds were singing sweetly, his wife Naomi was making a salad, we were sitting on the terrace gazing at the green mountains; I switched on the tape recorder, and once again a little boy ran screaming into Warsaw's burning Twarda Street, crying: 'Mama!'

The photographs hanging in Peter Osnos' study show him with princes, presidents and prime ministers. As a top journalist he interviewed all of them. Later on he worked for the famous publishing firm Random House. Now he has given up his brilliant journalistic career and his safe job to found his own small publishing firm. He is taking a risk, but he wants to prove what he can do. For himself? His family? The world? His ancestors in the world beyond? We wonder what gives us this inner drive that has complicated life for each of us in turn: 'You must become someone! You must demonstrate what you're capable of!' Whose genes have pushed us so hard all our lives?

Robert gave me an incredible gift: my mother's letters to his mother and to the Bychowskis, written from 1945 until her death. He had not thrown them away, which is why I am now able to quote from them and to wonder at the vast ocean of love that linked previous generations. In the intervals at the ballets he took me to, in the museums we visited with Monika, in Chinatown and in Italian cafés we talked about memory. Why had we run away from our parents' memories? Why had we drowned out our own? Why had the bond that tied us so strongly as children been broken? Why had we not tried to mend it for so many years? With some wonder and slight suspicion we watched as the closeness between us came back to life.

In May 2000, a year after my visit to New York, Monika and Robert flew to Kraków. This became the excuse for a larger get-together, which also included our relatives from Warsaw. A major event was the arrival from Moscow of Petya, Maks's son. We spread out our family photographs on the table and together we looked at pictures of his father – as a fiery young revolutionary, and as a tired old man, looking fatally dejected just before his tragic end. We drew new shoots on our family tree. On Petya's branches Lena, Maxim, Sergei, Ania and Tania appeared. On mine came Kasia, and then Maria.

The next stage in our flourishing adventure was a trip to Tuscany. Monika Bychowska-Holmes initiated the idea, and Robert Osnos and Maxim Valetsky jointly funded it. In April 2001, just before the Easter holidays, we all set off – from Warsaw, Kraków, New York, San Francisco, Moscow, Boston, and even from Stockholm, where Monika's daughter Deborah was at a conference. Once we were there, we found that of the twenty-six people who had answered the call twenty were descendants of Gustaw and Julia. So once we had sat down to the pasta he had cooked for us, Monika's husband, our co-host Douglas Holmes, raised the first toast in honour of that couple – the son of a Viennese rabbi and the daughter of a Warsaw merchant.

'It seems miraculous', he said, 'that after two world wars, after all the historical and personal catastrophes that their nine children went through, as many as five of them are represented at this table.' We took a look around us, and it was true.

Representing the oldest, the energetic, resourceful Flora, there was her great-grandson, Marek Beylin, a journalist for Poland's leading daily newspaper, *Gazeta Wyborcza*.

The mild, melancholy Gizella was represented by two of her grandchildren: Robert and Monika; and four great-grandchildren: Gwyn, who is an economist, Jean, a lawyer, Deborah, also a lawyer, and Pamela, a medical student; and one great-great-grandson, four-year-old Eli.

Janina was represented by me, her granddaughter; her great-granddaughter Kasia, who is a journalist and translator; and by her great-great-granddaughter, sixteen-year-old Maria.

Maksymilian Horwitz was represented by a five-person Russian and American group. His son Petya, a chemist, had flown in from Moscow, as had his granddaughter Lena, who is a businesswoman; his grandson Maxim, a businessman, was there from San Francisco; and two of his great-grandchildren, twenty-year-old Ania and fourteen-year-old Tania were also present.

Kamilla, the youngest, was represented by her granddaughter Nina, who works at Warsaw University, and three of her great-grandchildren: Piotr, who works in information technology, Marta, who is a biologist, and seventeen-year-old Asia.

Fifteen people were missing (not counting Róża's descendants, with whom none of us is in touch), above all Janek Kancewicz, the senior member of the clan, and Pierre Pfeffer from Paris, whom we could not persuade to come on the trip. It is hard to list all the missing people here, but even without them there was quite a din filling the Italian dining room, with six wives and husbands watching from the sidelines with loving interest. I shall not try to summarise the conversations that were going on around the tables in five different languages at once until late into the night. I shall not admit how many bottles of chianti we drank. Some of us were meeting for the first time in our lives, and we could not get the hang of who belonged to which generation. We did not know what sort of tone to adopt: serious or joking; how to overcome our own reservations, and whether to allow ourselves to be emotional or keep our feelings in check. Fortunately, we were saved by our common sense of humour. The process of getting close to each other in the course of a few days was a difficult experience, too complex to be summarised in a couple of sentences. There is just one incident I would like to describe.

One evening Robert Osnos gave a festive dinner to celebrate his seventieth birthday and – as a psychiatrist – proposed that we attempt a rather risky psychodrama. Each of the twenty-six people present had to say a few words about himself or herself. To begin with we were all numb with terror, then each of us spoke in turn. The first to burst into tears of emotion was my daughter Kasia, and immediately after her, so did Monika. After that everyone was more or less noticeably wiping away their tears. There was something mystical about it, as if we were reporting on our lives not only to those gathered around the table but also to our common ancestors.

When it came to her turn, my granddaughter Maria made a speech affirming the value of a life in which such happy surprises as the discovery of so many formerly unknown relatives can happen. Until recently the world had seemed vast and alien, but now it had grown smaller and she felt safe in it, like at home – because now she knew that in countries as far away as Russia or America she had people who were her relatives.

Petya got the biggest ovation. He said that he regarded our get-together as a great victory over fate. Two diabolical forces had sworn to annihilate us: Nazi totalitarianism had committed slaughter; Soviet totalitarianism had killed and destroyed people, and severed the ties between them. It had deprived them not only of their dignity and sense of security but also of their social affiliation, family tradition and personal identity. People who have been uprooted and stripped of the memory, attachments and values passed down by preceding generations do not know what they are living for and have nothing to pass on to their own children. Fortunately we had survived all those dangers, found each other again, and rediscovered our common past, which would allow us to understand better who we were and where we were heading.

To finish he asked us to raise our glasses in honour of the youngest member of the family, his grandson Leon, son of Sergei. Then we drank to the health of all the children: long live Leon from Moscow, Sam, Jonah and Eli from New York, and Nils from Riga.

'Enough!' cries the booming voice of my great-grandmother Julia. She does not like pathos or exaggerated sentiments. She summons her husband, children, sons-in-law, daughters-in-law and grand-children into the blue parlour, where the portrait of the Viennese rabbi hangs on the wall, for the final scene in this story. At once they will all start arguing dreadfully over the details. Red-haired Henrietta will be offended that I have forgotten about the Margulies family, and the good-natured Róża will worry that I have written so little about her sons. With the instincts of a peda-gogue, my grandmother will point out a few mistakes I have made, and my mother will defend me. They will call for me to correct the errors, sort out the dates, delete and add to the text. But I think my ancestors will probably be pleased with what has happened. They always placed the highest value on family bonds. I looked for the lost traces of our family and rediscovered some emotions. I sum-moned up the Shades and was answered by the Living. And that was how we found each other again, in the garden of memory.

SOURCES OF QUOTATIONS

———————— ✳ ————————

1. UNPUBLISHED

Maria Belin: 'Memoirs'.

Katarzyna Bielska: 'Memoirs'.

Jan Ryszard Bychowski: 'The Road Led through Wilno' (dedicated to the memory of Nachum Zynger of Warsaw).

Hanna Mortkowicz-Olczak: 'Memoirs'.

Janina Mortkowicz: 'Memoirs'.

2. PUBLISHED

Władysław Bartoszewski: *1859 dni Warszawy* ['1859 days of Warsaw'], Kraków 1974.

Karolina Beylin: *Dni powszednie Warszawy w latach 1880–1900* ['Warsaw Weekdays 1880–1900'], Warsaw 1967.

Karolina Beylin: *W Warszawie, w latach 1900–1914* ['In Warsaw, 1900–1914'], Warsaw 1972.

Celina Budzyńska: *Strzępy rodzinnej sagi* ['Scraps of a Family Saga'], Warsaw 1997.

Jan Ryszard Bychowski: *'List do ojca'* ['A Letter to my Father'], *Zeszysty Literackie* 1991, No. 34.

Alina Cała: *Asymilacja Żydów w Królestwie Polskim (1864–1897)* ['The Assimilation of the Jews in the Polish Kingdom (1864–1897)'], Warsaw 1989.

Bohdan Cywiński: *Rodowody niepokornych* ['The Origins of the Non-Submissives'], Warsaw 1967.

Czarna księga komunizmu ['The Black Book of Communism'], Warsaw 1999.

Norman Davies: *White Eagle, Red Star: The Polish–Soviet War 1919–1920* (Pimlico, London 2003).

Stanisław Helsztyński: *Przybyszewski* ['Przybyszewski'], Warsaw 1973.

Ludwik Hirszfeld: *Historia jednego życia* ['The Story of a Life'], Warsaw 2000.

Ferdynand Hoesick: *Dom rodzicielski* ['My Parents' House'], Kraków 1935.

Jan Kancewicz: *'Wuj Maks'* ['Uncle Maks'], in *Ludzie bliscy* ['Close People'], Warsaw 1960.

Jan Karski: *Tajne państwo*, Warsaw 2000 [published in English as *Story of a Secret State*, Houghton Mifflin Company, Boston 1944].

Stefan Korboński: *'W imieniu Rzeczypospolitej'* ['In the Name of the Republic'], in *Ten jest z ojczyzny mojej. Polacy z pomocą Żydom 1939–1945*, edited by Władysław Bartoszewski and Zofia Lewin, Kraków 1969 [published in English as *Righteous Among Nations – How Poles Helped the Jews 1939–1945*, Earlscourt Publications Ltd, London 1969].

Witold Leder: *'Przeżylem tamten proces'* ['I Survived that Process'], *Polityka* 1988, No. 49.

Sister Maria Ena: *Gdzie miłość dojrzewala do bohaterstwa* ['Where Love Matured into Heroism'], Niepokalanów 1999.

Hanna Mortkowicz: *Gorycz wiośniana* ['The Bitterness of Springtime'], Warsaw 1928.

Hanna Mortkowicz-Olczak: *Bunt wspomnień* ['A Riot of Memories'], Warsaw 1961.

Hanna Mortkowicz-Olczak: *Pod znakiem kłoska* ['At the Sign of the Ear of Corn'], Warsaw 1962.

Hanna Mortkowicz-Olczak: *'Ryś (wspomnienie o Ryszardzie Bychowskim)'* ['Ryś (a Memoir of Ryszard Bychowski)], *Tygodnik Powszechny* 1946.

Hanna Mortkowicz-Olczak: *'Wspomnienie o Irenie Grabowskiej'* ['Reminiscences of Irena Grabowska'] in *Ten jest z ojczyzny mojej. Polacy z pomocą Żydom 1939–1945*, op. cit.

Janina Mortkowicz: *Anulka* ['Anulka'], Warsaw 1928.

Janina Mortkowicz: *Stacho* ['Stacho'], Warsaw 1906.

Zofia Nałkowska: *Dzienniki 1909–1917* ['Diaries 1909–1917'], Warsaw 1976.

Jan Nowak-Jeziorański: *Kurier z Warszawy*, Kraków 2000 [published in English as *Courier from Warsaw*, Collins/Harvill Press, London 1982].

The final letter of Szmul Zygielbojm, in *Ten jest z ojczyzny mojej. Polacy z pomocą Żydom 1939–1945*, op. cit.

Leszek Podhorecki: *Historia Polski 1796–1997* ['A History of Poland 1796–1997'], Warsaw 1998.

Michał Sokolnicki: *Czternaście lat* ['Fourteen Years'], Warsaw 1936.

Henryk Walecki: *Wybór pism* ['Selected Works'], Warsaw 1967.

Wymiana więźniów politycznych pomiędzy II Rzeczpospolitą a Sowietami w okresie międzywojennym ['The Exchange of Political

Prisoners between the Second Republic and the Soviets in the Interwar Period'], Warsaw 2000.

Tadeusz Żeleński: *O Krakowie* ['About Kraków'], Kraków 1968.

Stefan Żeromski: *Na probostwie w Wyszkowie* ['At the Presbytery in Wyszków'], Warsaw 1929.

INDEX